FINDING
Funding
4TH EDITION

Grantwriting From Start to Finish,
Including Project Management and Internet Use

Ernest W. Brewer
Charles M. Achilles
Jay R. Fuhriman
Connie Hollingsworth

CORWIN PRESS, INC.
A Sage Publications Company
Thousand Oaks, California

For information address:

Corwin Press, Inc.
A Sage Publications Company
2455 Teller Road
Thousand Oaks, California 91320
E-mail: order@corwinpress.com

Sage Publications Ltd.
6 Bonhill Street
London EC2A 4PU
United Kingdom

Sage Publications India Pvt. Ltd.
M-32 Market
Greater Kailash I
New Delhi 110 048 India

Printed in the United States of America

Library of Congress Cataloging-in-Publication Data

Main entry under title:
    Finding funding: Grantwriting from start to finish, including project management
and Internet use / Ernest W. Brewer . . . [et al.]. — 4th ed.
      p. cm.
    Rev. ed. of: Finding funding / Ernest W. Brewer. 3rd ed. © 1998.
    Includes bibliographical references (p.) and index.
    ISBN: 0-7619-7797-X — ISBN 0-7619-7798-8 (pbk.)
    1. Educational fundraising—United States—Handbooks, manuals, etc. 2. Proposal
writing in education—United States—Handbooks, manuals, etc. 3. Federal aid to education—
United States—Handbooks, manuals, etc. 4. Government aid to education—United States—
Handbooks, manuals, etc. I. Brewer, Ernest W. II. Brewer, Ernest W. Finding funding.
III. Title.
    LB2825 .F522 2000
    379.1'2'0973 dc21   00-065984

This book is printed on acid-free paper.

01 02 03 04 05 06 07 7 6 5 4 3 2 1

Corwin Editorial Assistant: Kylee Liegl
Production Editor: Nevair Kabakian
Editorial Assistant: Kathryn Journey
Cover Designer: Tracy E. Miller

Contents

Preface

$\mathbf{R}$esponse to our first, second, and third editions of *Finding Funding* has been very inspiring, and we are pleased to be able to bring you *Finding Funding, Fourth Edition*. The first edition of this text ap-peared over 10 years ago and what a 10 years it has been in grantwriting. Because the world of grants and government funding changes rapidly, we are striving to keep the information in this book as current and useful as possible. The fourth edition has undergone some major changes but still retains its easy readability and the latest updates of telephone numbers, addresses, and web sites, as well as including some new resources. One major change in this edition is the addition of two new chapters, Chapter 7 on "Components of a Foundation Proposal" and Chapter 9 on "Helpful Hints From Grantwriting Professionals." You will find these chapters very helpful for exploring and writing foundation grant proposals and some tried and true tips from grant writing professionals. You'll also find current information about the programs available through the *Catalog of Federal Domestic Assistance* (*CFDA*) and the latest listings of centers and labs funded by Office of Educational Research and Improvement (OERI). Another new feature of this edition is an index of terms used in the book.

We feel that it is important to note that since the first edition, technology has changed significantly. This rapid growth in technology has greatly enhanced our ability to access and process grant information. Yet it continually challenges us to stay abreast of these changes so that we may provide the latest information to our readers. It comes as no surprise that from the time we send the fourth edition to press and it reaches bookstores, some aspects of the electronic grantwriting world will have changed. We embrace these changes because we feel it is making our work easier.

We would like to thank everyone who adopted the first, second, or third edition of this book, and we trust that you will find this fourth edition even more helpful in your work. We also wish to express appreciation to the many persons who have helped us by providing ideas, encouragement, and information. During our collective 85 years of proposal preparation and project administration, we have regularly attended and have given seminars, workshops, and briefing sessions related to grant proposal development and project implementation and have attended in the past 20 years more proposal-preparation sessions and seminars than we can recall. We also have served as readers— evaluating grant applications submitted for funding. We have carefully read newsletters, articles, "Dear Colleague" letters, government publications and circulars, application packets, the *Federal Register (FR)*, the *Catalog of Federal Domestic Assistance (CFDA)*, the *Code of Federal Regulations (CFR)*, and other books about funding. In preparing this book we have cited sources whenever possible. As collectors of useful and potentially useful items, our files are full of examples, samples, worksheets, and the like. Where we have included examples obtained at a workshop or seminar, we have given credit if the materials were identified by any citation.

If the materials did not include information about sources, and if we could not reconstruct the workshop or session where we obtained the materials, we still included them if we felt they would help this collection. We did not purposefully omit any source. If anyone using this book recognizes materials and sources, please send us the source information so we can make appropriate amends in future revisions.

We have developed numerous grant and contract proposals. Each proposal-development process is a learning experience—we have learned much from those who have cooperated, collaborated, or coauthored in the process. We have also learned from various funding source administrators and personnel who have helped us over difficult times. Given the extent of the aid we have received, it is not possible to list everyone who has contributed to our collective ideas about proposal development. Perhaps some of the people will be partially rewarded by seeing that we have incorporated into this vol-ume ideas that we have acquired from these many interactions.

We also relied on many other sources of ideas, such as publications from The Grantsmanship Center, the Education Funding Research Council, and other grant service groups. We have benefited from federal circulars and publications relating to proposal development. We have improved because of comments of other proposal writers, friends in various offices and agencies, and review panels who evaluated our proposals. We thank our students and seminar participants who have worked through portions of this material and who have made helpful comments.

All of the authors express their appreciation to the Corwin Press staff for their guidance and support during this revision. Their valuable advice and suggestions have improved this book greatly. In addition, the staff of Corwin Press are the best in the field—they made this task easy.

Our thanks also go to our family members who encouraged and supported us in the completion of this fourth edition.

Finally, we have synthesized information from others, from experience, and from "doing proposals." In the final analysis, any deficiencies in the text are the authors' own.

Ernest W. Brewer
Charles M. Achilles
Jay R. Fuhriman
Connie Hollingsworth

About the Authors

Ernest W. Brewer is Professor and Principal Investigator/Director in the Department of Human Resource Development and Department Head of Child and Family Studies at The University of Tennessee, Knoxville (UTK). He is currently serving as the Principal Investigator/Project Director of six federally funded grants. Prior to joining the university in 1976, he earned his doctorate degree from UTK in Technological and Adult Education and served as the Executive Director of the Institute of Human Resources.

Over the years he has acquired external funds for a variety of research, service, and developmental activities. During this time he has served as both editor and editorial board member of professional journals, and he has authored a variety of grant proposals, professional articles, and annual performance reports. His grants have ranged from five thousand to over a million dollars with more than $45,000,000 in grant support to date. As time permits, he serves as a "field reader" of proposals submitted to Washington, D.C.

In addition to administering funded projects, Brewer has taught graduate courses, given seminars, and participated in a variety of grantwriting, project design, and program implementation workshops. A favorite graduate course that he has repeatedly taught is his "Grantwriting and Program Implementation" course. He also teaches a noncredit course entitled "Grantwriting and Project Administration: Foundations to Federal" that is available to community agency personnel and nonprofit organizations.

Charles M. Achilles is Professor of Educational Leadership, College of Education, Eastern Michigan University (EMU). He received his doctorate in Educational Administration from the University of Rochester and worked briefly at the (former) U.S. Office of Education; for 21 years at the Bureau of Educational Research and Service, The University of Tennessee, Knoxville; for 6 years at the University of North Carolina at Greensboro; and since 1994 at EMU.

Since March 1968, Achilles has had continuous grant support for research, development, service, education, or training activities. He has served as author, coauthor, member of a proposal-development team, or adviser for more than 400 proposals. Not counting all multiple-year continuations, this work has resulted in more than 230 funded projects for more than $40,000,000 in support of education and education-related agencies.

He has taught graduate classes, seminars, and short workshops on application and proposal development for grants and contracts. He has also reviewed proposals for the federal government.

Jay R. Fuhriman is Professor of Bilingual Education and English as a Second Language at Boise State University, Boise, Idaho. He currently directs two undergraduate and one graduate program in bilingual education/ESL. He earned his doctorate degree from Texas A&M University (formerly Texas A&I) in Kingsville, TX, in Curriculum and Instruction and worked as a consultant and teacher prior to joining the teaching staff in 1977.

Fuhriman's grantwriting experience dates back to 1982 and has resulted in more than $22,000,000 worth of grant support to a variety of educational programs. During this period he has provided grant application consulting and review services to approximately 25 universities and school districts in the United States and has presented many national and regional grantwriting workshops. He also teaches a graduate-level grantwriting course at the university. On several occasions he has served as a field reader for proposals submitted to the U. S. Office of Education, Office of Bilingual Educaiton and Minority Languages Affairs. His contribution to the present work comes from the perspective of a grant proposal writer, a proposal reviewer, and a program director.

He has served as both editor and editorial board member of several professional journals and has published articles in the field of grantwriting. He has served as a member of the board of directors of national, regional and state professional organizations that deal with federal grants. Currently, he is president of the Idaho Association for Bilingual Education, Inc.

Connie Hollingsworth is Adjunct Assistant Professor and Director of Pre-College Programs in the College of Human Ecology, Department of Human Resource Development, The University of Tennessee, Knoxville (UTK). She received her Ph.D. in Human Ecology from UTK in 1995. Since beginning her tenure at UTK she has been directly involved in securing $6,000,000 in federal funds including 10 years of securing and administering USDA contracts.

She has been actively involved in grant administration since 1987. She teaches a graduate grantwriting class each year at UTK, conducts grantwriting workshops, consults, and is a contributing author for several grant related articles. Hollingsworth has also served as a peer reviewer for the U.S. Department of Education. Prior to coming to UTK she was employed by the University of Montevallo (AL) with a federally funded program.

Introduction

$\mathbf{F}$or some people writing a grant proposal is a chore or burden. For others putting ideas down clearly so people can read, understand, and appreciate them is exciting; if the ideas are funded, it may be a near-religious experience that elicits the urge to compete for yet another chance to finance needed activities or projects.

Historical Development

History shows that the Lewis and Clark Expedition was funded by the federal government in 1803. However, the actual grantmaking process dates back to 1842 when the 27th Congress made a grant award of $30,000 to Professor Samuel F. B. Morse. The funds allowed expense money and personal reimbursement to field test the electro-magnetic telegraph system and explore the feasibility of the system for public use. The grant award was significant in that it represented the first time Congress fully participated in the grantmaking process. Later in the 19th century congressional interest in research was manifested by the enactment of the Hatch Act, Smith-Hughes Act, Bankhead-Jones Act, and the Morrill Act all of which established land-grant colleges throughout the United States.

In the beginning there *was* federal support for education, but the Northwest Ordinances were not the grantwriter's dream. The opportunity to develop proposals to the federal government for support of an individual's or a group's ideas did not really blossom until the 1950s with the Cooperative Research Act (1956) and the National Defense Education Act (1958). The 1960s began the grantwriter's utopia with the Civil Rights Act, the Vocational Education Act, the Higher Education Act, the Elementary and Secondary Education Act, and the many reauthorizations of these and other acts serving special categories, such as bilingual education or handicapped children.

The increase in opportunities to secure external funds brought a new grants business—newsletters, seminars, grantwriters, and offices of proposal development. Consulting firms, grants offices, and specialized grantwriters became the supermarkets of the trade, severely challenging individuals and small agencies who were the Mom and Pop grocery stores serving the needs of local areas.

Increased Competition for Grant Monies

Still, new individuals enter the arena each year, both as aspiring grantwriters and as new project directors; there are seminars or workshops on proposal development and graduate courses in "Grants and Contracts" or "State and Federal Relations" at some universities. The materials collected, developed, and compiled in this volume are mostly related to grant proposal development for education, but the push for uniformity in grants among the various federal agencies (begun in 1977 with the uniform requirements) means that the materials have wider application. Some of the ideas and tips—especially in Part II, "Writing Grant Proposals"—may be of general interest and value to a grantwriter; some ideas about "project management" in Part III should benefit anyone operating a project.

Organization of Book

This book is divided into three major *parts* and several additional supporting sections, such as this Introduction, References, and Appendixes. Part I, "Exploring in the Grants World," includes Chapters 1-5 and discusses the planning and some of the major "tools of the trade" needed to get started in the grant/project field and using the Internet to access funding resources. Part II, "Writing Grant Proposals," includes Chapters 6-12 and covers some important steps in developing a successful grant application. Part III, "Implementing, Operating, and Terminating a Project," includes Chapters 13-16 and discusses both closing out a project annually and the often difficult but realistic element of terminating the project at the end of external support. Appendixes include potentially useful information, lists, and addresses that seemed inappropriate for the regular text.

Funding Questions: What Are the Federal Levels of Support for Education?

The grantwriter needs to know about the funding potential for grant support. According to the United States Office of Management and Budget (OMB),[1] the federal government provides support for

---

[1] United States Department of Education, National Center for Education Statistics, United States Office of Management and Budget, *Budget of the United States Government,* http://nces.ed.gov/pubs2000/2000019.pdf

education well beyond programs funded through the Department of Education (ED). Federal support for education, excluding estimated federal tax expenditures, was an estimated $115.6 billion in fiscal year 1999 (FY 99), an increase of $52.8 billion, or 84%, since FY 1990. After adjustment for inflation, federal support for education increased 47% between FY 1990 and FY 1999. Between FY 1980 and FY 1999, federal on-budget program funds for elementary and secondary education increased 24%; postsecondary education funds declined 18%; other education funds (which include funds for libraries, museums, cultural activities, and miscellaneous research) increased 87%; and funds for research and development and university-administered research and development centers increased 66%.

As an example, the federal budget for the United States Department of Education is outlined in Table I.1. It lists the 1998 and 1999 appropriations and President's budget for 2000.

Table I.1 Budget Appropriations for 1998 and 1999 and Requests by the President

Major Program Areas	1998[1] Appropriations	1999[1] Appropriations	2000[1, 2] President's Budget
Education Reform	$ 1,315,035,000	$ 1,514,100,000	$ 1,947,000,000
Elementary and Secondary Education	10,280,765,000	7,671,654,000	12,565,454,000
Bilingual Education and Minority Languages Affairs	354,000,000	380,000,000	415,000,000
Special Education and Rehabilitation Services	7,535,168,000	8,124,371,000	6,384,028,000
Vocational and Adult Education	1,519,698,000	1,555,970,000	1,750,250,000
Postsecondary Education	13,695,622,000	14,286,969,000	13,129,740,000
Educational Research and Improvement (OERI)	391,438,000	464,867,000	540,282,000

[1] U.S. Department of Education Fiscal Year 2000 Report. [2] Estimated; final budget not yet adopted by Congress at press time.

Table I.2 provides FY2000 to FY2004 estimates of discretionary spending by federal agencies. So those who are not directly interested in grants in the field of education, may want to explore a more detailed budget of the federal, state, or local area that you may be interested in seeking grants and contracts.

AAA Phenomenon

With the passage of a law or the start of a new federal initiative, there may be considerable hoopla and hype about the amount of money *authorized*. Don't get excited yet! It is a long way from funds authorized to support something and funds actually *allocated* to do the job. Along the way is the *appropriations* process. Familiarity with the

Table I.2 Discretionary Spending by Selected Federal Agencies

Federal Agency	2000[1]	2001[1]	2002[1]	2003[1]	2004[1]
Agriculture	3,000,000	3,000,000	3,000,000	3,000,000	3,000,000
Commerce	17,000,000	17,000,000	17,000,000	17,000,000	17,000,000
Defense	278,000,000	279,000,000	285,000,000	294,000,000	303,000,000
Education	34,000,000	35,000,000	39,000,000	40,000,000	41,000,000
Energy	17,000,000	18,000,000	19,000,000	19,000,000	20,000,000
Health and Human Services	43,000,000	46,000,000	50,000,000	50,000,000	51,000,000
Justice	17,000,000	17,000,000	21,000,000	21,000,000	21,000,000
Labor	10,000,000	11,000,000	12,000,000	12,000,000	13,000,000
Transportation	44,000,000	47,000,000	49,000,000	50,000,000	51,000,000
National Science	3,000,000	4,000,000	4,000,000	5,000,000	5,000,000

[1] Discretionary spending is appropriated by the Congress each year, in contrast with mandatory spending, which is automatic under permanent law.

———— **Grant Tip** ————

Find out the distribution of the allocated funds. This is the most important step in the whole process for the grantwriter.

three steps—authorization, appropriation, and allocation, or the AAA phenomenon—is vital to the grantwriter, because those steps give clues to the importance of, political impetus behind, and actual funds available for a project. Perhaps the best way to think of the AAA phenomenon is that *authorization* is the *ceiling,* or the most that a program could receive if it, in fact, *receives any funds.* An *authorization* level is built into each Public Law (PL), but an authorization does not guarantee that any funds will ever be appropriated or allocated. An authorization is typically set to provide flexibility in case the law is ever "funded."

Appropriation of funds to support federal activity is a separate step from passing public laws to put activities "on the books." An appropriations bill begins in the House of Representatives and after being finally negotiated and passed, provides the maximum that an agency can use to operate the program for which funds were appropriated. *Allocation* of funds is the administrative activity of disbursement of funds for specific purposes of the authorizing legislation. In a given year this could be less than the appropriation due to impoundments or recisions. The distribution of the allocated funds is the most important step in the whole process for the grantwriter. How many dollars are actually available for the program from which the proposer seeks support; how many projects will be funded, and what will be the expected range of the awards? If this information is not in the *Federal Register* notice or in the grant application package, a call to the agency to find out is a good investment. Once assigned to the agency, the appropriated funds may have many purposes other than support for your project: those other purposes might include program administration, obligations for multiyear funding, or earmarked funds to support inter- or intra-agency efforts. *If information on the actual availability of funds is not readily available, seek it out.*

Authorization • Appropriation • Allocation

Should You Seek Federal Support?

Certainly it is an honor and great achievement when an agency evaluates your proposal as worthy of funding, and there are positive benefits to receiving funding support. People usually emphasize the positive. There are, however, some potential negatives that are seldom mentioned. One should try to negate these negatives.

Potential Benefits From External Funding Support

Perhaps the biggest *plus* in getting a grant is that you now have some resources to meet an important need and to work toward a goal that is of interest to your organization. Funds for your project may support new equipment, books, or other resources and may provide some salaries. The activity may expand your capability, as well as that of your organization and others associated with the project, through training and professional growth; in fact, the project may even create new areas of skill or knowledge (expertise) among personnel. Persons who work assiduously on the project may be able to conduct financed research (or evaluation) that could provide material for a professional paper or published article. "Soft money" jobs often pay slightly more than regular positions because of the job insecurity. However, while they also have a predetermined length, they may allow you to demonstrate skills that will support your move to a regular position. Having control over funds may provide some autonomy, some opportunity to secure support personnel, and expanded options for professional travel and for meeting new professional experts. Not insignificantly, there are the personal benefits of a challenging task and the recognition that can come from operating a successful project that achieves positive results. Figure I.1 summarizes some potential positive outcomes from securing grant support.

Figure I.1. Benefits From Securing External Funds

* Meeting a Need
* Financial Support for Your Organization
* Autonomy/Released Time
* Challenging Opportunities
* Ability to Secure Support Personnel
* Financed Research (perhaps for a professional article)
* New Equipment
* Recognition/Model Program
* Salary Increases
* Expanded Capabilities
* Create New Areas of Expertise
* Advanced Training from Experts in New Fields
* Professional Travel and Presentation(s) at Professional Meetings

Potential Negative Aspects From External Funding

———**Grant Tip**———

Don't forget the probable "hassle" in trying to serve both the funding agency and your own organization. Trying to serve two masters is never easy.

What you need to do for the project may run afoul of the usual policies or operations of your organization (such as your need to travel extensively or to stay in places not covered by regular travel expense policy). The managerial and legal responsibilities of a project carry high levels of paperwork (red tape) and often unrealistically high expectations for "super success." As a grant administrator you will be subjected to site visits, audits, or both, and to an outrageous level of accountability. As the "new kid on the block," you may get limited or second-class space, equipment, furnishings, and priorities—unless the grant is large enough to support autonomous action. Project-related uncertainties, often over deadlines and about continued funding, can add stress to the job. There may be no firm intraorganizational support for the project, and if project personnel appear to have extra benefits (real or perceived), personality conflicts may develop (jealousy over travel, for example). The project may be assigned a subordinate role in the organization, and project activities may suffer if the funding agency has a shift in priorities. Don't forget the probable "hassle" in trying to serve both the funding agency and your own organization. Trying to serve two masters is *never* easy. Some potential negative aspects of receiving external funding support are listed in Figure I.2.

Figure I.2. Negative Factors of Securing External Funding Support

- Managerial/Legal Responsibilities
- Priority Shift May Cause Disharmony
- Lack of Strong Internal Support
- Personalities/Jealousies
- Subordinate Role of Project in Organization's Total Operations
- Skewed Priories at the Institution if Dependent on External Funds
- Uncertainty for Continuity
- Stress Increase Due to Ambiguity and the Success Syndrome
- High Level of Accountability
- Paperwork/Red Tape
- Sometimes Impossible Expectations
- Implementation in a Timely Manner/Time Tensions
- Limited or Second-Class Space, Materials, Equipment, and Support
- Dealing with Policies and Purposes of Two Masters: Funding Agency and Your Organization

Various Roles the Grant Administrator Must Play

The person who writes the grant typically implements and maintains the project throughout its funding cycle. However, some professionals just write proposals. If one of their proposals is funded, they turn it over to someone else to implement and direct. The individual who implements and maintains the grant often has to wear a variety of hats in performing the work requirements that are associated with external funding support. Figure I.3 lists various roles

Figure I.3. Major Activities or Roles of a Grant Administrator in Operating a Funded Project

• Administrator/Supervisor	• Evaluator
• Public Relations Activities	• Planner
• Marketer	• Innovator
• Researcher	• Persuader
• Negotiator	• Devil's Advocate
• Fiscal Officer	• Interpreter
• Entrepreneur	• Personnel Manager
• Strategist	• Visionary

in which grant administrators might find themselves while operating a funded project.

Summary

In reality, if people never write a *formal* proposal for a state or federal grant, at some point they will probably develop at least one proposal to do something of professional interest. That document will include many of the elements discussed in this handbook: problem definition, analysis of need, goals and objectives, activities, some management details—timelines, personnel, budget, reports—evaluation, and probably dissemination of results.

Prior to the actual writing of the document, there will be a period of exploring the feasibility of what is being proposed: planning, seeking a sponsor (or funding source if appropriate), and strategies to sell the idea or project. If the idea (proposal) is accepted, the project developer will be concerned with implementing the project to do what was proposed. At some point the project will be closed down and terminated. That is what this volume is all about—exploring, writing, implementing, and terminating your successful idea as a strong proposal and as an operating project.

PART I

Exploring in the Grants World

In Part I, Chapters 1-5, we present some prewriting elements that will help you get started in grant proposal development. These include some general, useful information about grants and the funding game, a review of some of the aids to help the grant seeker and proposal writer, and a chapter each on two major tools of the trade. In addition, we provide a chapter on the grant resources that are available to the novice and experienced grantwriter via the Internet.

1

Unraveling the Mystique in Grant Applications

Introduction

External funding is often available to support program development efforts. Getting external funding is not usually easy, but there are procedures and techniques (i.e., rules of the game) that can help you prepare a competitive proposal. Persons trained in proposal writing, institutions of higher education personnel, and employees of consulting firms that specialize in proposal development get the majority of external funds. Nevertheless, some tips, guidelines, and ideas will help newcomers and part-time proposal writers develop proposals that are competitive in the funding game. This book presents a summary of ideas about proposal development, specific information to help a proposal writer, examples from successful proposals, and some tips to help a person become more successful in proposal writing. The major emphasis in this book and the examples are programs funded through the United States Department of Education (USDE), but the concepts, techniques, and tips will help a person writing proposals for other agencies. The book provides strategies, vocabulary, examples, sources of ideas, and general information to aid both the novice and the experienced proposal writer in improving their proposals for funding support.

———Grant Tip———
Getting external funding is not usually easy, but there are procedures and techniques that will help you prepare a competitive proposal.

Proposal Development

Proposal development is hard work, but the result can be rewarding. Contrary to the opinion of some cynics, getting a grant is not entirely the result of politics or chance. Undoubtedly, the successful proposal is a fortuitous blend of certain ambiguous ingredients, but the serious proposal writer can gain the upper hand by careful attention to ideas and strategies that have been proven to be successful. It seems fair to say that although there is some luck in obtaining funding through the development of a proposal, there are also ways to improve the odds. Development of a successful proposal is not entirely style and technique. First, you need a good idea that connects with the particular interests of some funding source. Through planned approaches, study, and attention to detail, you can dramatically increase your chances of success.

Besides needing a good idea, writing ability, and a general knowledge of proposal processes, you will also need access to information and to "tools of the trade" that help in the writing of a proposal. In developing a proposal for the federal government, you will need access to some primary sources, including the *Federal Register (FR),* the *Catalog of Federal Domestic Assistance (CFDA),* and when necessary, the *Code of Federal Regulations (CFR).* These are covered in detail in Chapter 3, "Using the *Federal Register (FR)* and the *Code of Federal Regulations (CFR)*"; Chapter 4, "Using the *Catalog of Federal Domestic Assistance (CFDA)*"; and Chapter 5, "Using the Internet to Access Funding Resources." Other primary sources are the program guidelines or application packet and some Federal Management Circulars (FMCs). Secondary sources include articles and reference books about grants, newsletters from professional associations, and professional reading that helps explain various programs and grant processes.

What Is a Proposal?

——**Grant Tip**——
The formal proposal, in the required form and format, connects your ideas and interests with the ideas, interests, and programs of a funding source.

A formal proposal for funding, as the term is used here, is a written document developed in accordance with specific rules or guidelines. The document, in the required form and format, connects your (a person's or institution's) ideas and interests with the ideas, interests, and programs of a funding source. Usually, the proposal is the only direct contact with the funding agency during the competition period. A *competition* is initiated by the funding agency inviting institutions or agencies to submit proposals. Deadlines are established, and all parties submit their proposals to the funding source. The proposals are reviewed and rated. Certain ones are selected to receive funds. The competition process is explained in detail in Chapter 11. Therefore, your proposal should be clear, cogent, and concise and should clearly convey your ideas and the relationship of your project to the funding agency's goals. Any project that does not explicitly advance the purposes of the program or agency to which it is submitted will not be considered for funding.

In its simplest form, a proposal expresses a relationship among three important variables: *performance, time,* and *cost.* The proposer offers to perform something in a specified amount of time for a related cost. These three variables—performance, time, and cost—are carefully integrated and interrelated in the proposal.

The overall relationship among these variables as expressed in the proposal should remain constant. Therefore, during budget negotiations for a grant that has been accepted (see Chapter 11, "Understanding How Grants Are Awarded"), if the Grants/Contracts Officer disallows a specific expenditure, the proposer must realign the time, performance, or cost variables to maintain the integrity of the relationships among the three variables. For example, assume that your original budget was for $296,318 and the negotiator allows only $222,526. At that time the proposer should adjust the performance and time variables to correlate with the new cost. Having clearly established relationships among these three variables is an important basis for a strong proposal and project. In this handbook a proposal is treated as a rational expression of relationships among performance, time, and cost as expressed in a formal document to a funding agency.

In spite of the seeming complexity of many proposals, you can generally express the relationship among these variables by relying on the guiding questions of successful media reporters: what, why, how, who, when, and how much? In form and structure, a proposal often moves from the very general **why and what** to the very specific **when and how much**. A budget, although only an estimate of proposed expenditures, must relate specific costs for particular activities and staff persons staff. Figure 1.1 identifies the general flow of the proposal from general to specific.

——**Grant Tip**——
A proposal is a rational expression of relationships among performance, time, and cost as expressed in a formal document to a funding agency.

Terminology

A *grant* is awarded based upon an *application* developed in response to a Request for Applications (RFA). A *contract* is awarded based upon a *proposal* developed in response to a Request for Proposal (RFP). In reality, proposal writers speak of writing grants in response to RFPs.

A *program* is the agency's large-scale initiative. The application or proposal is to operate a *project* to meet and carry forth the purposes of the agency's *program*.

Figure 1.1. Proposal Guiding Questions: General to Specific

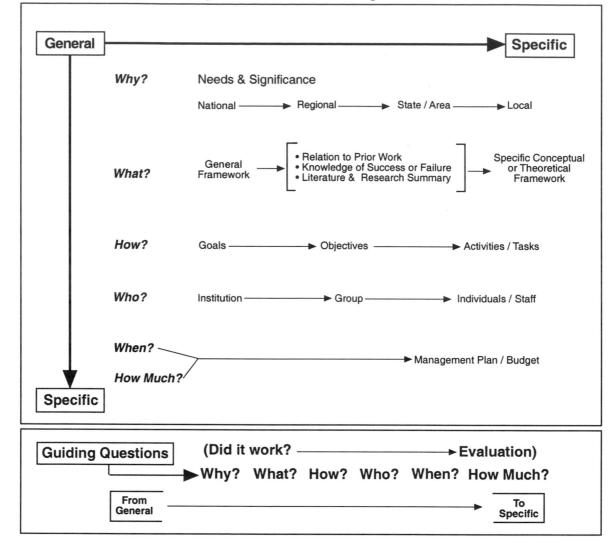

Grants and Other Funding Instruments

There are many ways to think about and to categorize types and sources of external support. This book focuses primarily on a source of support known as a grant and specifically a grant from the federal government. Examples are drawn primarily from grants available through the United States Department of Education.

Broadly speaking, the federal government has three categories of instruments for supporting funding. These three categories are the grant, the contract, and the cooperative agreement. There are many differences between and among these categories. The basic differences are fairly easy to understand.

Grant • Contract • Cooperative Agreement

A *grant* is an award made to advance the purposes of a specific federal program, such as Education of the Handicapped, Title I, Upward Bound, and the Women's Educational Equity Act. Chapter 10, "Reviewing a Funded Proposal," presents the proposal of the College Assistance Migrant Program (CAMP), which is a grant. Program personnel specify fairly broad and general guidelines describing the program's purpose and announce a competition inviting people to design projects to carry forth the purposes of the program. The proposer has considerable latitude and flexibility in determining what to do within the purposes and general guidelines of the program. Typically there are several successful grant proposals, depending on the amount of funds available to support the program. The government announces the grant competition in the *Federal Register*. The proposal writer obtains a copy of the grant application package, which contains guidelines to help in preparing the grant proposal. This book is designed primarily to help you develop a successful application or proposal for *grant* funding.

A *contract* is the government's way of soliciting for work that has been clearly specified. The government personnel know what needs to be done, have developed a set of specifications, and are looking for a qualified entity to conduct the work. Typically, there is only one, or at best a few, successful bidders to conduct the specified work. Solicitation for a contract is made public through a Request for Proposals (RFP). Government personnel announce many RFPs in a daily publication titled the *Commerce Business Daily*.

A *cooperative agreement* falls between a contract and a grant. In a cooperative agreement the funding agency personnel know in general what needs to be done, and although the funds are awarded to allow considerable discretion in their eventual use, the government works very closely with the recipient agency in defining, clarifying, and conducting the work requested in the cooperative agreement. Cooperative agreements are often used for large-scale projects such as Federal Research and Development (R&D) Centers. Cooperative agreement competitions are announced through the *Federal Register*,

——Grant Tip——
A grant is made to advance the purposes of a specific federal program. You have considerable latitude and flexibility within the guidelines of the program.

which is published every working day. The *Federal Register,* one of the necessary *tools of the trade* for a grant writer, is explained in detail in Chapter 3, "Using the *Federal Register (FR)* and the *Code of Federal Regulations (CFR)."* In a cooperative agreement competition, there is usually a very limited number of successful competitors. Once grantees have been awarded a cooperative agreement, they will coordinate with government personnel to achieve the cooperative agreement's goals. Figure 1.2 is a summary of some key differences among grants, contracts, and cooperative agreements. (This is a modification of a handout that was gathered from a workshop [source is unknown]).

Figure 1.2. Summary of Differences Among Three Funding Instruments

PROCEDURE	FEDERAL AGENCY	RELATIONSHIP
Grant	Patron	The grantee is responsible for performance with little or no federal or state agency involvement during performance. The agency supports the grantee's well-defined and well-written ideas.
Cooperative Agreement	Partner	The federal or state agency is involved during the performance and shares responsibility for performance. The agency and grantee plan together and maintain a cooperative working arrangement.
Contract	Purchaser	The federal or state agency is procuring for direct or third party use. The successful bidder will conform to predetermined activities.

The Grant Application Package

The grant application package or guidelines is a packet of material prepared by personnel at the funding agency. Material in the packet explains the purposes of a particular program and the specific processes for developing a proposal to seek funding from that agency. The guidelines usually consist of a copy of the federal regulations that govern the program, the forms required in the proposal, and supporting or helpful information about the program. As soon as the program personnel announce a grant competition in the *Federal Register,* the proposal writer must contact the funding source and obtain the application packet or guidelines. The guidelines will include a closing date for proposals in the competition. The proposer is responsible for seeing that the proposal is mailed or delivered on or before the closing date. The proposal deadline is an extremely important factor in determining whether or not you should even attempt to prepare a proposal. You need enough time to prepare a quality proposal, and the deadline is a fixed target. There is no such thing as a late proposal. *Proposals that do not meet the deadline date established in the application guidelines may be returned unopened.*

———**Grant Tip**———
There is no such thing as a late proposal. Proposals that do not meet the deadline may be returned unopened.

Categories of Grants and Sources of Support

There are many sources of support for projects built upon sound ideas. Although the focus of this book is federal funding in the Department of Education, the reader needs to understand the variety of support sources available. A simple categorization of support sources will help you organize and plan a grant-seeking strategy. For purposes of this categorization, consider that there are two sectors that provide funds: the *public sector* (or government), and the *private sector*.

Public ••• Private

Within the *public sector* support may be available through city, county, or other levels of government, but primarily public sector grant support usually comes from the federal and state levels of government. Some federal money for particular programs flows through to state government, which, in turn, distributes the funds in accordance with federal guidelines, often imposing some additional state restrictions as well. These funds, once they flow through to the state level, are thought of as state funds, and state personnel administer grants awarded from that funding source. To manage these funds, the federal government typically requires the state government to prepare a *state plan* or *contract* that spells out how the state will administer the funds in accordance with federal program guidelines.

Within the *private sector* the primary sources of funding are philanthropic foundations established by major companies or by families wishing to designate gifts to support humanitarian purposes. Some large, local businesses and industries contribute significantly to local improvement. These funds may be used to your benefit.

A third category of support, community foundations, is emerging, although in some cases it would be categorized under either a public or private sector. A community foundation set up to support specific purposes or community activities. With passage of limiting legislation on funding, community foundations have become fairly popular to support activities of public schools. Quasi-public corporations are generally established for the sole purpose of administering community foundation funds; they typically have boards of directors that represent the community at large.

Essentially, two types of grants are available: *competitive* and *noncompetitive*. A noncompetitive grant is typically awarded based on a formula and it is sometimes called an *entitlement*. The proposer agrees to conduct activities within a restricted range of options to achieve specific purposes of an established program. An entitlement or formula grant is more like a contract than a grant. Funds are available to the requesting agency if that agency develops a proposal in accordance with fairly definitive guidelines. Funding is based upon a formula, such as the number of youths who come from families with a particular income level.

———Grant Tip———
A noncompetitive grant is sometimes called an entitlement and is more like a contract than a grant.

Competitive ••• Noncompetitive

Of considerable interest to the grant seeker are *competitive grants*. Support under the *competitive* category is generally open, although certain programs may be limited to applicants in broad ranges of categories, such as public schools, private schools, higher education, and state education agencies. These programs are advertised in the case of the federal government, in the *Federal Register*, and the proposer must take the initiative in seeking the funds. Unlike entitlements where a designated amount of money is set aside for a specific purpose usually administered by a designated agency, in the competitive grants arena the proposer must specify what will be done in a particular time frame and what the costs (within reason) should be.

Some people categorize the type of funds according to the focus of the funds. Some funds have a very narrow or special purpose called *categorical funding.* Categorical funding is popular with politicians because it targets special interest groups, thus pleasing lobbyists and the special purpose groups and giving politicians content for speeches to constituencies. Additionally, if aid is targeted to a particular category, accountability seems easier, and evaluations can show changes relative to the status of that category.

Categorical ••• General

General aid is for general purposes. The logic behind general aid is that those closest to the problems should identify the problems and establish procedures to remediate them. Because the federal government or funding source cannot know the problems as well as local personnel, the responsibility for designating recipient groups should rest with the grant application developers.

Access to Information

Even with a good idea, adequate writing skills, and a supporting organization, you still need access to information about grant programs. Access to information may not be sufficient. Therefore, you also need to know what information is most important and how to use it. Primary sources of information include documents produced by the funding source, such as the *Federal Register,* which is addressed in Chapter 3, the *Catalog of Federal Domestic Assistance (CFDA),* which is covered in Chapter 4, and the application guidelines provided by the funding source. Secondary sources include news media, newsletters of professional associations, and even word of mouth. Persons who work in organizations with grant and contract offices may obtain information through those offices. Persons may obtain information by attending meetings or by talking with people who have previously received support for specific programs. The successful proposal writer will take an active interest in seeking information from many different sources.

Judging the importance of information and using it correctly are valuable skills. For instance, the proposal developer needs to know the total amount of funding available in a given year for a program, but sometimes finding out the details of available funds requires mathematical ability. It is not enough to know that the legislature has appropriated a particular sum for a program; you also need to know how much of that appropriation is available for new projects. This information may be in an application packet. If not, you should contact the funding agency to determine the amount available for new projects, the agency's estimate of the number of projects to be funded, and the general funding range for the projects. One confusing aspect in determining a funding level is that some programs allow multiple-year projects wherein the proposal writer develops a project for two, three, or more years. The agency may approve the project for a multiple-year time frame. In this case a portion of the agency's budget each year is obligated to support the continuing project's activities. The cumulative total of funding for continuing projects will not be available for new projects.

A continuing project becomes a *noncompeting continuation.* Near the end of each project year, project personnel must show that they have successfully achieved objectives for that year. If the project has been successful and funds continue to be available, the project becomes a noncompeting continuation, and project personnel do not need to develop a full, new competitive proposal. They prepare a much shorter continuation document. Generally, a noncompeting continuation proposal reviews activities from the preceding year and expresses a scope of work—including objectives, major activities, and a proposed budget—for the coming year.

Some programs reserve portions of their annual appropriations for administration and evaluation or for other costs. *Earmarked funds* reduce funding available for new projects. Thus you need to obtain some indication of funds available for new projects and use that information as a guideline in developing the scope of a new project. Next, apply some good common sense. If an agency has only $3,000,000 and hopes to fund 15 or 30 projects, you probably should not develop a proposal requesting $750,000.

A productive source of information about successful grants is the federal government. Successful, funded proposals arc in the public domain—they are public information. Under the Freedom of Information Act, you can go to government offices and review successful proposals. (Some proposal sections, such as budget, salaries, or personnel, may be excluded from public review.) Grant seekers should notify the agency in advance and identify exactly what they wish to review.

Besides access to and knowing how to use the information available, you need access to tools of the trade. *Tools of the trade* are those documents, books, newsletters, outlines, and other elements

———Grant Tip———
Funded proposals are in the public domain. You can go to government offices and review successful proposals.

that help the proposal writer develop successful proposals. (This book could qualify as a *tool of the trade*.) A tool might be a network that provides support and information. Special information sessions and grantwriting seminars are part of the communication network that arguably are some of the most important tools of the trade. This book addresses some major tools of the trade in subsequent chapters.

Planning to Be Competitive

Deadlines for ongoing grant competitions come around each year, usually at about the same time. Occasionally there are new initiatives for competitions. A small measure of planning and organizing will facilitate the orderly approach to entering the competitions.

Reserve some section of a file for your grants information. This file should contain components you would include as a part of most proposals, so the file will save you the time and effort required to write these segments each time. Some useful items for the files:

- Keep an up-to-date general summary of your organization written in clear, jargon-free prose. This synopsis will introduce a proposal reader to your organization. Be positive. This should sound almost as though the Chamber of Commerce wrote it.

- Have a brief explanation of your organization's capacity to operate a project. Comment on special features, such as computers or cooperative working agreements that can help, such as a college or university or major business or industry. List any special recognitions or awards. Do you have access to libraries or special databases?

- Demographic information should be easily accessible. Figure 1.3 is a suggested list of the types of information that will help. At the beginning of each year, update a file containing the descriptive items. Keep files for at least three years because some projects require data from previous years (example: local tax rate and per pupil expenditure). Also, data from past years can be used to show changes over time, such as changes in test scores, which may be helpful in evaluation and showing project success. Keep the data organized in the manner used by your system and state. Keep information in a file system with headings such as System Information or Student Information.

- Keep a handy list of charts and forms that you use in the proposal. These may relate to planning, timelines, showing

Grant Tip

Deadlines for ongoing grant competitions come around each year, usually at about the same time. Occasionally there are new initiatives or opportunities for competitions.

Figure 1.3. Demographic Data to Help in Proposal Writing in a Public School System

SYSTEM INFORMATION

1. Map(s) showing location of system in state and location of schools in system.
2. Written description of school system: proximity to major cities; airline service; census data such as population of area; major businesses and industries; education level of adults; organizational structure of school system square miles in city or county; per capita income (1-2 pages).
3. Federal Identification Number (Federal Employer ID Number).
4. Number of schools in system and grades included in each school.
5. Advisory boards.
6. Demographic data on pupils and employees: systemwide and by building units.

STUDENT INFORMATION (Use Numbers and Percents)

1. Total enrollment K-12 and by elementary/secondary, such as K, 1-8, 9-12, Preschool, and Adult.
2. Enrollment for each grade by school (monthly attendance report for system) and totals for each.
3. Number and percent of all minorities, by building and, if possible, by programs.
4. Retention rate (failures); absentee rate; dropout rate.
5. Reading and math standardized test scores by school, by grade, and averages for each.
6. Number served by special education, vocational programs, and enrollment.

TEACHER AND PERSONNEL INFORMATION

1. Total number of teachers; total administrative and professional staff.
2. Number of teachers by grade/subject, by school, and totals for each.
3. Level of training: Bachelor's, Master's, Master's + 45, Specialist, Doctorate (include administration).
4. Number of black, white, other minority and percentage (number of male and female).
5. Turnover rate.
6. Average years of experience.
7. Pertinent personnel policies.

FINANCIAL INFORMATION

1. All salary schedules.
2. Fringe benefits rates — social security, hospital, retirement (teacher and nonteacher), life insurance — and how each is computed.
3. Local tax rate.
4. Per pupil expenditure.
5. Percentage of local supplement—percentage of local vs. state funds vs. federal funds.
6. Pertinent fiscal/financial policies.

PRIVATE SCHOOL INFORMATION

1. List of private schools in system—administrators' names, addresses, and phone numbers. Have the private schools been approved by State Education Agency as eligible for federal and state funds?
2. Number of students in private schools in system by grade.

OTHER

1. Forms file: blank standard forms, blank "boilerplate" forms.
2. Copies of timelines, management charts, and organizational chart.
3. Public announcements for newspapers.
4. Copies of any assurance forms for civil rights, Title IX, handicapped.
5. Any information on court orders or important court cases influencing your district.

personnel responsibilities. In the "forms file" keep extra, blank copies of standard forms and "boilerplate" or minimal forms.

For the serious grantwriter, yet another planning step is important. Write to each grant competition of interest and request the grant application package. After you review the application, whether or not you prepare an application, make a note on a master list of (a) the date of the competition, (b) ideas you have for the competition, (c) priority of this grant for your organization, and (d) the address (name and phone of contact) of the office where you will write for next year's application packet. Next, circulate a general description of the competition, along with a statement of your interest, and solicit from your colleagues their interest, ideas, or commitment in developing a project for the next competition. Follow up on this solicitation and get plans started six to ten months in advance of *the usual* application deadline. Know that the regulations, guidelines, and approximate due date for proposals seldom change much from year to year. Nevertheless, *check the dates each year, and read carefully all new application packets.*

Develop a list of interesting programs, a file of applications, a list of past and approximate future due dates, names of people interested in a project, and some good ideas as the basis of planning and preparing a project for the next year. If there is substantial interest, initiate some planning, brainstorming, and writing sessions. Contact the federal office to get names and locations of funded projects. Get into the *mainstream* of project ideas. These steps, completed nearly a year in advance of your formal application, will prepare you for the competition.

If you are unsuccessful when you submit your proposal the first time, don't despair. Get the reviewers' comments. Review and study your proposal. Don't slavishly follow all reviewer comments. There will be new reviewers next year. Visit a successful project. Find and save good ideas. Speak with program personnel so they will know about your continuing interest. Plan to succeed the next time. Stalk each grant carefully.

——— **Grant Tip** ———
If you are unsuccessful the first time, don't despair. Don't slavishly follow all reviewer comments. There will be new reviewers next year.

Types of Grants: Competitive or Noncompetitive

The *noncompetitive grant* is typically a response to an entitlement established by some formula (e.g., Title I entitlement). The grant seekers (e.g., Local Education Agency [LEA] personnel) complete forms developed by the funding source (for Title I this would be the federal agency and State Education Agency [SEA] personnel in the particular state). These forms provide some minimum standards and uniformity to help SEA persons monitor the project to ensure that it meets federal and state regulations.

These noncompetitive grants require little creativity and not much project development; the proposer completes forms and assurances much like a contract. Most projects will be very similar as they are developed and administered under the SEA master plan (State Plan) that governs how the SEA will handle that particular program.

A *competitive grant,* however, is not awarded until the grantwriter develops a proposal that can compete successfully on established criteria with other proposals submitted in the same competition. The money is available to support projects to carry forth the purposes of the program, but it is *not* earmarked for a particular organization (e.g., LEA) or held as an entitlement based upon a preset formula. Applications for competitive grants extend and test the grantwriter's skills and creativity. Within the broad guidelines of a program's purposes, the competitive grant will support a project developed to serve the needs of a client group. Each project may be quite different as the funding agency only provides general guidelines and criteria.

Figure 1.4 provides a brief overview of two major types of grants, competitive and noncompetitive, and some classification of noncompetitive grants (i.e., some of the vocabulary or terminology for these grants). The purposes of and approaches to competitive and noncompetitive grants are quite different. In developing a *competitive* proposal the writer undertakes a large writing and development task; in a noncompetitive grant the funds are there and the person need only complete the minimal boilerplate forms and program descriptions.

Eligible recipients for competitive grants are LEAs, SEAs, institutions of higher education (IHEs), public and private profit and nonprofit agencies, and individuals. Eligible recipients for noncompetitive grants are governmental units or occasionally other nonprofit agencies. Figure 1.5 summarizes some of the differences between competitive and noncompetitive grants.

Government Contracts

It is no secret that the U.S. Government is the largest purchaser of products and services in the world. All of the requirements for

---

—— Grant Tip ——

Every 20 seconds of each working day, the U.S. Government awards a contract worth an average of $465,000. That totals over $800 billion per year.

At latest count, there are 22 million small businesses in the United States, yet only about 1% of them participate in government contracts.

Figure 1.4. An Outline Summary of Types of Grants

Grant: Award of money or direct assistance to perform an activity or project whose outcome is seen as less certain than that from a contract, with expected results described in general terms. Application can be submitted without having been solicited, an unsolicited proposal, or through a program announcement (Request for Application or RFA). Most federal grants fall into the following categories:

- **Competitive Grants:** awarded for specific types of research, demonstration, training, or service to program participants. (These are the grants dealt with in detail in this book.)

- **Entitlement or Noncompetitive Grants:** awarded automatically or based on a minimum "proposal" on the basis of legally defined formula to all agencies or institutions that qualify (state or medical schools). These are sometimes called formula grants when given to governmental agencies for distribution and monitoring under a state plan or state grant process.

- **Formula Grants:** awarded by federal agencies on the basis of a set formula such as so many dollars for population, per capita income, or enrollment. Chief recipients are state governments.

- **Block Grants:** sometimes called "bloc" grants; refers to grants in which the federal government merely stipulates in broad terms how the state and local government should spend federal aid. The tactical decision on where the money should be spent is left to the discretion of state and local officials. One purpose of block grants is to decentralize federal decision-making powers and let those closest to the problem define how to allocate the available funds. These are not "categorical" in the traditional sense.

- **Categorical Grants:** a restrictive version of the block grants are designated to serve only a specific group or category specified in the enabling legislation. Examples are funds for handicapped, bilingual education, or Title I. Grants may be competitive or noncompetitive.

---

doing business with the government are published daily in the *Commerce Business Daily*. The *CBD* is available through subscription. Copies are available at dispository libraries, or via the Internet. See Chapter 5, "Using the Internet to Access Funding Resources," for the Internet address.

Because the United States Government is the world's largest purchaser of goods and services, it is necessary for the government to contract with private businesses to provide the needed services. "Every 17 seconds of each working day, the United States Government awards a contract with an average value of $465,000" (retrieved at *Resources Offers Commerce Business Daily Free Trial*. URL: http://www.gcswin.com/opp1.htm). The purpose of this section is to make you aware of the enormous potential that exists in the governmental contracting business. It is not the intent of this book to teach you everything you always wanted to know about government contracts; however, we do not want you to overlook this area of funding.

There is a vast amount of information to assist you in learning more about contracts. Some of this information is good and some of

Figure 1.5. Two Types of Grants: Competitive and Noncompetitive

FACTOR	COMPETITIVE GRANT	NONCOMPETITIVE GRANT
Purpose	Typically supports the cost of special and/or exemplary project, demonstration and/or research project, etc.	Typically provides support for conducting—such as block grant—Title I or Chapter 2. This may include salaries, equipment, or supplies.
Structure of Document	Development of a narrative document in accordance with general guidelines.	Completion of specific forms.
Eligible Recipients	IHEs, SEAs, community agencies and/or individuals. Must check proposal guidelines that you are interested in.	Typically LEAs and SEAs, and some other government agencies.
Creativity	High degree of creativity required.	Little creativity is required.
Length of Document	Long and detailed; perhaps between 20-80 pages, or more.	Several pages.
Amount of Work Required	Requires extensive planning and development of written materials that respond to funding agency established criteria.	Typically involves filling in the blanks (boilerplate forms) and providing support explanations.
Preparation Dates	Notice dates are published in the *FR*. Grant periods are from 1-5 years.	Typically prepared on an annual basis.
Selection Criteria	Criteria established by the Secretary of Education and agency seeking to support innovative projects.	Must meet established guidelines, often a plan developed by another level of government.

it leaves something to be desired. You be the judge. The point here is that you should begin to accumulate contract information for your personal reference library. One category of sources that you should not overlook is governmental agencies' references and resources. For instance, if you are interested in contracts offered through the U.S. Department of Energy (DOE), then by all means obtain a copy of the *Acquisition Guide: A DOE Guide to the Award and Administration of Contracts* available free on the Internet at http://www.pr.doe.gov/acqguide.html. The National Institutes of Health (NIH), the National Science Foundation (NSF) and the U.S. Department of Education provide similar information, as do other federal agencies. Generally, these informative guides are free.

Perhaps you have a product or service you would like to sell to the government. If this is the case, it may be worth your while to learn more about the U.S. General Service Administration (GSA). Simply stated, the GSA is the government's purchasing agent and business manager. One of the hallmarks of the GSA is its strong support of small businesses, women-owned businesses, and minority-owned businesses. One of the best ways to find out more about GSA's services is to contact your local Small Business Center.

There are many similarities between grants and contracts. However, there are also notable differences that must be taken into account. Be sure to follow your institution's policies and procedures before submitting contracts through your institution.

Research Grants

Let's look at some of the points that characterize research grants and make them significantly different from nonresearch grants, such as the sample proposal presented in Chapter 10. For all grants and contracts that are awarded, institutions must comply with many different rules, regulations, laws, and policies. However, research grants generally pose a number of additional areas of compliance, including human subjects, care and use of laboratory animals, biosafety, radiation safety, drugs and controlled substances, and misconduct in scientific research. Institutions may vary on how these compliances are monitored, but frequently monitoring is through an Institutional Research Office or Review Board.

Institutions will vary in how they process and review research grants. For instance, your proposal may be classified as a research grant. However, your institution may classify it as exempt from the more elaborate review process or it may receive an expedited review classification. It would be a good idea to visit your institution's research office and get to know the individuals who are responsible for making decisions regarding research proposals. If you are associated with an institution or agency that has a research office, get a copy of the latest policies and procedures that your organization may have available. Then read and review them carefully. If you do not, you may miss an important deadline, causing you to miss the grant application submission date. If you are mainly dealing with research grants, it makes sense to set up files to keep all of the needed forms handy.

Most institutions have in place a set of rigid policies and procedures for all employees to follow when submitting research grants. For instance, when submitting a research grant to work with Head Start children, you should expect to complete detailed forms outlining how the human subjects you propose to study are going to be protected. At times it may be necessary for you to appear before a Human Subjects Compliance Panel at your institution to address any questions or concerns they might have before final approval is given to your proposal. It may be necessary for you to rewrite parts of your proposal and resubmit it for final approval. Given the time constraints in grantwriting, it is imperative that you begin your institutional compliance early.

Depending on the type of research you are proposing, there are numerous additional forms to be completed prior to submitting your proposal. Forms will vary from institution to institution, but generally they will all ask for similar assurances from you, the researcher. For example, you may have to complete a Human Subjects Compliance form, a Hazardous Agents Compliance form, or an Application for Controlled Substance Compliance form. Most research application guidelines require that you provide your institution's compliance forms when you submit your proposal.

Some Tips and Sobering Thoughts About Grants

Be familiar with the legislation, regulations, agency, and program. You don't need to be sophisticated, but do your homework.

Understand what has been funded; know what has worked and what has not.

Your idea doesn't need to be brand-new, but it should be new to your area or have some distinctive twist.

Relate your idea to current and important theories in your field or in some field of human behavior. If pertinent, rely on accepted theories (e.g., motivation, communication, change) to support what you propose.

Although you will express project need in terms of *your* particular population, the funding agency is *primarily* interested in how a project such as yours has fairly wide and general application. By relating your project to appropriate theories, you help the agency understand how project ideas can be useful in other sites and with other people. A brief but focused literature review will help you build a conceptual framework to show how your idea fits with current research and thinking.

Although you may explain that your evaluation is related to your objectives, the *real test* of project success is a reduction of the need that precipitated the project. Good projects should put themselves out of business in a few years—or be so successful that hordes flock to your doors. Get and keep good baseline data. At some point three to five years later, a comparison of the original baseline data with new baseline data will show the true measure of your project's success.

If your state has several electoral votes, is politically conservative, has legislators in key positions on key committees, and is located on a coast or near interesting places to visit, you may have an advantage in the proposal chase. In Figure 1.6, for example, the locations of the major, federally funded education initiatives (ERIC Clearinghouses and Support Components, Research and Development Centers, Regional Educational Laboratories). These are supported by the Education Department's Office of Educational Research and

————Grant Tip————
Proposal development is probably best approached with a businesslike effort buoyed by a sense of competition and play.

Figure 1.6. Distribution of OERI's Major Funding[1]

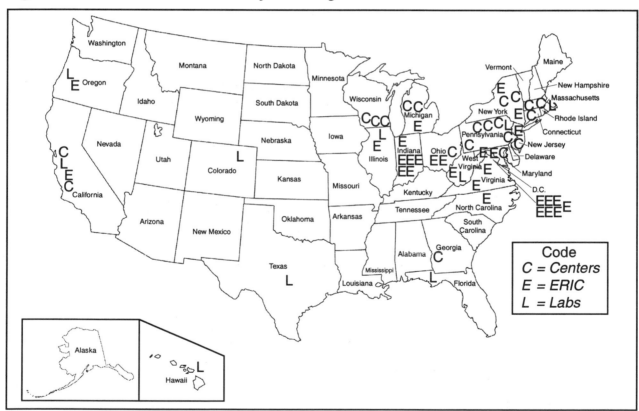

Source: U.S. Department of Education, OERI, 1997.

[1]Distribution of major OERI-funded Centers/Labs/ERIC prior to "At Risk" Center Competition. Some Centers are located in several sites.

Improvement (OERI). Figure 1.7 provides an OERI Organizational Chart that shows the national centers (Office of Educational Research and Improvement, 2000). A similar chart using influential congressional committee chairs might also be informative.

The "peer review" process is designed to give everyone a fair chance in competitions. On the other hand, some competitions award "performance points" for current projects, so those projects start with a 5-15 point advantage.

If a proposal meets an agency's "fundable" criterion, there is room for considerations other than a project's absolute value as rated by reviewers. Considerations could include past performance, geographic distribution requirements, prior submissions, and even some political influence. Don't panic or be naive. The funding process is generally protected by the peer review process—but not absolutely. A good proposal with influence probably will beat a good proposal with little or no influence.

Some Concluding Thoughts

Much skill and knowledge are involved in successful proposal writing, along with some luck and serendipity. Proposal development is best approached with a businesslike effort buoyed by a sense of competition and play. The Ancient Mariner "stoppeth one in three"

Figure 1.7. Office of Educational Research and Improvement Organizational Chart

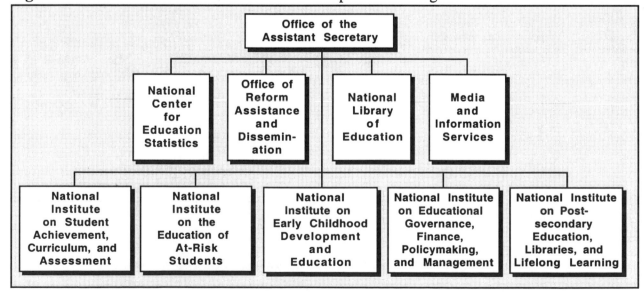

and everyone loves a .333 hitter in baseball. Why should you extend the odds? Seek 100%, but know that your grant application "hit rate" will begin to average out. That holds true for when you *start.* If you lose the first or second try, you will begin to win as you gain experience. It is not mystique; it is experience, skill, perseverence, and savvy. It is a serious game.

You can't win if you don't get in the game and play. You can't win with just an idea. You must put "pencil to paper" and express a good idea clearly.

Don't quit after one loss. Winners persevere.

2

How to Explore Grant Possibilities in Education

Introduction

You can become an effective proposal writer for grants in education. However, you must become familiar with the various U.S. Department of Education programs, their purposes and requirements, and their deadline dates before you respond to a Request for Application (RFA). You must be familiar with the various funding sources and the individuals who inform you about solicited education programs, and about the money that has been appropriated and allocated by the federal government. This chapter summarizes some important documents that provide this information. Although this chapter addresses selected basic information sources for grant seekers, Chapters 3 and 4, "Using the *Federal Register* and the *Code of Federal Regulations*" and "Using the *Catalog of Federal Domestic Assistance*," respectively, will cover these key federal documents in more detail. Chapter 5, "Using the Internet to Access Funding Resources," provides a variety of different funding sources on the internet. You must identify and use reference materials (the "tools of the trade") in planning for and responding to an RFA effectively. Know about new and old programs, frequent changes in regulations, and deadline dates for submitting the proposals. The Taft Corporation highlights this by saying that "modern fundraising is 90% research, 10% solicitation." In responding to federal grants, research and detailed knowledge are equally important.

Points to Consider Before Responding

Some questions you should consider and answer before you begin to develop a contract or an application can be divided into two major categories: personal and institutional. Examine your areas of interest, your time commitment, your qualifications, and your expertise to develop the proposal. Answers to the questions in Figure 2.1 will help you decide if you should proceed. While you may say "yes" to these questions, you must also examine institutional or organizational

———— **Grant Tip** ————
Examine your instititional or organizational commitment for the proposal before you commit your own time and resources.

Figure 2.1. Personal Questions Concerning Proposal

- Will I write the proposal?
- Do I have enough time to write the proposal and submit it by the deadline date?
- Can I maintain current job responsibilities and activities while developing a grant proposal?
- Do I have the necessary support personnel—clerical, printing, etc.—to write a competitive proposal?
- Do I have the authority to commit staff to respond quickly to write the proposal?
- Am I willing to put a high level of energy into the proposal to make sure it is competitive and not just mediocre?

Figure 2.2. Institutional Commitment Questions

- Is this grant activity within the scope of my institution or agency?
- Will the institution's priorities be skewed by responding or by conducting the project?
- Does my institution have the necessary facilities and resources to conduct the activities of the project?
- If matching funds are required, can or will my institution meet these requirements?
- How many different people and departments will be involved?
- If the funds are cut off and the program is dropped, what effect would it have on my institution?
- What are the hiring requirements at my institution for soft-money positions?
- Will it take two or three months to hire someone after I have been notified of the grant award?
- Can I still meet the requirements of the grant if I do not hire the personnel in a timely manner?

commitment for the proposal. Figure 2.2 provides some questions you should consider and answer before proceeding to the writing stage.

Individuals who begin to write proposals without considering the above questions often end up not completing the proposal or not meeting the deadline.

Identifying and Using Reference Material

There are over 2,500 daily information sources describing what is going on in the U.S. Capitol. Although one main characteristic of a successful proposal writer is never to leave a stone unturned, there are limits as to which data sources are the most appropriate and how much information you can review, such as federal information sources, subscription services, sources that monitor legislation, and other references and sources that may be appropriate.

Federal Information Sources

Federal Register (FR)

The *Federal Register (FR)* is published every weekday, except on legal holidays, by the Office of the Federal Register, National Archives and Records Administration, under the Federal Register Act and the regulations of the Administrative Committee of the *Federal Register*. The *FR* is the federal government's uniform system for making available to the public regulations and legal notices issued by federal agencies. It includes presidential proclamations and executive orders, federal agency documents having general applicability and legal effect, documents required to be published by acts of Congress, and other federal agency documents of public interest. The *Federal Register* is published in paper, 24x microfiche, and as an online database through GOP Access, a service of the U.S. Government Printing Office. It is available at most major libraries, and its distribution is through the Superintendent of Documents, Washington, D.C. 20402. The telephone number is (202) 512-1800 for paper or fiche and (202) 512-1530 for online database. In 2000 the *Federal Register* was furnished by mail to subscribers for $697 per year or $220 per year in microfiche form. Individual copies were $8.00 each. The online database is available on a Wide Area Information Servicer (WAIS) through the Internet. Chapter 3, "Using the *Federal Register* and the *Code of Federal Regulations*," discusses this important federal information source in more detail.

———Grant Tip———
The Federal Register *is the government's uniform system for making available to the public regulations and legal notices issued by federal agencies.*

Catalog of Federal Domestic Assistance (CFDA)

The *Catalog of Federal Domestic Assistance* is a government-wide compendium of federal programs, projects, services, and activities that provide assistance or benefits to the public. This source is published annually by the Office of Management and Budget (OMB) in loose-leaf form, using the most current data available to describe the status of programs at the time the *Catalog* or the *Update* to the

——— Grant Tip ———
The CFDA *is a government-wide compendium of federal programs, projects, services, and activities that provide assistance or benefits to the public.*

Catalog is compiled. The basic edition of the *Catalog*, usually published by June, reflects completed congressional action on program legislation. The *Update*, usually published in December, reflects completed congressional action on the President's budget proposals and on substantive legislation as of the date of compilation and includes information on federal programs that was not available at the time the latest edition of the *Catalog* was released. This *Catalog*, which is addressed in more detail in Chapter 4, "Using the *Catalog of Federal Domestic Assistance*," describes all federal programs that distribute funds to states, organizations, and individuals. Program descriptions contain uniform, detailed information about individual grant programs. The objectives, types of assistance, and eligibility requirements are provided so applicants can determine whether they are eligible for the assistance and whether it meets their program needs. The *CFDA* is available at most major libraries or by subscription from the Superintendent of Documents, Government Printing Office, Washington, D.C. 20402. The telephone number is (202) 512-1800. The 2000 domestic subscription price was $87 annually, which included periodically updated materials.

Federal Assistance Program Retrieval System (FAPRS)

The *Federal Assistance Program Retrieval System (FAPRS)* is a computerized question-answer system of rapid access to federal domestic assistance program information. The system provides information on federal programs that meet the developmental needs of the applicant and for which the applicant meets basic eligibility criteria. Program information provided by *FAPRS* is determined from information input supplied by the requestor. Upon receipt of an inquiry specifying the type of organization and its needs, the system can provide a printout of all of the domestic assistance programs that might be useful to that particular applicant. The primary output provided by *FAPRS* consists of a list of the titles and identifying numbers of the applicable programs from the *Catalog of Federal Domestic Assistance (CFDA)*. After you review this list of programs, you can obtain additional program information by (a) requesting the system to print complete program description(s) by program number(s), (b) requesting the system to print selected sections of program description(s), (c) requesting a list of applicable Office of Management and Budget (OMB) circular coordination requirements for each program, or (d) referring directly to the *CFDA* for specific information on a program. Individual

Grant Tip
The FAPRS *provides information on federal programs that meet the developmental needs of the applicant and for which the applicant meets basic eligibility criteria.*

FAPRS printouts can be obtained from access points located throughout the country; for volume users, direct access on a cost-reimburs-
able basis is available through the General Services Administration.
For further information and a specific price, call (202) 708-5126 or
toll-free answering service: (800) 669-8331, or write to the Federal
Domestic Assistance Catalog Staff, Reporters Building—Room 101,
300 7th Street, SW, Washington, D.C. 20407.

Commerce Business Daily (CBD)

The *Commerce Business Daily (CBD)* is published every
weekday, except holidays, by the U.S. Department of Commerce.
The *CBD* lists all federal procurement invitations, including the
Department of Education's requests for proposals (RFPs) for contracts. Although the *CBD* does not deal with grant competitions
directly, some institutions and agencies that traditionally seek grant
funds may benefit from materials included in the *CBD*. This publication is available at most major libraries or by subscription from the
Superintendent of Documents, U.S. Government Printing Office,
Washington, D.C. 20402. The telephone number is (202) 512-1800
and the on-line database number is (202) 482-0632. The 2000 domestic subscription price was $324 annually by first-class priority mail
or $343.75 annually by regular second-class mail. A six-month
subscription was $162.00 by first-class priority mail and $137.50 by
regular second-class mail.

> ——**Grant Tip**——
> *The* CBD *lists all federal procurement invitations, including the Department of Education's request for proposals (RFPs) for contracts.*

Code of Federal Regulations (CFR)

The *Code of Federal Regulations (CFR)* is published annually
by the Office of the Federal Register. This publication is a codification
of the general and permanent rules published in the *Federal Register*
by the executive departments and agencies of the federal government.
The *CFR* is divided into 50 titles that represent broad areas subject to
federal regulations. Each title is divided into chapters that usually bear
the name of the issuing agency. The *CFR* is kept up-to-date by the
individual issues of the *Federal Register*. These two publications
must be used together to determine the latest version of any given rule.
The price for the *CFR* differs according to the number of books that
cover the title of the agency in which you are interested. For example,
there are three books for education at a total cost of about $110 per
year. This publication is available at most major libraries or by

subscription from the Superintendent of Documents, U.S. Government Printing Office, Washington, D.C. 20402. The telephone number is (202) 512-1800.

United States Government Manual

The *United States Government Manual* is the official handbook of the federal government. The *Manual,* 868 pages in length, is the best source of information on the activities, functions, organization, and principal officials of the agencies of the legislative, judicial, and executive branches of government. It includes information on quasi-official agencies, international organizations in which the United States participates, and boards, committees, and commissions. A typical agency description includes a list of principal officials, a summary statement of the agency's purpose and role in the federal government, a brief history of the agency, including its legislative or executive authority, a description of its programs and activities, and a "Sources of Information" section. The 2000 price for this annual publication was $46 from the Superintendent of Documents, U.S. Government Printing Office, Washington, D.C. 20402. The telephone number is (202) 512-1800.

Resources in Education

Resources in Education provides up-to-date information about educational research sponsored by the Office of Educational Research and Improvement (OERI), Department of Education. It is designed to keep grant proposal writers, teachers, administrators, research specialists, others in the educational community, and the public informed about findings from educational research. The 2000 price for this annual publication was $102 from the Superintendent of Documents, U.S. Government Printing Office, Washington, D.C. 20402. The telephone number is (202) 512-1800.[1]

Information on Monitoring Upcoming Legislation

Grant seekers not only must remain up-to-date with current programs and new developments and policies within the U.S. Department

[1]Prices, addresses, phone numbers, publication information, and other details of these sources may change without notice. We have included the most recent information we have, but we cannot be responsible for changes.

of Education but they must also monitor the legislative developments in Congress so they can plan accordingly and respond to changes in a timely manner. Numerous publications and newsletters are helpful here. The *Congressional Record* and *Congressional Quarterly* are two major publications that provide information on legislation.

Congressional Record

The *Congressional Record* is the daily record of activities conducted within Congress. The *Record* contains a verbatim official report of the floor debates and information on new bills being introduced. In 2000 this publication cost $325 per year or $165 for six months or $2.75 per issue. Contact Government Printing Office, Washington, D.C. 20402. Phone (202) 512-1800.

Congressional Quarterly

The *Congressional Quarterly* is a weekly report of major action taken in Congress. This *Quarterly* documents how members of Congress voted on various bills. Contact *Congressional Quarterly*, Inc., 1414 22nd Street, NW, Washington, D.C. 20037.

Other Publications Monitoring Legislation

Other publications, such as newspapers, weekly journals, and newsletters of professional lobbying organizations monitor congressional activities and can help the grant seeker find out about new developments. The *Washington Post* and *New York Times* provide daily information on congressional activities, while the *Wall Street Journal* and *USA Today* frequently refer to activities taking place in Congress. Professional publications and subscription newsletters often print timely information on Congress, but the *Congressional Quarterly* and the *Congressional Record* are the most comprehensive publications in this area. Weekly news magazines (e.g., *U.S. News & World Report, Time*, and *Newsweek*) are also excellent sources for monitoring new developments in Congress.

Subscription Service Sources

An almost endless selection of subscription service sources is available on a daily, weekly, and monthly basis. Typically, subscription

―――Grant Tip―――
Not only do you need to keep up with current programs and new developments and policies within the U.S. Department of Education, you must also monitor legislative developments.

―――Grant Tip―――
Subscription service sources typically provide timely information and good summaries that help you avoid having to read basic information sources.

service sources gather some of their information from the previously mentioned federal information sources, other sources that monitor legislation, and news releases from departments in the U.S. government. However, some subscription services provide very timely information. Good summaries help you avoid having to read a lot of basic information sources; they screen and abstract the information you may be specifically interested in. Some subscription services described here are especially helpful.

Education Daily

——Grant Tip——
Education Daily
provides accurate,
timely reports on
activities of
Congress, the U.S.
Department of
Education, and the
White House.

Education Daily is the education community's independent news subscription service. It is printed daily, except weekends and legal holidays, and provides accurate, timely reports on activities of Congress, the U.S. Department of Education, and the White House. It also provides weekly legislative updates, reports on the latest educational research findings and activities, and other newsworthy items. The 2000 subscription cost for this daily educational newsletter service was $604 per year or $302 for six months. Contact Capitol Publications, Inc., 7201 McKinney Circle, Frederick, MD 21704. Phone (800) 655-5597 or (703) 683-4100.

Federal Research Report

The *Federal Research Report* is available on a weekly basis. This report includes federal contract opportunities and federal notes. The 2000 subscription rate was $284 per year. Multiple-year and six-month rates are available on request. Contact *Federal Research Report*, Business Publishing, Inc., 8737 Colesville Road, Room 1100, Silver Spring, MD 20910-3925. To order, phone (301) 589-5103 or (800) 274-6737.

Federal Grants and Contracts Weekly

The *Federal Grants and Contracts Weekly* is published every Monday except Labor Day and Christmas week. It focuses on project opportunities in research, training, and service. This *Weekly* is a timely and complete newsletter about new federal grants and contracts available. A monthly supplement focuses on foundation funding, profiles of key agencies, and updates on new developments, legislation, and regulations. This highly recommended newsletter helps the grant seeker to keep in touch with various project opportunities. The 2000 price was $398 per year or $210 for six months. Contact Capitol Publications, Inc., 7201 McKinney Circle, Frederick, MD 21704. Phone (800) 655-5597 or (703) 683-4100.

Education Funding News

The *Education Funding News,* in publication for over 25 years, produced by the Education Funding Research Council is published weekly except the last week in August and the last week in December. This publication provides information on what is happening in Washington and features grant opportunities in the field of education. Subscribers also receive exclusive access to the Online Funding Deadline Database, an updated, searchable deadline funding database accessible over the internet. The 2000 subscription price was $298 per year for 50 issues. Contact Thompson Publishing Group, P.O. Box 26185, Tampa, FL 33633-0922. Phone (800) 677-3789.

What Works in Teaching and Learning

What Works in Teaching and Learning provides up-to-date news of breakthrough programs and studies from around the United States. It includes coverage of federal research activities, research results, and funding. This biweekly newsletter also reports on testing, and evaluation, education reforms, and related topics of interest to individuals who are researchers or administrators in education. The 2000 price was $277 per year or $163 for six months. Contact Capitol Publications, Inc., 7201 McKinney Circle, Frederick, MD 21704. Phone (800) 655-5597 or (703) 683-4100.

The Chronicle of Higher Education

The *Chronicle of Higher Education* is published weekly except during the last two weeks in August and the last two weeks in December. It provides timely news in all fields of higher education, government policies affecting education, grant deadline dates, grant awards, and much more information that will be of interest to the grant seeker. The 2000 price was $75 per year for 49 issues or $40.50 for 24 issues. Contact *The Chronicle of Higher Education*, P. O. Box 1955, Marion, Ohio 43306-2055. Phone (800) 728-2803 or (202) 466-1032.

Other Publications Concerning Education and Technology

Capitol Publications produces a biweekly newsletter titled *Special Education Report,* which in 2000 cost $308 per year or $156 for six months. This newsletter deals with current and pertinent information about federal legislation, regulations, programs, and funding for educating children with disabilities. This newsletter also deals with federal and state litigation on educating disabled persons and reviews innovations and research in the field. Contact Capitol Publications, Inc., 7201 McKinney Circle, Frederick, MD 21704. Phone (800) 655-5597 or (703) 683-4100.

The *Education Technology Monitor* is a monthly newsletter that reports on developments in education technology. Also available to subscribers is free access to online funding and grant resources. The cost for this newsletter is $177 annually and is published by the Education Funding Research Council. Contact Thompson Publishing Group, P.O. Box 26185, Tampa, FL 33633-0922. Phone (800) 677-3789.

The *Vocational Training News* covers the Federal Job Training Partnership Act and the Carl D. Perkins Vocational Act. This newsletter also covers illiteracy, Private Industry Councils, and state education and training initiatives. The 2000 cost for this weekly publication was $325 per year for 50 issues or $162.50 for six months for 25 issues. Contact Capitol Publications, Inc., 7201 McKinney Circle, Frederick, MD 21704. Phone (800) 655-5597 or (703) 683-4100.

The *Health Grants and Contracts Weekly* contains timely and comprehensive coverage of health-related federal grants and contracts. This weekly also profiles key funding agencies and provides legislative and regulatory updates. The 2000 cost was $383 per year for 50 issues or $191.50 for six months for 25 issues. Contact Capitol Publications, Inc., 7201 McKinney Circle, Frederick, MD 21704. Phone (800) 655-5597 or (703) 683-4100.

Annual Resource Documents

The following annual resource documents are excellent tools to use in exploring grants in education. They usually provide a general overall view of the programs and grant administration activities. A couple of these publications also provide information on the past and current funding levels, the contact person, and so forth.

——— Grant Tip ———
Annual resource documents provide a general overview of programs and grant administration activities, and some may provide information on past and current funding levels.

Guide to Federal Funding for Education

The annual *Guide to Federal Funding for Education* provides an accurate, detailed description of the federal programs offering financial assistance to local and state educational agencies (LEAs and SEAs), postsecondary institutions (PSIs), and other public and private organizations and agencies working in the field of education. For each program, the *Guide* provides a program purpose, quick check (eligible applicant, type of aid, and requirements), key facts and any restrictions about the program, the grantmaking process (administering agency, application procedure, and selection criteria), award information, and the person to contact for more information about the program. In addition to this 1,300-plus page document, the *Guide* issues monthly *Grant Updates* that provide information on new funding opportunities and important statutory, regulatory, and budgetary initiatives. The *Updates* include summaries of recent regulations and selected funding invitations published in the *Federal Register* and the *Commerce Business Daily*. This *Guide* and the monthly *Grant Updates* provide convenient and economical access to basic information regarding the various programs being funded in the U.S. Department of Education. The 2000 cost for the *Guide to Federal Funding for Education* with *Grant Updates* was $297 per year plus shipping and handling. Another guide provided by the Government Information Services is the *Guide to Federal Funding for Governments and Nonprofits* (including monthly *Grant Updates* at $339 plus postage and handling). Contact Thompson Publishing Group, P.O. Box 26185, Tampa, FL 33633-0922. Phone (800) 677-3789.

Annual Register of Grant Support

The *Annual Register of Grant Support—A Directory of Funding Sources* is a comprehensive compendium of over 3,000 gifts and awards. This annual publication provides grant support information in four major areas: *public funding sources* among government departments and agencies; *private funding sources* that include private and family foundations; *corporate sources* that include corporate foundations and giving programs; and the *nontraditional sources* including educational associations, special interest groups, professional associations, and community trusts. The education section deals with the four major headings: *educational projects and research* (general), *elementary and secondary education, higher education projects and research,* and *scholar aid programs* (all disciplines). Each listing comes directly from the source and provides name, address, telephone numbers, fields of interest, names and purposes of grant programs, total funding available, money per award, eligibility requirements, and deadlines. It also notes the number of applicants, recipients, and representative awards in the most recent year. The 2000 cost for the *Annual Register of Grant Support—A Directory of Funding Sources* was $210 plus shipping and handling charges. Contact the Order Department, Reed Elseveir, 121 Chanlon, P.O. Box 31, New Providence, NJ 07974-9904. Phone (800) 521-8110 or (908) 508-7696 [fax].

Federal Grants Management Handbook

The *Federal Grants Management Handbook* is a loose-leaf handbook and monthly update service for individuals who manage federal grants. The publisher states the *Handbook* "cuts through the jargon to provide practical advice and straightforward answers to help grants managers comply with complex administrative requirements." The *Handbook* outlines the management of a federal grant by providing practical advice and information on the following: how to organize receipt of grants funds; how to administer federal grants; how to develop and maintain a satisfactory grant accounting system; how to develop and negotiate an indirect cost rate; the basic principles in purchasing and procurement under grants; an overview of audit requirements of federal grants; how to comply with "strings attached" to federal grants; and much more grant management information. This *Handbook* also provides monthly page updates and "Current Developments" newsletters that cover a wide range of topics and events that affect federal grants management. The 2000 annual cost was $269 including the monthly updates with a $237 renewal rate. Contact Thompson Publishing Group, Subscription Service Center, P. O. Box 26185, Tampa, FL 33623-6185. For instant service, call toll free (800) 677-3789 or (202) 872-4000.

Guide to Department of Education Programs

The *Guide to Department of Education Programs* is published by the Office of Public Affairs, U.S. Department of Education. This annual *Guide* provides, in compact form, information necessary to begin the process of applying for federal education program funds. The guide's contents include the following offices: Office of Elementary and Secondary Education; Office of Postsecondary Education;

——Grant Tip——

Sometimes it is difficult to ascertain what information is correct. Contact the U.S. Department of Education directly. The application package is comprehensive and will serve as your main resource.

Office of Educational Research and Improvement; Office of Bilingual Education and Minority Languages Affairs; Office of Vocational and Adult Education; and Office of Special Education and Rehabilitation Services. Contact the U.S. Department of Education, 400 Maryland Avenue, SW, Washington, D.C. 20202. Phone (877) 433-7827.

Other Information Sources

The Grantsmanship Center

The Grantsmanship Center offers a loose-leaf collection of reprints from *The Grantsmanship Center News* that provides practical advice and information on program planning and proposal writing, funding strategies, and many more areas of interest to nonprofit grant seekers. Contact The Grantsmanship Center, 1125 W. Sixth Street, Fifth Floor, P.O. Box 17220, Los Angeles, CA 90017. Phone (213) 482-9860.

Office of Educational Research and Improvement (OERI)

The U.S. Department of Education's Office of Educational Research and Improvement (OERI) supports and conducts research on education; collects and analyzes education statistics; administers grant and contract programs to improve libraries and library education; and disseminates information to teachers, school administrators, policymakers, researchers, and grant seekers. One avenue that they use is the OERI-funded Regional Educational Laboratories. These laboratories "plan programs through an ongoing assessment of regional needs, a knowledge of the current trends in research and practice, and interaction with the many other agencies and institutions that assist communities and schools with educational improvement" (*Institutional Projects Funded by OERI,* 2000). These laboratories and their respective phone numbers are shown in Figure 2.3.

The OERI also oversees and funds an Education Resources Information Center (ERIC) system, a network of clearinghouses and a small number of adjunct clearinghouses, and four support components. "ERIC is the largest education database in the world—containing nearly 700,000 bibliographic records of documents and journal articles; approximately 2,600 records are added monthly. Papers, conference proceedings, literature reviews, and curriculum materials, along with articles from nearly 800 education-related journals, are

Figure 2.3. Regional Educational Labratories Funded by OERI

Laboratory	Location	Telephone
Appalachia Educational Laboratory (800.624.9120)	Charleston, WV 25325	304.347.0400
Far West Lab for Educational Research and Development	San Francisco, CA 94107	415.565.3000
Mid-Continent Regional Educational Laboratory	Aurora, CO 80014	303.337.0990
North Central Regional Educational Laboratory	Oakbrook, IL 60521	708.571.4700
Northwest Regional Educational Laboratory	Portland, OR 97204	503.275.9500
Pacific Regional Educational Laboratory	Honolulu, HA 96813	808.532.6000
Regional Lab for Educ. Improvement of the NE & Islands	Andover, MA 01810	508.470.0098
Research for Better Schools	Philadelphia, PA 19123	215.574.9300
Southeastern Regional Vision for Education	Tallahassee, FL 32301	904.922.2300
Southwest Educational Development Laboratory	Austin, TX 78701	512.476.6861

——Grant Tip——
OERI's Labs, ERIC Centers, and National Research and Development Centers should come in handy when providing a review of literature, a state of the art.

indexed and abstracted for entry into the ERIC database" (*All About ERIC,* 1990, p. 1). Figure 2.4 provides a list of the clearinghouses, phone numbers, and e-mail addresses. About 900 locations are designated as ERIC information service providers. ERIC offers free reference and referral services to the grantwriter through its network of clearinghouses and its toll-free number. For assistance or more information, call 1-800-LET-ERIC.

In addition to the labs and ERIC centers, the OERI funds and oversees the National Research and Development Centers. These centers conduct research on topics of national significance to educational policy and practice. Each center's role is to exercise leadership in its mission area; conduct research and development that advance theory and practice; attract the sustained attention of expert researchers to concentrate on problems in education; create a long-term interaction between researchers and educators; participate in a network for collaborative exchange in the education community; and disseminate research findings in useful forms to education policymakers and practitioners. Figure 2.5 lists each center and provides respective phone numbers and e-mail addresses (when available). All of these centers address nationally significant problems and issues in education and help to strengthen learning for all students in the United States.

The OERI provides publications available from OERI's Education Information Branch (EIB) or from the Government Printing Office (GPO). Contact the National Library of Education, 400 Maryland Avenue, SW, Washington, DC. Phone (800) 424-1616.

Figure 2.4. ERIC Clearinghouses and System Components

ERIC Clearinghouses	URL	Location	Telephone
Support Components			
ACCESS ERIC • 2277 Research Boulevard, 6L	accesseric.org	Rockville, MD	800.538.3742
ERIC Document Reproduction Service (EDRS)	edrs.com	Springfiled, VA	703.440.1400
ERIC Processing and Reference Facility (Facility)	ericfac.piccard.csc.com	Lanham, MD	800.799.ERIC
Adjunct ERIC Clearinghouse			
Child Care (ADJ/CC)	nccic.org	Vienna, VA	800.616.2242
Clinical Schools (ADJ/CL)	aacte.org/menu2.html	Washington, DC	800.822.9229
Consumer Education (ADJ/CN)	nice.emich.edu	Ypsilanti, MI	734.487.2292
Educational Opportunity	trioprograms.org	Washington, DC	202.347.2218
Entrepreneurship Education (ADJ/EE)	celcee.edu	Kansas City, MO	888.423.5233
ELS Literacy Education (ADJ/LE)	cal.org/ncle	Washington, DC	202.362.0700
International Civic Education (ADJ/ICE)		Bloomington, IN	800.266.3815
Postsecondary Education and the Internet		Charlottesville, VA	804.924.3880
School Counseling Services	library.unt.edu/ericscs	Denton, TX	940.565.2910
Service Learing (ADJ/SL)	umn.edu/~serve	St. Paul, MN	800.808.4378
Test Collection	ericae.net/testcol.htm	Princeton, NJ	609.734.5689
U.S.-Japan Studies (ADJ/UJ)	indiana.edu/~japan	Bloomington, IN	800.266.3815
ERIC Clearinghouses			
Adult, Career, and Vocational Education (ERIC/CE)	ericacve.org	Columbus, OH	800.848.4815
Assessment and Evaluation (ERIC/TM)	ericae.net	College Park, MD	800.464.3742
Community Colleges (ERIC/JC)		Los Angeles, CA	800.832.8256
Counseling and Student Services (ERIC/CG)	uncg.edu/edu/ericcass	Greensnboro, NC	800.414.9769
Disabilities and Gifted Education (ERIC/EC)	ericec.org	Reston, VA	800.328.0270
Educational Management (ERIC/EA)	eric.uoregon.edu	Eugene, OR	800.438.8841
Elementary & Early Childhood Education (ERIC/PS)	ericeece.org	Champaign, IL	800.583.4135
Higher Education (ERIC/HE)	eriche.org	Washington, DC	800.773.3742
Information & Technology (ERIC/IR)	ericir.syr.edu/ithome	Syracuse, NY	800.464.9107
Languages & Linguistics (ERIC/FL)	cal.org/ericcll	Washington, DC	800.276.9834
Reading, English, & Communication (ERIC/CS)	indiana.edu/~eric_rec	Bloomington, IN	800.759.4723
Rural Education & Small Schools (ERIC/RC)	ael.org/eric	Charleston, WV	800.624.9120
Science, Mathematics, & Environmental Education	ericse.org	Columbus, OH	800.276.0462
Social Studies/Social Science Educ. (ERIC/SO)	edu/~ssdc/eric_chess.htm	Bloomington, IN	800.266.3815
Teaching and Teacher Education (ERIC/SP)	ericsp.org	Washington, DC	800.822.9229
Urban Education (ERIC/UD)	eric-web.tc.columbia.edu	New York, NY	800.601.4868
Affiliate Clearinghouse			
National Clearinghouse for Educational Facilities	edfacilities.org	Washington, DC	888.552.0624
ERIC Publishers			
ORYX Press (ORYX)	oryxpress.com	Phoenix, AR	800.279.6799
United States Government Printing Office (GPO)	access.gpo.gov	Pittsburg, PA	202.512.1800

Figure 2.5. National Research and Development Centers

Facility	URL	Location	Telephone
Center for Research on Education, Diversity and Excellence	crede.ucsc.edu	Santa Cruz, CA	831.459.3500
Center for Research on the Education of Students Placed At-Risk	crespar.law.howard.edu	Baltimore, MD	410.516.8800
Center for Research on Evaluation, Standards, and Student Testing	cresst96.cse.ucla.edu	Los Angeles, CA	310.206.1532
Center for the Improvement of Early Reading Achievement	ciera.org	Ann Arbor, MI	734.647.6940
Center for the Study of Teaching and Policy		Seattle, WA	206.221.4114
Nat'l Center for Early Development and Leadership	fpg.unc.edu/~ncedl	Chapel Hill, NC	919.966.4250
Nat'l Center for Improving Student Learning Math and Science		Madison, WI	608.265.6240
Nat'l Center for Postsecondary Improvements	ncpi.stanford.edu	Stanford, CA	650.723.7724
Nat'l Center for the Study of Adult Learning and Literacy	gseweb.harvard.edu/~ncsall	Cambridge, MA	617.495.4843
Nat'l Center on Increasing the Effectiveness of Reform Efforts		Philadelphia, PA	215.573.0700
Nat'l Research & Dev. Center on English Learning & Achievement		Albany, NY	518.442.5026
Nat'l Research Center on the Gifted and Talented	gifted.uconn.edu/nrcgt.html	Storrs, CT	860.486.4676

Depository Library Program

Information from the federal government is available at Depository Libraries around the U.S. and its territories. Each working day, federal agencies provide these libraries with information. As noted in Figure 2.6, there are two Depository Libraries designated in any part of the state by each Senator, two in each congressional district,

Figure 2.6. Types of Libraries Designated

870	2 libraries for each congressional district designated by the Representative
200	2 libraries for each state designated by each Senator
2	2 libraries designated by the Resident Commissioner from Puerto Rico
2	2 libraries designated by the Mayor of the District of Columbia
1	1 library designated by the Governor of American Samoa
1	1 library designated by the Governor of Guam
2	2 libraries designated by the Governor of the Virgin Islands
55	Highest state appellate court libraries
50	State libraries
72	Libraries of the land-grant colleges
14	Libraries of the executive departments in Washington
125	Libraries of the independent agencies and of major bureaus/divisions of departments and agencies
5	Libraries of the U.S. military academies
175	Law school libraries

Figure 2.7. Number of Depository Libraries Per State

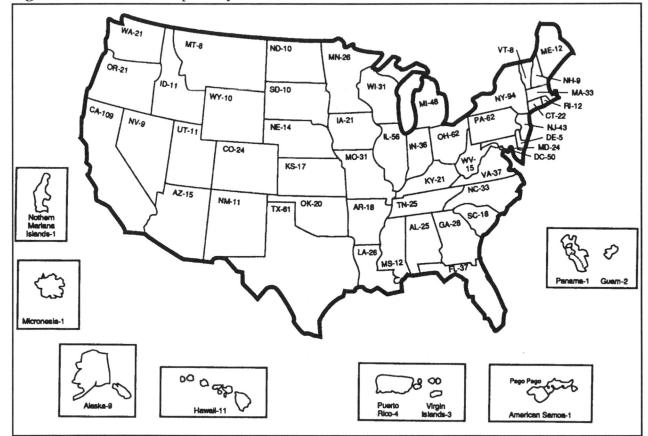

one at each land-grant university. According to *Joint Committee Print* (*A Directory of U.S. Government Depository Libraries,* 1990), almost 1,400 libraries have been designated as depositories. These libraries participate in the Depository Library Program established by Congress to allow the public free access to government publications. Each year Depository Libraries select titles from more than 25,000 new government publications. Fifty regional Depository Libraries receive every unclassified government publication of interest to the public and have undertaken the responsibility of retaining this material permanently, on paper or microfiche. Figure 2.7 is a map with the number of Depository Libraries per state. Interlibrary loan and reference services are also provided. To find the Depository Library in your area, contact your local library or write to the Superintendent of Documents, Washington, D.C. 20402.

——**Grant Tip**——

Almost 1,400 Depository Libraries that are free for use by the public each year select titles from more than 25,000 new government publications.

Foundation and Corporation Directories

Many foundation and corporation directories are on the market. the *Foundation Directory* is a major publication describing over 7,900 of the largest foundations in the U.S. Financial data (assets, number of grant awards, etc.) are provided along with information on the types of support generally awarded, geographic and other giving restrictions, application deadlines, etc. There is also a *Foundation Directory Supplement* that provides updates six months after publication of the *Directory* itself. To make this set complete, the *Foundation Directory, Part 2* is available and provides information on midsize foundations ($50,000 to $200,000) whereas the other publication addresses those foundations with annual grants totaling at least $200,000. The 2000 costs for these publications were $215 for the hardcover of the *Foundation Directory,* $300 for the *Foundation Directory Supplement*, and $185 for the *Foundation Directory, Part 2.* The Foundation Center produces a variety of publications (*National Data Book of Foundations, Foundation Grants Index, National Directory of Corporate Giving, Grant Guides,* etc.). Write The Foundation Center, 79 Fifth Avenue, New York, New York 10003-3076. Phone (800) 424-9836 or (212) 620-4230.

The Foundation Center also provides a *Grant Guide* series that is directed toward specific fields. These *Guides* have descriptions of hundreds of foundation grants of $10,000 or more that were recently awarded in a specific subject area. The subject areas for which there is a specific *Grant Guide* provided by The Foundation Center at a 2000 cost of $75 each include the following: *Aging; Alcohol and Drug Abuse; Arts, Culture and the Humanities; Children and Youth; Community Development, Housing and Employment; Crime, Law Enforcement, and Abuse Prevention; Elementary and Secondary Education; Environmental Protection and Animal Welfare; Film, Media, and Communications; Foreign and International Programs; Health Programs for Children and Youth; Higher Education; Homeless; Hospitals, Medical Care and Research, Libraries and Information Services; Literacy, Reading, and Adult/Continuing Education; Matching and Challenge Support; Medical and Professional Health Education; Mental Health, Addictions and Crisis Services; Minorities; Physically and Mentally Disabled; Public Health and Diseases; Public Policy and Public Affairs; Recreation, Sports, and Athletics; Religion, Religious Welfare and Religious Education; Scholarships, Student Aid, and Loans; Science and Technology Programs; Social and Political Science Programs; Social Services;* and *Women and Girls.* These are available from The Foundation Center. The phone number and address are noted.

The Taft Corporation publishes a two-volume set of reference directories that combines information on corporate and foundation funding sources. *The Directory of Corporate and Foundation Givers* provides information on approximately 8,000 private foundations, corporate foundations, and corporate direct giving programs. The *Foundation Reporter* gives detailed information (foundation philosophy, financial summaries, typical recipients, enumerates recent grants, etc.) on approximately 600 leading foundations in the U.S. The 2000 cost was $270 for the *Directory* and $435 for the *Reporter.* For more information on these publications, contact The Taft Group, P.O. Box 9187, Farmington Hills, MI 48333-9187. Phone (800) 877-8238.

National Science Foundation (NSF)

The National Science Foundation (NSF) funds many educational programs. The NSF's *Grants for Research and Education in Science and Engineering Guide* provides guidance for the preparation of unsolicited proposals to NSF. Some NSF programs operate from more specific program announcements or solicitations. The general provisions of this *Guide* apply to all NSF programs to the extent that they are not modified by individual program announcements or solicitations. Information about program deadlines and target dates for proposals appears in the *NSF Bulletin,* issued monthly except July and August; copies may be obtained from the Editor, *NSF Bulletin,* NSF, Washington, D.C. 20550. General information about NSF programs may be found in the *Guide to Programs,* available from the Forms and Publications Unit of NSF. Information about special requirements of NSF programs may be obtained from the appropriate program offices.

For information about the NSF grant process, refer to the NSF *Grant Policy Manual,* NSF 77-47, or Chapter VI of Title 45 of the *Code of Federal Regulations.* The *Manual* is a compendium of basic NSF policies and procedures for use by the grant community and NSF staff. NSF grants are subject to the specific provisions contained in the grant instruments, including Grant General Conditions. The *Manual* is available for $15.00 from the Superintendent of Documents, Government Printing Office, Washington, D.C. 20402. The phone number is (202) 512-1800. Copies of the Grant General Conditions may be obtained from Forms and Publications, National Science Foundation, Division of Human Resource Development, Directorate for Education and Human Resources, Room 1225, Washington, D.C. 20550. Phone (202) 357-7350.

———**Grant Tip**———

The NEA Guide *and the* NEH Overview *are both* free *and they provide valuable information for developing proposals to NEA and NEH.*

National Endowment for the Arts (NEA)

The *National Endowment for the Arts Guide to Programs* provides step-by-step instructions on who is eligible, how to apply, deadlines, and amounts available. Currently, there is a lot of debate between the U.S. House of Representations and the U.S. Senate concerning future funding for the NEA. But at this time, the NEA is currently fully funded and you can contact the appropriate NEA Program Director and get the *Guide* free of charge by writing to the National Endowment for the Arts, Public Information Office, 1100 Pennsylvania Avenue NE, Washington, D.C. 20506. Phone (202) 682-5400.

National Endowment for the Humanities (NEH)

The *National Endowment for the Humanities Overview of Endowment's Programs* is the sister publication to the NEA's *Guide*. It provides information about the history, purposes, policies, and organization of NEH to help individuals and organizations determine whether proposed projects and activities in the humanities may be eligible for support. It provides information on the activities supported by the Endowment's grantmaking programs, as well as a current schedule of application deadlines. The publication is available free by writing to the National Endowment for the Humanities, 1100 Pennsylvania Avenue, SW, Washington, D.C. 20506. Phone (202) 606-8400.

Institutional or Agency Grants Newsletter

Many large institutions and agencies have a grants and research office that disseminates a monthly newsletter to other personnel in the organization. The agency usually abstracts information on upcoming grants and deadlines to advertise potential funding sources and new programs. However, information may not be all that helpful because it is a secondary source not the primary source.

Word of Mouth

Word of mouth sources can be helpful. Professional conventions and visits to institutions, agencies, or both, are excellent avenues to pertinent grant information. Talk to people who have been successful in obtaining grants. Scan professional newsletters and journals but be aware that this may be old information and not as helpful as other sources identified in this chapter.

Summary

This chapter has provided selected information regarding various reference sources to aid in the processes of grant seeking and grant administration. The chapter does not include all sources on the market; it concentrates on the sources most frequently used by proposal writers and administrators in education. The listing is not intended to be comprehensive, and omission or inclusion of a source does not imply endorsement or rejection. The most essential and basic publications for federal sources of grant support and administration requirements are the *Federal Register, Code of Federal Regulations,* and the *Catalog of Federal Domestic Assistance,* which are explained in more detail in subsequent chapters.

Many good newsletters and grant information services cover government funding sources; however, the government is the original source for its information. Because information on grants is so widely disseminated, do not get absorbed with information that is outdated or of little value. It is sometimes difficult to ascertain what information is pertinent or what the full scope is of an anticipated program coming up for funding. If that is the case, contact the U.S. Department of Education directly for answers to specific questions. The grant application package is the comprehensive word and serves as the main resource for directions that will help you respond to a program with a competitive proposal document.

3

Using the *Federal Register (FR)* and the *Code of Federal Regulations (CFR)*

Introduction

Chapter 2, "How to Explore Grant Possibilities in Education," identified and provided a brief description of some basic information sources that are important in responding to requests for federal educational grants. Some sources, such as the *Federal Register (FR)*, *Code of Federal Regulations (CFR)*, and the *Catalog of Federal Domestic Assistance (CFDA)*, deserve more attention because they are the official federal government documents to inform the public and, more specifically, the grant seeker and grant administrator of the various grant programs. This chapter provides detailed information both on the *Federal Register* and the *Code of Federal Regulations*, which often must be used together. Chapter 4 covers the *Catalog of Federal Domestic Assistance* in more detail and explains how to use the *CFDA* effectively in responding to federal grants in education.

There are many excellent commercial newsletters and information services regarding federal grants in education. However, the federal government is the original source for their information. Therefore, the *Federal Register* and the *Code of Federal Regulations* are the two most essential publications for federal sources of funding and grant administration requirements.

The Federal Register System

The Federal Register System is composed mainly of two major publications, the daily *Federal Register* and the annual *Code of Federal Regulations*. These two publications provide a current version of any federal agency's regulations. Congress established the Federal Register Publication System as a unified method of informing the public of regulations. In the surge of New Deal legislation enacted in the 1930s, Congress delegated more responsibility to federal departments and agencies in the form of authority to issue detailed regulations dealing with complex social and economic issues. As programs were in the making and more regulations were written, a serious communications problem evolved. With no central publication system, there was no efficient way for the public to know about the various regulations that affected them. Therefore, a central publication system was established to manage effectively the increased number and expanded scope of federal regulations.

Federal Register Act

The Federal Register Act became law on July 26, 1935 and established a systematic approach for handling agency regulations (44 U.S.C. Chapter 15). Prior to 1935 you would have to go directly to the federal agency and review a couple of typed or handwritten pages. The act established a uniform system for handling agency regulations by requiring the following:

- Submitting and filing documents with the Office of the Federal Register.

- Placing documents on public inspection.

- Publishing documents in the *Federal Register*.

- After a 1937 amendment to the Act, codifying rules in the *Code of Federal Regulations*.

Administrative Procedure Act

The Administrative Procedure Act became law on June 11, 1946 and added several new dimensions to the Federal Register System (5 U.S.C. 551 et seq.). This act specifically provided for

───**Grant Tip**───
The daily FR *and the annually revised* CFR *work together to provide an up-to-date version of any agency's regulations.*

- Giving the public (but with some stated exceptions) the right to participate in the rule-making process by commenting on proposed rules.

- Requiring that the effective date for a regulation be not less than 30 days from the date of publication of the final rules unless there was good cause for an earlier date.

- Providing for publication of agency statements of organization and procedural rules.

The Federal Register Act and the Administrative Procedure Act, as outlined above, define the basic functions of the Federal

Register System and provide the framework for the promulgation of government regulations. As mentioned before, the System is composed primarily of two major publications, the daily *Federal Register* and the annually revised *Code of Federal Regulations*. These two publications work together to provide an up-to-date version of any agency's regulations. To understand the system, one needs to understand each separate publication as well as the relationship between the two publications. Figure 3.1 displays how this total system works together.

Figure 3.1. The Federal Register System Flowchart

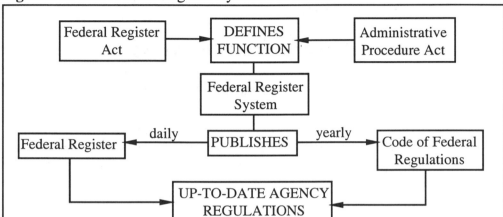

The *Federal Register (FR)*

The executive branch's two official daily publications are the *Federal Register* and the *Commerce Business Daily*. Typically, grant programs are announced in the *Federal Register* and contract solicitations appear in the *Commerce Business Daily*. In harmony with the scope of this book, we do not go into great detail discussing the *Commerce Business Daily* but focus our attention on the *Federal Register*.

The *Federal Register* is published every federal working day by the Office of the Federal Register (OFR), National Archives and Records Administration in Washington, D.C. The *Federal Register* provides a uniform system for making available to the public regulations and legal notices issued by federal agencies and the President. These include presidential proclamations and executive orders and federal agency documents having general applicability and legal effect, documents required to be published by act of Congress, and other federal agency documents of public interest. Documents are on file for public inspection in the Office of the Federal Register (OFR) the day before publication, unless earlier filing is requested by the issuing agency. Distribution is made only by the Superintendent of Documents, United States Government Printing Office.

To provide a uniform system, the documents are categorized and published under the five main title headings: Presidential Documents, Rules and Regulations, Proposed Rules, Notices, and Sunshine Act Meetings. These document categories are reviewed in the following paragraphs.

Document Categories of the *Federal Register*

Presidential Document

These are documents signed by the President and submitted to the Office of the Federal Register (OFR) for publication. Documents in this category include:

- Proclamations
- Executive orders
- Memorandums
- Orders
- Presidential determinations
- Reorganization plans

There is an example of a proclamation (Figure 3.2) on page 59. This document was issued by the President of the United States and put in the *Federal Register* immediately after it was signed.

Rules and Regulations

These are regulatory documents that have general applicability and legal effect. The *Federal Register* publication system considers the terms "rules" and "regulations" as similar. According to the OFR's *Document Drafting Handbook* (Fox, Nanovic, & Sowada, 1994), documents in this category are classified as follows:

Figure 3.2. An Example of a Presidential Document

Federal Register Vol. 64, No. 145 Friday, July 29, 1999	**Presidential Documents**	38873

Title 3—   **Proclamation 6708 of July 26, 1999**

The President **Anniversary of the Americans with Disabilities Act, 1999**

By the President of the United States of America

A Proclamation

The Americans with Disabilities Act is a national monument to freedom. Contained within its broad pillars of independence, inclusion, and empowerment is the core ideal of equality that has defined this country since its beginnings. For when America's founders set down the guiding words of freedom, first among them, proudly were, "We the People." Our young Nation would be governed not by kings or tyrants—America would be led by farmers and doctors, artists and merchants, teachers and parents, each possessing widely different knowledge and skills. Some would be active participants in community life. Others would embrace the quiet joys of home. But all of the people would make an essential contribution to the character and quality of America.

On this, the fourth anniversary of the Americans with Disabilities Act (ADA), we mark the full extension of the ADA's employment provisions to our Nation's small businesses. In 1990, members of both political parties resolved to make laws of inclusion, and today, telephone relay systems connect deaf and hard-of-hearing individuals to Americans everywhere. Four years ago, we pledged to build bridges to independence, and today, architectural barriers are coming down in office buildings and movie theaters across the country, making room for new passageways to participation. We moved to craft policies of empowerment, and today, leaders in public and private sectors alike are recognizing the vast potential of every citizen and the breathtaking determination of each to create and to achieve. With this Act, we began a new era for 49 million of our fellow citizens. And today, celebrating the rights of people with disabilities, we declare in no uncertain terms that "We the People" means all of us, with our myriad differences and doubts, with our infinite talents and aspirations.

This day—a wonderful, vigorous celebration of the progress and possibilities for equal opportunity—must also include an equally vigorous commitment to continue the fight. Now is the time to act on our understanding that having a physical or mental disability is a part of the human experience. We must work to fully implement the provisions of the ADA and to see that these and related laws are aggressively enforced in our schools and workplaces, in our national government and local councils. Most important, we must finally overcome the remaining handicaps of prejudice and stereotype. Discrimination, ignorance, intolerance— these barriers are a far greater tragedy than any common limitation of the human mind or body. And it is only in overcoming these that America will truly be worthy of its people.

NOW, THEREFORE, I, WILLIAM J. CLINTON, President of the United States of America, by virtue of the authority vested in me by the Constitution and laws of the United States, do hereby proclaim July 26, 1999, as the Anniversary of the Americans with Disabilities Act. I call upon the people of the United States to observe this day with appropriate ceremonies and activities.

IN WITNESS WHEREOF, I have hereunto set my hand this twenty-sixth day of July, in the year of our Lord nineteen hundred and ninety-four, and of the Independence of the United States of America the two hundred and nineteenth.

(FR Doc. 94-18733
Filed 7-28-99; 10:48 am)
Billing code 3195-01-P

[Original has President Clinton's Signature]

Editorial note: For the President's remarks on signing this proclamation, see issue 30 of the *Weekly Compilation of Presidential Documents.*

1. **Documents that amend the CFR.** These documents amend the *Code of Federal Regulations (CFR)* by adding new text or by revising or removing existing text. A document that amends *CFR* text must publish each change to the *CFR* in full and state the effective date for any change.

2. **Documents that are interim or temporary rule.** Interim or temporary rule documents are effective immediately for a short or definable period of time. They have the same effect as a final rule in that they amend the *CFR* and give an effective date. However, in issuing an interim or temporary rule, the agency often asks for public comment. After the comment period expires, the agency may consider adjustments to the interim or temporary rule before issuing the final rule.

3. **Documents that affect other documents.** These documents affect other documents previously published in the rules and regulations section and typically include the following:

   • Corrections to previously published rules

   • Any change of the effective date of a previously published rule

   • Any document changing the comment period of an interim or temporary rule

   • Suspension of a previously published rule

   • Withdrawal of a previously published rule not yet in effect

   • Petition for reconsideration of a previously published rule

4. **Documents that have no regulatory text.** These documents have no regulatory text and do not amend the *CFR* but either affect the agency's handling of its regulations or are of continuing interest to the public in dealing with an agency. The Administrative Conference of the United States, in Recommendation No. 76-2, recommends that these documents be preserved in the *CFR*. These types of documents are as follows:

   • General policy statements

   • Interpretations of agency regulations

   • Statements of organization and function

Figure 3.3, on pages 61-66, is a copy of this type of document. This rules and regulations document issued by the United States

(text continues on page 67)

Figure 3.3. An Example of a Rules and Regulations Document

DEPARTMENT OF EDUCATION

34 CFR Part 644

RIN 1840-AB65

Educational Opportunity Centers

AGENCY: Department of Education.

ACTION: Final regulations.

SUMMARY: The Secretary amends the regulations governing the Educational Opportunity Centers program. The Educational Opportunity Centers program is authorized under title IV of the Higher Education Act of 1965 (HEA), and these final regulations implement changes made to the HEA by the Higher Education Amendments of 1992. In addition to incorporating statutory changes, the regulations also clarify and simplify requirements governing the program and revise one funding criterion.

The purposes and allowable activities of the Educational Opportunity Centers program support the National Education Goals. Specifically, the program funds projects designed to improve the academic competency of program participants (Goal #3).

DATES: These regulations take effect either 45 days after publication in the Federal Register or later if the Congress takes certain adjournments. If you want to know the effective date of these regulations, call or write to the Department of Education contact person. A document announcing the effective date will be published in the **Federal Register**.

Applicability: The criteria listed under § 644.22 will apply on and after June 1, 1999. Until June 1, 1999, the existing criteria will continue to apply.

FOR FURTHER INFORMATION CONTACT: Margaret A. Wingfield, U.S. Department of Education, 400 Maryland Avenue, SW., room 5065, Washington, DC 20202-5249. Telephone: (202) 708-4804. Individuals who use a telecommunications device for the deaf (TDD) may call the Federal Information Relay Service (FIRS) at 1-800-877-8339 between 8 a.m. and 8 p.m., Eastern time, Monday through Friday.

SUPPLEMENTARY INFORMATION: These regulations implement the Higher Education Amendments of 1992 (Pub. L. 102-325, enacted July 23, 1992). The Educational Opportunity Centers program provides grants to institutions of higher education; public and private agencies and organizations; combinations of institutions, agencies and organizations; and secondary schools under special circumstances. The purposes of the program are to (1) provide information regarding financial and academic assistance available for individuals who desire to pursue

a program of postsecondary education; and (2) assist individuals in applying for admission to institutions that offer programs of postsecondary education, including preparing necessary applications for use by admissions and financial aid officers.

On October 26, 1999, the Secretary published a notice of proposed rulemaking (NPRM) for this program in the **Federal Register** (58 FR 57704). The NPRM included a summary of regulations proposed to implement statutory changes and other regulations proposed to clarify and simplify requirements governing the program.

Analysis of Comments and Changes

In response to the Secretary's invitation in the NPRM, 45 persons submitted comments on the proposed regulations. An analysis of the comments and the changes that have been made in the regulations since publication of the NPRM is published as an appendix to these final regulations.

Major Changes in the Regulations

The major differences between the NPRM and these final regulations are as follows:

1. Section 644.21 (Selection Criteria—Plan of Operation)

The criterion listed under § 644.21(c)(5) has been modified to encourage applicants to include information about their plan to coordinate with other projects for disadvantaged students.

2. Section 644.30 (Allowable Costs)

Section 644.30 has been revised to include, as allowable costs, transportation, lodging, and meals for project participants and staff during visits to postsecondary institutions or for participation in "College Day" and career awareness activities. Also, fees for college admissions applications and college entrance examination fees are now permissible under certain circumstances.

3. Section 644.31 (Unallowable Costs)

This section has been revised to conform to the changes made in the allowable costs section.

4. Section 644.32 (Recordkeeping)

The language in § 644.32(d)(1) has been modified to lessen the recordkeeping burden on grantees.

Intergovernmental Review

This program is subject to the requirement of Executive Order 12372 and the regulations in 34 CFR part 79. The objective of the Executive order is to foster an intergovernmental partnership and a strengthened federalism by relying on processes

developed by State and local governments for coordination and review of proposed Federal financial assistance.

In accordance with the order, this document is intended to provide early notification of the Department's specific plans and actions for this program.

Assessment of Educational Impact

In the notice of proposed rulemaking, the Secretary requested comments on whether the proposed regulations would require transmission of information that is being gathered by or is available from any other agency or authority of the United States.

Based on the response to the proposed rules and on its own review, the Department has determined that the regulations in this document do not require transmission of information that is being gathered or is available from any other agency or authority of the United States.

List of Subjects in 34 CFR Part 644

Colleges and Universities, Education of disadvantaged, Grant programs—education, Reporting and recordkeeping requirements, Secondary education.

(Catalog of Federal Domestic Assistance Number 84.066 Educational Opportunity Centers Program.)

Dated: January 10, 1999.

Richard W. Riley,

Secretary of Education.

The Secretary revises part 644 of title 34 of the Code of Federal Regulations to read as follows:

PART 644—EDUCATIONAL OPPORTUNITY CENTERS

Subpart A—General

Sec.

644.1   What is the Educational Opportunity Centers program?

644.2   Who is eligible for a grant?

644.3   Who is eligible to participate in a project?

644.4   What services may a project provide?

644.5   How long is a project period?

644.6   What regulations apply?

644.7   What definitions apply?

Subpart B—Assurances

644.10   What assurances must an applicant submit?

Subpart C—How Does the Secretary Make a Grant?

644.20   How does the Secretary decide which new grants to make?

Figure 3.3. Continued. An Example of a Rules and Regulations Document

2659   Federal Register / Vol. 65, No. 11 / Tuesday, January 18, 2000 / Rules and Regulations

644.21   What selection criteria does the Secretary use?

644.22   How does the Secretary evaluate prior experience?

644.23   How does the Secretary set the amount of a grant?

Subpart D—What Conditions Must Be Met by a Grantee?

644.30   What are allowable costs?

644.31   What are unallowable costs?

644.32   What other requirements must a grantee meet?

Authority: 20 U.S.C. 1070a-11 and 1070a-16, unless otherwise noted.

Subpart A—General

§ 644.1 What is the Educational Opportunity Centers program?

The Educational Opportunity Centers program provides grants for projects designed to provide—

(a) Information regarding financial and academic assistance available for individuals who desire to pursue a program of postsecondary education; and

(b) Assistance to individuals in applying for admission to institutions that offer programs of postsecondary education, including assistance in preparing necessary applications for use by admissions and financial aid officers.

(Authority: 20 U.S.C. 1070a-16)

§ 644.2 Who is eligible for a grant?

The following are eligible for a grant to carry out an Educational Opportunity Centers project:

(a) An institution of higher education.

(b) A public or private agency or organization.

(c) A combination of the types of institutions, agencies, and organizations described in paragraphs (a) and (b) of this section.

(d) A secondary school, under exceptional circumstances such as if no institution, agency, or organization described in paragraphs (a) and (b) of this section is capable of carrying out an Educational Opportunity Centers project in the target area to be served by the proposed project.

(Authority: 20 U.S.C. 1070a-11)

§ 644.3 Who is eligible to participate in a project?

(a) An individual is eligible to participate in an Educational Opportunity Centers project if the individual meets all of the following requirements:

(1)(i) Is a citizen or national of the United States;

(ii) Is a permanent resident of the United States;

(iii) Is in the United States for other than a temporary purpose and provides evidence from the Immigration and Naturalization Service of his or her intent to become a permanent resident;

(iv) Is a permanent resident of Guam, the Northern Mariana Islands, or the Trust Territory of the Pacific Islands (Palau); or

(v) Is a resident of the Freely Associated States—the Federated States of Micronesia or the Republic of the Marshall Islands.

(2)(i) Is at least 19 years of age; or

(ii) Is less than 19 years of age, and the individual cannot be appropriately served by a Talent Search project under 34 CFR part 643, and the individual's participation would not dilute the Educational Opportunity Centers project's services to individuals described in paragraph (a)(2)(i) of this section.

(3) Expresses a desire to enroll, or is enrolled, in a program of postsecondary education, and requests information or assistance in applying for admission to, or financial aid for, such a program.

(b) A veteran as defined in § 644.7(b), regardless of age, is eligible to participate in an Educational Opportunity Centers project if he or she satisfies the eligibility requirements in paragraph (a) of this section other than the age requirement in paragraph (a)(2) of this section.

(Authority: 20 U.S.C. 1070-11 and 1070a-16)

§ 644.4 What services may a project provide?

An Educational Opportunity Centers project may provide the following services:

(a) Public information campaigns designed to inform the community about opportunities for postsecondary education and training.

(b) Academic advice and assistance in course selection.

(c) Assistance in completing college admission and financial aid applications.

(d) Assistance in preparing for college entrance examinations.

(e) Guidance on secondary school reentry or entry to a General Educational Development (GED) program or other alternative education program for secondary school dropouts.

(f) Personal counseling.

(g) Tutorial services.

(h) Career workshops and counseling.

(i) Mentoring programs involving elementary or secondary school teachers, faculty members at institutions of higher education, students, or any combination of these persons.

(j) Activities described in paragraphs (a) through (i) of this section that are specifically designed for students of limited English proficiency.

(k) Other activities designed to meet the purposes of the Educational Opportunity Centers program stated in § 644.1.

(Authority: 20 U.S.C. 1070a-16)

§ 644.5 How long is a project period?

(a) Except as provided in paragraph (b) of this section, a project period under the Educational Opportunity Centers program is four years.

(b) The Secretary approves a project period of five years for applications that score in the highest ten percent of all applications approved for new grants under the criteria in § 644.21.

(Authority: 20 U.S.C. 1070a-11)

§ 644.6 What regulations apply?

The following regulations apply to the Educational Opportunity Centers program:

(a) The Education Department General Administrative Regulations (EDGAR) as follows:

(1) 34 CFR Part 74 (Administration of Grants to Institutions of Higher Education, Hospitals, and Nonprofit Organizations).

(2) 34 CFR Part 75 (Direct Grant Programs), except for § 75.511.

(3) 34 CFR Part 77 (Definitions that Apply to Department Regulations), except for the definition of "secondary school" in § 77.1.

(4) 34 CFR Part 79 (Intergovernmental Review of Department of Education Programs and Activities).

(5) 34 CFR Part 82 (New Restrictions on Lobbying).

(6) 34 CFR Part 85 (Governmentwide Debarment and Suspension (Nonprocurement) and Governmentwide Requirements for Drug-Free Workplace (Grants)).

(7) 34 CFR Part 86 (Drug-Free Schools and Campuses).

(b) The regulations in this part 644.

(Authority: 20 U.S.C. 1070a-11 and 1070a-16)

§ 644.7 What definitions apply?

(a) Definitions in EDGAR. The following terms used in this part are defined in 34 CFR 77.1:

Applicant
Application
Budget
Budget period
EDGAR
Equipment
Facilities
Fiscal year
Grant
Grantee
Private
Project
Project period
Public

Figure 3.3. Continued. An Example of a Rules and Regulations Document

Secretary
Supplies

(b) *Other definitions.* The following definitions also apply to this part:

HEA means the Higher Education Act of 1965, as amended.

Institution of higher education means an educational institution as defined in sections 1201(a) and 481 of the HEA.

Low-income individual means an individual whose family's taxable income did not exceed 150 percent of the poverty level amount in the calendar year preceding the year in which the individual initially participated in the project. The poverty level amount is determined by using criteria of poverty established by the Bureau of the Census of the U.S. Department of Commerce.

Participant means an individual who—
(i) Is determined to be eligible to participate in the project under § 644.3; and
(ii) Receives project services.

Postsecondary education means education beyond the secondary school level.

Potential first-generation college student means—
(i) An individual neither of whose parents received a baccalaureate degree; or
(ii) An individual who regularly resided with and received support from only one parent and whose supporting parent did not receive a baccalaureate degree.

Secondary school means a school that provides secondary education as determined under State law, except that it does not include education beyond grade 12.

Target area means a geographic area served by an Educational Opportunity Centers project.

Veteran means a person who served on active duty as a member of the Armed Forces of the United States—
(i) For a period of more than 180 days, any part of which occurred after January 31, 1955, and who was discharged or released from active duty under conditions other than dishonorable; or
(ii) After January 31, 1955, and who was discharged or released from active duty because of a service-connected disability.

(Authority: 20 U.S.C. 1070a-11, 1070a-16, and 1141)

Subpart B—Assurances

§ 644.10 What assurances must an applicant submit?

An applicant shall submit, as part of its application, assurances that—
(a) At least two-thirds of the individuals it serves under its proposed Educational Opportunity Centers project will be low-income individuals who are potential first-generation college students;
(b) Individuals who are receiving services from another Educational Opportunity Centers project or a Talent Search project under 34 CFR

Part 643 will not receive services under the proposed project;
(c) The project will be located in a setting or settings accessible to the individuals proposed to be served by the project; and
(d) If the applicant is an institution of higher education, it will not use the project as a part of its recruitment program.

(Authority: 20 U.S.C. 1070a-16)

Subpart C—How Does the Secretary Make a Grant?

§ 644.20 How does the Secretary decide which new grants to make?

(a) The Secretary evaluates an application for a new grant as follows:
(1)(i) The Secretary evaluates the application on the basis of the selection criteria in § 644.21.
(ii) The maximum score for all the criteria in § 644.21 is 100 points. The maximum score for each criterion is indicated in parentheses with the criterion.
(2)(i) For an application for a new grant to continue to serve substantially the same populations or campuses that the applicant is serving under an expiring project, the Secretary evaluates the applicant's prior experience in delivering services under the expiring project on the basis of the criteria in § 644.22.
(ii) The maximum score for all the criteria in § 644.22 is 15 points. The maximum score for each criterion is indicated in parentheses with the criterion.
(3) The Secretary awards additional points equal to 10 percent of the application's score under paragraphs (a) (1) and (2) of this section to an application for a project in Guam, the Virgin Islands, American Samoa, the Trust Territory of the Pacific Islands (Palau), or the Northern Mariana Islands if the applicant meets the requirements of subparts A, B, and D of this part.
(b) The Secretary makes new grants in rank order on the basis of the applications' total scores under paragraphs (a) (1) through (3) of this section.
(c) If the total scores of two or more applications are the same and there are insufficient funds for these applications after the approval of higher-ranked applications, the Secretary uses the remaining funds to serve geographic areas and eligible populations that have been underserved by the Educational Opportunity Centers program.
(d) The Secretary may decline to make a grant to an applicant that carried out a project that involved the fraudulent use of funds under section 402A(c)(2)(B) of the HEA.

(Authority: 20 U.S.C. 1070a-11, 1070a-16, and 1144a(a))

§ 644.21 What selection criteria does the Secretary use?

The Secretary uses the following criteria to evaluate an application for a new grant:
(a) *Need for the project* (24 points). The

Secretary evaluates the need for an Educational Opportunity Centers project in the proposed target area on the basis of the extent to which the application contains clear evidence of—
(1) A high number or percentage, or both, of low-income families residing in the target area;
(2) A high number or percentage, or both, of individuals residing in the target area with education completion levels below the baccalaureate level;
(3) A high need on the part of residents of the target area for further education and training from programs of postsecondary education in order to meet changing employment trends; and
(4) Other indicators of need for an Educational Opportunity Centers project, including the presence of unaddressed educational or socioeconomic problems of adult residents in the target area.
(b) *Objectives* (8 points). The Secretary evaluates the quality of the applicant's proposed project objectives on the basis of the extent to which they—
(1) Include both process and outcome objectives relating to each of the purposes of the Educational Opportunity Centers program stated in § 644.1;
(2) Address the needs of the target area;
(3) Are clearly described, specific, and measurable; and
(4) Are ambitious but attainable within each budget period and the project period given the project budget and other resources.
(c) *Plan of operation* (30 points). The Secretary evaluates the quality of the applicant's plan of operation on the basis of the following:
(1) (4 points) The plan to inform the residents, schools, and community organizations in the target area of the goals, objectives, and services of the project and the eligibility requirements for participation in the project;
(2) (4 points) The plan to identify and select eligible participants and ensure their participation without regard to race, color, national origin, gender, or disability;
(3) (2 points) The plan to assess each participant's need for services provided by the project;
(4) (12 points) The plan to provide services that meet participants' needs and achieve the objectives of the project; and
(5) (8 points) The management plan to ensure the proper and efficient administration of the project including, but not limited to, the project's organizational structure, the time committed to the project by the project director and other personnel, and, where appropriate, its coordination with other projects for disadvantaged students.
(d) *Applicant and community support*

Figure 3.3. Continued. An Example of a Rules and Regulations Document

2661   **Federal Register** / Vol. 65, No. 11 / Tuesday, January 18, 2000 / Rules and Regulations

(16 points). The Secretary evaluates the applicant and community support for the proposed project on the basis of the extent to which the applicant has made provision for resources to supplement the grant and enhance the project's services, including—

(1) (8 points) Facilities, equipment, supplies, personnel, and other resources committed by the applicant; and

(2) (8 points) Resources secured through written commitments from schools, community organizations, and others.

(e) *Quality of personnel* (9 points). (1) The Secretary evaluates the quality of the personnel the applicant plans to use in the project on the basis of the following:

(i) The qualifications required of the project director.

(ii) The qualifications required of each of the other personnel to be used in the project.

(iii) The plan to employ personnel who have succeeded in overcoming the disadvantages or circumstances like those of the population of the target area.

(2) In evaluating the qualifications of a person, the Secretary considers his or her experience and training in fields related to the objectives of the project.

(f) *Budget* (5 points). The Secretary evaluates the extent to which the project budget is reasonable, cost-effective, and adequate to support the project.

(g) *Evaluation plan* (8 points). The Secretary evaluates the quality of the evaluation plan for the project on the basis of the extent to which the applicant's methods of evaluation—

(1) Are appropriate to the project's objectives;

(2) Provide for the applicant to determine, using specific and quantifiable measures, the success of the project in—

(i) Making progress toward achieving its objectives (a formative evaluation); and

(ii) Achieving its objectives at the end of the project period (a summative evaluation); and

(3) Provide for the disclosure of unanticipated project outcomes, using quantifiable measures if appropriate.

(Approved by the Office of Management and Budget under control number 1840-0065)
(Authority: 20 U.S.C. 1070a-16)

§ 644.22 How does the Secretary evaluate prior experience?

(a) In the case of an application described in § 644.20(a)(2)(i), the Secretary reviews information relating to an applicant's performance under its expiring Educational Opportunity Centers project. This information includes performance reports, audit reports, site visit reports, and project evaluation reports.

(b) The Secretary evaluates the applicant's prior experience in delivering services on the basis of the following criteria:

(1) (3 points) (i) Whether the applicant provided services to the required number of participants who resided in the target area; and

(ii) Whether two-thirds of all participants served were low-income individuals and potential first-generation college students.

(2) (6 points) The extent to which the applicant met or exceeded its objectives' regarding the provision of assistance to individuals in applying for admission to, or financial aid for, programs of postsecondary education.

(3) (6 points) The extent to which the applicant met or exceeded its objectives regarding the admission or reentry of participants to programs of postsecondary education.

(Approved by the Office of Management and Budget under control number 1840-0065)
(Authority: 20 U.S.C. 1070a-16)

§ 644.23 How does the Secretary set the amount of a grant?

(a) The Secretary sets the amount of a grant on the basis of—

(1) 34 CFR 75.232 and 75.233, for new grants; and

(2) 34 CFR 75.253, for the second and subsequent years of a project period.

(b) If the circumstances described in section 402A(b)(3) of the HEA exist, the Secretary uses the available funds to set the amount of the grant beginning in fiscal year 1994 at the lesser of—

(1) $180,000; or

(2) The amount requested by the applicant.

(Authority: 20 U.S.C. 1070a-11)

Subpart D—What Conditions Must Be Met by a Grantee?

§ 644.30 What are allowable costs?

The cost principles that apply to the Educational Opportunity Centers program are in 34 CFR part 74, subpart Q. Allowable costs include the following if they are reasonably related to the objectives of the project:

(a) Transportation, meals, and, with specific prior approval of the Secretary, lodging for participants and staff for—

(1) Visits to postsecondary educational institutions to obtain information relating to the admission of participants to those institutions;

(2) Participation in "College Day" activities; and

(3) Field trips to observe and meet with people who are employed in various career fields in the target area and who can serve as role models for participants.

(b) Purchase of testing materials.

(c) Fees required for college admissions of entrance examinations if—

(1) A waiver is unavailable; and

(2) The fee is paid by the grantee to a third party on behalf of a participant.

(d) In-service training of project staff.

(e) Rental of space if—

(1) Space is not available at the site of the grantee; and

(2) The rented space is not owned by the grantee.

(f) Purchase of computer hardware, computer software, or other equipment for student development, project administration, and recordkeeping, if the applicant demonstrates to the Secretary's satisfaction that the equipment is required to meet the objectives of the project more economically or efficiently.

(Authority: 20 U.S.C. 1070a-11 and 1070a-16)

§ 644.31 What are unallowable costs?

Costs that are unallowable under the Educational Opportunity Centers program include, but are not limited to, the following:

(a) Tuition, fees, stipends, and other forms of direct financial support for participants.

(b) Research not directly related to the evaluation or improvement of the project.

(c) Construction, renovation, and remodeling of any facilities.

(Authority: 20 U.S.C 1070a-11 and 1070a-16)

§ 644.32 What other requirements must a grantee meet?

(a) Eligibility of participants. (1) A grantee shall determine the eligibility of each participant in the project at the time that the individual is selected to participate.

(2) A grantee shall determine the status of a low-income individual on the basis of the documentation described in section 402A(e) of the HEA.

(b) Number of participants. In each budget period, a grantee shall serve a minimum of 1,000 participants who reside in the target area. However, the Secretary may reduce the minimum number of these participants if the amount of the grant for the budget period is less than $180,000.

(c) Recordkeeping. For each participant, a grantee shall maintain a record of—

(1) The basis for the grantee's determination that the participant is eligible to participate in the project under § 644.3;

(2) The services that are provided to the participant; and

(3) The specific educational benefits received by the participant.

(d) Project director. (1) A grantee shall employ a full-time project director unless paragraph (d)(3) of this section applies.

(2) The grantee shall give the project director sufficient authority to administer the project effectively.

(3) The Secretary waives the requirement in paragraph (d)(1) of this section if the applicant demonstrates that the requirement will hinder

Figure 3.3. Continued. An Example of a Rules and Regulations Document

coordination—
(i) Among the Federal TRIO Programs (sections 402A through 402F of the HEA); or
(ii) Between the programs funded under sections 402A through 410 of the HEA and similar programs funded through other sources.

(Approved by the Office of Management and Budget under control number 1840-0065) (Authority: 20 U.S.C. 1070a-11 and 1070a-16).

Note: This appendix will not be codified in the Code of Federal Regulations.

Appendix—Analysis of Comments and Responses

The following is an analysis of the comments and changes in the regulations since the publication of the NPRM on October 26, 1999 (58 FR 57704). Substantive issues are discussed under the section of the regulations to which they pertain. Minor changes—and suggested changes that the Secretary is not legally authorized to make under applicable statutes— are not generally addressed.

How long is a project period? (§ 644.6)
Comment: One commenter suggested that the Secretary change the regulations so that a competition for Educational Opportunity Center (EOC) grants would be held once every two years. The commenter noted that such a schedule would be more efficient than a 4-year schedule and would be more fair because applicants who were not funded could reapply more quickly.
Discussion: The length of EOC project periods is prescribed in the Higher Education Act. Section 644.6 of these regulations merely reflects the statutory requirement.
Changes: None.
What selection criteria does the Secretary use? (§ 644.21)
Comment: Several commenters recommended that § 644.21(c)(5) be changed to require the Secretary to consider an applicant's plan to coordinate its EOC project with other projects that serve disadvantaged students. The commenters maintained that allotting points based on such a plan would encourage coordination among projects. Some commenters offered specific language suggesting that the Secretary evaluate an applicant's plan of operation based in part on "the plan, including the project's organization structure, its coordination with other programs for disadvantaged students sponsored by the sponsoring entity, and the time committed to the project by administrative and other staff, to ensure the proper and efficient administration of the project."
Discussion: The Secretary agrees that an applicant's plan to coordinate activities with other projects should be considered in the selection criteria and that such consideration will encourage coordination. However, the Secretary recognizes that in some cases an

EOC project may be the only project for disadvantaged students administered by a particular institution or agency. Therefore, the Secretary has adopted much of the suggested language but has included the modifier "where appropriate" to ensure that applicants who administer only an EOC project will not be disadvantaged by their inability to coordinate with other projects.
Changes: Section 644.21(c)(5) has been changed to read: "The management plan to ensure the proper and efficient administration of the project including, but not limited to, the project's organizational structure, the time committed to the project by the project director and other personnel, and, where appropriate, its coordination with other projects for disadvantaged students."
How does the Secretary evaluate prior experience? (§ 644.22)
Comment: Many commenters suggested that the Secretary change § 644.22, relating to prior experience points. None of the commenters asked the Secretary to change the wording of the criteria; all requested that the Secretary describe in greater detail how the criteria are applied. Some commenters argued the regulations should require the Secretary to notify grantees as to the number of points they received for prior experience before the funding determinations are made. Commenters argued that such a procedure would allow grantees to "correct errors" in the Secretary's evaluation of their prior experience. Other commenters suggested that the regulations should require the Secretary to award a portion of the prior experience points each year based on a grantee's annual performance report. They suggested that each grantee should be informed within a specified period as to how well each performance report was scored.
Commenters also noted that the regulations should require the Secretary to award prior experience points based only on a grantee's performance during the first two years of its grant. This procedure, they argued, would ensure that a grantee's prior experience would be measured against actual outcomes rather than speculation about what the grantee is likely to have accomplished by the end of the project period. Several commenters offered suggestions on how prior experience points should be allocated under the two-year evaluation schedule.
Discussion: The comments suggest a high degree of anxiety over how the Secretary rates prior experience. The comments imply that the assessment process should be continuous, extensive, and interactive. The Secretary, however, has no intention of unnecessarily burdening grantees with such a process. Under § 644.20(2)(i) of the regulations, the Secretary only evaluates prior experience when a grantee submits an application for "a new grant to continue to serve substantially the same populations or campuses that the applicant is

serving under an expiring grant." Prior experience is not evaluated until the Secretary receives such an application. This procedure reflects the mandate expressed in section 402(A)(c)(1) of the Higher Education Act, which states: "In making grants * * * the Secretary shall consider prior experience." The law requires the Secretary to evaluate prior experience only when the Secretary is deciding to make a grant; the Secretary only decides to make a grant if an application has been submitted. Thus, the final assessment of prior experience is conducted as part of the overall process for selecting new grants. This process begins when applications are received and ends when applicants are notified of the Secretary's funding decisions.
The application process is not an interactive process. After the closing date, no additional information is accepted or considered. Therefore, any information that an applicant feels should be considered during the course of the selection process should be provided before the closing date. The Secretary does not disclose information relating to the rank of applications until all applicants are notified of the Secretary's funding decisions. After applicants receive notification, they may request copies of documents that reflect the prior experience assessments.
Changes: None.
What are allowable costs? (§ 644.30)
Comment: Many commenters suggested that the Secretary amend § 644.30 of the proposed regulations to include college admission fees and college entrance examination fees in the list of allowable costs. The commenters noted that many adult EOC participants cannot afford to pay examination and application fees and are therefore discouraged from pursuing postsecondary education.
Discussion: The Secretary agrees that admission fees should be included in the list of allowable costs because some adult participants may be discouraged from applying to postsecondary institutions because of the expense associated with examination and application fees. However, the Secretary strongly encourages Educational Opportunity Centers to work with higher educational institutions to secure waivers whenever possible. Further, application fees will not be an allowable cost under § 644.30 if the fee is paid to the grantee institution because the Secretary encourages grantees to provide meaningful support to the Educational Opportunity Centers that they administer.
Changes: The Secretary has changed § 644.30 so that the list of allowable costs includes fees required for college admissions applications or entrance examination fees if (1) a waiver of the fee is unavailable; and (2) the fee is paid by the grantee to a third party on behalf of a participant.
What are unallowable costs? (§ 644.31)

Figure 3.3. Continued. An Example of a Rules and Regulations Document

2663   Federal Register / Vol. 65, No. 11 / Tuesday, January 18, 2000 / Rules and Regulations

Comment: Many commenters requested that the Secretary remove transportation, meals, and lodging from the list of unallowable costs in § 644.31. The commenters further requested that the Secretary include transportation, meals, and lodging in the list of allowable costs in § 644.30. Several commenters argued that campus visits are necessary to help participants choose an appropriate postsecondary placement. Other commenters noted that such visits are often impossible for EOC participants who reside in rural areas. Finally, some commenters argued that transportation, meals, and lodging should be allowable costs because they are allowable under the Talent Search program.

Discussion: The Secretary believes that college visits are often necessary to help adult participants gain the confidence and insight that they need to feel comfortable in applying for college admission. The Secretary agrees with the commenters that it would be unfortunate if the cost of such visitations prevented some participants from pursuing postsecondary education. Therefore, on a case-by-case basis, transportation, lodging, and meals may be allowable costs under the circumstances described in the regulations.

Changes: The Secretary has removed transportation, lodging, and meals from the list of unallowable costs in § 644.31. The Secretary has also changed § 644.30 so that the list of allowable costs includes: "(a) Transportation, meals, and, with specific prior approval of the Secretary, lodging for participants and staff for—(1) Visits to postsecondary educational institutions to obtain information relating to the admission of participants to those institutions; (2) Participation in "College Day" activities: and (3) Field trips to observe and meet with people who are employed in various career fields in the target area and who can act as role models for participants."

What other requirements must a grantee meet? (§ 644.32)

Comment: Some commenters suggested that the Secretary should change § 644.32(d)(1) to read: "Unless a part-time director furthers coordination of the project with other programs for disadvantaged clients operated by the sponsoring institution or agency, or unless a waiver is granted, a grantee shall employ a full-time project director." The commenters argued that the change was necessary because the language in the NPRM does not reflect the intent of the 1992 Amendments to the Higher Education Act, which requires the Secretary to encourage coordination among TRIO programs and other programs for disadvantaged students and to allow for a less-than-full-time director.

One commenter recommended that the Secretary require a full-time project director at all Educational Opportunity Centers. The commenter noted that the degree of detail to which a director must be attentive requires a

full-time commitment. The commenter further suggested that coordination among projects is desirable and can be accomplished when various directors work together for the mutual benefit of all projects on a single campus.

Discussion: The Secretary strongly supports coordination of EOC activities between and among projects to extent that the coordination fosters—

(1) Improved services for the EOC participants;

(2) More efficient or effective means of delivering services; or

(3) An increase in the resources available to participants.

There is no magic formula for coordination. It only occurs when all partners see it in their best interest to cooperate and coordinate activities to obtain some beneficial objectives. Projects do not have to share staff to coordinate activities. Coordination can occur in a number of ways by staff at all levels. Having a part-time director does not guarantee that coordination of activities will occur. Having a full-time director does not guarantee that the coordination of activities will not occur.

Each project is different in terms of its setting, resources, and support systems. The Secretary recognizes that a project may effectively operate with less than a full-time director if other support personnel are in place to assist in shared management duties. However, coordination can take many other forms. For example, coordination may be achieved by planning and conducting joint or cooperative field trips, lectures, career days, or test-preparation sessions. Coordination may also be achieved by sharing space or equipment.

Section 644.32(d)(1) accurately reflects both the intent of the 1992 Amendments to the HEA and the Secretary's commitment to coordination. Waivers of the requirement for a full-time director are available under § 644.32(d)(3) if an applicant can show that efforts to coordinate among projects will be hindered by not allowing one person to direct more than one project.

The Secretary believes that in many cases the size and scope of an EOC project require the attention of a full-time director. The average EOC project receives more than a million dollars over the course of a project period and serves more than eight thousand participants. Given the size and scope of EOC projects, the Secretary believes that the appropriateness of allowing a part-time director must be evaluated with great care.

Changes: None.

Comment: Several commenters suggested that the Secretary should change § 644.32(c)(3), relating to records of educational benefits. The commenters requested that the Secretary eliminate the phrase "the specific educational benefits to the participants that resulted from the services" because keeping a record of how each participant benefited from the services would be

too burdensome. The commenters suggested that § 644.32(c)(3) require only that grantees keep a record of "the specific educational benefits received by the participant."

One commenter suggested that the Secretary should not change the recordkeeping requirement in § 644.32(c)(3) because it formed the basis for collecting valuable statistics.

Discussion: The Secretary agrees that the phrase "that resulted from the services" implies that a grantee must demonstrate and record a causal relationship between services and benefits. The Secretary believes that such a record is not necessary to indicate a benefit, particularly in instances where the services provided can be deemed to be benefits in and of themselves.

Changes: The recordkeeping requirement at § 644.32(c)(3) is changed to read "the specific educational benefits received by the participant."

[FR Doc. 94-903 Filed 1-14-94; 8:45 am]

BILLING CODE 4000-01-P

Department of Education identifies the specific office (Office of Elementary and Secondary Education), the *CFR* number, the title, and the action taken in reference to the regulations.

Proposed Rules

These documents notify the public of the issuance of proposed rules and regulations. The OFR classifies the following types of documents as proposed rules for publication in the *Federal Register:*

- Documents that suggest changes to agency regulations in the *CFR* and request public comments on those suggested changes. Most of the documents in this section are required to be published as proposals by section 553 of the Administrative Procedure Act or other statutory authority. Some regulations are exempted from notice and comment requirements. Many agencies voluntarily publish these regulations in proposed form to allow public comment.

- Documents that affect other documents previously published in the proposed rule section. These documents may do the following:

  — Extend the comment period

  — Announce a public hearing

  — Publish or announce the availability of supplemental information

  — Withdraw a proposed rule or terminate a proposed rule proceeding

  — Correct a previously published proposed rule document

- Any document that serves as the first public notice that a rule-making proceeding is anticipated. These include the following documents:

  — Advance Notices of Proposed Rule Making

  — Notices of Inquiry

  — Notices of Intent

Federal agencies issue these documents early in the rule-making process to receive public reaction as early as possible. These documents describe a problem or situation that implies the possibility of regulatory action by the agency. In accordance to the following, they seek public response concerning the necessity for regulations in the area and the adequacy of the agency's potential regulatory response.

- Certain petitions for rule making are placed in the proposed rule section because the petition proposes to amend, revise, add to, or remove existing regulations in the *CFR,* and the agency requests public comment.

- A document that announces a meeting or hearing that may be the first step in a rule-making proceeding is placed in the proposed rule section.

- The documents also provide the public with advance notice of anticipated agency rule making and allows for comments.

Figure 3.4, pages 69-74, shows the first page of six pages of a Proposed Rules Document issued by the Office of Elementary and Secondary Education. Notice the *action (Notice of proposed rule making)* that is to be taken. The Department of Education is proposing to amend the regulations and is seeking comments concerning these proposed regulations. Comments must be received on or before October 3, 2000.

Notices

These are documents other than rules and proposed rules that are applicable to the public and are published for public information. The typical notice documents announce the following:

- Grant application deadlines

- Meetings

- Applications

- Issuance or revocation of licenses

- Availability of environmental impact statements

- Certain petitions

- Orders or decisions affecting named parties

Figure 3.5 on page 75 is a Notice Document. The notice document example states that the deadline to submit this application is March 14, 2000. It also provides valuable information such as the deadline date for intergovernmental review, the date when applications are available, the amount of funds available, the estimated range

——— **Grant Tip** ———

Notice Documents provide valuable information, ranging from deadline dates to estimated number of grants to be funded under this program.

(text continues on page 76)

Figure 3.4. An Example of a Proposed Rules Document

| Federal Register / Vol. 64, No. 170 / Friday, September 2, 1999 / Proposed Rules | 45964 |

DEPARTMENT OF EDUCATION

34 CFR Part 645

RIN 1840-AB65

Upward Bound Program

AGENCY: Notice of proposed rulemaking.
SUMMARY: The Secretary proposes to amend the regulations governing the Upward Bound Program. These regulations are needed to further implement statutory changes made to the Upward Bound Program by the Higher Education Amendments of 1992, and to clarify and simplify certain requirements governing the program. The selection criteria, prior experience criteria, and grantee accountability provisions are affected by these proposed changes.

The purposes and allowable activities of the Upward Bound Program support the National Education Goals. Specifically, the program funds projects designed to increase high school graduation rates, increase competency over challenging subject matters, encourage more students to pursue programs in mathematics and science, and help gain parental participation in the social, emotional and academic growth of their children.
DATES: Comments must be received on or before October 3, 1999.
ADDRESSES: All comments concerning these proposed regulations should be addressed to Richard T. Sonnergren, U.S. Department of Education, Room 5065, FOB-6, 400 Maryland Avenue, SW., Washington, DC 20202-5249.

A copy of any comments that concern information collection requirements should also be sent to the Office of Management and Budget at the address listed in the Paperwork Reduction Act section of this preamble.
FOR FURTHER INFORMATION CONTACT: Prince Teal or Carlos Stewart, U.S. Department of Education, 400 Maryland Avenue, SW., Room 5065 Washington, DC 20202-5249. Telephone: (202) 708-4804. Individuals who use a telecommunications device for the deaf (TDD) may call the Federal Information Relay Service (FIRS) at 1-800-877-8339 between 8 a.m. and 9 p.m., Eastern time, Monday through Friday.

SUPPLEMENTARY INFORMATION:

Background

The Upward Bound Program provides grants to institutions of higher education; public and private agencies and organizations; combinations of institutions, agencies, and organizations; and secondary schools under special circumstances. The purpose of the program is to generate the skills and motivation necessary for success in education beyond high school.

On October 1, 1999, the Secretary published revisions to the Upward Bound Program regulations to implement changes required by the Higher Education Amendments of 1992 (58 FR 51520-21). This NPRM proposes program

improvements that were not covered by the October 1, 1999 regulations. The major provisions of these proposed regulations include the following:

•*Definitions (§ 645.5).* The proposed regulations revise or add definitions to clarify certain terms used in the regulations, including definitions of "participant," "independent student," and "organization/agency."

•*Kinds of Projects (§ 645.10).* The proposed regulations will define in general the three types of Upward Bound projects supported under the program, i.e., Regular Upward Bound projects, Math and Science Upward Bound projects, and Veterans Upward Bound projects.

•*Upward Bound services and activities (§§ 645.11-645.14).* Section 645.11 of the proposed regulations lists the services that all Upward Bound projects must provide. Section 645.12 describes the manner in which services are provided in Regular Upward Bound projects. Section 645.13 lists additional services that the Math and Science Upward Bound project must provide and the manner in which services are provided. Section 645.14 lists additional services that the Veterans Upward Bound project must provide.

•*How does one apply for an award? (§§ 645.20-645.21).* Section 645.20 of the proposed regulation describes the condition under which the Secretary will accept more than one application from an eligible applicant. Section 645.21 describes the assurances an applicant must include in an application.

•*Selection criteria (§ 645.31).* The proposed regulations revise the order, weighting, and content of application selection criteria. The purpose for this revision is to simplify and clarify the review process and increase grantee accountability. In addition, the proposed regulations clarify and strengthen the requirements for a grantee's evaluation of a project.

•*Prior experience (§ 645.32).* The proposed regulations revise the criteria for the evaluation of a grantee's prior experience to focus on project outcomes.

•*Project size (§ 645.43(a)).* The proposed regulations establish a minimum number of participants residing in the target area who must be served by a project in each budget period, and permit that number to be reduced if the grant amount for the budget period is less than $190,000. The proposed regulations require that veterans Upward Bound projects serve at least 120 participants during each budget period, and that all other Upward Bound projects serve at least 50 participants in each budget period. Coupled with the new definition of "participant" in § 645.6 and the new recordkeeping requirements for participants in § 645.43(c), this provision is intended to ensure that projects provide a reasonable level of services to a significant number of recipients. This intended result is consistent with section 402A(b)(3) of the HEA, which establishes a $190,000 minimum grant level for awards beginning in fiscal year 1994, unless the

applicant requests a lesser amount.

•*Project period (§ 645.34).* The proposed regulations implement a statutory provision that expands the project period to four years—or five years in the case of applications that receive peer review scores in the highest 10 percent of all scores for approved new projects.

Executive Order 12866

Clarity of the Regulations

Executive Order 12866 requires each agency to write regulations that are easy to understand.

The Secretary invites comments on how to make these regulations easier to understand, including answers to questions such as the following: (1) Are the requirements in the regulations clearly stated? (2) Do the regulations contain technical terms or other wording that interferes with their clarity? (3) Does the format of the regulations (grouping and order of sections, use of headings, paragraphing, etc.) aid or reduce their clarity? Would the regulations be easier to understand if they were divided into more (but shorter) sections? (A "section" is preceded by the symbol "§" and a numbered heading; for example, § 645.20. (4) Is the description of the proposed regulations in the **SUPPLEMENTARY INFORMATION** section of this preamble helpful in understanding the proposed regulations? How could this description be more helpful in making the proposed regulations easier to understand? (5) What else could the Department do to make the regulations easier to understand?

A copy of any comments that concern whether these proposed regulations are easy to understand should also be sent to Stanley Cohen, Regulations Quality Officer, U.S. Department of Education, 400 Maryland Avenue, SW. (Room 5125, FOB-6), Washington, DC 20202-2241.

Regulatory Flexibility Act Certification

The Secretary certifies that these proposed regulations would not have a significant economic impact on a substantial number of small entities. The small entities that would be affected by these regulations are small institutions of higher education, other agencies and organizations, and secondary schools that receive Federal funds under this program. However, the regulations would not have a significant economic impact on the small entities affected because the regulations would not impose excessive regulatory burdens or require unnecessary Federal supervision. The regulations would impose minimal requirements to ensure the proper expenditure of program funds.

Paperwork Reduction Act of 1980

Sections 645.4, 645.31, 645.32, and 645.43 contain information collection requirements. As required by the Paperwork Reduction Act of 1980, the Department of Education will submit a copy of these sections to the Office of

Figure 3.4. Continued. An Example of a Proposed Rules Document

| 45965 | Federal Register / Vol. 64, No. 170 / Friday, September 2, 1999 / Proposed Rules |

Management and Budget (OMB) for its review. (44 U.S.C. 3504(h)).

Institutions of higher education; public and private agencies and organizations; combinations of institutions, agencies, and organizations; and secondary schools are eligible to apply for grants under these regulations. The Department needs and uses the application data and information to make grants. Annual grantee reporting is estimated to average 40 hours per response for over 600 respondents, including the time for reviewing instructions, searching existing data sources, gathering and maintaining the data needed, and completing and reviewing the collection of information.

Organizations and individuals desiring to submit comments on the information collection requirement should direct them to the Office of IRA, OMB, Room 10235, New Executive Office Building, Washington, DC 20504; Attention: Daniel J. Chenok.

Intergovernmental Review

This program is subject to the requirements of Executive Order 12372 and the regulations in 34 CFR Part 79. The objective of the Executive order is to foster an intergovernmental partnership and a strengthened federalism by relying on processes developed by State and local governments for coordination and review of proposed Federal financial assistance.

In accordance with the order, this document is intended to provide early notification of the Department's specific plans and actions for this program.

Invitation to Comment

Interested persons are invited to submit comments and recommendations regarding these proposed regulations.

All comments submitted in response to these proposed regulations will be available for public inspection during and after the comment period in Room 5065, FOB-6, 400 Maryland Avenue, SW., Washington, DC., between the hours of 8:30 a.m. and 4 p.m., Monday through Friday of each week except Federal holidays.

Assessment of Educational Impact

The Secretary particularly requests comments on whether the proposed regulations in this document would require transmission of information that is being gathered by or is available from any other agency or authority of the United States.

List of Subjects in 34 CFR Part 645

Colleges and Universities, Education of disadvantaged, Grant programs—education, Reporting and recordkeeping requirements, Secondary education.

Dated: August 17, 1999.
David A. Longanecker,
Assistant Secretary, Office of Postsecondary Education.
(Catalog of Federal Domestic Assistance

Number 84.047, Upward Bound Program.)

The Secretary proposes to amend Title 34 of the Code of Federal Regulations by revising Part 645 to read as follows:

PART 645—UPWARD BOUND PROGRAM

Subpart A—General

Sec.
645.1   What is the Upward Bound Program?
645.2   Who is eligible for a grant?
645.3   Who is eligible to participate in an Upward sound project?
645.4   What are the grantee requirements with respect to low income and first-generation participants?
645.5   What regulations apply?
645.6   What definitions apply to the Upward Bound Program?

Subpart B—What Kinds of Projects and Services Does the Secretary Assist Under This Program?

645.10   What kinds of projects are supported under the Upward Bound Program?
645.11   What services do all Upward Bound projects provide?
645.12   How are regular Upward Bound projects organized?
645.13   What additional services do Math and Science Upward Bound projects provide and how are they organized?
645.14   What additional services do Veterans Upward Bound projects provide?

Subpart C—How Does One Apply for an Award?

645.20   How many applications for an Upward Bound award may an eligible applicant submit?
645.21   What assurances must an applicant include in an application?

Subpart D—How Does the Secretary Make a Grant?

645.30   How does the Secretary decide which grants to make?
645.31   What selection criteria does the Secretary use?
645.32   How does the Secretary evaluate prior experience?
645.33   How does the Secretary set the amount of a grant?
645.34   How long is a project period?

Subpart E—What Conditions Must Be Met by a Grantee?

645.40   What are allowable costs?
645.41   What are unallowable costs?
645.42   What are Upward Bound stipends?

645.43   What other requirements must a grantee meet?
(Authority: 20 U.S.C. 1070a-11 and 1070a-13, unless otherwise noted)

Subpart A—General

§ 645.1 What is the Upward Bound Program?

(a) The Upward Bound Program provides Federal grants to projects designed to generate in program participants the skills and motivation necessary to persist in completing a program of secondary education and enter and complete a program of postsecondary education.
(b) The Upward Bound Program provides Federal grants for the following three types of projects:
(1) Regular Upward Bound projects.
(2) Upward Bound Math and Science projects.
(3) Veterans Upward Bound projects.
(Authority: 20 U.S.C. 1070a-11 and 1070a-13)

§ 645.2 Who is eligible for a grant?

The following entities are eligible to apply for a grant to carry out an Upward Bound project:
(a) Institutions of higher education.
(b) Public or private agencies or organizations.
(c) Secondary schools, in exceptional cases, if there are no other applicants capable of providing this program in the target area or areas to be served by the proposed project.
(d) A combination of the types of institutions, agencies, and organizations described in paragraphs (a) and (b) of this section.
(Authority: 20 U.S.C 1070a-11 and 1070a-13)

§ 645.3 Who is eligible to participate in an Upward Bound project?

An individual is eligible to participate in a Regular, Math and Science, or Veterans Upward Bound project if the individual meets all of the following requirements:
(a)(1) Is a citizen or national of the United States.
(2) Is a permanent resident of the United States.
(3) Is in the United States for other than a temporary purpose and provides evidence from the Immigration and Naturalization Service of his or her intent to become a permanent resident.
(4) Is a permanent resident of Guam, the Northern Mariana Islands, or the Trust Territory of the Pacific Islands.
(5) Is a resident of the Freely Associated States—the Federated States of Micronesia or the Republic of the Marshall Islands.
(b) Is—(1) A potential first-generation college student; or
(2) A low-income individual.
(c) Has a need for academic support, as determined by the grantee, in order to pursue successfully a program of education beyond high school.
(d) At the time of initial selection, has completed the eighth grade but has not entered the twelfth grade and is at least 13 years old, but

Figure 3.4. Continued. An Example of a Proposed Rules Document

Federal Register / Vol. 64, No. 170 / Friday, September 2, 1999 / Proposed Rules   45966

not older than 19. However, a veteran as defined in § 645.6, regardless of age, is eligible to participate in an Upward Bound project if he or she satisfies the eligibility requirements in paragraphs (a), (b), and (c) of this section.
(Authority: 20 U.S.C. 1070a-11 and 1070a-13)

§ 645.4 What are the grantee requirements with respect to low income and first-generation participants?
(a) At least two-thirds of the eligible participants a grantee serves must at the time of initial selection qualify as both low-income individuals and potential first-generation college students. The remaining participants must, at the time of initial selection, qualify as either low-income individuals or potential first-generation college students.
(b) For purposes of documenting a participant's low-income status the following applies:
(1) In the case of a student who is not an independent student, an institution shall document that the student is a low-income individual by obtaining and maintaining—
(i) A signed statement from the student's parent or legal guardian regarding family income;
(ii) Verification of family income from another governmental source;
(iii) A signed financial aid application; or
(iv) A signed United States or Puerto Rican income tax return.
(2) In the case of a student who is an independent student, an institution shall document that the student is a low-income individual by obtaining and maintaining—
(i) A signed statement from the student regarding family income;
(ii) Verification of family income from another governmental source;
(iii) A signed financial aid application; or
(iv) A signed United States or Puerto Rican income tax return.
(c) For purposes of documenting potential first-generation college student status, documentation consists of a signed statement from a dependent participant's parent, or a signed statement from an independent participant.
(d) A grantee does not have to revalidate a participant's eligibility after the participant's initial selection.
(Authority: 20 U.S.C. 1070d, and 1070d-1a)

§ 645.5 What regulations apply?
The following regulations apply to the Upward Bound Program:
(a) The Education Department General Administrative Regulations (EDGAR) as follows:
(1) 34 CFR Part 74 (Administration of Grants to Institutions of Higher Education, Hospitals, and Nonprofit Organizations);
(2) 34 CFR Part 75 (Direct Grant Programs), except for 34 CFR 75.511;

(3) 34 CFR Part 77 (Definitions that Apply to Department Regulations), except for the definition of "secondary school" in 34 CFR 77.1;
(4) 34 CFR Part 79 (Intergovernmental Review of Department of Education Programs and Activities);
(5) 34 CFR Part 82 (New Restrictions on Lobbying);
(6) 34 CFR Part 85 (Governmentwide Debarment and Suspension (Nonprocurement) and Governmentwide Requirements for Drug-Free Workplace (Grants)).
(7) 34 CPR Part 86 (Drug-Free Schools and Campuses);
(b) The regulations in this Part 645.
(Authority: 20 U.S.C. 1070a-11 and 1070a-13)

§ 645.6 What definitions apply to the Upward Bound Program?
(a) *Definitions in EDGAR.* The following terms used in this part are defined in 34 CFR 77.1:

Applicant	Grant
Application	Grantee
Award	Project
Budget	Project period
Budget period	Secretary
EDGAR	State
Equipment	Supplies
Facilities	

(b) *Other Definitions.* The following definitions also apply to this part:
Family taxable income means—
(1) With regard to a dependent student, the taxable income of the individual's parents;
(2) With regard to a dependent student who is an orphan or ward of the court, no taxable income.
(3) With regard to an independent student, the taxable income of the student and his or her spouse.
HEA means the Higher Education Act of 1965, as amended.
Independent student means a student who—
(1) Is an orphan or ward of the court;
(2) Is a veteran of the Armed Forces of the United States (as defined in this section);
(3) Is a married individual; or
(4) Has legal dependents other than a spouse.
Institution of higher education means an educational institution as defined in sections 1201(a) and 481 of the HEA.
Limited English proficiency with reference to an individual, means an individual whose native language is other than English and who has sufficient difficulty speaking, reading, writing, or understanding the English language to deny that individual the opportunity to learn successfully in classrooms in which English is the language of instruction.
Low-income individual means an individual whose family taxable income did not exceed 150 percent of the poverty level amount in the calendar year preceding the year in which the individual initially participates in the project.

The poverty level amount is determined by using criteria of poverty established by the Bureau of the Census of the U.S. Department of Commerce.
Organization/Agency means an entity that is legally authorized to operate programs such as Upward Bound in the State where it is located.
Participant means an individual who—(1) Is determined to be eligible to participate in the project under 645.3;
(2) Except for veterans, is enrolled in a target school; and
(3) Has received more than one month of project services.
Potential first-generation college student means—
(1) An individual neither of whose parents received a baccalaureate degree; or
(2) A student who, prior to the age of 18, regularly resided with and received support from only one parent and whose supporting parent did not receive a baccalaureate degree.
Secondary school means a school that provides secondary education as determined under State law.
Target area means a discrete geographic area—as determined by the applicant—to be served by an Upward Bound project.
Target school means a school designated by the applicant as a focus of project services.
Veteran means a person who served on active duty as a member of the Armed Forces of the United States—
(1) For a period of more than 180 days, any part of which occurred after January 31, 1955, and who was discharged or released from active duty under conditions other than dishonorable; or
(2) After January 31, 1955, and who was discharged or released from active duty because of a service-connected disability.
(Authority: 20 U.S.C. 1001 et seq., 1070a-11, 1070a-13, 1088, 1141, 1141a, and 3283(a)).

Subpart B—What Kinds of Projects and Services Does the Secretary Assist Under This Program?

§ 645.10 What kinds of projects are supported under the Upward Bound program?
The Secretary provides grants to the following three types of Upward Bound projects:
(a) Regular Upward Bound projects designed to prepare high school students for programs of postsecondary education.
(b) Upward Bound Math and Science projects designed to prepare high school students for postsecondary education programs and careers in the fields of math and science.
(c) Veterans Upward Bound projects designed to assist veterans to prepare for a program of postsecondary education.
(Authority: 20 U.S.C. 1070a-11 and 1070a-13)

§ 645.11 What services do all Upward Bound projects provide?
(a) An Upward Bound project that has

Figure 3.4. Continued. An Example of a Proposed Rules Document

45967   **Federal Register** / Vol. 64, No. 170 / Friday, September 2, 1999 / Proposed Rules

received funds under this part for at least two years must provide as part of its core curriculum, instruction in—

(1) Mathematics through pre-calculus;
(2) Laboratory science;
(3) Foreign language;
(4) Composition; and
(5) Literature.

(b) All Upward Bound projects may provide such services as—

(1) Instruction in subjects other than those listed in 645.11(a) that are necessary for success in education beyond high school;
(2) Personal counseling;
(3) Academic advice and assistance in secondary school course selection;
(4) Tutorial services;
(5) Exposure to cultural events, academic programs, and other educational activities not usually available to disadvantaged youths;
(6) Activities designed to acquaint youths participating in the project with the range of career options available to them;
(7) Instruction designed to prepare youths participating in the project for careers in which persons from disadvantaged backgrounds are particularly underrepresented;
(8) Mentoring programs involving elementary or secondary school teachers, faculty members at institutions of higher education, students or any combination of these person and other professional individuals; and
(9) Programs and activities such as those described in paragraphs (b)(1) through (b)(8) of this section that are specifically designed for individuals with limited proficiency in English.
(Authority: 20 U.S.C. 1070a-13)

§ 645.12 How are regular Upward Bound projects organized?

(a) Regular Upward Bound projects—
(1) Must provide participants with a summer instructional component that is designed to simulate a college-going experience for participants, and an academic year component; and
(2) May provide a summer bridge component to those Upward Bound participants who have graduated from secondary school and intend to enroll in an institution of higher education in the following fall term. A summer bridge component provides participants with services and activities, including college courses, that aid in the transition from secondary education to postsecondary education.
(b) A summer instructional component shall—
(1) Be six weeks in length unless the grantee can demonstrate to the Secretary that a shorter period will not hinder the effectiveness of the project nor prevent the project from achieving its goals and objectives, and the Secretary approves that shorter period; and
(2) Provide participants with the services described in 645.11 on a daily basis.
(c)(1) Except as provided in paragraph (c)(2)

of this section, an academic year component shall provide program participants with the services described in 645.11 on a weekly basis throughout the academic year, and to the extent possible shall not prevent participants from fully participating in academic and nonacademic activities at the participants secondary school.
(2) If an Upward Bound project's location or the project's staff are not readily accessible to participants because of distance or lack of transportation, the grantee may, with the Secretary's permission, provide project services to participants every two weeks during the academic year.
(Authority: 20 U.S.C. 1070a-13)

§ 645.13 What additional services do Math and Science Upward Bound projects provide and how are they organized?

(a) In addition to the services that must be provided under 645.11(a) and may be provided in 645.11(b), a Math and Science Upward Bound project must provide—
(1) Intensive instruction in mathematics and science including hands-on experience in laboratories, field-sites and state-of-the-art computer facilities;
(2) Activities that will involve participants with research faculty from the applicant institution;
(3) Activities that will involve participants with graduate and undergraduate science and mathematics majors who may serve as tutors and counselors for participants; and
(b) A Math and Science Upward Bound project must provide—
(1) A summer component in the manner described in 645.12(b); and
(2) An academic year component during which the project provides services to participants at least once a month.
(Authority: 20 U.S.C. 1070a-11 and 1070a-13)

§ 645.14 What additional services do Veterans Upward Bound projects provide?

In addition to the services that must be provided under 645.11(a) and may be provided under 645.11(b), a Veterans Upward Bound project must—
(a) Provide intensive basic skills development in those academic subjects required for successful completion of a high school equivalency program and for admission to postsecondary education programs;
(b) Provide short-term remedial or refresher courses for veterans who are high school graduates but who have delayed pursuing postsecondary education. If the grantee is an institution of higher education, these courses shall not duplicate courses otherwise available to veterans at the institution; and
(c) Assist veterans in securing support services from other locally available resources such as the Veterans Administration, State veterans agencies, veterans associations, and other State and local agencies that serve veterans.
(Authority: 20 U.S.C. 1070a-11 and 1070a-13)

Subpart C—How Does One Apply for an Award?

§ 645.20 How many applications for an Upward Bound award may an eligible applicant submit?

(a) The Secretary accepts more than one application from an eligible entity so long as the additional applications describe projects that serve different populations; i.e., a group of potential participants that cannot readily be served under the applicant's other application due to differences in geographical location, academic level, curricular emphasis, or age.
(b) Each application for funding under the Upward Bound program shall state whether the application proposes a Regular Upward Bound project, a Math and Science Upward Bound project, or a Veterans Upward Bound project.
(Authority: 20 U.S.C. 1070a-11 and 1070a-13)

§ 645.21 What assurances must an applicant include in an application?

An applicant must assure the Secretary that—
(a) Not less than two-thirds of the project's participants will be low-income individuals who are potential first-generation college students; and
(b) That the remaining participants be either low-income individuals or potential first-generation college students.
(Authority: 20 U.S.C. 1070a-13)

Subpart D—How Does the Secretary Make a Grant?

§ 645.30 How does the Secretary decide which grants to make?

(a) The Secretary evaluates an application for a grant as follows:
(1)(i) The Secretary evaluates the application on the basis of the selection criteria in § 645.31.
(ii) The maximum score for all the criteria in § 645.31 is 100 points. The maximum score for each criterion is indicated in parentheses with the criterion.
(2)(i) If an applicant for a new grant proposes to continue to serve substantially the same target population or schools that the applicant is serving under an expiring project, the Secretary evaluates the applicant's prior experience in delivering services under the expiring Upward Bound project on the basis of the criteria in § 645.32.
(ii) The maximum score for all the criteria in § 645.32 is 15 points. The maximum score for each criterion is indicated in parentheses with the criterion.
(b) The Secretary makes grants in rank order on the basis of the application's total scores under paragraphs (a)(1) and (a)(2) of this section.
(c) If the total scores of two or more applications are the same and there are insufficient funds for these applications after the approval of higher-ranked applications, the Secretary uses whatever remaining funds are available to serve geographic areas that have been underserved by the Upward

Figure 3.4. Continued. An Example of a Proposed Rules Document

Federal Register / Vol. 64, No. 170 / Friday, September 2, 1999 / Proposed Rules   45968

Bound program.

(d) The Secretary may decline to make a grant to an applicant that carried out a project that involved the fraudulent use of funds under section 402A(c)(2)(B) of the HEA. (Authority: 20 U.S.C. 1070a-11, 1070a-13)

§ 645.31 What selection criteria does the Secretary use?

The Secretary uses the following criteria to evaluate an application for a grant:

(a) *Need for the project* (24 points). In determining the need for an Upward Bound project, the Secretary reviews each type of project (Regular, Math and Science, or Veterans) using different need criteria. The criteria for each type of project contain the same total weight of 24 points and are as follows:

(1) The Secretary evaluates the need for a Regular Upward Bound project in the proposed target area on the basis of—(i) High school dropout rates in the target area;

(ii) College-going rates of the high schools in the target area;

(iii) Student/counselor ratios of the high schools in the target area;

(iv) Income level of families within the target area;

(v) Education attainment levels of families within the target area; and

(vi) Unaddressed academic, social, or economic problems of low-income, potentially first-generation students in the target area.

(2) The Secretary evaluates the need for an Upward Bound Math and Science project in the proposed target area on the basis of—

(i) The extent to which student performance on standardized aptitude or achievement tests in mathematics and science in the proposed target schools, is lower than State and national norms.

(ii) The extent to which target schools lack the resources to offer a full range of mathematics and science courses, which are prerequisites for entry into postsecondary programs in mathematics, science, or engineering;

(iii) The extent to which attendance data, dropout rates, college-going rates and student/counselor ratios in the target schools indicate the importance of having additional educational opportunities available to low-income, first-generation students; and

(iv) The extent to which there are eligible students in the target schools who have demonstrated interest and capacity to pursue academic programs and careers in mathematics and science and who could benefit from an Upward Bound Math and Science program.

(3) The Secretary evaluates the need for a Veterans Upward Bound project in the proposed target area on the basis of clear evidence that shows—

(i) The proposed target area lacks the services for eligible veterans that the applicant proposes to provide;

(ii) A large number of veterans who reside in the target areas are low income and

potential first generation;

(iii) A large number of veterans who reside in the target area, have not completed high school or, have completed high school but have not enrolled in a program of postsecondary education; and

(iv) Other indicators of need for a Veterans Upward Bound project, including the presence of unaddressed academic or socio-economic problems of veterans in the area.

(b) *Objectives* (9 points). The Secretary evaluates the quality of the applicant's proposed project objectives on the basis of the extent to which they—

(1) Include both process and outcome objectives relating to the purpose of the applicable Upward Bound programs for which they are applying;

(2) Address the needs of the target area or target population; and

(3) Are measurable, ambitious, and attainable over the life of the project.

(c) *Plan of operation* (30 points). The Secretary determines the quality of the applicant's plan of operation by assessing the quality of—

(1) The plan for identifying, recruiting, and selecting participants to be served by the project;

(2) The plan for assessing individual participant needs and for monitoring the academic growth of participants while they are in an Upward Bound project;

(3) A follow-up plan for tracking the academic accomplishments of participants after they are no longer participating in the Upward Bound project;

(4) The plan for locating the project within the applicant's organizational structure, and the plan to inform the applicant community of the goals and objectives of the project;

(5) The various services and activities to be provided to project participants and their parents;

(6) The extent to which the timelines presented are appropriate for accomplishing critical elements of the project;

(7) The extent to which proposed services and activities relate logically to the needs in the target area;

(8) The plan to ensure effective and efficient administration of the project, including, but not limited to matters such as financial management, quality control, student records management, personnel management, and the plan for coordinating the Upward Bound project with other programs for disadvantaged students;

(9) The quality of the applicants plan to use its resources and personnel to achieve project objectives; and

(10) The plan to work cooperatively with key administrative, teaching and counseling personnel at the target schools to achieve project objectives.

(d) *Applicant and community support* (16 points). The Secretary evaluates the applicant and community support for the proposed

project on the basis of the extent to which the applicant demonstrates that—

(1) The applicant is committed to supplementing the project with resources such as space, furniture and equipment, supplies, and personnel that enhance the project;

(2) The applicant has secured written commitments of support from schools, community organizations, and businesses, including the commitment of resources that will enhance the project as described in paragraph (d)(1) of this section.

(e) *Quality of personnel* (8 points). To determine the quality of personnel the applicant plans to use, the Secretary looks for information that shows—

(1) The qualifications required of the project director, including formal educational training in fields related to the objectives of the project and experience in designing, managing, or implementing similar projects;

(2) The qualifications required of each of the other personnel to be used in the project, including formal educational training and work experience in fields related to the objectives of the project; and

(3) The quality of the applicant's plan for employing personnel who have succeeded in overcoming barriers similar to those confronting the project's target population.

(f) *Budget and cost effectiveness* (5 points) The Secretary reviews each application to determine the extent to which—

(1) The budget for the project is adequate to support planned project services and activities, and

(2) Costs are reasonable in relation to the objectives and scope of the project.

(g) *Evaluation plan* (8 points). The Secretary evaluates the quality of the evaluation plan for the project on the basis of the extent to which the applicant's methods of evaluation—

(1) Are appropriate to the project and include both quantitative and qualitative evaluation measures; and

(2) Examine in specific and measurable ways the success of the project in—

(i) Making progress toward achieving its process objectives; and

(ii) Achieving its outcomes objectives. (Authority: 20 U.S.C. 1070a-16)

§ 645.32 How does the Secretary evaluate prior experience?

(a) In the case of an application described in 645.30(a)(2), the Secretary reviews information relating to an applicant's performance under its expiring Upward Bound grant. This information includes information derived from annual performance reports, audit reports, site visit reports, project evaluation reports, and any other verifiable information submitted by the applicant.

(b) The Secretary evaluates the applicant's prior experience in delivering services on the basis of the following criteria:

(1) (3 points) Whether the applicant consistently provided services to the number of participants required to be served under the approved application;

(2) (3 points) The extent to which project participants' competencies, aptitude and

Figure 3.4. Continued. An Example of a Proposed Rules Document

motivation necessary for entry into an educational program beyond high school have improved;

(3) (3 points) The extent to which project participants are retained in the project throughout their secondary education program;

(4) (3 points) The extent to which project participants undertake programs of postsecondary education upon completion of project activities and secondary education; and

(5) (3 points) The extent to which former project participants succeeded in education beyond high school, including the extent to which they graduate from postsecondary education programs;
(Authority: 20 U.S.C. 1070a-11 and 1070a-13)

§ 645.33 How does the Secretary set the amount of a grant?

(a) The Secretary sets the amount of a grant on the basis of—

(1) 34 CFR 75.232 and 75.233, for new grants; and

(2) 34 CFR 75.232, for the second and subsequent years of a project period.

(b) If the circumstances described in section 402A(b)(3) of the HEA exist, the Secretary uses the available funds to set the amount of the grant beginning in fiscal year 1995 at the lesser of—

(1) $190,000; or

(2) The amount requested by the applicant.
(Authority: 20 U.S.C. 1070a-11)

§ 645.34 How long is a project period?

(a) Except as provided in paragraph (b) of this section, a project period under the Upward Bound program is four years.

(b) The Secretary approves a project period of five years for applications that score in the highest ten percent of all applications approved for new grants under the criteria in § 645.31.
(Authority: 20 U.S.C. 1070a-11)

Subpart E—What Conditions Must Be Met by a Grantee?

§ 645.40 What are allowable costs?

The cost principles that apply to the Upward Bound Program are in 34 CFR Part 74, Subpart Q. Allowable costs include the following if they are reasonably related to the objectives of the project:

(a) In-service training of project staff.

(b) Rental of space if space is not available at the host institution and the space rented is not owned by the host institution.

(c) For participants in an Upward Bound residential summer component, room and board—computed on a weekly basis—not to exceed the weekly rate the host institution charges regularly enrolled students at the institution.

(d) Room and board for those persons responsible for dormitory supervision of participants during a residential summer component.

(e) Educational pamphlets and similar materials for distribution at workshops for the parents of participants.

(f) Student activity fees for participants.

(g) Admissions fees, transportation, Upward Bound T-shirts, and other costs necessary to participate in field trips, attend educational activities, visit museums, and attend other events that have as their purpose the intellectual, social, and cultural development of participants.

(h) Costs for one project-sponsored banquet or ceremony.

(i) Tuition costs for postsecondary credit courses at the host institution for participants in the summer bridge component.

(j)(1) Accident insurance to cover any injuries to a project participant while participating in a project activity; and

(2) Medical insurance and health service fees for the project participants while participating full-time in the summer component.

(k) Courses in English language instruction for project participants with limited proficiency in English, only if these classes are not available at a target school.

(l) Transportation costs of participants for regularly scheduled project activities.

(m) Transportation, meals, and overnight accommodations for staff members when they are required to accompany participants in project activities such as field trips.

(n) Purchase of computer hardware, computer software, or other equipment for student development, project administration and recordkeeping, if the applicant demonstrates to the Secretary's satisfaction that the equip-ment is required to meet the objectives of the project more economically or efficiently.
(Authority: 20 U.S.C. 1070a-11 and 1070a-13)

§ 645.41 What are unallowable costs?

Costs that may not be charged against a grant under this program include the following:

(a) Research not directly related to the evaluation or improvement of the project.

(b) Meals for staff except as provided in § 645.40(d) and (m) and (c) of this section.

(c) Room and board for administrative and instructional staff personnel who do not have responsibility for dormitory supervision of project participants during a residential summer component, unless these costs are approved by the Secretary.

(d) Room and board for participants in Veterans Upward Bound projects.

(e) Construction, renovation or remodeling of any facilities.

(f) Tuition, stipends, or any other form of student financial support for project staff.
(Authority: 20 U.S.C. 1070a-11 and 1070a-13)

§ 645.42 What are Upward Bound stipends?

(a) A project may provide stipends for all participants who participate on a full-time basis.

(b) In order to receive the stipend, the participant must show evidence of satisfactory participation in activities of the project including—

(1) Regular attendance; and

(2) Performance in accordance with standards established by the grantee and described in the application.

(c) The grantee may prorate the amount of the stipend according to the number of the scheduled sessions in which the student participated.

(d) The following rules govern the amounts of stipends a grantee is permitted to provide:

(1) For Regular Upward Bound projects and Upward Bound Math and Science projects—

(i) For the academic year component, the stipend may not exceed $40 per month; and

(ii) For the summer component, the stipend may not exceed $60 per month.

(2) For Veterans Upward Bound projects, the stipend may not exceed $40 per month.
(Authority: 20 U.S.C. 1070a-11 and 1070a-13)

§ 645.43 What other requirements must a grantee meet?

(a) *Number of participants.* (1) In each budget period, Regular Upward Bound projects shall serve between 50 and 150 participants and Upward Bound Math and Science projects shall serve between 50 and 75 participants.

(2) Veterans Upward Bound projects shall serve a minimum of 120 veterans in each budget period.

(3) The Secretary may waive the requirements of paragraphs (a)(1) and (a)(2) of this section if the applicant can demonstrate that the project will be more cost effective and consistent with the objectives of the project if a greater or lesser number of participants will be served.

(b) *Project director.* (1) A grantee shall employ a full-time project director unless paragraph (b)(3) of this section applies.

(2) The grantee shall give the project director sufficient authority to administer the project effectively.

(3) The Secretary waives the requirement in paragraph (b)(1) of this section if the applicant demonstrates that the requirement will hinder coordination—

(i) Among the Federal TRIO Programs; or

(ii) Between the programs funded under sections 402A through 410 of the HEA and similar programs funded through other sources.

(c) *Recordkeeping.* For each participant, a grantee shall maintain a record of—

(1) The basis for the grantee's determination that the participant is eligible to participate in the project under § 645.3;

(2) The basis for the grantee's determination that the participant has a need for academic support in order to pursue successfully a program of education beyond secondary school;

(3) The services that are provided to the participant;

(4) The educational progress of the participant during high school and, to the degree possible, during the participant's pursuit of a postsecondary education program.
(Authority: 20 U.S.C. 1070a-11 and 1070a-13).

[FR Doc. 94-21744 Filed 9-1-99; 8:45 am]

BILLING CODE 4000-01-P

Figure 3.5. An Example of a Notice Document

Federal Register / Vol. 65, No. 11 / Tuesday, January 18, 2000 / Notices	**2664**

DEPARTMENT OF EDUCATION

[CFDA No.: 84.066]

Educational Opportunity Centers; Notice Inviting Applications for New Awards for FY 2000

Purpose of Program: To provide grants to permit applicants to conduct projects designed to: (1) Provide information regarding financial and academic assistance available for individuals who desire to pursue a program of postsecondary education, and (2) assist individuals to apply for admission to institutions that offer programs of postsecondary education. This program supports the National Education Goals. Specifically, the program funds projects designed to increase education opportunities for adults (Goals 5).

Eligible Applicants: Institutions of higher education, public and private agencies and organizations, combinations of institutions, agencies and organizations, and, in exceptional cases, secondary schools, such as if no other applicants are capable of providing an Educational Opportunity Centers project in the proposed target area.

Deadline for transmittal of applications: March 14, 2000.

Deadline for intergovernmental review: May 13, 2000.

Applications available: January 28, 2000.

Available funds: $22.5 million.

Estimated range of awards: $180,000-$750,000.

Estimated average size of awards: $346,000.

Estimated number of awards: 65.

Note: The Department is not bound by any estimates in this notice.

Project period: Up to 60 months.

Budget period: 12 months.

Applicable regulations: (a) The Education Department General Administrative Regulations (EDGAR) in 34 CFR parts 74, 75, 77, 79, 82, 85, and 86; and (b) The regulations for this program in 34 CFR part 644, as published in this same issue of the **Federal Register**.

For applications or information contact: Margaret Wingfield, U.S. Department of Education, 400 Maryland Avenue, SW., room 5065, Washington, DC 20202-5249. Telephone: (202) 708-4804. Individuals who use a telecommunications device for the deaf (TDD) may call the Federal Information Relay Service (FIRS) at 1-800-877-8339 between 8 a.m. and 8 p.m. Eastern Standard Time, Monday through Friday.

Information about the Department's funding opportunities, including copies of application notices for discretionary grant competitions, can be viewed on the Department's electronic bulletin board (ED Board), telephone (202) 260-9950; or on the Internet Gopher Server at GOPHER.ED.GOV (under Announcements, Bulletins, and Press Releases). However, the official application notice for a discretionary grant competition is the notice published in the **Federal Register.**

Program Authority: 20 U.S.C. 1070a-11 and 1070a-16.

Dated: January 4, 1994.

David A. Longanecker,
Assistant Secretary for Postsecondary Education.

[FR Doc. 94-904 Filed 1-14-2000; 8:45 am]

BILLING CODE 4001-01-P

of awards, and the estimated number of grants to be funded under this program.

Sunshine Act Meetings

These are notices of meetings published as required by the government in the Sunshine Act (5 U.S.C. 552b(e)(3)). Figure 3.6 on page 77 is a Sunshine Act Meeting Document. This section of the *Federal Register* contains notices of meetings published under the Federal Government in the Sunshine Act.

Structure of the *Federal Register*

The *Federal Register* is organized and formatted according to date, day, volume, numbers, and pages. For example, the volume for the 2000 calendar year was 65, with numbers 1 to 251, meaning that the *Federal Register* was issued 251 days in 2000, with the pages being numbered cumulatively from 1 to over 50,000 pages for the calendar year. Each issue of the *Federal Register* contains the following elements:

- Preliminary pages of finding aids concerning the contents of that issue
- Documents arranged under the headings of
  - Presidential documents (see example on page 59)
  - Rules and regulations (see example on pages 61-66)
  - Proposed rules (see example on pages 69-74)
  - Notices (see example on page 75)
  - Sunshine Act meetings (see example on page 77)
  - Corrections
- Documents published as separate parts to allow the issuing agency to order reprints
- Pages of general reader aids

Steps to Using the *Federal Register*

To use the *Federal Register* effectively to respond to requests for federal applications for grants in education, you need access to the daily *Federal Register*. This could be obtained through the research and grants' office at your institution, through the nearest depository

Figure 3.6. An Example of a Sunshine Act Meeting Document

Sunshine Act Meetings

Federal Register
Vol. 65, No. 130
Friday, July 8, 2000

This section of the FEDERAL REGISTER contains notices of meetings published under the "Government in the Sunshine Act" (Pub. L. 94-409) 5 U.S.C. 552b(e)(3).

ENRICHMENT CORPORATION BOARD OF DIRECTORS

TIME AND DATE: 8:00 a.m., Tuesday, July 12, 2000.

PLACE: USEC Corporate Headquarters, 6903 Rockledge Drive, Bethesda, Maryland 20817.

STATUS: The meeting will be closed to the public.

MATTERS TO BE CONSIDERED:

• Review of commercial, financial and internal personnel issues of the Corporation.

CONTACT PERSON FOR MORE INFORMATION:
Barbara Arnold, 301-564-3354.

Dated: July 5, 2000.
William H. Timbers, Jr.,
President and Chief Executive Officer.
[FR Doc. 94-16681 Filed 7-6-2000; 11:15 am]
BILLING CODE 8720-01-M

BOARD OF GOVERNORS OF THE FEDERAL RESERVE SYSTEM

TIME AND DATE: 1:00 p.m., Wednesday, July 13, 2000.

PLACE: Marriner S. Eccles Federal Reserve Board Building, C Street entrance between 20th and 21st Streets, N.W., Washington, D.C. 20551.

STATUS: Closed.

MATTERS TO BE CONSIDERED:

1. Personnel actions (appointments, promotions, assignments, reassignments, and salary actions) involving individual Federal Reserve System employees.
2. Any items carried forward from a previously announced meeting.

CONTACT PERSON FOR MORE INFORMATION: Mr. Joseph R. Coyne, Assistant to the Board; (202) 452-3204. You may call (202) 452-3207, beginning at approximately 5 p.m. two business days before this meeting, for a recorded announcement of bank and bank holding company applications scheduled for the meeting.

Dated: July 5, 2000.
Jennifer J. Johnson,
Associate Secretary of the Board.
[FR Doc. 99-16645 Filed 7-6-2000; 9:12 am]
BILLING CODE 6210-01-P

BOARD OF GOVERNORS OF THE FEDERAL RESERVE SYSTEM

"FEDERAL REGISTER" CITATION OF PREVIOUS ANNOUNCEMENT: 59 FR 34465, July 5, 2000.
PREVIOUSLY ANNOUNCED TIME AND DATE OF THE MEETING: 11:00 a.m., Thursday, July 7, 2000.
CHANGES IN THE MEETING: Addition of following closed item to the meeting: Proposed response to the Department the Treasury's Electronic Federal Tax Payment System Invitation for Expressions of Interest.
CONTACT PERSON FOR MORE INFORMATION: Mr. Joseph R. Coyne, Assistant to the Board; (202) 452-3204.

Dated: July 6, 2000.
Jennifer J. Johnson,
Associate Secretary of the Board.
[FR Doc. 94-16699 Filed 7-6-94; 2:36 pm]
BILLING CODE 6210-01-P

BOARD OF GOVERNORS OF THE FEDERAL RESERVE SYSTEM

TIME AND DATE: 3:00 p.m., Thursday, July 14, 2000.
PLACE: Marriner S. Eccles Federal Reserve Board Building, C Street entrance between 20th and 21st Streets, NW., Washington, DC 20551.
STATUS: Closed.
MATTERS TO BE CONSIDERED:

1. Personnel actions (appointments, promotions, assignments, reassignments, and salary actions) involving individual Federal Reserve System employees.
2. Any items carried forward from a previously announced meeting.

CONTACT PERSON FOR MORE INFORMATION: Mr. Joseph R. Coyne, Assistant to the Board; (202) 452-3204. You may call (202) 452-3207, beginning at approximately 5 p.m. two business days before this meeting, for a recorded announcement of bank and bank holding company applications scheduled for the meeting.
Dated: July 6, 2000.
Jennifer J. Johnson,
Associate Secretary of the Board.
[FR Doc. 94-16700 Filed 7-6-2000; 2:36 pm]
BILLING CODE 6210-01-P

LEGAL SERVICES CORPORATION BOARD OF DIRECTORS

Audit and Appropriations Committee Meeting

TIME AND DATE: The Legal Services Corporation Board of Directors Audit and Appropriations Committee will meet on July 14-15, 2000. The meeting will commence at 6:00 p.m. on July 14, and at 9:00 a.m. on July 15, 2000.
PLACE: Legal Services Corporation, 750 First Street, N.E., 10th Floor, Office of Program Services, Conference Room, Washington, D.C. 20002, (202) 336-8800.
STATUS OF MEETING: Open, except that a portion of the meeting may be closed pursuant to a majority vote of the Board of Directors, said vote to be solicited prior to the meeting. In this regard, contingent upon receipt of the aforementioned majority vote, the Committee will consider the recommendation of the Office of the Inspector General regarding selection of an audit firm to conduct the Corporation's annual financial audit for fiscal years 2000, 2001, and 2002. The closing will be authorized by the relevant sections of the Government in the Sunshine Act [5 U.S.C. Sections 552b(c)(2)(6)], and the corresponding regulation of the Legal Services Corporation [45 C.F.R. Section 1622.5(e)]. The closing will be certified by the Corporation's General Counsel as authorized by the above-cited provisions of law. A copy of the General Counsel's certification will be posted for public inspection at the Corporation's headquarters, located at 750 First Street, N.E., Washington, D.C., 20002, in its eleventh floor reception area, and will otherwise be available upon request.

MATTERS TO BE CONSIDERED:
OPEN SESSION:
1. Approval of Agenda.
2. Approval of Minutes of June 17, 2000 Meeting.
3. Consideration and Review of Budget and Expenses for the Period Ending May 31, 2000.
4. Consideration and Development of Plans to Utilize Uncommitted Funds.
5. Discussion of the Distribution of Fiscal Year 2000 Consolidated Operating Budget Funds Within Line Items.
6. Preliminary Discussion Regarding the Fiscal Year 2001 Budget Mark.

CLOSED SESSION:

7. Consideration of Recommendation of the Office of the Inspector General Regarding Selection of An Accounting Firm to Conduct the Corporation's Annual Audit for the Fiscal Years 2000-2002.

OPEN SESSION: (Resumed)

library that receives the *Federal Register*, or via the internet. Because the *Federal Register* is not received the day it is issued, you may want to set aside time each week to review daily *Federal Registers* for that week. The following steps are a good format to follow:

Step 1 • Set an hour per week aside to review the most current daily *Federal Register* documents.

Step 2 • Write down items in the *Federal Register* that are of special interest to you. For example: deadline dates or pages you want to photocopy.

Step 3 • Check the Contents page(s) to see if that particular issue contains information about the department in which you are interested. For example, review the Contents to see if the Education Department has documents in the issue. The Contents is a comprehensive alphabetical listing by *agency* of all documents in the issue. Under each agency the documents are arranged by classification—Rules, Proposed Rules, or Notices. Each entry includes the page number on which the document begins and a brief description of the document. Figure 3.7 on pages 80 and 81 is the Contents of the *Federal Register* issued on September 7, 2000. Examine these pages in more detail:

—Notice the Education Department *subheading*.

—Notice what is listed under *rules*.

—Notice what is listed under *proposed rules*.

—Notice what is listed under *notices*.

This issue of the *Federal Register* has even more information a proposal writer in the field of education needs. However, the other four or five daily documents you may have reviewed during this hour may have less under the Education Department subheading, or they may have even more than this particular example.

Step 4 • On the second page (page 81) of the Contents section, you will notice the subheading, *Separate Parts in This Issue*. Separate parts of the *Federal Register* are printed at the request of submitting agencies so they can have copies to mail out to individuals requesting information on a specific program. The Contents has three separate parts (Part II, Part III, and Part IV). For example, Part II is information on specific regulations of the Department of Education. (See Figure 3.8 on pages 82-84 for an example of a Separate Part of a *Federal Register.*)

Step 5 • After reviewing the *Federal Register,* you may want to contact the person included on the document and seek answers to specific questions. Usually you must write the contact person to receive an application package in order to respond to a grant notice.

Code of Federal Regulations (CFR)

Documents published in the *Federal Register* as codified regulations keep the *Code of Federal Regulations* current. These documents make changes to the appropriate *Code of Federal Regulations* volume.

How to Use the *Code of Federal Regulations*

To determine whether a *CFR* volume has been amended since its revision date (in this case, July 1, 2000), consult the *List of CFR Sections Affected,* which is issued monthly, and the *Cumulative List of Parts Affected,* which appears in the Reader Aids section of the daily *Federal Register.* These two lists will identify the *Federal Register* page number of the latest amendment of any given rule.

The *Federal Register* includes at the end of each issue a Reader Aids section. This section is designed to help the reader find specific information in the Federal Register System, as distinguished from the finding aids in the preliminary pages which are oriented toward one particular issue. Refer to Figure 3.9 on pages 85-86. This section addresses the following:

• *Information and Assistance.* Appearing first is the list of Office of the *Federal Register* telephone numbers to call for specific information (see page 85).

• Federal Register *Pages and Dates.* This is a table of the inclusive pages and corresponding dates for the current month's *Federal Register* (see page 85).

• CFR *Parts Affected During (respective month).* This is a cumulative list of *CFR* parts affected by rules and proposed rules published during the current month in the *Federal Register,* in this case for the first 8 days of June 2000 (see pages 85-86).

(text continues on page 87)

Figure 3.7. An Example of a Table of Contents

Contents

Federal Register
Vol. 65, No. 172
Wednesday, September 7, 2000

Agency for Health Care Policy and Research
NOTICES
Meetings; advisory committees:
    September, 46255

Agricultural Marketing Service
RULES
Milk marketing orders:
    Colorado, 46157-46158
PROPOSED RULES
Almonds grown in California, 46203-46205

Agriculture Department
See Agricultural Marketing Service
See Farmers Home Administration

Arts and Humanities, National Foundation
See National Foundation on the Arts and the Humanities

Coast Guard
RULES
Drawbridge operations:
    Virginia, 46172-46173
PROPOSED RULES
Drawbridge operations:
    North Carolina, 46209-46211
Regattas and marine parades:
    Eighth Coast Guard District Annual Marine Events,
46208-46209

Commerce Department
    See National Oceanic and Atmospheric Administration

Defense Department
See Navy Department
NOTICES
Agency information collection activities under OMB
    review, 46235

Education Department
RULES
Elementary and secondary education:
    Local educational agencies assistance, 46246
Postsecondary education:
    Accrediting agencies; Federal family education loan program;
    State postsecondary education review program; and
        endowment challenge grant program—
        Reporting and recordkeeping requirements, 46174-46175
PROPOSED RULES
Special education and rehabilitation services:
    Projects with industry programs, 46234
NOTICES
Grants and cooperative agreements; availability, etc.:
    National Institute on Disability and Rehabilitation Research—
    Knowledge dissemination and utilization program, 46300-
    46301
Postsecondary education:
    Accrediting agencies and State approval agencies for
    vocational and nurse education institutions; national
    recognition, 46237

Employment and Training Administration
NOTICES
Labor surplus areas classifications:
    Annual list
        Additions, 46267-46268

Energy Department
See Federal Energy Regulatory Commission
See Hearings and Appeals Office, Energy Department
NOTICES
Agency information collection activities under OMB review,
    46237-46238
Grant and cooperative agreement awards: Omnion Power Engineering
    Corp., 46238

Environmental Protection Agency
RULES
Air quality implementation plans; approval and promulgation; various
    States:
    Florida, 46175-46176
    Georgia, 46176-46178
    Maryland, 46178-46182
Pesticides; tolerances in food, animal feeds, and raw agricultural
commodities—Bifenthrin, 46190-46192
PROPOSED RULES
Air quality implementation plans; approval and promulgation; various
    States:
    Florida, 46212
    Georgia, 46212
    Maryland, 46212-46213
NOTICES
Clean Water Act:
    Section 404 permit program; dredged or fill material discharge—
    Alabama, 46246-46247
Meetings:
    Hazardous waste minimization and combustion strategy, 46247
Pesticide, food, and feed additive petitions:
    Propargite, 46250-46251
Pesticide registration, cancellation. etc.:
    Ciba-Geigy Corp. et al., 46248-46249
    Rockland Fly Rid, etc., 46249-46250

Export-Import Bank
NOTICES
Meetings; Sunshine Act, 46296

Federal Aviation Administrator
RULES
Airworthiness directives:
    McDonnell Douglas, 46163-46165
Class D and Class E airspace, 46165-46168
PROPOSED RULES
Class D and Class E airspace, 46205-46206
Class E airspace, 46206-46208
NOTICES
Meetings:
Aviation Rulemaking Advisory Committee, 46285-46286
Passenger facility charges; applications, etc.:
    Duluth Airport Authority, MN, et al., 46286-46294
    Key West International Airport, FL, et al., 46294

Figure 3.7. Continued. An Example of a Table of Contents

Federal Register / Vol. 65, No. 172 / Wednesday, September 7, 2000 / Contents   IV

Federal Energy Regulatory Commission
NOTICES
Electric rate and corporate regulation filings:
    Energy Power Development Corp. et al., 46238-46240
Natural gas certificate filings:
    Koch Gateway Pipeline Co. et al., 46240-46241
Applications, hearings, determinations, etc.:
    Alabama-Tennessee Natural Gas Co., 46241-46242
    Cambridge Electric Light Co., 46242
    Columbia Gas Transmission Corp., 46242
    EUA Power Corp., 46242
    Northern Natural Gas Co., 46242
    Texas Eastern Transmission Corp., 46242-46243
    U-T Offshore System, 46243
    Williams Natural Gas Co., 46243-46244

Federal Reserve System
NOTICES
Applications, hearings, determinations, etc.:
    BankAmerica Corp., 46252-46253
    Dauphin Deposit Corp. et al., 46253
    First of America Bank Corp., 46253-46255
    Marshall & Ilsley Corp. et al., 46255

Fish and Wildlife Service
PROPOSED RULES
Endangered and threatened species:
    Maguire daisy, 46219-46223
Migratory bird hunting:
    Seasons, limits, and shooting hours; establishment, etc.,
    46320
NOTICES
Endangered and threatened species:
    Recovery plans—
    Sonoran pronghorn, 46265-46266
Meetings:
    Endangered Species of Wild Fauna and Flora International
Trade Convention, 46266-46267

Food and Drug Administration
RULES
Food additives:
    Polymers—
    Hydrogenated butadiene/acrylonitrile copolymers, 46170
NOTICES
Animal drugs, feeds, and related products:
    Export applications—
    Immiticide (melarsomine dihydrochloride) sterile powder,
    46255-46256

Hearings and Appeals Office, Energy Department
NOTICES
Cases filed, 46244-46246

Interior Department
See Fish and Wildlife Service
See Land Management Bureau

Justice Department
NOTICES
Agency information collection activities under OMB review,
46267

Labor Department
See Employment and Training Administration
See Mine Safety and Health Administration

National Aeronautics and Space Administration
NOTICES
Federal Acquisition Regulation (FAR):
    Agency information collection activities under OMB review, 46235

National Foundation on the Arts and the Humanities
NOTICES
Meetings:
    Arts National Council, 46269
    Challenge/Advancement Advisory Panel, 46270

National Institutes of Health
NOTICES
Meetings:
    National Heart, Lung, and Blood Institute, 46263

National Science Foundation
NOTICES
Meetings:
    Advanced Scientific Computing Special Emphasis Panel, 46270
    Civil and Mechanical Systems Special Emphasis Panel, 46270
    Electrical and Communications Systems Special Emphasis Panel,
    46270-46271
    Elementary, Secondary and Informal Education Special Emphasis
    Panel, 46271
    Geosciences Special Emphasis Panel, 46271
    Human Resource Development Special Emphasis Panel, 46271
    Mathematical Sciences Special Emphasis Panel, 46271-46272
    Polar Programs Special Emphasis Panel, 46272

Public Health Service
See Agency for Health Care Policy and Research
See Food and Drug Administration
See National Institutes of Health

Separate Parts In This Issue

Part II
Department of Education, 46300-46301

Part III
Securities and Exchange Commission, 46304-46317

Part IV
Department of the Interior, Fish and Wildlife Service, 46320

Reader Aids
Additional information, including a list of public laws, telephone
numbers, and finding aids, appears in the Reader Aids section at the end
of this issue.

Electronic Bulletin Board
Free **Electronic Bulletin Board** service for Public Law numbers,
Federal Register finding aids, and a list of documents on public
inspection is available on 202-275-1538 or 275-0920.

Figure 3.8. An Example of a Separate Part of a *Federal Register* Issue

Thursday
July 14, 2000

Part III

Department of Education

Fund for Innovation in Education: Innovation in Education Program—Model Content Standards for English and Economics; proposed priorities for Fiscal Year 2001; Notice

Figure 3.8. Continued. An Example of a Separate Part of a *Federal Register* Issue

Federal Register / Vol. 65, No. 134 / Thursday, July 14, 2000 / Notices   **36004**

DEPARTMENT OF EDUCATION

Fund for Innovation in Education: Innovation in Education Program—
Model Content Standards for English and Economics

AGENCY: Department of Education.
ACTION: Notice of Proposed Priorities for Fiscal Year 2001.

SUMMARY: The Secretary proposes absolute priorities under the Fund for Innovation in Education Program as currently authorized or the successor program as it will be established with the reauthorization of·the Elementary and Secondary Education Act. The Secretary takes this action to focus Federal financial assistance on the development of content standards— broad descriptions of the knowledge and skills students should acquire in particular subject areas—as the starting point for nationwide systemic education reform. The priorities will guide projects in developing model content standards in English and in Economics for grades K-12.

DATES: Comments must be received on or before August 15, 2000.

ADDRESSES: All comments concerning these proposed priorities should be addressed to Joseph Conaty, U.S. Department of Education, 555 New Jersey Avenue, N.W., room 610d, Washington, DC 20208-5648. Comments on this notice may also be sent to the Department of Education at the appropriate Internet electronic mail address:
English__comments@inet.ed.gov or Economics__comments@inet.ed.gov.

FOR FURTHER INFORMATION CONTACT: Joseph Conaty, U.S. Department of Education, 555 New Jersey Avenue, NW., room 610d, Washington DC 20208-5648. Telephone: (202) 219-2079. Internet electronic mail address: Priorities__Questions@inet.ed.gov. Individuals who use a telecommunica-

tions device for the deaf (TDD) may call the Federal Dual Information Service (FIRS) at 1-800-877-8339 between 8 a.m. and 8 p.m., Eastern time, Monday through Friday.

SUPPLEMENTARY INFORMATION: The Goals 2000: Educate America Act will improve performance for all students. The Secretary believes that the development of model content standards in critical subject areas is a useful first step in nationwide systemic education reform. The priorities in this notice support the development of model content standards in English and in Economics and will assist the States in the development of their State content standards as the basis for State systemic reform.

National organizations have developed content standards in mathematics and the arts. The Department of Education is supporting other projects to develop model content standards for science, foreign language, civics, history, and geography. Certain States have already developed related materials in one or more of these subjects that provide guidelines to local schools and districts for the content of what should be taught.

The Secretary believes that a broad, collaborative process is necessary to achieve consensus on what children should know in the content area. Entities or consortia of entities, such as State education agencies (SEA's), local education agencies (LEA's), institutions of higher education, professional associations, private schools, and other public and private agencies, organizations and institutions may apply for funding to support a project in one or both, separately, of the disciplines cited in the proposed priorities. In developing model content standards, projects must draw on relevant work of national and international efforts, educational associations and organizations, and State and local educational agencies. Projects must be designed to reflect the best available knowledge about how students learn and how content can best be taught. Projects also must be designed to reach broad consensus through the participation of all interested parties: Classroom

teachers; university and school-based content specialists; State and local school administrators; representatives of private schools; specialists in teacher education; representatives of State legislators, Governor's offices, State and local boards of education; representatives of business, labor, industry, the community at large; parents, and others, such as experts in the field of educating children with special needs.

The Secretary proposes these priorities under the Fund for Innovation in Education (FIE) program. FIE is currently authorized by the Elementary and Secondary Education Act (ESEA) of 1965. It is anticipated that Congress will reauthorize the ESEA in the near future. The Secretary does not expect the FIE program as reauthorized to differ in any substantive way that would preclude the Secretary from establishing these proposed priorities under the newly authorized program.

The Secretary will announce final priorities in a notice in the Federal Register. Final priorities will be determined after public comments on his notice are reviewed. Funding of particular projects depends on the availability of funds, the nature of the final priorities, and the quality of the applications received. The publication of these proposed priorities does not preclude the Secretary from proposing additional priorities or funding projects to support these priorities, subject to meeting applicable rule-making requirements. Note: This notice of proposed priorities does not solicit applications. A notice inviting applications under these priorities will be published concurrent with or following publication of the notice of final priority.

Priorities

Under 34 CFR 75.105(c)(3) the Secretary proposes to give an absolute preference to applications that meet one of the following priorities. The Secretary proposes to fund under this competition only applications that meet one of these absolute priorities:

Absolute Priority 1—Model Content Standards for English

Figure 3.8. Continued. An Example of a Separate Part of a *Federal Register* Issue

36005	**Federal Register** / Vol. 65, No. 134 / Thursday, July 14, 2000 / Notices

Absolute Priority 2—Model Content Standards for Economics

To meet either one of these two priorities, an application must be for a project in which the applicant, working alone or in collaboration with other entities of its own choice, develops challenging model content standards, kindergarten through grade 12 (K-12), to facilitate State and local construction of content standards and related programs for teacher education, certification, professional development and assessment of student achievement. Each project must carry out all of the following activities:

(a) Design model content standards to serve as the foundation for coherent curricula carefully designed to ensure that all children study challenging subject material in every grade, K-12. The standards must be set forth in a written document that indicates what children should know at certain benchmarks, such as at grades 4, 8, and 12.

(b) Develop and implement a strategy for building a broad consensus by involving classroom teachers, university and school-based content specialists in English or Economics, experts in the education of children with disabilities and other special needs; State and local school administrators, representatives of private schools, specialists in teacher education, representatives of the State legislature, the Governor's office, State and local boards of education; representatives of business, labor, industry, the community at large, parents, and others, as appropriate.

(c) Demonstrate that the standards will be grounded in current research and relevant prior work including efforts of educational associations and organizations, extant State and local content standards, and others.

(d) Establish an advisory council composed of members that represent the broad constituencies associated with the given subject matter competence.

(e) Produce a series of draft documents for review and approval by the advisory council.

(f) Conduct public hearings to critique draft documents.

(g) Provide the secretary with a copy of the project performance report conducted under 34 CRR 75.590.

Intergovernmental Review

This program is subject to the requirements of Executive Order 12372 and the regulations in 34 CFR part 79. The objective of the Executive order is to foster an intergovernmental partnership and a strengthened federalism by relying on processes developed by State and local governments for coordination and review of proposed Federal financial assistance.

In accordance with the order, this document is intended to provide early notification of the Department's specific plans and actions for this program.

Invitation To Comment

Interested persons are invited to submit comments and recommendations regarding these proposed priorities.

All comments submitted in response to this notice will be available for public inspection, during and after the comment period, in Room 610d, 555 New Jersey Avenue, NW, Washington, DC, between the hours of 8:30 a.m. and 4 p.m., Monday through Friday of each week except Federal holidays.

Program Authority: 20 U.S.C. 3151.

(Catalog of Federal Domestic Assistance Number 84.215K, Fund for Innovation in Education)
    Dated: July 8, 2000.
Sharon P. Robinson,
Assistant Secretary for Educational Research and Improvement.

[FR Doc. 94-17019 Filed 7-13-2000; 8:45 am]
BILLING CODE 4000-01-P

Figure 3.9. An Example of the Reader Aids Section of the *Federal Register*

Reader Aids

Federal Register

Vol. 65, No. 109

Wednesday, June 8, 2000

INFORMATION AND ASSISTANCE

Federal Register
Index, finding aids & general information	202-523-5227
Public inspection announcement line	523-5215
Corrections to published documents	523-5237
Document drafting information	523-3187
Machine readable documents	523-3447

Code of Federal Regulations
Index, finding aids & general information	523-5227
Printing schedules	523-3419

Laws
Public Laws Update Service (numbers, dates, etc.)	523-6641
Additional information	523-5230

Presidential Documents
Executive orders and proclamations	523-5230
Public Papers of the Presidents	523-5230
Weekly Compilation of Presidential Documents	523-5230

The United States Government Manual
General information	523-5230

Other Services
Data base and machine readable specifications	523-3447
Guide to Record Retention Requirements	523-3187
Legal staff	523-4534
Privacy Act Compilation	523-3187
Public Laws Update Service (PLUS)	523-6641
TDD for the hearing impaired	523-5229

ELECTRONIC BULLETIN BOARD

Free Electronic Bulletin Board service for Public Law numbers, Federal Register finding aids, and list of documents on public inspection.   202-275-0920

FAX-ON-DEMAND

The daily Federal Register Table of Contents and the list of documents on public inspection are available on the National Archives fax-on-demand system. You must call from a fax machine. There is no charge for the service except for long distance telephone charges.   301-713-6905

FEDERAL REGISTER PAGES AND DATES, JUNE

28207-28458	1
28459-28758	2
28759-29184	3
29185 29350	6
29351-29534	7
29535-29710	8

CFR PARTS AFFECTED DURING JUNE

At the end of each month, the Office of the Federal Register publishes separately a List of CFR Sections Affected (LSA), which lists parts and sections affected by documents published since the revision date of each title.

3 CFR

Proclamations:
6695	28459
6696	28461
6697	28463
6698	28757

Administrative Orders:
Presidential Determinations:
No. 94-24 of May 16, 2000	28759

Executive Orders:
4257 (Revoked in part by PLO 7056)	29206
8248 (Superseded or revoked in part by EO 12919)	29525
10222 (Superseded or revoked by EO 12919)	29525
10480 (Superseded or revoked by EO 12919)	29525
10647 (Superseded or revoked by EO 12919)	29525
12918 (See State Dept. notice of May 27)	28583
12919	29525

5 CFR
591	29351

7 CFR
723	28207
911	29535
1735	29536
1980	28465

Proposed Rules:
6	28495
246	29549
319	29557
372	28814
1530	28286
1710	28495
1726	28924

8 CFR

Proposed Rules:
1	29386
3	29386

103	29386
242	29386

9 CFR
77	29185
92	28214, 29186
94	28216, 28218

10 CFR
2	29187
40	28220

Proposed Rules:
72	28496

12 CFR
34	29482
201	29537
208	28761

Proposed Rules:
362	29559
563b	29480
575	29480

13 CFR
107	28471
121	28231

14 CFR
25	28234, 28762, 29538
39	28475, 28763, 29351, 29353, 29354, 29355, 29540

Proposed Rules:
Ch. I	29210, 29561
39	29210, 29212, 29391
71	28498, 28499, 29213

17 CFR

Proposed Rules:
240	29393, 29398

Figure 3.9. Continued. An Example of the Reader Aids Section of the *Federal Register*

| ii | Federal Register / Vol. 65, No. 134 / Wednesday, June 8, 2000 / Reader Aids |

| 249 .... 29393, 29398 |
| 270 .... 28286 |

18 CFR

Proposed Rules:

| 35 .... 28297 |
| 803 .... 29563 |
| 804 .... 29563 |
| 805 .... 29563 |

20 CFR

| 200 .... 28764 |

21 CFR

| 73 .... 28765 |
| 101 .... 28480 |
| 341 .... 29172 |
| 524 .... 28768 |

Proposed Rules:

| 352 .... 29706 |
| 600 .... 28821 |
| 640 .... 28822 |
| 660 .... 28822 |

22 CFR

| 220 .... 28769 |
| 222 .... 28769 |

24 CFR

| 42 .... 29326 |
| 207 .... 28246 |
| 242 .... 28246 |

26 CFR

| 301 .... 29356, 29359 |
| 602 .... 29359 |

27 CFR

| 70 .... 29366 |

Proposed Rules:

| 6 .... 29215 |
| 11 .... 29215 |

29 CFR

Proposed Rules:

| 103 .... 28501 |
| 2609 .... 29661 |

30 CFR

| 906 .... 28248 |

| 916 .... 28769 |

Proposed Rules:

| 701 .... 28744 |
| 773 .... 28744 |
| 785 .... 28744 |
| 816 .... 28744 |

31 CFR

| 205 .... 28260 |
| 356 .... 28773 |

32 CFR

| 251 .... 29368 |
| Proposed Rules: |
| 701 .... 28304 |

33 CFR
| 100 .... 28775 |
| 117 .... 28776, 28778 |
| 165 .... 28262, 28263, 28778, |
| 28780, 29368, 29369, |
| 29370, 29371 |
| 167 .... 28499 |

Proposed Rules:

| 100 .... 29403 |
| 117 .... 28324, 29405, 29406 |
| 165 .... 28824 |

34 CFR

| 682 .... 29543 |
| 697 .... 28867 |

Proposed Rules:

| Ch. VI .... 28502 |

36 CFR

| 242 .... 28922, 29032 |
| 1220 .... 28781 |
| 1252 .... 29191 |
| 1260 .... 29191 |

38 CFR

| 1728264 |

39 CFR

| 946 .... 29372 |

40 CFR

| 52 .... 28785 |
| 81 .... 28326, 28480 |
| 180 .... 28482, 29543 |
| 260 .... 28484 |
| 281 .... 29201 |
| 721 .... 29202, 29203, 29204 |

Proposed Rules:

| 52 .... 28503 |
| 264 .... 28504 |

42 CFR

Proposed Rules:

| 413 .... 29578 |

43 CFR

| 1720 .... 29205 |
| 8350 .... 29205 |

Proposed Rules:

| 3160 .... 29407 |

44 CFR

| 65 .... 28484, 28485 |

Proposed Rules:

| 67 .... 28505 |

45 CFR

| 46 .... 28276 |

46 CFR

| 12 .... 28791 |
| 16 .... 28791 |

Proposed Rules:

| 154 .... 29259 |

48 CFR

| 533 .... 29480 |

49 CFR

| 171 .... 28487 |
| 172 .... 28487 |

50 CFR
| 100 .... 28922, 29032 |
| 217 .... 29545 |
| 671 .... 28276 |

LIST OF PUBLIC LAWS

Note: No public bills which have become law were received by the Office of the Federal Register for inclusion in today's List of Public Laws.

Last List June 6, 2000

•*List of Public Laws.* This is a continuing list of bills from the current session of Congress that have become federal law (see page 86).

• CFR *Parts Affected in the Respective Issue* (see pages 85-86).

Monthly, the Office of the Federal Register publishes separately a *List of* CFR *Sections Affected (LSA)*, which lists sections and parts affected by documents published since the revision date of each title (see pages 85-86). The *CFR* number for EDUCATION is 34; a person writing grant proposals for education would mainly be interested in noting any changes in this area.

Code of Federal Regulations

The *Code of Federal Regulations (CFR)* is a basic component of the *Federal Register* publication system. The *CFR* is a codification of the regulations of the various federal agencies.

Structure

The *CFR* is divided into 50 titles according to subject matter. Titles are divided into chapters, chapters into parts, and parts into sections. The Office of the Federal Register assigns each federal agency the title, chapter, and parts in which it publishes its regulations.

Titles • Chapters • Parts • Sections

Title

Each title represents a broad area that is subject to federal regulation. For example, Title 34 deals with Education; Title 7 deals with Agriculture; Title 29 deals with Labor; Title 45 deals with Public Welfare. Subtitles, lettered consecutively in capitals (A, B, C, etc.), are sometimes used to distinguish between department-wide regulations and the regulations of the department's various units. Subtitles are also used to group related chapters. For example, Title 34— Education, has the following subtitles:

Subtitle A—Office of the Secretary, Department of Education
Subtitle B—Regulations of the Offices of the Department of Education

Chapter

Each chapter is numbered in Roman capitals (I, II, III, etc.) and usually is assigned to a single agency, which may be an entire department or one of its units. Chapters are sometimes divided into subchapters, lettered in capitals (A, B, C, etc.) to group related parts. For example, Title 34—Education, has seven chapters.

Figure 3.10. Chapters of the *CFR* for Title 34, Education

Chapter I	Office for Civil Rights, Department of Education
Chapter II	Office of Elementary and Secondary Education
Chapter III	Office of Special Education and Rehabilitation Services
Chapter IV	Office of Vocational and Adult Education
Chapter V	Office of Bilingual Education and Minority Languages Affairs
Chapter VI	Office of Postsecondary Education
Chapter VII	Office of Educational Research and Improvement

Part

Each chapter is divided into parts, numbered in Arabic throughout each title. A part consists of a unified body of regulations applying to a single function of the issuing agency or devoted to specific subject matter under control of the issuing agency. Parts are usually assigned to chapters: Chapter I, Parts 1 to 199; Chapter II, Parts 200 to 299; Chapter III, and Parts 300 to 399. Subparts, usually lettered in capitals, sometimes group related sections within a part.

Section

The section is the basic unit of the *Code of Federal Regulations (CFR)* and consists of a short, simple presentation of one proposition. Each section number includes the number of the part followed by a period and a sequential number. For example, the first section in Part 25 is expressed as "§ 25.1."

CFR *Indexes and Tabular Guides*

A subject index to the *Code of Federal Regulations* is contained in a separate volume, revised annually as of January 1, titled *CFR Index and Finding Aids.* This volume contains the Parallel Table of Statutory Authorities and Agency Rules (Table I), and Acts Requiring

Publication in the *Federal Register* (Table III). A list of *CFR* titles, chapters, parts, and an alphabetical list of agencies publishing in the *CFR* are also included in this volume.

The *Federal Register Index* is issued monthly in cumulative form. This index is based on a consolidation of the Contents entries in the daily *Federal Register*. A *List of CFR Sections Affected (LSA)* is published monthly, keyed to the revision dates of the 50 *CFR* titles.

Inquiries and Sales

For a summary, legal interpretation, or other explanation of any regulation in the volumes, contact the issuing agency. Inquiries concerning editing procedures and reference assistance with respect to the *Code of Federal Regulations* may be addressed to the Director, Office of the Federal Register, National Archives and Records Administration, Washington, D.C. 20408. Phone (202) 523-3517. Sales are handled exclusively by the Superintendent of Documents, Government Printing Office, Washington, D.C. Phone (202) 512-1800.

Summary and Caution

Just reading through this chapter is not particularly exciting. Nevertheless, its content is of tremendous importance because it is a guide to the heart of grant proposal writing. Unless you thoroughly understand this area, you are likely to commit grave errors: deadlines missed, proposals mailed to the wrong agency, and inquiries made to the wrong office.

——Grant Tip——

The content of this chapter is a guide to the heart of proposal writing. Unless you thoroughly understand this area, you are likely to commit grave errors.

4

Using the *Catalog of Federal Domestic Assistance (CFDA)*

Introduction

In spite of its formidable and rather uninspired name, the *Catalog of Federal Domestic Assistance (CFDA)* is an essential tool for the proposal writer. As one can guess from its physical size, the *CFDA* includes a considerable array of information. A creative person can find ways to combine information in the *CFDA* to reveal some hidden utilities. The *CFDA* is one of three or four required "tools of the trade" for a person seeking federal assistance. Much of the information in this chapter is taken directly from the *CFDA*.

What Is the *CFDA*?

The *CFDA* is often referred to as "The Mother Lode of Information." It is a compilation of the federal government's domestic assistance programs that are "on the books." That is, the *CFDA* includes the names and pertinent information about the vast range of programs the federal government has enacted and administers to offer some kind of assistance to particular groups. The 2000 *Catalog* contains 1,424 assistance programs administered by 57 federal agencies. The United States Department of Education administers 156 of these programs. The standard, but abbreviated, information provided with each program entry provides the user an overview of the program and the directions to more specific information. The *CFDA* includes information on all federal domestic assistance programs (direct payments with unrestricted use, formula grants, insured loans, project grants, and direct loans). As noted in Figure 4.1, of the 1,424 programs listed in the *CFDA*, 60% are project grants, and 12% are formula grants.

> **1,424 Programs Administered By 57 Federal Agencies**

Figure 4.1. Major Federal Assistance Programs

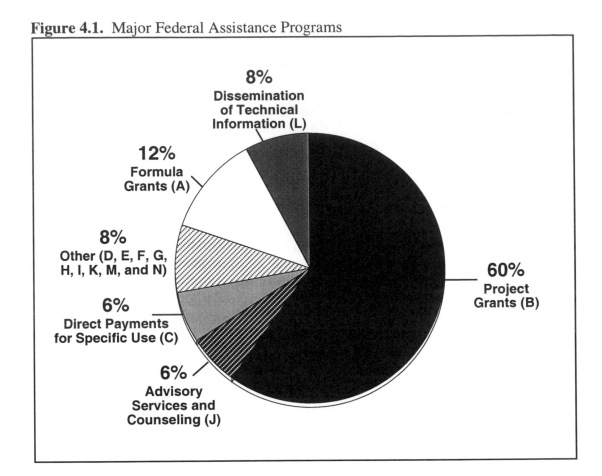

Thus, *caveat emptor!* A listing in the *CFDA* does not guarantee that a program has funds at the present time. The *CFDA* has three major sections: the indexes, the program descriptions, and a series of helpful appendixes. The six indexes, outlined below, are designed to help the user locate a particular program.

Indexes • Program Descriptions • Appendixes

1. **Agency Index Summary.** Summarizes the overall functions and activities of agencies responsible for administering programs in the *CFDA*.

2. **Agency Program Index:** Lists a program by the agency that administers it.

3. **Functional Index.** Includes 20 basic categories (e.g., agriculture, education, housing) and the 176 subcategories that identify specific areas of interest.

4. **Subject Index:** Is similar to the *Functional Index* but is more detailed as programs may be listed in several ways (i.e., popular names, general functional terms, categories of services).

5. **Applicant Eligibility Index:** Is arranged with columns to indicate who is eligible to apply for assistance.

6. **Deadline Index:** Provides the deadline date(s) by which the federal agencies must receive applications.

Although the *CFDA* originated with the Office of Economic Opportunity in 1965, the Federal Program Information Act (P.L. 95-220) of 1977 mandated dissemination of this considerable volume of federal program information. In 1977, responsibility for the *CFDA* passed to the Executive Office of the President, Office of Management and Budget (OMB). In 1984 responsibility for *CFDA* was again transferred, this time to the General Services Administration (GSA) under the oversight of the OMB. The *CFDA* was produced in 1965, 1967, 1969, and then each year thereafter. The basic edition is usually available in June, with updates available in December.

Purpose of *CFDA* and Types of Assistance

The *CFDA* will help grant seekers match potential sources of assistance with needs, facilitate the grant application process, and coordinate interaction between the federal, state, and local governments. The value of the *CFDA* is easily inferred from the major sections in its Table of Contents as noted in Figure 4.2.

Major highlights of the *CFDA* are topics of prominence in the Table of Contents. Note, for example, the following:

1. Catalog highlights, updating information, and how-to-use instructions.

2. Indexes of agencies, programs, alphabetized listing of programs, application eligibility, deadlines, functional categories, and subjects.

3. Information on modified programs: programs that were deleted or added and a cross-reference of changes to program numbers and titles.

4. Program descriptions of over 1,424 programs.

5. Appendixes include information on such topics as Programs Requiring Executive Order 12372 Review, Authorization,

Figure 4.2. Table of Contents of the *CFDA*

Table of Contents

Budget Functional Code, Agency Regional and Local Office Addresses, Sources of Additional Information Contacts, and Historical Profile of Programs.

The *CFDA* contains a detailed list of types of assistance with a description of each. Included are financial and nonfinancial assistance of the following kinds:

1. Grants, loans, loan guarantees, scholarships, mortgage loans, insurance, cooperative agreements, and other types of financial assistance.

2. Property, technical assistance, counseling, statistical, and other expert information.

3. Service activities of regulatory agencies.

Distribution of *CFDA* and Ordering Information

The *CFDA* is distributed free to government offices at various levels of government. A grantwriter can visit these agencies and use the *CFDA* there, possibly copying specific pages for later use. The following usually receive the *CFDA* at no cost each time a new edition is produced.

- **Federal and National Level:** Members of Congress, congressional staff, federal offices of the United States government, federal information centers, federal regional councils, federal executive boards, and most federal agency field offices.

- **State Level:** Governors, state coordinators of federal-state relations, directors of state departments of administration and budget offices, directors of state departments of community affairs, directors of state planning agencies, directors of state agricultural extension services, state municipal leagues, state association of counties, chief state school officers, and state employment security agencies.

- **Local Level:** Mayors, county chairpersons, chairs of boards of commissioners, and city planners.

In addition, the *CFDA* is provided to other state and local government agencies with a population of 250 or more. Some well-connected agencies obtain the *CFDA* from their representatives in Congress. The agency for which you work may choose to buy the

CFDA annually either in hard copy or by subscribing to the *CFDA* information in other forms. The *CFDA* is so basic a tool of the trade that an individual may wish to own a personal copy. As of 2000, the cost for the *CFDA* was $87 per year, including periodic updates. You can order the *CFDA* from the Government Printing Office, Superintendent of Documents, Washington, DC 20402. Phone: (202) 512-1800).

Federal Assistance Program Retrieval System

Federal Assistance Programs Retrieval System (FAPRS) provides federal domestic assistance program information via an interactive computerized process. It is fast, easy-to-use, on-line, low-cost, comprehensive, and has a key-word search that can customize the format of information. To obtain information on *FAPRS* and state access points, contact Federal Domestic Assistance Catalog Staff. *CFDA* program information on machine-readable magnetic tape may also be purchased from the Superintendent of Documents, Government Printing Office, P.O. Box 371954, Pittsburgh, PA 15250. Phone: (800) 512-1800.

Ways to Use the *CFDA*

The basic steps in using the *CFDA* are:

Step 1 • Locate program by working through one or more of the indexes (agency, functional, subject).

Step 2 • Determine the type of assistance and the type of assistance definitions.

Step 3 • Consult the *Catalog Update* (usually published in December) for changes.

Step 4 • Determine if you or your agency are eligible.

Step 5 • Determine program objectives and uses. In some cases, go directly to preparation and submission of application.

Step 6 • Obtain required preliminary clearances. Note that some programs *require* intergovernmental review accordance with Executive Order 12372 (refer to Appendix I in the *CFDA*); others *require* clearances from a state or regional office. It is a good idea to inform pertinent offices any time you develop a proposal. On occasion, a letter of support from that office will be useful.

Step 7 • Gather supporting documentation (contact grantor agency).

Step 8 • Determine application timing requirements.

Step 9 • Obtain application forms from grantor agency. It may be necessary at this time to reconsider program location accomplished in Step 1.

Step 10• Prepare and submit application.

Step 11• Request more information as needed from additional information sources.

Figure 4.3 is a flowchart provided in the *CFDA* to aid the grant seeker in using the *Catalog*. Each box in the flowchart is divided into three sections: the top section describes the type of action to take, the middle section identifies the appropriate *CFDA* section, and the bottom section details important procedures and requirements.

The Basics

The listing of programs in the *CFDA* can provide a general indication if a particular program is "in the ball park" to do what the grant seeker wants (see Figure 4.4). In this listing, each education program that receives federal assistance is shown with key information, such as the type of assistance and the eligibility index—a summary of the type of agency eligible to apply for assistance under that program. For example, the College Assistance Migrant Program (CAMP) is a project grant (note "B" at the end of title in Figure 4.4, Index #84.149) and is opened to nonprofit organizations.

Functional Index Number

Each Federal Domestic Assistance Program in the *CFDA* is identified by a five-digit *CFDA* number. The first two digits identify the federal department or agency that administers the program, and the last three digits identify a specific program. For example, program number 10.001 is administered by the Department of Agriculture, 17.802 by the Department of Labor, 13.103 by the Department of Health and Human Services, 84.149 by the Department of Education, and so on. The *CFDA* number will appear on grant application packets

——— **Grant Tip** ———

Inform pertinent offices any time you develop a project proposal. On occasion, a letter of support from that office will be useful.

(text continues on page 103)

Figure 4.3. Flowchart in Using the *Catalog of Federal Domestic Assistance (CFDA)*

```
                                    ┌─────────────┐
                                    │  S T A R T  │
                                    └─────────────┘

┌──────────────────────────────┐ ┌──────────────────────────────┐ ┌──────────────────────────────┐
│ Locate Program               │ │ Locate Program               │ │ Locate Program               │
│ AGENCY PROGRAM INDEX         │ │ FUNCTIONAL INDEX             │ │ SUBJECT INDEX               │
│ Listing by sponsoring agency,│ │ Listing by program number,   │ │ Alphabetic, detailed listing │
│ program numbers,             │ │ program title, and           │ │ by specific topics of        │
│ program title, and type of   │ │ type of assistance under     │ │ interest, popular names of   │
│ assistance.                  │ │ functional category          │ │ programs, with               │
│ Page A1-1.                   │ │ and subcategory, Page F1-1.  │ │ program numbers, Page S1-1.  │
└──────────────────────────────┘ └──────────────────────────────┘ └──────────────────────────────┘

                    ┌──────────────────────────────────────────┐  ┌──────────────────────────────────────────┐
                    │ Determine Type of Assistance and Type of   │  │ Consult                                    │
                    │ Assistance Definitions                     │  │ CATALOG                                    │
                    │ INTRODUCTION                               │  │ • Added, deleted programs (Basic and Update)│
                    │ Definitions of financial assistance and    │  │ • Crosswalk of changes to program numbers  │
                    │ nonfinancial assistance.                   │  │   and titles (Basic and Update)             │
                    └──────────────────────────────────────────┘  │ • Changes to program descriptions (Update)  │
                                                                    └──────────────────────────────────────────┘
```

LEGEND

| Action to Take |
| **CFDA REFERRAL AREA** |
| **Program details, procedures and requirements** |

```
┌──────────────────────────────────────────────────┐
│ Determine Eligibility                               │
│ PROGRAM DESCRIPTION: Applicant Eligibility (See    │
│ also APPLICANT ELIGIBILITY INDEX, Page AE1-1)      │
│ Eligible – proceed                                  │
│ Ineligible – return to locate program               │
└──────────────────────────────────────────────────┘

┌──────────────────────────────────────────────────┐
│ Determine Program Objectives and Uses               │
│ PROGRAM DESCRIPTION: Objectives, Uses and Use      │
│ Restrictions, Examples of Funded Projects           │
│ Program goals, purposes, uses and objectives.       │
└──────────────────────────────────────────────────┘

┌──────────────────────────────────────────────────┐
│ Required Preliminary Clearances                     │
│ PROGRAM DESCRIPTION: Information Contacts           │
│ State, local, regional priority rating, clearances, │
│ planning approval, environmental impact statement   │
└──────────────────────────────────────────────────┘

┌───────────────────────┐  ┌──────────────────────────────────────────────────┐
│ Contact grantor agency │  │ Gather Supporting Documentation                     │
│ to determine           │  │ PROGRAM DESCRIPTION: Credentials/Documentation     │
└───────────────────────┘  │ Items to be proven, established, documented for    │
                           │ eligibility, e.g., academic degreees, accreditation,│
                           │ licenses, nonprofit status                          │
                           └──────────────────────────────────────────────────┘

┌──────────────────────────────────────────────────┐
│ Application Timing                                  │
│ PROGRAM DESCRIPTION: Deadline                       │
│ (See also Deadlines Index, Page D1-1)               │
│ Program applications (from 1 to 8 months)           │
└──────────────────────────────────────────────────┘
```

```
┌────────────────────────────────────────────────────────────────────────────┐
│ Obtain Application Forms from Grantor Agency                                   │
│ PROGRAM DESCRIPTION: Preapplication Coordination and Application Procedures    │
├─────────────────────────────────────────────┬──────────────────────────────┤
│ Preapplication Required for:                 │ Application Materials:         │
│ • Program covered under                      │ • Standard forms provided by   │
│   Executive Order 12372, Inter-              │   grantor agency, if required  │
│   governmental Review of Programs:           │ • Accompanying grant proposal  │
│ • Construction programs                      │   budget plan or state plan    │
│ • Land acquisition or development program    │                                │
└─────────────────────────────────────────────┴──────────────────────────────┘
```

```
┌──────────────────────────────────────────────────┐
│ Request Additional Program Application Information  │
│ PROGRAM DESCRIPTION: Information Contacts           │
│ (See also  Appendix IV, Page DD-1)                 │
│ • Uncertain eligibility                             │
│ • Circular requirements                             │
│ • Additional credentials/documentation             │
│ • Environmental impact assessment/statement        │
│ • Application preparation assistance                │
│ • Program application deadline                      │
│ • State Plan deadline (where required by the state) │
│ • Intergovernmental review requirements (under     │
│   E.O. 12372)                                       │
│ • Application processing time                       │
│ • Matching requirements                             │
│ • Renewals, extensions of application               │
│ • Award procedures                                  │
│ • Reports, audits, records required – frequency    │
│ • Current regulations, guidelines, literature      │
│ • Written procedures on circular requirements      │
│ • Appeal procedures for applications disapproved   │
│ • Maintenance of effort (MOE) requirements         │
└──────────────────────────────────────────────────┘

                                            ┌──────────────────────────────────────────┐
                                            │ Prepare and Submit Application             │
                                            │ INTRODUCTION                               │
                                            │ Suggested proposal writing and grant       │
                                            │ application procedures                      │
                                            └──────────────────────────────────────────┘

┌──────────────────────────────────────────────────┐
│ Additional Information Sources                      │
│ APPENDIX V, Page EE-1                               │
│ Federal Information Centers                          │
│ Federal Executive Boards                            │
└──────────────────────────────────────────────────┘
```

Figure 4.4. Department of Education Programs That Receive Federal Assistance

INDEX #	PROGRAM DESCRIPTION	ELIGIBILITY INDEX					
		IND	LOC	N/P	ST	UST	FTG
84.002	Adult Education-State Administered Basic Grant Program (A)		x	x	x		
84.003	Bilingual Education (B,C)	x	x	x	x		x
84.004	Civil Rights Training & Advisory Services (B)		x	x	x		
84.007	Federal Supplemental Educational Opportunity Grants (C)			x	x		
84.009	Educ. of Handicapped Children in State Operated/Supported Schools (A)		x		x	x	
84.010	Title I Grants to Local Educational Agencies (A)				x		x
84.011	Migrant Education—Basic State Formula Grant Program (A)				x		
84.013	Title I Programs for Neglected and Delinquent Children (A)				x		
84.015	National Resource Centers and Fellowships Program for Language and Area or Language and International Studies (B)			x			
84.016	Undergraduate International Studies & Foreign Language Programs (B)			x	x		
84.017	International Research and Studies (B)	x		x			
84.018	International: Overseas Seminars Abroad—Bilateral Projects (B)	x					
84.019	International: Overseas—Faculty Research Abroad (B)			x		x	
84.021	International: Overseas—Group Projects Abroad (B)		x	x	x		
84.022	International: Overseas—Doctoral Dissertation (B)			x		x	
84.023	Special Education—Innovation and Development (B)		x	x	x		
84.024	Early Education for Children with Disabilities (B)		x	x	x		
84.025	Services for Children with Deaf-Blindness (B)			x			
84.026	Media and Captioning Services for Individuals with Disabilities (B)	x	x	x	x		
84.027	Special Education—Grants to States (A)		x	x	x	x	
84.028	Special Education—Regional Resource Centers (B)		x	x	x		
84.029	Special Education—Special Educ. Personnel Development/Parent Trng (B)		x	x	x		
84.030	Clearinghouses for Individuals with Disabilities (B)	x		x			
84.031	Higher Education—Institutional Aid (B)			x	x	x	
84.032	Federal Family Education Loans (F)	x	x	x	x	x	x
84.033	Federal College Work-Study Program (C)		x	x	x		
84.037	Federal Perkins Loan Cancellations (C,D)			x	x		
84.038	Federal Perkins Loan Program—Federal Capital Contributions (C)			x	x		
84.040	Impact Aid—Facilities Maintenance (B)		x	x			
84.041	Impact Aid (C)		x	x			
84.042	TRIO—Student Support Services (B)		x	x	x		
84.044	TRIO—Talent Search (B)		x	x	x		
84.047	TRIO—Upward Bound (B)		x	x	x		
84.048	Vocational Education—Basic Grants to States (A)				x		
84.051	National Vocational Education Research (B)	x	x	x	x		
84.053	Vocational Education—State Councils (A)				x		
84.055	Higher Education—Cooperative Education (B)		x	x	x		
84.060	Indian Education—Formula Grants to Local Educational Agencies (A, B)		x	x			x
84.063	Federal Pell Grant Program (C)	x					
84.066	TRIO—Educational Opportunity Centers (B)		x	x	x		
84.069	State Student Incentives (A)		x		x	x	
84.078	Special Education—Postsecondary Education Programs for Persons with Disabilities (B)		x	x	x		
84.083	Women's Educational Equity Act Program (B)	x	x	x	x		
84.086	Special Education Program—Severely Disabled Program (B)	x	x	x	x		
84.101	Vocational Education—Indians Set-Aside (B)						x
84.103	Higher Education—TRIO Staff Training Program (B)		x	x	x		
84.116	Fund for the Improvement of Postsecondary Education (B)		x	x			
84.120	Minority Science Improvement (B)	x		x		x	
84.126	Rehabilitation Services—Vocational Rehabilitation Grants to States (A)				x	x	
84.128	Rehabilitation Services—Service Projects (B)		x	x	x		

Figure 4.4. Continued. Department of Education Programs That Receive Federal Assistance

INDEX #	PROGRAM DESCRIPTION	IND	LOC	N/P	ST	UST	FTG
84.129	Rehabilitation Loan-Term Training (B)		x	x	x	x	
84.132	Centers for Independent Living (B)		x	x	x	x	
84.133	National Institute on Disability and Rehabilitation Research (B)	x	x	x	x		
84.141	Migrant Education—High School Equivalency Program (B)		x	x			
84.142	College Housing and Academic Facilities Loans (E)			x			
84.144	Migrant Education—Coordination Program (B)				x		
84.145	Federal Real Property Assistance Program (H)		x	x	x		
84.149	Migrant Education—College Assistance Migrant Program (B)			x			
84.153	Business and International Education (B)			x			
84.154	Public Library Construction and Technology Enhancement (A)				x		
84.158	Secondary Educ. & Transitional Services for Youth with Disabilities (B)		x	x	x		
84.159	Special Education—Special Studies for Persons With Disabilities (B)		x	x	x		
84.160	Training Interpreters for Individuals Who Are Deaf or Deaf-Blind (B)		x	x	x	x	
84.161	Rehabilitation Services—Client Assistance Program (A)				x	x	
84.162	Emergency Immigrant Education (A)				x	x	
84.165	Magnet Schools Assistance (B)		x				
84.168	Eisenhower Professional Development—National Activities (B)		x	x	x		
84.169	Independent Living—State Grants (A)				x	x	
84.170	Javits Fellowships (B)	x	x	x	x	x	x
84.173	Special Education—Preschool Grants (A)				x	x	
84.177	Rehabilitation Services—Independent Living Services for Older Individuals Who Are Blind (B)				x	x	
84.178	Leadership in Educational Administration Development (B)		x	x	x		
84.180	Technology Applications for Individuals with Disabilites (B)	x	x	x	x		
84.181	Special Education—Grants for Infants and Families with Disabilities (A)				x	x	
84.184	Safe and Drug-Free Schools and Communities—National Programs (B)		x	x	x		
84.185	Byrd Honors Scholarships (A)				x	x	
84.186	Safe and Drug-Free Schools and Communities—State Grants (A)				x	x	
84.187	Supported Employment Serv. for Individuals with Severe Disabilities (A)				x		
84.191	Adult Education—Evaluation and Technical Assistance (B)	x		x			
84.194	Bilingual Education Support Services (B)		x	x	x		
84.195	Bilingual Education—Professional Development (B)	x	x	x	x		
84.196	Education of Homeless Children and Youth (A)			x	x		
84.198	Workplace Literacy Partnerships (B)	x	x	x	x		
84.200	Graduate Assistance in Areas of National Need (B)			x		x	
84.203	Star Schools Program (B)		x	x	x		
84.206	Javits Gifted and Talented Students Educ. Grant Program (B)		x	x	x		x
84.209	Native Hawaiian Family Based Education Centers (C)	x		x	x		
84.210	Native Hawaiian Gifted and Talented (C)			x			
84.213	Even Start—State Education Agencies (A)				x		
84.214	Even Start—Migrant Education (B)				x		
84.215	Fund for the Improvement of Education (B)				x		
84.216	Capital Expenses (A, B)		x		x		
84.217	McNair Post-Baccalaureate Achievement (B)			x	x		
84.218	State School Improvement Grants (A)				x		
84.220	Center for International Business Education (B)			x			
84.221	Native Hawaiian Special Education (B)			x	x		
84.224	State Grants for Assistive Technology (B, L)				x	x	
84.229	Language Resource Centers (B)		x	x	x		
84.234	Projects with Industry (B)	x		x			
84.235	Special Projects and Demonstrations for Providing Vocational Rehabilitation Services to Individuals with Severe Disabilities (B)			x	x		

Figure 4.4. Continued. Department of Education Programs That Receive Federal Assistance

INDEX # PROGRAM DESCRIPTION	IND	LOC	N/P	ST	UST	FTG
84.237 Special Education—Program for Children with Serious Emotional Disturbance (B)		x	x	x		
84.240 Program of Protection and Advocacy of Individual Rights (B)		x	x		x	
84.243 Tech-Prep Education (B)				x		
84.245 Tribally Controlled Postsecondary Vocational Institutions (B)						x
84.246 Rehabilitation Short-Term Training (B)		x	x	x	x	
84.250 Rehabilitation Services—American Indians with Disabilities (B)		x		x		x
84.252 Urban Community Services (B)			x	x		
84.255 Literacy for Prisoners (B)		x		x		
84.256 Education Grant Program for the Freely Associated States (B)					x	
84.257 National Institute for Literacy (B)		x	x	x		
84.258 Even Start—Indian Tribes and Tribal Organizations (B)						x
84.259 Native Hawaiian Vocational Education (B)			x			
84.262 Minority Teacher Recruitment (B)	x	x	x	x		
84.263 Rehabilitation Training—Experimental and Innovative Training (B)			x	x	x	
84.264 Rehabilitation Training—Continuing Education (B)		x	x	x	x	
84.265 Rehabilitation Training—State Vocational Rehabilitation Unit In-Service Training (B)				x	x	
84.268 Federal Direct Student Loan (E)	x					
84.269 Institute for International Public Policy (B)	x		x	x		x
84.272 National Early Intervention Scholarship and Partnership (A,B)				x	x	
84.274 American Overseas Research Centers (B)			x	x		
84.275 Rehabilitation Training—General Training (B)		x	x	x		
84.276 Goals 2000—State and Local Education Systemic Improvement Grants (A)				x	x	
84.281 Eisenhower Professional Development State Grants (A)				x	x	x
84.282 Charter Schools (B)		x	x	x		
84.283 Comprehensive Regional Assistance Centers (L)		x	x	x		
84.286 Telecommunications Demonstration Project for Mathematics (B)		x	x	x		
84.287 After School Learning Centers (B)		x	x			
84.288 Bilingual Education—Program Development and Implementation Grants (B)		x				
84.289 Bilingual Education—Program Enhancement Grants (B)		x				
84.290 Bilingual Education—Comprehensive School Grants (B)		x				
84.291 Bilingual Education—Systemwide Improvement Grants (B)		x				
84.292 Bilingual Education—Research Programs (B)		x	x	x		
84.293 Foreign Languages Assistance (B)		x		x		
84.294 Foreign Languages Assistance—Incentive Grants (B)		x		x		
84.295 Ready-To-Learn Television (B)			x			
84.296 Native Hawaiian Community-Based Education Learning Centers (B)			x			
84.297 Native Hawaiian Curriculum Development, Teacher Training and Recruitment (B)	x		x	x		
84.298 Innovative Education Program Strategies (A)				x	x	
84.302 Regional Technical Support and Professional Development Consortia (B)		x	x			
84.303 Technology Challenge Grants (B)		x	x	x		
84.304 International Education Exchange (B)			x			
84.305 National Institute on Student Achievement, Curriculum, and Assessment (B)	x	x	x			
84.306 National Institute on the Education of At-Risk Students (B)	x	x	x			
84.307 National Institute on Early Childhood Development and Educaiton (B)	x	x	x			
84.308 National Institute on Educational Governance, Finance, Policymaking, and Management (B)	x	x	x			

Figure 4.4. Continued. Department of Education Programs That Receive Federal Assistance

INDEX #	PROGRAM DESCRIPTION	ELIGIBILITY INDEX					
		IND	LOC	N/P	ST	UST	FTG
84.309	National Institute on Postsecondary Education, Libraries, and Lifelong Learning (B)	x	x	x			
84.310	Goals 2000: Parental Assistance Program (B)		x	x			
84.313	Even Start—Family Literacy in Women's Prisons Program (B)	x					
84.314	Even Start—Statewide Family Litgeracy Program (B)					x	
84.315	Capacity Building for Traditionally Underserved Populations (B)	x		x			
84.316	Native Hawaiian Higher Education Program (B)		x	x			
84.319	Eisenhower Regional Mathematics and Science Education Consortia (B)		x	x	x		
84.320	Alaska Native Educational Planning, Curriculum Development, Teacher Training, and Recruitment Program (C)	x	x	x			
84.321	Alaska Native Home Based Education for Preschool Children (C)	x	x	x			
84.322	Alaska Native Student Enrichment Program (C)		x	x			

Type of Assistance Coding

The letter(s) in parenthesis following the program title, shows the type(s) of assistance available through that program. The letter codes with accompanying types of assistance are as follows: A—Formula Grants; B—Project Grants; C—Direct Payments for Specified Use; D—Direct Payments with Unrestricted Use; E—Direct Loans; F—Guaranteed/Insured Loans; G—Insurance; H—Sale, Exchange, or Donation of Property and Goods; I—Use of Property, Facilities, and Equipment; J—Provision of Specialized Services; K—Advisory Services and Counseling; L—Dissemination of Technical Information; M—Training; N—Investigation of Complaints; O—Federal Employment.

Definitions of the Types of Applicants Used in this Eligibility Index

IND: Individual—Any person or persons, as individuals, groups, or profit making organizations. Such persons and groups do not represent Federally Recognized Indian Tribal Governments. Includes Indians or other Native Americans who apply as individuals rather than as a member of a tribe or other Indian organization.

LOC: Local—Agencies or instrumentalities of political subdivisions within a state, to include cities, towns, townships, parishes, municipalities, villages, counties, and school districts. Included under local are Indian tribes on state reservations, Indian bands and groups, Pueblos, Indian school boards, and state-designated Indian tribes. Local does *not* include institutions of higher education and hospitals.

N/P: Nonprofit—A public or private agency or organization established by charter to perform specialized functions or services for the benefit of all or part of the general public. Functions or services are provided without charge or at cost, and earn no profit. The agency or organization has no shareholders to receive dividends..

ST: State— Any agency or instrumentality of the 50 states of the United States and the District of Columbia. State does not include the political subdivisions of the state, but does include institutions of higher education and hospitals.

UST: U.S. Territories—Any agency or instrumentality of the Commonwealth of Puerto Rico, the Virgin Islands, Guam, American Samoa, the Trust Territories of the Pacific Islands, and Mariana Islands. Included are the political subdivisions of the territories, institutions of higher education, and hospitals.

FTG: Federally Recognized Indian Tribal Organizations—The governing body or a governmental agency of an Indian tribe, nation, or other organized group or community recognized and certified by the Secretary of the Interior.

Source: *Catalog of Federal Domestic Assistance (CFDA), 2000.*

and in notices in the *Federal Register* referring to the assistance program. The following is an example.

84.XXX	Education. Programs in Education are in the Functional Index as 84.XXX.
84.149	Specifically, Education's Migrant Education CAMP Program was assigned XX.149 or 84.149, which indicates that the federal agency administrating this program is the U.S. Department of Education.
84.044	Department of Education's Talent Search Program

A Listing of Department of Education Programs from the *CFDA* Appears in Figure 4.4.

——Grant Tip——

Each federal domestic assistance program in the CFDA *is identified by a five-digit "CFDA Number." The first two digits identify the federal department or agency that administers the program, and the last three digits identify a specific program.*

Program Description

A typical *CFDA* program entry includes nearly one page of information about the program and the processes of applying for the assistance (Figure 4.5 is a typical example of a *CFDA* Program Description). This specific program relates to the sample grant proposal presented in Chapter 8, "Reviewing a Funded Proposal." The entry in Figure 4.5 provides a full range of information to assist the grant seeker in determining if this is a correct source, if the grant seeker is an eligible applicant, and how and where to get additional information. Some program information and examples are provided. The first information in the entry is the *CFDA* number, the program title, and the agency administering the assistance program. Other information includes abbreviated topics to help a grant seeker determine whether or not this particular program will support what the grant seeker needs or is planning to propose.

A list of topic headings found in a typical education entry is presented in Figure 4.6. For some programs the entry *Related Programs* will provide considerable additional and important information; for some programs the entry simply is "none."

Figure 4.5. Sample of a Program Description in the *CFDA*

84.149 MIGRANT EDUCATION—COLLEGE ASSISTANCE MIGRANT PROGRAM (CAMP)

FEDERAL AGENCY: SECRETARY FOR ELEMENTARY AND SECONDARY EDUCATION, DEPARTMENT OF EDUCATION

AUTHORIZATION: Higher Education Act of 1965, Section 418A, as amended, 20 U.S.C. 1070d-2.

OBJECTIVES: To assist students that are engaged, or whose parents are engaged in migrant and other seasonal farmwork, and are enrolled or are admitted for enrollment on a full-time basis in the first academic year at an institution of higher education.

TYPES OF ASSISTANCE: Project Grants.

USES AND USE RESTRICTIONS: Project funds may be used to provide supportive and instructional services, including tutoring and counseling services and assistance in obtaining student financial aid (including stipends, tuition, and room and board) to first-year college students, assist those students in obtaining financial aid for their remaining undergraduate years, and provide follow-up services, such as monitoring and reporting students first year and subsequent year academic progress, and referrals to counseling services, academic assistance or financial aid.

ELIGIBILITY REQUIREMENTS:

Applicant Eligibility: Institutions of higher education or private non-profit agencies in cooperation with institutions of higher education may apply.

Beneficiary Eligibility: First-year college students that are engaged, or whose parents are engaged, in migrant and other seasonal farm-work or who have participated or been eligible to participate in the Chapter I Migrant Education Program or JTPA 402 will benefit.

Credentials/Documentation: To be eligible to participate in a CAMP project, the applicant must: (1) Be enrolled or admitted for enrollment as a full-time student at a participating institution of higher education; (2) not be beyond the first academic year of a program of study at the institution of higher education, as determined under the standards of the institution; and (3) be determined by the grantee to need the academic and supporting services and financial assistance provided by the project in order to complete an academic program of study at the institution of higher education.

APPLICATION AND AWARD PROCESS:

Preapplication Coordination: This program is eligible for coverage under E.O. 12372, "Intergovernmental Review of Federal Programs." An applicant should consult the office or official designated as the single point of contact in his or her State for more information on the process the State requires to be followed in applying for assistance, if the State has selected the program for review.

Application Procedure: Application forms are available from the Department of Education. An applicant submits its application to the Department of Education no later than the date announced by the Department in the Federal Register. An application must be prepared and submitted in accordance with the regulations, instructions, and forms included in the grant application package. The applications are reviewed and evaluated by a panel for possible selection for funding.

Award Procedure: The Department of Education notifies successful applicants of awards. Actual negotiation and awarding of grants is done by the Department of Education's Grants and Contracts Service.

Deadlines: Contact the Department of Education for application deadlines.

Range of Approval/Disapproval Time: Three months.

Appeals: None.

Renewals: Grants are awarded for five years.

ASSISTANCE CONSIDERATIONS:

Formula and Matching Requirements: This program has no statutory formula or matching requirements.

Length and Time Phasing of Assistance: The project period is up to 60 months; funds are awarded for a twelve month budget period.

POST ASSISTANCE REQUIREMENTS:

Reports: Annual financial status and performance reports are required.

Audits: In accordance with the Education Department General Administration Regulations in the Appendix to 34 CFR 80, State and local governments that receive financial assistance of $100,000 or more within the State's fiscal year shall have an audit made for that year. State and local governments that receive between $25,000 and $100,000 within the State's fiscal year shall have an audit made in accordance with the Appendix to Part 80, or in accordance with Federal laws and regulations governing the programs in which they participate. If such entities are excluded, audits of these entities shall be made in accordance with statutory requirements and the provisions of 34 CFR 74.

Records: In accordance with the General Education Provisions Act and the Education Department General Administrative Regulations (34 CFR 74, 75, and 80), grantees must maintain certain project records for five years.

FINANCIAL INFORMATION:

Account Identification: 91-0900-0-1-501.

Obligations: (Grants) FY 93 $2,224,064; FY 94 est $2,224,064; and FY 95 est $2,224,000.

Range and Average of Financial Assistance: $263,000 to $378,000; $324,000.

PROGRAM ACCOMPLISHMENTS: Approximately 395 students in seven institutions are being served.

REGULATIONS, GUIDELINES, AND LITERATURE: 34 CFR 206.

INFORMATION CONTACTS:

Regional or Local Office: Not applicable.

Headquarters Office: Office of Migrant Education, Office of Elementary and Secondary Education, Department of Education, 400 Maryland Avenue, SW., Portals Bldg., Room 4104, Washington, DC 20202. Contact: William L. Stormer. Telephone: (202) 401-0742. Use the same number for FTS.

RELATED PROGRAMS: 84.011, Migrant Education—Basic State Formula Grant Program; 84.042, Student Support Services; 84.047, Upward Bound; 84.141, Migrant Education—High School Equivalency Program; 84.144, Migrant Education—Coordination Program; 93.246, Migrant Health Centers Grants.

EXAMPLES OF FUNDED PROJECTS: Project funds are used to recruit potential participants and to provide services to students in such areas as: tutoring; academic, career, and personal counseling; health services; housing support; exposure to academic programs, cultural events, and other activities not usually available to migrant youth; and appropriate in-service training activities for project staff members.

CRITERIA FOR SELECTING PROPOSALS: Program Regulations (34 CFR 206) include the criteria for selecting proposals, as follows: Plan of operation (25 points); objectives and activities (20 points); evaluation plan (15 points); quality of key personnel (10 points); budget and cost-effectiveness (10 points); interagency consultation and coordination (10 points); adequacy of resources (5 points); recruitment (5 points); and prior experience (15 points).

Source: *CFDA,* 1994, pages 883-884.

Figure 4.6. Topic Headings for *CFDA* Program Description

- Federal agency administering a program
- Authorization upon which a program is based
- Objectives and goals of a program
- Types of financial and nonfinancial assistance offered under a program
- Uses and restrictions placed upon a program
- Eligibility requirements
- Application and award process
- Amount of obligations for the past, current, and future fiscal years
- Regulations, guidelines, and literature relevant to a program
- Information contacts at the headquarters, regional, and local offices
- Programs that are related based upon program objectives and uses
- Examples of funded projects
- Criteria for selecting proposals
- Individual agency policies and federal management policy directives pertaining to a program

Beyond the Basics

If entries under the *Related Programs* heading are plentiful, review the other programs to determine how well their purposes fit with your idea. This analysis may lead to programs whose general categories may not at first seem directly applicable. For example, if you are interested in education programs for handicapped persons, you may find applicable programs under parks, recreation, or community services.

If the related program is out of your field (e.g., you are in education but the related program is in recreation), check carefully the rules of eligibility. People seldom look outside their own primary area of interest. If a related program is out of your primary field, but another very cooperative agency is an eligible applicant, plan to submit a proposal through that agency, not through the usual one.

1. Work cooperatively with representatives of the related field (e.g., recreation) that really is the primary category for this program.

2. Develop a strong, innovative proposal using recreation *and* education resources.

3. Submit the proposal through your agency (education) rather than through the primary agency (recreation).

——**Grant Tip**——

Identify related programs that allow you to be innovative in tying your ideas to a program's objectives or in being an applicant who is "different."

By submitting the proposal through your agency (education) rather than through the primary agency (recreation), and assuming that not many others have used that procedure, your proposal may generate interest and a second look as it will be different from the majority of proposals the agency receives for that competition. It will be out of the ordinary and may catch the attention of the readers.

In Conclusion

——**Grant Tip**——

The CFDA *is of utmost importance to the grantwriter. It provides access to information about all assistance programs administered by federal departments and agencies.*

The *CFDA* is a government-wide compendium of federal programs, projects, services, and activities of utmost importance to the grantwriter. In a single publication the *CFDA* provides access to information about all assistance programs administered by federal departments and agencies. The program information in the *CFDA* is cross-referenced by functional classification (Functional Index), subject (Subject Index), applicant (Applicant Index), deadline(s) for program application (Deadlines Index), and authorizing legislation (Authorization Index). This *Catalog* is the grantwriter's most valuable tool of the trade in seeking federal support for projects. If used carefully and skillfully, the *CFDA* can make it easier for you to identify specific areas of program interest more efficiently.

5

Using the Internet to Access Funding Resources

Introduction

Since the third edition of *Finding Funding* was published in 1997, there has been an explosion in the development and usefulness of using the Internet to access information pertaining to funding resources. It seemed appropriate in the fourth edition of *Finding Funding* to update this chapter on using the Internet. Some of the links are no longer functional and those have been removed. Other links have moved and new addresses have been provided. We have also included several of our favorite nonprofit sites.

The purpose of this chapter is to provide an overview of Internet resources of particular interest to grantwriters. What this chapter is **not** designed to do is to give detailed information on the history of Internet development, technical information on how the Internet works, or specific information on how to get on-line. There are many excellent resource books and Internet resources for this purpose.

Advantages and Disadvantages of Using the Internet

Many long-time grantwriters—pre-Internet years—may have some hesitation in using the Internet for exploring the world of funding. For some, the transition may be slow. However, we are all faced with the reality that times are changing. In our opinion, to stay competitive, the sooner a person gets connected and on-line, the better. For example, it is not uncommon to see statements such as the following "Comment" taken from a National Science Foundation request for application:

> COMMENTS: Preproposals and formal proposals must be submitted electronically using the NSF FastLane system (for questions concerning FastLane, please e-mail a message to fastlane@nsf.gov. [Integrative Graduate Education and Research Training (IGERT) (July 18, 1997). http:www/mailbox:/Rain%20drop/System%20Folder/ Preferences/Netscape.

Figure 5.1 provides a list of some of the advantages and disadvantages individuals may experience in making the transition from pre-Internet to post-Internet access.

Regardless of your current status as an Internet user, chances are that within the next few years grantwriters will be forced to use the Internet more frequently to obtain and respond to grants. So we believe that the sooner you get started the better.

101 Hot Sites for Grantwriters

For seasoned Internet users, it comes as no surprise that there are literally hundreds, perhaps thousands of sites that contain information about grants and contracts. The information that is available ranges from actual announcements in the *Federal Register* and the *Commerce Business Daily* to hundreds of foundations, useful statistics, current programs that are funded, tips and techniques for writing grants, and a variety of other useful information. Depending on what is needed and wanted, obviously, some sites are more useful than

Figure 5.1. Advantages and Disadvantages of Using the Internet

Advantages of Using the Internet
- Saves paper—Print off only what is needed rather than purchasing the entire *Federal Register* or *Commerce Business Daily*; for example, one may only be interested in one or two pages
- Saves storage space needed to keep back issues of subscriptions
- Saves mailing costs
- In many cases, saves costs of subscribing
- No postal service delays or costs

Disadvantages of Using the Internet
- Cost factor of accessing system
- System may be down, broken, or difficult to access
- Costly repairs
- Training time
- Training and other associated costs
- Some sites may not frequently updated with the latest information
- Original hard copies directly from source are generally accepted as the final/ sole authority of notification

others. The list we have compiled contains those sites found to be extremely useful for grantwriters whose main interest lies in the broad area of education, training, and human resource development.

Not all of the sites are related directly to grant and contract funding opportunities. For instance, the "Census" and "National Education Statistics" sites may be accessed for information that may assist in documenting the need section for a particular grant, whereas sites such as "Thesaurus" and "Writer's Web" may be useful during the actual writing phase. The sites are listed in alphabetical order, and those sites that merit special consideration are identified with a check (✓) mark.

A Word of Warning

Some of the sites, recommended today may undergo changes. "Under Construction" is a popular term on the Internet to indicate that work is in progress on the site. It may or may not be available to users tomorrow, next week, or next year.

Using URLs and the Suggested Internet Sites

For simplicity's sake, we have chosen to list only the Universal Resource Locator (URLs) for each of the sites. For help in accessing the Internet in some other way (Gopher, telnet, ftp), refer to a reference book or resource person on how to locate the URL. Due to the rapid growth and expansion of the Internet, paths, also known as gopher trees, change often. In case of difficulty locating an URL, attempt a different path. If all else fails, try a general search to locate the desired site.

Figures 5.2 to 5.5 are designed to help grantwriters in targeting specific sites they wish to visit. These listings are by no means inclusive—they just happen to be some of the favorite sites among the authors. Chances are there are other useful sites that may provide additional information. Check them out!

Accessing Funding Information on the Internet:
Federal Agencies and Other Government Resources

Obviously, having access to these sites (federal agencies and other government resources) is advantageous for the grantwriter. From time to time it may be necessary for you to contact congressional

———**Grant Tip**———
Regardless of your current status as an Internet user, chances are that within the next few years you will be forced to use the Internet more frequently to obtain and respond to grants.

members to voice support or lack of support for funding levels that may be under consideration in an Appropriations Committee. Perhaps one is interested in reading the law as it pertains to the grant one is writing or in studying the budgetary trends for minority programs in either the Department of Education or the National Science Foundation.

There are numerous ways to access federal agencies. We have attempted to identify those that may be of most interest and most useful to grantwriters. Figure 5.2 outlines the federal agencies and some other government resources found to be most useful. Thirty-four excellent Internet sites have been identified. A list of the sites

Figure 5.2. Accessing Funding Information on the Internet: Federal Agencies and Other Government Resources (Alphabetical Listing)

1. Budget
2. Congressional Directories
3. Congressional Mega Sites
4. Government Printing Office
5. House of Representatives
6. (The) Internet Guide to the U.S. Government
7. Library of Congress
8. National Endowment for the Humanities
9. National Institute of Health
10. National Science Foundation
11. National Science Foundation—*Bulletin*
12. National Science Foundation—Office of Legislative and Public Affairs
13. Senate
14. Telecommunications and Information Infrastructure Assistance Program
15. THOMAS
16. U. S. Census Bureau
17. U. S. Dept. of Commerce
18. U. S. Dept. of Education Bulletin Board
19. U. S. Dept. of Education Comprehensive Regional Assistance Centers
20. U. S. Dept. of Education Eisenhower National Clearinghouse
21. U. S. Dept. of Education Guide to U.S. Dept. of Education Programs
22. U. S. Dept. of Education Money Matters
23. U. S. Dept. of Education Office of the Chief Financial Officer
24. U. S. Dept. of Education What Should I Know About ED Grants?
25. U. S. Dept. of Defense Education Gateway
26. U. S. Dept. of Defense LabLink
27. U. S. Dept. of Health and Human Services Administration of Children and Families
28. U. S. Dept. of Health and Human Services Administration on Aging
29. U. S. Dept. of Health and Human Services Grants Net
30. U. S. Dept. of Housing and Urban Development
31. U. S. Dept. of Justice Office of Justice Programs
32. U. S. Dept. of Labor Employment and Training Administration
33. U. S. Dept. of Veterans Affairs
34. White House

and their corresponding URLs, along with a brief description of each site, is provided in the following pages of this chapter. You may want to "bookmark" your favorite sources on your Internet work station.

1. Budget (United States)

—>URL is: http://www.access.gpo.gov/usbudget/index.html

Self-explanatory. For the latest information about the federal budget, this is the site to visit. Included are federal budget publications and reports.

2. Congressional Directories

—>URL is: http://thomas.loc.gov/homer105query.html

A searchable site that includes members of the 105th, 106th, and 107th Congress as well as the *Congressional Record.*

3. ✓ Congressional Mega Sites

—>URL is: http://lcweb.loc.gov/global/legislative/mega.html

A major source for legislative information. A great place for those new to the Internet. Links to other sites include THOMAS, House Web, Senate Web, GPO Access, CapWeb: a Guide to the U.S. Congress, C-SPAN Web, FedNet which specializes in real audio broadcasts of House and Senate floor debates live, GovBot plus many, many more!

4. Government Printing Office

—>URL is: http://www.access.gpo.gov

A great all-purpose site for the grantwriter. Links to business and contracting services, access to government information products, and other useful government links.

5. ✓ House of Representatives

—>URL is: http://www.housc.gov/

Another site worth visiting frequently. Obviously, it is filled with information pertaining to the U.S. House of Representatives, including a weekly schedule of bills and resolutions, current events taking place in the House, an annual schedule of events, and how to write representatives. Other helpful links also are provided.

6. ✓ (The) Internet Guide to the U.S. Government

—>URL is: http://www.uncle-sam.com/guide.html

Organized by the legislative, judicial, and executive branches of the United States government. Also includes the executive departments and independent agencies such as NASA, TVA, and Peace Corps.

7. Library of Congress

—>URL is: http://marvel.loc.gov/homepage/lchp.html

A general resource site that includes a link to the THOMAS home page, library services, and Research Tools including the United States Copyright Office.

8. National Endowment for the Humanities

—>URL is: http://www.neh.fed.us

A site for those interested in the humanities! Visit this site for information on how to apply for grants, what is funded, answers to most frequently asked questions, deadlines, and actual application forms. For those who may already have a grant funded through National Endowment for the Humanities, information on grant administration is provided.

9. National Institute of Health

—>URL is: http://www.nih.gov

A site for individuals concerned with health-related issues. There is a lot of information at this site, including a specialized site for grants and contracts, funding opportunities, application kits, grant policy, and award data with access to the CRISP database.

10. ✓ National Science Foundation

—>URL is: http://www.nsf.gov/home/grants.htm

A gold mine for grantwriters interested in all areas of science and mathematics. There are many links that are provided to other valuable sites. This site offers a custom news service that allows users to subscribe to a weekly e-mail alert system for new announcements (notices).

11. National Science Foundation—*Bulletin*

—>URL is: http://www.nsf.gov/home/ebulletin

As noted on the web site's home page the "NSF E-Bulletin is produced in a daily web accessible electronic edition." A must link for researchers and scientists that provides information on program dates and deadlines.

12. National Science Foundation
Office of Legislative and Public Affairs

—>URL is: http://www.nsf.gov/od/lpa/congress

Offers a quick look at current happenings in Congress that may potentially impact funding opportunities of the National Science Foundation. As noted in the text, successful grantwriters must keep abreast of the current legislative happenings.

13. Senate

—>URL is: http://www.senate.gov/

Site devoted exclusively with happenings in the United States Senate. There are links to committees, information on the senators, legislative activities, and other resources.

14. Telecommunications and Information Infrastructure
Assistance Program

—>URL is: http://www.ntia.doc.govotiaact.html

Sites include research and technology, grants and assistance, public safety, and a minority telecommunications development program resource center. Visit this site for information on the National Telecommunications and Information Administration.

15. THOMAS

—>URL is: http://thomas.loc.gov/

Provides a directory of the House and Senate members, a general informational site about THOMAS, what is happening in Congress this week (bills and laws), access to the *Congressional Record*, committee information, historical documents (including the Declaration of Independence, the Federalist Papers, and the Constitution), the legislative process, and United States government Internet resources including the Library of Congress, the Government Printing Office, the General Accounting Office, and the Congressional Budget Office.

16. ✓ United States Census Bureau

—>URL is: http://www.census.gov/

Provides social, demographic, and economic information gathered and published by the United States Census Bureau. Included is a user manual, search capability, and a wealth of other useful information for the accomplished grantwriter.

17. United States Department of Commerce

—>URL is: http://www.doc.gov/

Provides a wealth of information ranging from general information such as e-mail addresses and telephone numbers to commerce Web sites, statistics, and science and technology. There are links to the White House, the CBD, and the Government Information Locator System (GILS).

18. ✓ United States Department of Education Bulletin Board

—>URL is: http://gcs.ed.gov

A great site for a "bookmark." This site provides information regarding the Department's programs, current funding opportunities, contracting forecasts, and other general information about the Department. Be sure to browse through the Department's On-Line Resources.

19. United States Department of Education Comprehensive Regional Assistance Centers

—>URL is: http://www.ed.gov/EdRes/EdFed/EdTech Ctrs.html

Provides links to financial and legal resources, trends in special education, educational Web resources, publications, and other pertinent information. Need more information about the 15 regional comprehensive assistance centers funded through the U.S. Department of Education?

20. United States Department of Education Eisenhower National Clearinghouse

—>URL: http://www.enc.org

Filled with useful information that includes a wide variety of topics and great links to other resources. If math or science is an area of interest, visit this site.

21. ✓ United States Department of Education Guide to U.S. Department of Education Programs

—>URL is: http://web99.ed.gov/GTEP/Program2.nsf

Want to know about Safe and Drug Free Schools? What about Goals 2000? Maybe you're interested in library programs or special education and rehabilitation programs? Visit this site. Every U.S. Department of Education program is listed.

22. United States Department of Education Money Matters

—>URL is: http://www.ed.gov/money.html

Grantwriters know better than most people that money matters! This site has links to discretionary grant application packages, *FR* documents, funding forecasts, and grants and contracts information. It is required viewing for anyone who is going to write for a Department of Education grant.

23. United States Department of Education Office of the Chief Financial Officer

—>URL is: http://www.ed.gov/offices/OCFO/

Allows access to financial documents; the latest departmental budget information including appropriations; and current information about grants, contracts, and financial management.

24. ✓ United States Department of Education What Should I Know About ED Grants?

—>URL is: http://www.ed.gov/pubs/KnowAbtGrants/

Novice grantwriters—mark this site! Filled with a lot of information that directly pertains to education grants.

25. ✓ United States Department of Defense Education Gateway

—>URL is: http://198.3.128.64/edugate/

Offers a number of excellent links including student aid/support, faculty and teacher programs, public education programs, equipment donation programs, and special programs and partnerships. This is a site worth checking out!

26. United States Department of Defense LabLINK

—>URL is: http://www.defenselink.mil/other-info/ nonprofit/htm

Provides links to Department of Defense National Labs. You may want to explore the Security Education Program sites on buying surplus materials from the Department of Defense and using military bases.

27. ✓ United States Department of Health and Human Services Administration of Children and Families

—>URL is: http://www.acf.dhhs.gov/programs/ ofs/grants form.htm

A super site loaded with grant-related documents and forms including application forms, certificates, disclosures, and assurances.

28. ✓ United States Department of Health and Human Services Administration on Aging

—>URL is: http://www.aoa.dhhs.gov/

Housed in the United States Department of Health and Human Services, the Administration on Aging site provides a wealth of information on the Older Americans Act and its reauthorization. Other information available includes budget information, accomplishments, a resource page, and related press releases.

29. ✓ United States Department of Health and Human Services Grants Net

—>URL is: http://www.hhs.gov/progorg/grantsnet/index.html

Provides a wealth of information that includes links to administering awards, a grants administration manual, grants policy directives, grant resources, public laws, reinvention, streamlining and continuous improvement activities, cost principles and procedures, how to find grant information, the ability to search for funding, how to apply, and other useful information. This is a site worth browsing!

30. United States Department of Housing and Urban Development

—>URL is: http://www.hud.gov

For anyone interested in HUD grants this site should be bookmarked. There is a direct link to their Notices of Funding Availability (NOFAs).

31. United States Department of Justice Office of Justice Programs

—>URL is: http://afterschool.gov/

This site offers a database of more than 100 grants and loan programs as well as a publications and clearinghouse link.

32. United States Department of Labor
Employment and Training Administration

—>URL is: http://www.dol.gov/

A site filled with a wealth of information about the Department of Labor. Grantwriters will want to visit the library to view the latest Department of Labor *FR* notices.

33. United States Department of Veterans Affairs

—>URL is: http://www.va.gov

For grantwriters interested in knowing more about the Department of Veterans Affairs. An informative site with many related sites.

34. ✓ White House

—>URL is: http://www.whitehouse.gov

Not only visually inviting, this home page has a number of great links that you will want to check out. From this site you can e-mail the President and Vice President, take a tour of the White House, check out daily press releases, and get lost in the virtual library.

Accessing Funding Information on the Internet: Specific Grant Services

Figure 5.3 outlines a number of Internet sites for locating specific grant services, including foundations and an assortment of publications that may be useful to grantwriters. The Foundation Center site is a great place to browse around. Many useful links are provided to corporations and foundations offering funding opportunities. Other grant resources including the Yahoo Web Site "Education Grants," the Grant Getter's Guide to the Internet, Grants Web WWW, and the URL List for Grant Seekers are all sites worth visiting. These sites include numerous links to other sites that are of interest to grantwriters.

A discussion about grant resources would not be complete without mentioning some of the standard government publications that are now available on the Internet. The *Catalog of Federal Domestic Assistance*, the *Code of Federal Regulations*, the *Commerce Business Daily*, the *Congressional Record,* the *Daily Report Card*, *Education*

Week on the Web, and the *Federal Register* are all easily accessible. Other publications that may be of interest and worth checking out are *Academe This Week* and *EDUCAUSE*. Both of these publications will help to keep users abreast of the current educational issues and trends—a must for the successful grantwriter.

Many of the sites that are included in this section—*Catalog of Federal Domestic Assistance, Code of Federal Regulations, Commerce Business Daily,* and the *Federal Register*—are also referred to within other chapters of *Finding Funding*. For greater detail, refer to these chapters prior to searching via the Internet.

Foundations and Grant Resources

In addition to the wealth of information available on government funding opportunities, there are also a number of sites that provide information about funding through foundations. Be sure to check out The Foundation Center site. Accessing this site will give you the capability to link to numerous other resources. Alternatively, if you happen to know the foundation in which you are interested, you can do a general search to see if a particular foundation is on-line.

35. ✓ (The) Foundation Center

—>URL is: http://fdncenter.org/

Award-winning site that links to hundreds of private foundations and corporate grantmakers on the Internet, including a simple-to-

Figure 5.3. Accessing Funding Information on the Internet: Specific Grant Services

Foundations and Nonproft Giving	Publications, Government
35. The Foundation Center	46. *Catalog of Federal Domestic Assistance*
36. Education Grants (Yahoo Web Site)	47. *Code of Federal Regulations*
37. Grant Getter's Guide to the Internet	48. *Commerce Business Daily*
38. The Grants Library	49. *Congressional Record*
39. Bobst Library at NYU, Grants in the Arts	50. *Education Week on the Web*
40. The Learning Institute for Nonprofit Organizations	51. *Federal Register*
41. Guide to Funding: A Reference Directory to Public and Private Giving for Artists and Scholars	**Publications, Other**
42. Nonprofit Gateway	
43. Philanthrophy News Network Online	52. *Academe This Week*
44. Nonprofit Resources Catalogue	53. EDUCAUSE
45. Internet Nonprofit Center	

use Grantmaker Search that allows you to search their listings by subject or geographical location, as well as sites for private foundations, community foundations, and grantmaking public charities.

36. ✓ Education Grants (Yahoo Web Site)

—>URL is: http://dir.yahoo.com/education/index.html

A great place to start surfing the Web if you are a novice Internet user. There are many wonderful and informative topics. One is bound to spark your interest!

37. ✓ Grant Getter's Guide to the Internet

—>URL is: http://web.calstatela.edu/academic/orsp
grantguide.html

This may very well be the first stop for those who are new to the Internet. A must for your grantwriter's toolkit. It is an amazing compilation of useful information.

38. ✓ The Grants Library

—>URL is: http://www.thegrantslibrary.com

A relatively new site whose mission is to be the world's largest compilation of grant-related web sites. Check it out.

39. Bobst Library at NYU, Grants in the Arts

—>URL is: http://www.nyu.edu/library/bobst/research/
hum/art/grants.htm

This site provides two basic articles on how to research foundations and a short course in proposal writing. There are also links to arts deadlines and dealines in academe. You will also find a listing of links to major funding sources in the arts.

40. The Learning Institute for Nonprofit Organizations

—>URL is: http://www.uwex.edu/li/nonprofit/learner/
sites.htm

A great starting point for anyone wanting to begin a basic research into nonprofit web sites. The site also provides information about courses and degrees, a listserv, and other pertinent information.

41. Guide to Funding: A Reference Directory to Public and Private Giving for Artists and Scholars

—>URL is: http://www.amherst.edu/~erreich/pcah_html/ fundingguide.html

Mark this site! It is a super site with over 17 pages of links to everything from major grant-making organizations to a publications list on fundraising. You will want to visit this site frequently.

42. NonProfit Gateway

—>URL is: http://www.nonproft.gov/links/depts/html

A site that provides links to a government directory, key information sites, and nonprofit resources within the federal government.

43. Philanthropy News Network Online

—>URL is: http://www.pnnonline.org/giving/nea0114.cfm

For those interested in nonprofit information, be sure to check out this site. It is filled with many useful links and current information related to nonprofit funding. You will want to bookmark this site!

44. Nonproft Resources Catalogue

—>URL is: http://www.clark.net/pub/pwalker/General_ Nonprofit_Resources/

A site that provides meta-links to to various related sites including a link to international philanthrophy and volunteering.

45. Internet Nonprofit Center

—>URL is: http://www.nonprofit.org/

The site provides information for and about nonprofit organizations. There are links to a nonprofit locator, the Form 990 Project, and a INC Library.

Publications, Government

46. ✓ Catalog of Federal Domestic Assistance

—>URL is: http://www.cfda.gov

The *CFDA* is considered to be one of the basic grantwriting tools. This site provides the opportunity to query the *CFDA*. Chapter 4 addresses the *CFDA* in-depth and provides an example of a *CFDA* entry.

47. ✓ Code of Federal Regulations

—>URL is: http://www.access.gpo.gov/nara/

A great site for the serious grantwriter. It is searchable and includes sites that provide *CFR* background information, answers to frequently asked questions, and a user's guide, as well as other useful links. Chapter 3 deals with the *Federal Register* and the *Code of Federal Regulations* and provides examples of these documents.

48. ✓ Commerce Business Daily

—>URL is: http://www.ld.com/cbd.shtml

This site provides access to today's *CBD* as well as the ability to search archived *CBD* notices at no charge. You will want to explore additional links that may be of interest to the grantwriter.

49. Congressional Record

—>URL is: http://thomas.loc.gov/home/r105query.html

A searchable site that includes members of the 105th, 106th, and 107th Congresses as well as the *Congressional Record.*

50. Education Week on the Web

—>URL is: http://www.edweek.org/

Billed as "American Education's Online Newspaper of Record." Education Week on the Web provides a number of options including the *Daily News*, the *Teacher Magazine*, archives, jobs, and special reports. The *Daily News* provides links to the most current educational articles being published around the country.

51. ✓ *Federal Register*

—>URL is: http://www.access.gpo.gov/su_docsaces. aces140.html

This is our preferred method for accessing the *Federal Register*— through the Government Printing Office. This site allows the user many different options for searching the *Federal Register*. Chapter 3 describes the *Federal Register* and provides a variety of examples of the various documents that are printed in this valuable resource.

Publications, Other

52. *Academe This Week (Chronicle of Higher Education)*

—>URL is: http://chronicle.merit.edu/

Updated weekly, *Academe This Week* provides a quick synopsis of *The Chronicle of Higher Education*. This site provides important information on how to subscribe to *The Chronicle* and how to register for *Academe This Week*.

53. EDUCAUSE

—>URL is: http://www.educause.edu/

Formally known as *Edupage* and CAUSE these two groups joined forces to pursue their interest of higher education and technology. Numerous links are provided to related information.

Accessing Funding Information on the Internet: *Databases and Other "Need" Information*

The Internet sites listed in Figure 5.4 include some databases and other sites that may be useful in writing your Need section. This listing is by no means inclusive. If health care is an area of interest, checkout Achoo. The ERIC database allows you to complete a general

Figure 5.4. Accessing Funding Information on the Internet:
Databases and Other "Need" Information

Databases

   54. Achoo (health care)
   55. Educational Resources Information Center (ERIC)

Statistics

   56. FEDSTATS
   57. Government Information Sharing Project
   58. Government Information Xchange
   59. National Center for Educational Statistics
   60. National Center for Educational Statistics—Education at a Glance
   61. National Center on Educational Outcomes

---

education search and Internic is more government related.

When completing a Need section of a grant proposal, it is frequently necessary to include statistics in order to dramatize the need. The Internet provides a number of sites that provide useful statistics such as FEDSTATS, the Government Information Sharing Project, the Government Information Xchange, the National Center for Education Statistics, and the National Center on Educational Outcomes. A writer may also find it useful to visit his or her state's home page to see if there are links to statistical information for specific targeted area.

Databases

54. Achoo

—>URL is: http://www.achoo.com/

A comprehensive health-care database that has over 7,000 indexed and searchable sites. Grantwriters interested in health care will want to visit this site; it includes communication and research tools.

55. ✓ Educational Resources Information Center (ERIC)

—>URL is: http://www.accesseric.org/

One of the sites found in every successful grantwriter's tool kit. From here, one can access all types of useful information by searching the ERIC database and its systemwide resources.

Statistics

56. FEDSTATS

—>URL is: http://www.fedstats.gov/

Did you know that there are more than 70 United States federal agencies that produce statistics? Federal Stats (FEDSTATS) allows easy access to this wealth of information. There are links to agencies, data access tools, programs, and regional statistics.

57. Government Information Sharing Project

—>URL is: http://govinfo.kerr.orst.edu/

Need demographics? Check out this site for statistics related to United States counties; census of population and housing; population estimates by age, sex, and race; equal employment opportunity file; and the school district data book profiles. There is also economic information related to the regional economic information system, the economic census, the census of agriculture, United States imports/exports, and the consolidated federal funds report.

58. Government Information Xchange (GIX)

—>URL is: http://www.info.gov/

This site provides direct links to most of the key federal sites including a federal directory, state and local information, a foreign and international link, and the yellow pages.

59. National Center for Educational Statistics

—>URL is: http://nces.ed.gov/index.html

The purpose of this site "is for collecting and analyzing data that are related to education in the United States and other nations." You will want to mark this site!

60. ✓ National Center for Educational Statistics— Education at a Glance

—> URL is: http://ncesol.ed.gov/NCES/indihome.asp

This site has a wealth of statistical information including a public school/district locator, data access tools, the Nation's Report Card, Public Elementary/Secondaary Data, Postsecondary Education Data, International Math/Science Study, and a Public Library Locator. There also are links to other special topics that should be of interest to the grantwriter. An excellent site with a lot of useful information.

61. National Center on Educational Outcomes

—>URL is: http://www.coled.umn.edu/NCEO/

If you need up-to-date information on educational outcomes for all students, you will want to visit this site. The main menu offers the following options: overview of NCEO, on-line publications, information exchange, technical assistance, publications list, links to related sites, and NCEO staff.

Accessing Funding Information on the Internet: Writing and Other

Figure 5.5 provides a list of some favorite and most-used sites during the actual writing phase. Undoubtedly, readers' lists may include some of the same sites. However, the important thing to remember is that what may be useful for some may or may not be useful others. All sites recommended should be used as a stepping stone to other sites that will provide the information needed to submit a winning proposal.

Arts

62. ArtsEdge

—>URL is: http://artsedge.kennedy-center.org/artsedge. html

This site is provided through the support of the Kennedy Center, the National Endowment for the Arts, and the Department of Education. The information that is available ranges from curriculum that supports the national education goals, a student-centered link, information for the global arts community, a news site with the latest developments in the arts education community, and a

Figure 5.5. Accessing Funding Information on the Internet: Writing and Other

---

Arts

    62. ArtsEdge (See also Foundations and Nonprofit Giving)

National Associations

    63. Council for Opportunity in Education
    64. National Education Association
    65. National Parent Teacher Organization

Other

    66. AskERIC
    67. Best Education Sites Today
    68. Consumer Information Center
    69. Corporation for National Service (AmeriCorps)
    70. EdWeb
    71. Federal Depository Library Program
    72. Federal Web Locator Service
    73. FEDIX
    74. FIPSE

    75. Goals 2000: Educate America Act
    76. Gopher Jewels
    77. Internet Public Library
    78. Learn and Serve America
    79. School-to-Work
    80. Scott Yanoff's Internet Connections
    81. UMass K12 Internet Bulletin Board System
    82. US RELnet (Regional Education Labs)
    83. Women's Educational Equity Act
           Resource Center

**Underrepresented Populations/
Special Education and Rehabilitation**

    84. Minority On-Line Information Service
    85. National Clearinghouse for Bilingual Education
    86. Council for Opportunity in Education
    87. National Rehabilitation Information Center
    88. National Research and Development Centers
    89. Office of Special Education Programs—Regional Resources and Federal Centers

Writing

    90. American Psychological Association
    91. Quotations
    92. Thesaurus
    93. Writer's Handbook

Nonprofit

    94. Appalachian Regional Commission: How to Apply for a Grant
    95. ArtDeadline.Com
    96. ArtsWire Current
    97. Funds Available Through HUD
    98. Fundsnet Services ONLINE
    99. Grants and Related Resources
  100. Guide to Funding: A Reference Directory to Public and
          Private Giving for Artists and Scholars.
  101. The Learning Institute for Nonprofit Organizations

link that allows one to search through a database of arts education directories and resources.

National Associations

63. Council for Opportunity in Education (COE)

—>URL is: http://www.trioprograms.org

A site for those interested in TRIO programs. Many useful links are provided as well as information about TRIO, government relations, TRIO clearinghouse, regional news, and publications.

64. National Education Association

—>URL is: http://www.nea.org

A comprehensive site with links to education statistics, resources, and works4me.tips. This is a site you will want to visit often.

65. National Parent Teacher Organization

—>URL is: http://www.pta.org

An all-purpose general education site for the latest happenings in education across America.

Other

66. AskERIC

—>URL is: http://ericir.syr.edu/

A service of the Educational Resources Information Center (ERIC). Contains five areas: (1) Questions and Answers, (2) a Virtual Library, (3) New and Noteworthy, (4) Lessons Plans, and (5) a searchable ERIC database. From this site one can link (connect) to the U.S. Department of Education and the ERIC system.

67. ✓ Best Education Sites Today

—>URL is: http://www.education-world.com/

Chocked full of current educational information. Definitely a site worth visiting on a regular basis.

68. ✓ Consumer Information Center

—>URL is: http://www.pueblo.gsa.gov/

Filled with a wealth of information on the best federal publications for consumers, including free materials as well as those with a nominal charge. Additionally, this site provides the Consumer Information Center World Wide Web Links to most of the Federal Agencies and Indexes.

69. Corporation for National Service (AmeriCorps)

—>URL is: http://www.cns.gov/americorps/index.html

Want to know more about AmeriCorps? Check out this site. A brief but informative introduction to this program is provided at this site with links to Learn and Serve America and National Senior Service Corps.

70. ✓ EdWeb

—>URL is: http://edweb.gsn.org/

A great site with many useful links to education resources and other Web links.

71. Federal Depository Library Program

—>URL is: http://www.access.gpo.gov/fdlp01.html

This site allows you to search a comprehensive catalog of government information products (MOCAT), browse government Internet sites by topic, browse electronic government information products by title, search for government information on selected Internet sites, search GILS, locate federal depository libraries, and obtain information on demand from U.S. Fax Watch.

72. ✓ Federal Web Locator Service

—>URL is: http://www.infoctr.edu/fwl/

As noted on the home page, The Federal Web Locator "is intended to be the one stop shopping point for federal government information on the World Wide Web." This site is worth a visit. Put this one in your grantwriting toolkit!

73. FEDIX

—>URL is: http://www.rams-fie.com

Through this site you can link to seven federal agencies and search either by subject or audience. Information is also provided on how to register for the free on-line service that delivers to you the targeted research and education funding opportunities you have selected.

74. FIPSE (Fund for the Improvement of Postsecondary Education)

—>URL is: http://www.ed.gov/offices/OPE/

A great site for information on FIPSE including competition guidelines; application materials; evaluation information; funding advice such as "How to Get a FIPSE Grant" by Eulalia Cobb, "12 Steps to Funding: General Advice for Grant Seekers"; illustrative essays about FIPSE projects; and information specifically for FIPSE grantees.

75. Goals 2000: Educate America Act

—>URL is: http://www.ed.gov/G2K/

For those who need to access information about Goals 2000 this site provides the full text of the Goals 2000: Education America Act, progress reports, state plans, and a variety of other information pertaining to this initiative.

76. ✓ Gopher Jewels (Education, includes K-12 Category)

—>URL is: http://galaxy.einet.net/GJ/education.html

Many, many useful educational sites are provided, ranging from A to Z. Sites that you can link to include Adult Educaton, Curriculum and Instruction, Distance Learning, and seven others.

77. Internet Public Library

—>URL is: http://www.ipl.org/

This site provides reference links to a number of different topics including Education. Additional information includes magazines and serials, newspapers, on-line texts, and sites for teens and youth.

78. Learn and Serve America

—>URL is: http://www.cns.gov/learn/index.html

Provides some basic information about the Learn and Serve America programs, including information about service learning, resources for programs, research materials, and national service-learning leader schools.

79. School-to-Work

—>URL is: http://www.stw.ed.gov/

A great site for those interested in the school-to-work initiative. The home page provides numerous links to related information. This site provides current grant award notices, information about tates, resources, evaluation and other related areas.

80. ✓ Scott Yanoff's Internet Connections

—>URL is: http://sirius.we.lc.ehu.ed/internet/inet.services.html

An award-winning comprehensive site covering many different topics. A great place for the novice Internet user to start "surfing." Indexed alphabetically be sure to scan the Education topics for those that may be of interest. Several useful links to other education sites are provided.

81. UMass K12 Internet Bulletin Board System

—>URL is: http://k12.oit.umass.edu/

A general information site. Many different links to educational information including encyclopedias, dictionaries, educational listservs, and a calendar of events.

82. US-RELnet (Regional Education Laboratories)

—>URL is: http://www. relnetwork.org

Users have the opportunity to visit each of the 10 regional educational laboratories to find out specific information about their activities. Addresses are provided as well as links to news archives and REL publications.

83. Women's Educational Equity Act Equity Resource Center

—>URL is: http://www.edc.org/WomensEquity/Index.html

For individuals interested in promoting gender-fair multicultural education. Links to publications, grantee information, and other related links.

Underrepresented Populations/Special Education and Rehabilitation

84. Minority On-Line Information Service (MOLIS)

—>URL is: http://web.fie.com/web/mol/molisfaq.htm

A great resource for individuals interested in information pertaining to minorities. There are a number of links to other sites including minority opportunities for minority institutions.

85. National Clearinghouse for Bilingual Education

—>URL is: http://www.ncbe.gwu.edu/

A site funded by the U.S. Department of Education. Users can find an online library, language and education links, and other useful links.

86. Council of Opportunity in Education (See National Associations, #63)

87. National Rehabilitation Information Center

—>URL is: http://www.naric.com

Interested in finding out more about disability and rehabilitation research? Then this site is for you. It provides online services with links to 60,000 disability-related records.

88. National Research and Development Centers

—>URL is: http://www.ed.gov/offices/OERI/ResCtr.html

This site provides links to many of the centers. As noted on its home page, the National Research and Development Centers "are designed to address nationally significant problems and issues in education."

89. Office of Special Education Programs—Regional Resource and Federal Centers

—>URL is: http://www.dssc.org/frc/rrfc.htm

This site can put you in touch with each of the six Regional Resource Centers for Special Education and the Referral Resource Center for Special Education. There are a number of other links to related sites.

Writing

90. American Psychological Association

—>URL is: http://www.beadsland.com/weapas/

With the expanded use of the Internet for research purposes, the popular American Psychological Association (APA) style has now outlined its proposed standards on how to reference documents that are found on-line and used in scholarly publications. The APA style provides excellent guidelines on style and format in writing that could be transferable to grantwriting.

91. Quotations

—>URL is: http://www.bartleby.com/99/

This happens to be one of the "related" sites that may be helpful during the writing stage. Quotations, if used judiciously, can add interest and spark to a grant proposal.

92. Thesaurus

—>URL is: http://thesaurus.com

A great tool for the grantwriter's tool kit! A site that allows you to browse Roget's Thesaurus with a dictionary link.

93. ✓ Writer's Handbook

—>URL is: http://www.english.uiuc.edu/cws/
wworkshop writer.html

An on-line resource for writers. Includes a grammar handbook, a bibliography of style handbooks, the best Web sites for writers, and links to reference texts and directories.

Nonprofit

94. Appalachian Regional Commission: How to Apply for a Grant

—>URL is: http://www.arc.gov/grants/grntmain.htm

For those who are interested in the Appalachian Region, this is a site you will want to check out. It is full of information about this regional grant-making commission including links to ARC project guidelines, news, events, and publications. For those living in other regions of the country, similar commissions may exist so you will want to explore this as a viable option.

95. ArtDeadline.Com

—>URL is: http://www.artsdeadline.htm

A site that is solely devoted to hundreds of art-related announcements. This site is by subscription ($12.00 for 90-day trial membership, $24.00 for a full one-year Internet version, and a $34.00 e-mail version for 12 issues). The site is indexed and provides a keyword search capability with easy print screens.

96. ArtsWire Current

—>URL is: http://www.fundingnews.htm

This site is for those who are interested in any aspect of social, economic, philosophical, and political issues related to arts and culture. This site combines recent articles related to arts and culture along with conferences, art events, funding news, and job opportunities.

97. Funds Available Through HUD

—>URL is: http://www.hud.gov/fundsavl.html

HUD has compiled most of its grants into what is referred to as SuperNOFA. Anyone interested in community development, drug elimination programs, economic development programs, fair housing and housing counseling programs, HOPEIV programs, housing opportunities for persons with AIDS, and numerous other HUD-related projects should visit this site often.

98. Fundsnet Services ONLINE

—>URL is: http://www.fundsnetservices.com

A comprehensive site that provides links to grants and fundraising resources. There are more than 1,500 sources! There is an extensive section of Latino web sites for Spanish-speaking visitors.

99. Grants and Related Resources

—>URL is: http://www.lib.msu.edu/harris23/grants/2educat.htm

This is a great site that has a huge listing of grants and funding sources for nonprofit organizations. It is easy to navigate through the alphabetical subject listing of 26 major categories. Many of the annotated listings provide quick hot links right to the funding information.

100. Guide to Funding: A Reference Directory to Public and Private Giving for Artists and Scholars

—>URL is: http://www.amherst.edu/~erreich/pcah_html/
       funding guide.html

As noted on the homepage, this site is a result of the President's Committee on the Arts and Humanities. It would be an excellent site for beginners to check out because it provides numerous links to some of the top Internet sites including major grantmaking organizations, fundraising resource centers, publications list on grants and funding, arts and humanities service organizations, the top 10 lists of corporate givers, the top 10 list of foundation givers, and the top 10 list of foundations ranked by giving to the arts.

101. The Learning Institute for Nonprofit Organizations

—>URL is: http://www.uwex.edu/li/

The site is a collaborative effort between the University of Wisconsin Extension Service and the Society for Nonprofit Organizations. Currently there are 16 links to related nonprofit grant sites including board development/governance, foundation information, fundraising and grantwriting, how to start nonprofit organizations, marketing, and outcome measurement.

Summary

The Internet is not going to solve every problem or answer all questions. It is simply a tool for the grantwriter that should be used to its best advantage.

No doubt by the time that readers finish reading this chapter, some of this information may be revised, removed, or located at a new address. Do not despair, this is all part of the process of using the information superhighway. As this incredible resource continues to expand and grow, there are certain to be some unexpected delays along the way including some detours and, yes, even some roadblocks. Don't give up—keeping trying. It will be worth the effort.

Suggested On-line Internet References

Big Dummy's Guide to the Internet, Adam Gaffin with Jorg Heitkotter. Texinfo Edition 1.04. January, 1994. URL is: http://www. physics.csbsju.edu/Help/bdg/bdg_1.html

EFF's (Extended) Guide to the Internet. Texinfo Edition 2.3, September, 1994. Adam Gaffin with Jorg Heitkotter. URL is: http:// www.hep.net/documents/eegtti/eeg_toc.html

Entering the World Wide Web: A Guide to Cyberspace, Kevin Hughes. URL is: http://www.its.unimelb.edu.au/courses/ wwwintro/guide.61/guide.toc.html

Glossary of Internet Terms, c. 1995 by Internet Advertising Southwest (TM). URL is: http://www.matisse.net/files/glossary.html

A Grant Seeker's Guide to the Internet: Revised and Revisited, Andrew J. Grant & Suzy D. Sonenberg. URL is: http://www. mind spring.com/~ajgrant/guide.htm

The Hitchhikers Guide to the Internet, E. Krol. September, 1989. URL is: http://www.ece.ntua.gr/facilities/documentation/internet/ hitchhikers-guide/thgtti.html

The Net: User Guidelines and Netiquette, Arlene H. Rinaldi. URL is: http://www.fau.edu/netiquette.ent

Patrick Crispen's Internet Roadmap. URL is: http://www. mobiusweb.com/~mobius/Roadmap/roadmap.html

The World Wide Web Unleashed. URL is: http://www.december.com/ works/wwwu.html

Zen and the Art of Internet: *A Beginner's Guide to the Internet,* First Edition, January 1992 (1.0), Kehoe. URL is: http://www. cs.indiana.edu/docproject/zen/zen-1.0_toc.html

---

Authors' Note: At the time of publication all links (URLs) were operational.

PART II

Writing Grant Proposals

In Part II, Chapters 6-12, we address the specifics of writing grant proposals. Information on the basic components of a standard proposal, tips on reviewing and responding to a request for proposal (RFP), and a sample funded proposal are presented. In addition, we outline the various steps an application goes through and introduce key players who are vital participants in the grant-making process.

6

What Are the Components of a Proposal?

Introduction and Some Background

In Chapter 6 we explore some ideas, tips, and strategies for developing proposals in *general;* in Chapter 8 we use *in detail* one specific Department of Education program and analyze the process of writing a proposal to that program. Chapters 1, 6, 8, and 9 together offer a roadmap for developing successful proposals for external funding excluding the private sector where a foundation or group may have specific requirements.

This chapter emphasizes developing competitive proposals and offers some samples and examples. The grantwriter will compile a file of forms and formats that suit the writer's own style and needs. A proposal must be well written; the proposal is the bridge between the funding agency with its goals, priorities, and regulations and your agency with its abilities, interests, staff, and approach to problems of concern to the funding source.

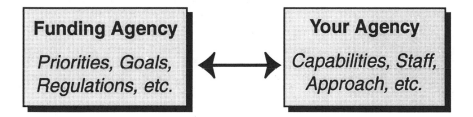

The proposal should be *clear, concise, cogent, compelling*, and *correct*—the *"five Cs"* of carefully crafted proposals. The language should be reasonably free of jargon. The ideas should be presented succinctly with minimum repetition. Use short sentences and the active voice. The plan should be clear and forceful. Your ideas should be refreshing and attractive with direct ties both to a major problem and to the key interests of the agency to which you will submit the proposal. Finally, the proposal should be as error free as possible: Attend well to tense, agreement, and other rules of grammar.

———Grant Tip———
The proposal should be clear, concise, cogent, compelling, and correct—the "five Cs" of carefully crafted proposals.

This chapter reviews the background of the "standard" federal proposal and explains each section briefly. Some explanations are pertinent for recent proposal formats that are reviewed later in the chapter, but the chapter has a special slant toward a "standard" federal proposal.

Although still directed toward Department of Education programs, Chapter 6 has relevance across other federal agencies. This is possible, in part, due to the general similarity among many federal proposal formats and other requirements. The desire for some commonality among federal program proposal requirements led, in 1974, to Federal Management Circular (FMC) 74-7 (9/13/74) "Uniform administrative requirements for grants-in-aid to state and local governments." In part, FMC 74-7 stated, "On March 27, 1969, the President ordered a 3-year effort to simplify, standardize, decentralize and otherwise modernize the Federal grant machinery." FMC 74-7 temporarily replaced Office of Management and Budget (OMB) Circular No. A-102 while standardization occurred. On 9/12/77 the OMB issued a new Circular A-102 as Part VII of the *Federal Register.* Figure 6.1 shows the "standard" proposal format as described in OMB

Figure 6.1. Parts of a Standard Proposal (OMB A-102, 1977)

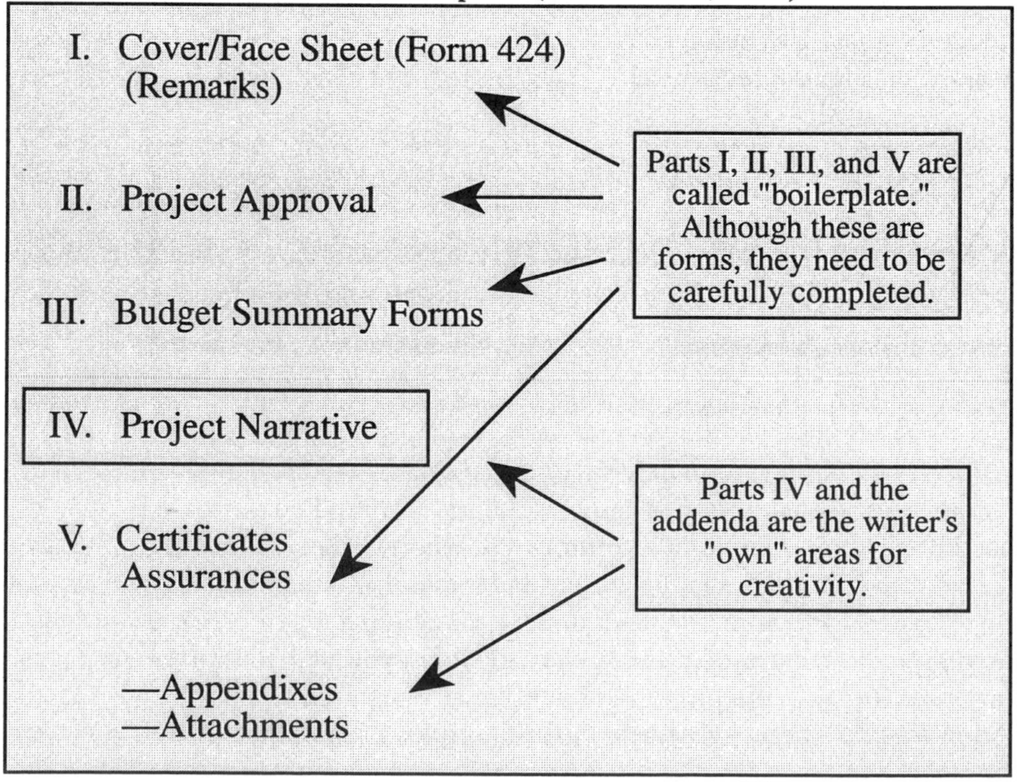

A-102; standard forms, including the face sheet (Form 424), a project approval form, budget summary forms, and various certifications and assurances become part of each proposal application. Between 1977 and the present, there have been some modest changes in the forms and the formats, but the 1977 standardization instilled the idea that the various agencies might be able to work from a similar proposal design. *The original (1977) plan is shown here for perspective. Newer examples are provided a few pages later.*

In proposal-preparation parlance, the standard forms that become part of the proposal package are collectively called "boilerplate." These are Parts I, II, III and V of the A-102 format. The boilerplate provides a similarity and continuity that assist in categorizing, comparing, and codifying the proposals at the agency, and it facilitates multiple-agency proposals and interagency funding of large projects. The boilerplate is usually completed last, or near last, in the proposal-writing process.

Part IV of the 1977 A-102 format is the Narrative, the opportunity for the writer to express what the project is about. Each proposal application may have some specific instructions, but the general parts of the narrative (9/77) are those shown in Figure 6.2, General Federal Proposal Format. Some programs *require* an *Abstract,* usually about 250 words. You will probably write this last. Although not required, a brief *Introduction* or *Background* may be useful, especially if your agency is not well known. Here you might *briefly* describe your agency and something of your agency's history, experience, and interest in the project being proposed. Comment on special strengths. Be brief and concise—try to keep this to less than two pages. The parts of the narrative required in A-102 are briefly described here. Later Education Department proposal applications have slightly different formats and follow specifics for the program and Education Division General Administrative Regulations, or *EDGAR,* as set forth in 34 *CFR,* Part 74 Administration of Grants; Part 75; Direct Grant Programs, and Part 77 Definitions that apply to Department Regulations. See Chapter 3 of this book for information on the *CFR* and Chapter 14 for information on using *EDGAR* and *GPRA.*

Objectives and Need for Assistance

You should work first on the needs, because the needs will help structure the objectives, the project activities, and the evaluation. Needs should be specific, employing compelling data. Move from general

Figure 6.2. General Federal Proposal Format, Part IV: Program Narrative for Standard Grant Applications

---

ABSTRACT

INTRODUCTION/BACKGROUND*

1. OBJECTIVES AND NEED FOR THIS ASSISTANCE

   Need (National, Regional, State, or Local). Get and use data. Objectives will be stated to show that progress toward them will be measurable.

2. RESULTS OR BENEFITS EXPECTED (GENERAL)

   This is a "philosophy" or overall goal for your effort. (This section has been dropped in later proposal format.)

3. APPROACH

   A. Plan of Action: Besides a clear statement of your activities, this section might include the theoretic considerations/conceptual base (literature, etc.)
   B. Time Frame or Time Projections
   C. Data to Be Collected; Evaluation Process/Design
   D. Organizations, Cooperators, Consultants

4. GEOGRAPHIC LOCATION (Attach a map or maps)

5. OTHER

   A. Director (Resume)
   B. Other Key Personnel
   C. References

CERTIFICATIONS, APPENDIXES, ATTACHMENTS FOLLOW THE NARRATIVE

*Usually, if there are no page limits, it is suggested that you make introduction and key points (1-5) as center headings (capitalized). The other dividers shown here (A, B, etc.) are freestanding side headings, and each starts a new page during proposal-writing time so that it is easy to make changes as you review the work or get feedback from others. In later application packets, there is a request for a 25-page (double-spaced) limit. Starting each section on a separate page may be a lost luxury.

---

needs (even those used to argue for the legislation at congressional hearings) to specific needs (at your local site). Where possible, use recognized sources such as census data and standard test scores. Consider needs at several levels, for example,

General Needs to Specific Needs

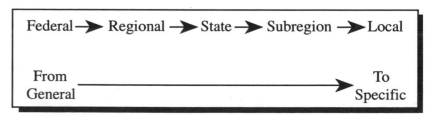

The *Needs* section, although emphasizing conditions that your project will address, should show that these *needs* relate to a *class* or *group* of people deserving help or assistance. Although you are seeking support for *your* clientele, the agency will want to support a worthy, innovative effort that can be generalized to others like your clients—a model that may be "transportable" and provide a cost-effective stable solution to a fairly common problem that has been clearly documented by the needs you have carefully compiled.

Besides being important in their own right, thoroughly documented needs are important to other aspects of the proposal and, ultimately, to the project. The needs become

- Baseline data to assist in the evaluation plan or design

- A"target" giving substance to each objective

- An organizing element around which you will structure key activities

The objectives provide an organizing framework for the proposal and for the activities you will complete to achieve the objectives. Objectives should be specific; as much as possible, they should be stated in *measurable terms*. Unless the project is extremely complex, 4-8 objectives will be adequate. You need an objective to guide each major concern but not for minor efforts; each objective will be the focus of several enabling activities. Often one objective will relate to dissemination of project outcomes.

Results or Benefits Expected

The *Results or Benefits Expected* section (seldom used in U.S. Department of Education applications now) provided an opportunity to state a general view of the project's potential. These points need not be *measurable* in the sense that objectives are, but they should tie things together, provide a view of how successes with this project may lead to a model or generalized solution, and express how this project may contribute to a stream of research or project development. In recent grant applications, this section has been dropped and points usually sought here may be addressed in such sections as *Meeting the Purposes of the Authorizing Statute* or *How Well the Objectives of the Project Relate to the Purposes of the Program.*

——— **Grant Tip**———
The objectives provide an organizing framework for the proposal; as much as possible, they should be stated in measurable terms.

Approach

This section delineates the proposer's unique way of addressing the needs and purposes of the authorizing statutes. In this section the proposer explains clearly a "plan of action" that includes such things as

- Theoretic considerations or a conceptual base

- A literature review showing how this project will *fit* with current thinking and extend the state-of-the-art

- A research review showing how this project uses current research knowledge

- Explanations of how each activity of note will contribute to project success

- A plan showing how personnel will be deployed to perform the activities and to achieve the objectives

- A management plan to show how the proposer will organize and operate the project in an efficient and effective manner

- A plan to guide formative and summative process and product evaluation

- A clear picture of ideas for disseminating project results to important audiences

The *Approach* section will include a timeline, time frame, or projections of approximately when things will be completed. The timeline may be in graphic form and will relate to the management plan. Figure 6.3 shows one format for a timeline that relates major activities to completion times by months or quarters of the project year. You do not need to specify *exact dates*—in fact, you may not be able to control these anyway. Use months or two-week intervals to show your checkpoints for progress.

An *Evaluation Plan* or design is also part of the approach. The evaluation plan will specify the data to be collected to assess the project's processes and products. The needs data, carefully developed, will be part of evaluation in that they serve as the *baseline* information. A project is successful if its activities reduce the need that generated the project in the first place. It is not enough to state that you will employ an external agency to do your evaluation. Your proposal must contain enough good evaluation information so the proposal readers can assess the rigor and utility of your evaluation

——Grant Tip——

Your proposal must contain enough good evaluation information so the proposal readers can assess the rigor and utility of your plan.

Figure 6.3. Major Activities Planning Form

Major Activities	Dates (By month or quarter)											
	Q 1			Q 2			Q 3			Q 4		
	Jan	Feb	Mar	Apr	May	Jun	Jul	Aug	Sep	Oct	Nov	Dec

plan. One simple plan to organize project evaluation is shown in Figure 6.4. Each point should be addressed in the evaluation narrative. This includes the evaluation purpose or focus, types of data, and perspective or focus of the evaluator(s).

Seldom does a single agency accomplish all of a project's outcomes by itself. A successful project has persons or agencies that *cooperate* in the project's efforts. Be sure to describe the cooperating entities and specify the particulars of the cooperation. Include any

Figure 6.4. A Simple Model to Structure Project Evaluation Efforts

Evaluation & Data Type	Evaluator Perspective	PURPOSE OR FOCUS OF EVALUATION		
		Formative (Process)	Summative (Product)	Project Management
Quantitative	External Internal			
Qualitative	External Internal			

special contributions of each "cooperator." The proposal may contain an appendix with letters or sample letters that describe a cooperator's involvement and contributions. Commitments of specifics (time, money, and space) are much more valuable than general support.

The *Geographic Location* section should specify why the funding agency can benefit from locating the project *here*. Explain ease of travel, special resources, unusual geographic characteristics, or demographic influences. One or two good maps will help the reader visualize the location. This brief section should not only be convincing, but the location should support project activities.

The *Other* section of the narrative will contain information about project personnel—the director and staff. If the project requires activities that staff do not have specific and particular skills to deliver, list by name and areas of special expertise consultants who will fill in the gaps. End this section with a listing of the references cited in the theoretic framework/conceptual basis for the project and other sources that *strongly* support what you anticipate doing. Try to have no references over 5-7 years old *unless* the reference is considered a "classic."

A later section in this chapter outlines some recent variations on the "standard" proposal format. The newer structures build on *EDGAR* and remove some repetition and extra materials that the original format seemed to engender. "General" and philosophic "stuff" has been removed, leaving only the "scientific." The normative, ethical, and moral elements of the proposal seem to have been removed for a more "businesslike" approach.

The Project: Planning and Design

The standard format, proceeding as it does from Objectives and Needs to Other, including personnel, seems to suggest a chronology and linear approach following that design. Indeed, some proposal-writing seminars and writing guides also suggest a flow of activity from *needs* to *objectives* to *activities*. Figure 6.5 shows the *usual* "flow" of project-development and proposal-writing efforts, including the theoretical or usual approach, as espoused in these training seminars. Realistically, however, most successful grantwriters do not follow the model taught in these seminars and workshops.

Perhaps this model would work easily if people started from "ground zero" and if there were no time limits or deadlines. Remember: *There is no such thing as a late proposal!* This idealized model, useful for instructional purposes and not revealing the actual approach

---

——Grant Tip——
Try to have no references over 5-7 years old, unless the reference is considered a "classic."

Figure 6.5. Flowchart of Project-Development/Proposal-Writing Efforts

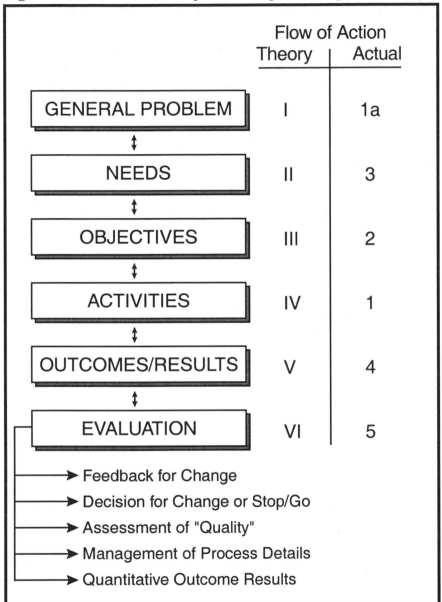

of successful grantwriters, suggests a seeking out of needs a "shotgun" approach, followed by a refining and shaping of needs to reflect your agency's clientele and to meet the funding agency's priorities.

The applying agency usually has existed for some time and agency personnel have analyzed what *really* needs to be done—and what local customs and mores will allow. They have used their Informed Professional Judgment (IPJ) to identify the activities needed to get the job done. Thus, the applying agency personnel know the *general problem* and the *activities* that make sense *given* the certainties and expectations of persons in the service areas. They know what they want to do and what they can do. Logically, then, they start their proposal planning and development with the problem and activities. They use what they already have concluded from their IPJ. Thus, in the real realm of the proposal-development process, the set of events goes something as follows:

1. **Activities** (IV on Figure 6.5). Activities are already known to the writer by IPJ of the agency staff or clients. The proposal writer then asks a logical question. . .

   Why do we want to do these activities? The answers, often beginning with "to" or "because," offer the outline of the. . .

2. **Objectives** (III on Figure 6.5). Several activities are likely to cluster under one objective. Then, for each rough objective, ask a logical question. . .

   Why are these objectives important or what generated these objectives? The answers, often beginning with "because," offer the outline of the. . .

3. **Needs** (II on Figure 6.5). Now, rather than *searching out* needs, a "shotgun" approach, your task is to *document* the needs, a "rifle" approach. Assign someone to find compelling evidence and proof for needs. Next, return to each objective (III on Figure 6.5) and ask a logical question. . .

   What will happen if we fulfill the objectives? The answers, usually stated as a benefit or improved condition, offer the working outline for the. . .

4. **Outcomes and Results** (V on Figure 6.5). The next logical questions stem from the projected outcomes and are. . .

   How will we recognize our success in obtaining the outcomes? What evidence will show that the outcomes have been attained? The answers to these questions will help in framing the plan or design for. . .

5. **Evaluation** (VI on Figure 6.5). The evaluation will then be refined to fulfill at least the four purposes shown at the bottom of Figure 6.5.

These steps, fairly easily and quickly done by agency staff and perhaps a consultant or two in a *brainstorming session,* provide a working outline or structure for a proposal. Each major section needs careful review, revision, and refinement, but this outline, in the "real world" sequence, will offer a guideline to get the proposal development process underway without the bickering that often slows down the process. This process asks and seeks resolution to the *What* questions and the *How* questions that avoid philosophy and values (the *Why* questions). This is *really* how grantwriting is done *successfully.*

- How will we measure the results?
- How will we do it?
- What shall we do?
- What can we do?

The Evolving Federal Standard "Proposal" Format

The OBM Circular A-102 got the standardization process for grants and applications off to a start (see Figure 6.6). The evolution of the standard definitions, rules and regulations, and criteria for judging applications, led to *EDGAR.* As program personnel became comfortable with *EDGAR,* the program's implementing rules and regulations from the *Federal Register* began to reflect *EDGAR's* criteria rather than promulgating program-specific implementing rules and regulations. Nevertheless, you should always review each program's specific rules and regulations to be sure *all* requirements are covered. Use of the process established in 9/77 by A-102 led to certain changes, such as usually dropping the original Part II (Project Approval Form—see Figure 6.1), and relying instead upon state clearinghouses or Single Points of Contact (SPOC) in each state to determine if the project proposal requires review by the SPOC to meet the mandate of Federal Executive Order 12372. Note that Appendix I of the *CFDA* includes the Executive Order 12372 information, but be sure to review this requirement each time you submit a proposal.

Recent federal grant applications substitute the SPOC for the former Part II and result in a three-part proposal rather than a four-part proposal (see Figure 6.6). Form 424, the Standard Cover Sheet, has been simplified and the new Narrative section is no longer usually restricted to the general headings (see Figure 6.2); the narrative format

Figure 6.6. The Evolving Federal Grant Application Format

I.   Cover/Face Sheet (Form 424)

II.   Budget Summary Forms and Data

III.   Project Narrative ◄──────────────────┐

IV.   Certifications/Assurances*

V.   Appendixes Attachments

> See Figure 6.7 for details of one competition's suggestions for preparing the narrative.

*Some writers include Certifications/Assurances after the Budget and before the Narrative; some establish these as Appendix A. Wherever each part of a proposal is located, a Table of Contents will help the reader/reviewer. Compare this five-part outline with the original OMB A-102 five-part outline shown in Figure 6.1.

—————Grant Tip—————
Every required section that gets points in the proposal evaluation process should have an entry in the Table of Contents.

is now tailored to *EDGAR* criteria and the specific idiosyncrasies of the particular competition (see Figure 6.7 for an example). Note that the instructions in the sample (Figure 6.7) ask the proposer to describe the proposed project following the selection criteria in the order in which the criteria are listed. Figure 6.8 shows the *EDGAR* selection criteria as used and weighted for this particular grant competition Secretary's Fund for Innovation in Education Program. Note that the criteria as listed total 85 points with an additional 15 points that can be distributed as the agency (Secretary) decides; for this competition the "floating" 15 points will be added to the Plan of Operation, making this section now worth 30 points. Thus the outline for this proposal (for Part III or the Narrative—see Figures 6.6 and 6.7) is the *EDGAR* outline as provided in Figure 6.8.

Table of Contents

The Table of Contents serves multiple purposes. It shows the location of the key ingredients of the proposal but—and perhaps more importantly—it shows the proposal reader where to locate the specific elements that constitute the points for criteria that guide the rating of the proposal. If some section of the proposal should receive points, the Table of Contents should make extremely clear where that section is located.

The Table of Contents should be the page immediately behind the cover sheet, Part I (Form 424). It is convenient and greets the reader as soon as the reader turns the cover page. If you have remarks related to an entry on Form 424, those should be on the reverse (back) of Form 424 so the Contents are on the first right-hand page after the cover sheet.

A sample Table of Contents conforming to the 25-page request is shown in Figure 6.9. This Contents section corresponds to the grant application shown in Figures 6.7 and 6.8. Note that because the Narrative (Part III) is supposed to be approximately 25 pages, the Certifications/Assurances are put ahead of the Narrative and designated with lower-case Roman numerals. Another proposal writer

Figure 6.7. Details of Suggestions for Preparing the Narrative for the Department of Education Grant Competition[1]

PART III — NARRATIVE

Before preparing the Narrative, an applicant should read carefully the Application Notice describing the priorities and selection criteria used to evelute applications.

The Narrative should encompass each function or activity for which funds are being requested and should

1. Begin with one-page Abstract; include statements about
   (i) the need for the project,
   (ii) the proposed plan of operation, and
   (iii) the project's significance and intended outcomes.

2. Describe the proposed project in light of each of the selection criteria (see Figure 6.8) in the order in which the criteria are listed in the Application Notice.

3. Include any other pertinent information that might be useful in reviewing the application.

The Secretary strongly requests the applicant to limit the Application Narrative to no more than 25 double-spaced, typed pages (on one side only), including appendixes, although the Secretary will consider applications of greater length. The Department has found that successful applications under this program meet this page limit.

[1]Note the requirement for an abstract and the strong suggestion for page limitations.

Figure 6.8. *EDGAR* Selection Criteria as Used and Weighted for the 2000 Secretary's Fund for Innovation in Education Program

(a) **How This Section Works**

(1) If a discretionary grant program does not have implementing regulations, the Secretary uses the criteria in this section to evaluate applications for new grants under the program.
(2) The maximum score for all of these criteria is 100 points.
(3) The maximum score for each criterion is indicated in parentheses.

(b) **The Criteria**

(1) *Meeting the purposes of the authorizing statute.* (30 points) The Secretary reviews each application to determine how well the project will meet the purpose of the stature that authorizes the program including consideration of—
   (i) The objectives of the project; and
   (ii) How the objectives of the project further the purposes of th authorizing statute.
(2) *Extent of need for the project.* (20 points) The Secretary reviews each application to determine the extent to which the project meets specific needs recognized in the statute that authorizes the program, including consideration of—
   (i)   The needs addressed by the project;
   (ii) How the applicant identified those needs;
   (iii) How those needs will be met by the project; and
   (iv) The benefits to be gained by meeting those needs.
(3) *Plan of operation.*✻ (15 points) The Secretary reviews each application to determine the quality of the plan of operation for the project, including —
   (i)   The quality of the design of the project;
   (ii) The extent to which the plan of management is effective and ensures proper and efficient administration of the project;
   (iii) How well the objectives of the project relate to the purpose of the program;

   (iv) The quality of the applicant's plan to use its resources and personnel to achieve each objective;
   (v)   How the applicant will ensure that project participants who are otherwise eligible to participate are selected without regard to race, color, national origin, gender, age, or handicapping condition; and
   (vi) For grants under a program that requires the applicant to provide an opportunity to participation of students enrolled in private schools, the quality of the applicant's plan to provide that opportunity.
(4) *Quality of key personnel.* (7 points)
   (i) The Secretary reviews each application to determine the quality of key personnel the applicant plans to use on the project, including —
       (A) The qualifications of the project director (if one is to be used);
       (B) The qualifications of each of the other key personnel to be used in the project;
       (C) The time that each person referred to in paragraph (b)(4)(i)(A) and (B) will commit to the project; and
       (D) How the applicant, as part of its nondiscriminatory employment practices, will ensure that its personnel are selected for employment without regard to race, color, national origin, gender, age, or handicapping condition.
   (ii) To determine personnel qualification under paragraphs (b)(4)(i)(A) and (B), the Secretary considers —
       (A) Experience and training in fields related to the objectives of the project; and
       (B) Any other qualifications that pertain to the quality of the project.

(5) *Budget and cost effectiveness.* (5 points) The Secretary reviews each application to determine the extent to which —
   (i) The budget is adequate to support the project; and
   (ii) Costs are reasonable in relation to the objectives of the project.
(6) *Evaluation plan.* (5 points) The Secretary reviews each application to determine the quality of the evaluation plan for the project, including the extent to which the applicant's methods of evaluation —
   (i) Are appropriate to the project; and
   (ii) To the extent possible, are objective and produce data that are quantifiable.

(Cross-reference: See 34 CFR 75.59 Evaluation by the grantee.)

(7) *Adequacy of resources.* (3 points) The Secretary reviews each application to determine the adequacy of the resources that the applicant plans to devote to the project, including facilities, equipment, and supplies.

(c) **Weighting the Criteria***

(15 points) The Secretary distributes an additional 15 points among the criteria listed in paragraph (b) of this section. The Secretary indicates in the application for the program how these 15 points are distributed.

*For purposes of this competition, the 15 additional points will be added to the Plan of Operation for a possible total of 30 points.

might have made the Certifications/Assurances into an Appendix. Note the cross-referenced sections (Budget Summary and Detail, pp. v-vii and the Narrative on Budget and Cost-Effectiveness, p. 19).

Figure 6.9. Example of a Table of Contents

Table of Contents

SAMPLE TABLE OF CONTENTS (for the program described in Figures 6.7 and 6.8 with an entry for each item that is eligible for POINTS as described in Figure 6.8).

Some proposals will not need a References Section. In the Appendix with Letters of Support and Participation, you can list the letters as "on file," because including 10-20 letters here will add unneeded bulk.

The Cover or Face Sheet

Part I of the proposal is usually a standard form that is used as the cover for the proposal. This is Form 424 or something similar. Take time to complete this carefully. You will identify the Federal Program. This will be the *CFDA* number; it may be preprinted or you may need to fill in the numbers. Use a good descriptive title. Include, where asked, the name of the person who knows the most about the project and proposal. This is the person the funding agency will contact for budget negotiations or if there are questions. Here you do not want the proposal-submitting agency's Chief Executive Officer who may know the project only by name—you want a person who can handle detailed questions. Follow instructions closely. This form is the agency's and the reader's first contact with your project. *First impressions count!*

Appendixes and Attachments

The Appendixes and Attachments are for supporting data. The program may call for a copy of your catalog or your IRS tax-exempt data. You may want to send along important letters or data to strengthen your application. Use the Appendixes wisely. Include only important and related materials. Refer to all Appendixes in the narrative. If there is a page limit for supporting information or for the total proposal, do **NOT** exceed it.

——Grant Tip——
Develop a clear, concise, and cogent Abstract that will "sell" your idea in 200-250 words.

Abstract

Now that you are finished, review the proposal carefully. Then develop a clear, concise, and cogent *Abstract* that will "sell" your idea in 200-250 words. You are now done, except for mailing or delivering the proposal *on time*.

A Research Proposal

Although this volume deals primarily with the project proposal, many of the ideas pertain also to research proposals. A couple of major differences are highlighted in Figure 6.10.

Figure 6.10. Primary Differences Between Project Proposal and
                Research Proposal

Project Proposal	Research Proposal
Director	Principal Investigator (PI)
Staff	Research Associates or Assistants
Objectives	Research Questions or Hypothesis
Evaluation	Actual Findings or Outcomes
Approach	Review of Research
	Theoretic and Conceptual Base
	Limitations
	Delimitations
	Design

In Conclusion

Write the proposal carefully. Treat it as if it were an article going
to a good publishing outlet with tough editors. The readers will be
thorough in reading and evaluating your work. Try to make the agency's
work easier by attending carefully to all elements of the proposal.

7

Components of a Foundation Proposal

Introduction

What do Emergency 911, the Hospice Movement, public libraries, pap smears, the polio vaccine, the invention of rocketry, *Sesame Street*, white lines on the highway, world hunger, and the yellow fever vaccine have in common? According to the Council on Foundations, all of these "great grants" came from private foundations and philanthropy (Council on Foundations, 2000).

The *Philanthropy News Digest* (2000) noted that in a report, *Foundation Giving Trends: Update on Funding Priorities, 2000 Edition,* "Giving grew by 22.2% in the latest year to $9.7 billion, while the number of grants rose 12.8% to 97,220. The growth resulted in increased support benefiting nonprofits in nearly every field and discipline." Further findings from this report noted "a record number of large grants [were awarded], including 350 of at least $25 million: 147 grants of at least $5 million; and 10 grants of at least $20 million."

According to Rebecca W. Rimel (1999), President and CEO of The Pew Trusts, "With the federal government beating a retreat, philanthropy is feeling increasing pressure to fill the void in health care, social services, education, the environment, and the arts" (p. 4). Rimel also noted that,

> In 1995 foundations gave $10.4 billion to the nonprofit sector. That is a lot of money, but minuscule compared with the $241 billion provided in 1995 by the federal government to states and localities for social programs alone and the nearly $143 billion contributed by individuals. Against these numbers, even the more than $213 million awarded by trusts in 1998 seems barely significant. (p. 4)

Budget squeezes resulting from maintaining aging physical plants, higher operating costs, and a growing need for research and services to underserved populations have created a growing demand from individuals and nonprofit organizations for resources and information about the best way to secure external funding. This demand is coming from both ends of the spectrum: requests for large grant awards and for relatively small grants. Kraft (1999) noted,

> It is often true that numerous smaller "mini-grants" that exist are overlooked in favor of the more substantial allocations. Not all teachers, however, need to make application for the large grants. Smaller grants, alternatively, range in available funds from a few hundred to a (very) few thousand dollars. They are ideal and many times more accessible to the . . . teacher in need of only a few hundred dollars to fund an innovative idea (p. 57).

One of the first questions most individuals who are seeking monetary support ask is, "Who might give me money to fund this idea?" That is a logical question. There are many resources, and we recommend that for smaller monetary amounts (under $25,000) you look at foundations as a starting point.

This chapter deals with obtaining smaller foundation grants ranging from mini-grants to $25,000. Applying for foundation grants that exceed this amount, in our opinion, in many cases can be very similar to submitting a federal grant proposal; and the process would be much the same as that outlined in other chapters. Therefore, this chapter deals exclusively with the relatively smaller foundation grant proposals.

This chapter also presents some important aspects of understanding foundation funding. The chapter outlines some of the major differences between foundation funding and federal funding, outlines six steps to getting funded (Brewer & Hollingsworth, 2001), and provides helpful information about obtaining foundation funding.

How Do Foundation Proposals Differ From Federal Grant Proposals?

Although there are some similarities between writing a proposal for federal grant monies and writing for foundation funding, there are some differences. According to Sliger (1998), "The procedures in small grant acquisition differ in several ways from those for obtaining large grants. For instance, small grants usually require much less time and effort than do large grants" (p. 10). Sliger also noted that the best bet for grants may be those that are local and that a proposal may not

Figure 7.1. Differences Between Federal Grant Proposals and Foundation Proposals ($1,000-$25,000)

	Federal	Foundations
Proposal Length	20+ pages	± 10 - 15 pages
Submission Requirements	Rigid time deadline	More flexible, often no deadline (typically)
Evaluation Requirements	Point-based and almost always peer reviewed	Director may screen first, then submit to board for consideration.
Award or Funding Period	Can be up to 4 or 5 years	Usually short-term, 1 year or less
Notification	Can take up to 6 months; required to notify you regardless of outcome	If funded they usually call. If not funded they may provide you with written notification, but some may not
Reporting Requirements	Vary, but usually very detailed; annual performance reports required	Usually require one short report at the end of the project
Personal Relations and Contact	Limited, usually rare	Expected, encouraged, usually required

be necessary in order to get smaller grant. A "letter of request" may be all that is needed.

Additional differences between submitting a federal grant proposal and submitting a foundation grant proposal are outlined in Figure 7.1 and are provided for those experienced federal grant writers who need to be aware of these basic differences. The transition from writing for federal grants to writing for foundation grants should not be difficult if the basic differences are considered.

According to Miller (1995), "There is no better deal in the nonprofit sector than grants. Yet many grants go unsolicited because of several major misconceptions" (p. 17). These misconceptions include things such as difficulty in grants administration and the level

—— **Grant Tip** ——

There is no better deal in the nonprofit sector than grants.

of competition in the grants arena. Miller went on to say, "the wise administrator views grants as 'venture capital'. . . . grants enable the administrator to launch new or to expand ongoing programs that, in turn, will generate critically needed new revenues" (p. 17).

Types of Private-Sector Funding

Corporate donations are just one type of private-sector funding that may be considered by nonprofit organizations and individuals who are seeking funding. Other types include federated funding (United Way), fees for services, foundation grants, fundraising events, individual donors, and profitmaking businesses.

Many excellent resources are available through public libraries, bookstores, and the Internet that explain and explore other types of private sector funding in more detail.

What Is a Foundation?

Simply stated, a foundation is a nonprofit organization that supports charitable activities. Foundations usually are created with endowments, or money given by individuals, families, or corporations. The income earned from investing the endowments is used to make grants. The Foundation Center (1996-1997) has defined a foundation as "a nonprofit, nongovernmental organization with a principal fund or endowment of its own which maintains or aids charitable, educational, religious, or other activities serving the public good, primarily by making grants to other nonprofit organizations" (p. xi).

Now that you have narrowed your focus to foundations, you need a clear understanding of the different types of foundations. Knowing and understanding the different types of foundations will assist you in your search for funding. Foundations can be divided into several categories: (a) private foundations, (b) community foundations, (c) operating foundations, (d) corporate foundations, and (e) grant-making public charities. Figure 7.2 provides examples of each type of foundation.

In addition to knowing the types of foundations, it is important to understand the types of support that are commonly available for nonprofit organizations. According to the Applied Research and Development Institute there are four categories of support for nonprofit organizations. These categories are outlined in Figure 7.3.

—— **Grant Tip** ——

Foundation guidelines will vary slightly, so it is critical when approaching foundations and writing proposals that you recognize and respect these individual differences.

Figure 7.2. Types of Foundations With Examples

Types	Examples
Private Foundations	The Frist Foundation J. Paul Getty Trust Bill and Melinda Gates Foundation The Andrew W. Mellon Foundation Alfred P. Sloan Foundation
Community Foundations	Foundation for the Mid-South Foundation for the Carolinas San Antonio Area Foundation The Oregon Community Foundation Boston Foundation
Operating Foundations	The Mustard Seed Foundation The Century Foundation Carnegie Endowment for International Peace Alcoholic Beverage Medical Research Foundation The Century Foundation
Grantmaking Public Charities	American Association of University Women American Hotel Association National Music Foundation Schwab Fund for Charitable Giving The Kristi Yamaguchi Always Dream Foundation
Corporate Grantmakers	AT&T Foundation ConAgra, Inc. Eastman Kodak Company Kmart Corporation Motorola, Inc.

Six Steps to Getting Funding

Six essential steps to funding include (a) identifying your need, (b) getting preapproval, (c) identifying sources of funding, (d) contacting sources, (e) writing a proposal, and (f) submitting your proposal. These steps provide a useful framework for responding to most foundation grant applications—specifically mini-grant applications and those under $25,000. Foundation guidelines will vary slightly, so when approaching foundations and writing proposals you must recognize and respect these individual differences.

Figure 7.3. Type of Foundation Support Commonly Available for Nonprofit Organizations

—— **Grant Tip** ——
One of the key differences between those who get funding for their ideas and those who don't can best be characterized as a driving force—an almost obsessive passion about their idea(s).

Operating (General Support). Covers costs of running the organization to meet community needs.

- Contributions from individuals (annual funds)
- Foundation and corporate grants
- Earned income
- Interest from endowment

Special Projects. Used to start up a new program or to fund a project with a limited time frame.

- Foundation and corporate grants
- Government agencies
- Individuals

Capital/Equipment. Used to build or renovate a physical plant, purchase land, or purchase major equipment.

- Capital campaigns
- Major gifts
- Foundations, corporations, government agencies

Endowment

- Principal held as long-term investment while income is used for operations.
- Individuals (planned gifts)
- Capital/Endowment campaigns

Source: Applied Research and Development Institute

Step 1. Identifying Your Need

Let's say that you need extra funds to enhance your middle-school classroom's curriculum so that you can spark a real interest in rocket science. You realize that the funds are simply not available through your school's budget or from your district to provide each student with a rocket-building kit, to purchase some videotapes that will significantly extend the textbook, and to take your students on an all-day field trip to the closest space and air museum. You realize that these things are needed for you to provide your students with an optimum learning experience. However, you also realize that your school board doesn't necessarily see things your way.

One of the key differences between those who get funding for their ideas and those who don't can best be characterized as a driving force—an almost obsessive passion about their idea(s) that make some grant seekers persistent in the search. Seldom do these individuals just find extra money, nor do they receive telephone calls from strangers asking them if they could use an extra $5,000 for the school year. Plain and simple, most who get funded ask for the funds by writing a proposal. Until you put pen to paper, chances are that you will not get the funds you want for your rocket-building unit. Rejection usually doesn't deter these individuals. Because of their passion for their idea or project, they are willing to ask over and over again.

Step 2. Getting Preapproval

Getting approval from your own organization before beginning to search for funding sources may head off embarrassing or potentially damaging funding conflicts (Brewer & Hollingsworth, 2001, p. 124). If you do not know your organization's policies for requesting external funds, by all means ask before you go out on the proverbial limb. Doing so is a sign of professional courtesy and could prevent your being in an embarrassing situation later.

A common occurrence in larger organizations like a university that has many departments is for one department to request funds from XYZ Foundation only to find out later that the university's top official has been courting the same foundation for months for a major contribution. If several of the university's departments are requesting funds from the XYZ Foundation, officials could see this as excessive or even worse, disorganized. It could easily jeopardize the larger donation from which all departments or students might ultimately benefit. Before you approach a foundation, you should take into consideration questions such as your agency or institutional procedures for seeking external funding, channels your proposal must go through for approval and how long this usually takes, where the new program will be housed, and the procedures for handling indirect costs.

———**Grant Tip**———
If you do not know your organization's policies for requesting external funds, by all means ask before you go out on the proverbial limb.

Step 3. Identifying Sources of Funding

The Foundation Center

One comprehensive source for information on foundations is The Foundation Center. Perhaps you live near one of their libraries located in New York; Washington, DC; Atlanta; Cleveland; or San Francisco. These sites provide access to periodicals, free educational programs, and fee-based training programs. There are many other places from which to obtain foundation information. Check at your local public library, or the nearest college or university library. The Internet has a wealth of information, including online directories and multiple electronic databases, which are relatively easy to use and provide a wide range of useful information.

What are some "areas of interests" that foundations fund? The list is long, according to the Foundation Center. In a recent Foundation Center publication index there were over 300 areas of interests listed, including education, health, art, social services, and technology. However, some of the lesser-known areas of interest were also listed, including rural development, voluntarism promotion, peace, folk arts, and nonprofit management. Chances are that for whatever project or idea you are promoting, there is a foundation to match your idea.

What and who determine a foundation's funding decisions? Ferguson (1996) noted that "foundations and corporations differ in how they establish their funding priorities. Foundations often rely on the personal bent of their trustees, while corporations follow their business interests" (p. 12). Regardless of a foundation's interest(s), it is not wise to seek funds for your class rocket science project from a foundation that clearly only funds community healthcare projects.

Prewriting Checklist

There are several important steps to be taken prior to beginning to write your proposal. First, determine exactly what/why you need funds and write it down: for example, to provide a comprehensive rocket science project for 150 middle-school students. Next, determine exactly how much you will need in grant funds to provide the materials and services. Write down what you anticipate that you will need and how much you anticipate it will cost: a preliminary budget. There are numerous considerations when thinking about a budget. Gitlin and Lyons (1996) suggested some questions to be asked during the budget-writing stage, including, what are your organization's fringe benefit and travel reimbursement rates? Figure 7.4 shows some questions and prewriting considerations.

Once you have gathered this preliminary information, seek support for the ideas from your supervisor. Now you are ready to contact the foundation for a copy of the annual report and grant

—— Grant Tip ——
Chances are that for whatever project or idea you are promoting, there is a foundation to match your idea.

Figure 7.4. Some Prewriting Considerations

- Salary schedule of your organization/institution?
- What is your organization's fringe benefits package?
- Can I give stipends?
- What is the indirect cost rate?
- How do I handle cash donations?
- What is the procedure for petty cash expenditures and reimbursements?

application form(s). Carefully read everything you receive, highlighting important information. A simple prewriting checklist will enable you to see readily if a foundation may be a good match. Figure 7.5 is a sample of a prewriting checklist. Be sure your donor research is current, because foundations' areas of interests may change from time to time. You cannot assume that because ABC Foundation funded a HIV/Aids Community Forum last year that 3 years from now this will be one of the foundation's areas of interests. Furthermore, you cannot assume that foundations continue forever. In a 1996-1997 publication, The Foundation Center reported that 27 foundations recently terminated or dissolved.

Many foundations limit their awards to organizations. Although there may be exceptions to this from time to time, the number of grants awarded to individuals are usually rare in comparison to those awarded to organizations. Individual grants when awarded are generally for research or training activities.

Step 4. Contacting Sources

Once you have determined that a foundation represents a solid match with your interests and ideas, contact the foundation. Ask what the foundation's preferred method of contact is if it is not clearly stated in the written materials. Generally, initial contacts may be one of three types: telephone, visit to the office, or a brief written preproposal or letter of inquiry that may be mailed, faxed, or e-mailed. Proposal development experts generally agree on two things: (a) The importance of establishing personal relationships is one of the basic differences between securing federal and foundation funds, and (b) securing foundation funds and finding a perfect match is critical. Always put your best foot forward and remember the adage, "First impressions are the most important." Common sense and intuition are

——**Grant Tip**——
Creating a simple prewriting checklist will enable you to see if a foundation may be a good match for your idea.

Figure 7.5. Prewriting Checklist

Name of Foundation	ABC Foundation	MNO Foundation	XYZ Foundation
Purpose	Art Music Minorities	HIV/AIDS	Pre-College Higher Education Minority Education Environment Concerns
Areas of Interests	Fellowships Scholarships	Research	General/operating Support Scholarships
Limitations	Iowa organ- izations only	No grant to individuals No loans	No grants to individuals No construction or building or for endowment funds
Application Procedures	Application form required	No application form	Common application/ budget accepted
Due Dates	4 wks. prior to quarterly board meeting	None	1 month prior to twice- annual board meeting
Contact Information	Letter only	Letter only	Proposal
Final Notification	3 months	Unknown	Upon receipt of pro- proposal
Other Information	Submit 3 copies	Must submit annual re- port	Board meets as needed Spring and fall meet- ings are when they consider proposals

also important! For each foundation, you should record a mailing address, telephone number, web address, date of initial contact, to whom you spoke, and the outcome of the conversation.

Heezen (1991) reported "that the chances for success are increased by over 300% through the preproposal contact" (p. 63). Consider several important elements when making this all-important contact. First, make sure that your needs match those of the funder. Ask for tips on ways that could make your proposal more appealing to the foundation. Listen. Listen carefully, and read the foundation's materials for details. Then carefully follow the directions. If you have any concerns about budgeting, try to get an experienced individual to give you some pointers on critical elements that need to be included. Brewer and Hollingsworth (2001) noted, "Before you make your first call, spend some time rehearsing what you plan to say. It might be helpful for you to jot down the important points that you want to include in your introduction. Always have a pen and paper close by so you can write down important names, titles, addresses, telephone numbers, submission dates, and other pertinent information" (p. 127). Figure 7.6 outlines seven tips Brewer and Hollingsworth provided for making contact with potential grant givers.

Stowe (1995) also noted the importance of agency contacts: "The perfect proposal is a document that builds on your personal contacts at the foundation. In addition to clearly and concisely communicating about your program, outcomes, and methods of evaluation, it also speaks to the heart" (p. 28).

Figure 7.6. Tips for Contacting Potential Grant Givers

• Be on your best professional behavior by being polite and courteous.
• Avoid using a speaker telephone. Using a speaker telephone is annoying and often appears too impersonal.
• Be brief and to the point. The offices of many charitable institutions are understaffed, and the employees are very busy. They appreciate callers who are clear and concise.
• Find out the name and preferred title of the person you speak with. Keep detailed records of whom you spoke with and when.
• Ask the individual to send you any printed information about his or her organization and its policy for making donations or contributions. Usually this will include some type of brief outline or description that you should follow in requesting funding.
• If you are supposed to call back, be sure to find out the best time to do so. You will save time and avoid appearing pushy or unorganized.
• Thank the individual for allowing you to submit your proposal for consideration, and act quickly.

Source: Brewer & Hollingsworth. (2001).

Step 5. Writing a Proposal

Letters of Inquiry

A foundation may request that you provide a "Letter of Inquiry," a type of pre-proposal. On the other hand, some foundations discourage preliminary letters of inquiry. You must read the literature to see what the foundation prefers.

Let's assume that the foundation you have selected requires a Letter of Inquiry: Foundations receive many such letters; make yours stand out. Do not underestimate this step because you must first get your idea past this stage to move to the next round. Inquiry letters should follow all of the basics of technical letter writing: be free of erasures, have perfect spelling, and be grammatically correct. According to Reif-Lehrer (1995), if there are no specific instructions, you may want to consider "writing the letter from the point of view of the opportunity the agency has in supporting your project, *not* how their funding will fill *your* needs" (p. 315).

Deborah Koch, Director of Foundation Relations at Massachusetts University, Amherst coordinates a university-wide program for foundation fundraising that focuses on projects and programs in support of the University's research, academic, and community service priorities. Koch (2000) provided the following tips to make your proposal more attractive to a foundation. You need to convince your prospective funder that

- Funding your project will benefit many people in need. Foundations want to change the world for the better but do not have the resources to meet all needs. Show them how far their investment will go with your project.

- What you propose is novel, a new way of looking at things, and shows exciting promise. Foundations want to be associated with new, cutting-edge work, especially if it becomes a standard by which others operate or if it changes policy in a way that supports their targeted constituencies and issues.

- Your work will be done collaboratively with local government, nonprofit and community groups, higher education, and/or business.

- Your project is inclusive of those you seek to help, either in planning, directing, or execution.

- Your organization has made its own investment into the project. The nonprofit best shows the value it places on a project by the degree to which it tries to make it happen.

- The outcomes of your work are replicable so as to benefit many more. Foundations want their investments to go as far as possible.

- You can demonstrate that the work will be continued after the foundation grant has ended (p. 18).

Figure 7.7 identifies some additional tips that you should remember as you write a letter of inquiry.

Some agencies require a fairly formal pre-proposal. These pre-proposals are evaluated, and only a small number of the proposers may be invited to submit a full proposal. Making this "first cut" does not ensure success in response to submission of the full proposal.

Figure 7.7. Tips for Writing Letters of Inquiry to Foundations

- Be clear, concise, cogent, and correct.
- Use standard English. Proofread your letter carefully.
- Ask someone not familiar with your idea to provide a critical analysis.
- Stick to one page. A separate page for your project summary may be appropriate.
- Use the correct names and titles of individuals at the foundation.
- Use current references or resources if you are going to cite these in your letter. Make sure that any documentation, charts, or tables directly support your case. Do not add statistics just because you think that they are impressive.
- Be clear the way in which your idea is a perfect match for the foundation.
- State how much money you are requesting.
- Be precise (name, address, telephone number, fax number, and e-mail address) about how you contact the foundation.
- Make your writing interesting and creative. Remember: Foundations may get hundreds of letters. You want yours to stand out—not bore the reader!

———**Grant Tip** ———
"If instructions are unclear, call the foundation and ask for an explanation."

Make a simple outline for your letter, from a short introduction to a closing paragraph. Figure 7.8 is an example of a Letter of Inquiry.

Letter Proposals

It is not uncommon for foundations to request a letter proposal. In other words, there is no formal application package required, as for a federal proposal. This should be clearly evident in their proposal guidelines. You may be asked to attach a copy of your organization's annual budget and other fiscal-related items. Letter proposals should be kept to around five pages.

Figure 7.8. Example of a Letter of Inquiry

March, 15, 2001

Ms. Anna B. Goode, Director
XYZ Foundation
123 Corporate Place
Anywhere, US 11111

Dear Ms. Adams:

I am writing to inquire about the XYZ Foundation's interest in funding a class science project for 300 middle school students for Spring Semester. I am specifically interested in obtaining $10,350 to provide these students with a holistic experience, including actually building their own rocket, having competitions for awards, supplemental resource materials, and a culminating field trip to the nearby Space Camp facilities.

My major objectives are to spark these students' interest in science as a career and to foster their desire to become lifelong learners. Secondarily, I want to nurture their spirit of competition, teamwork, collaborative learning, and higher order thinking skills.

As a teacher in the Central City School District, it appears that I am eligible to receive a grant from the XYZ Foundation. I have been fortunate to have the cooperation of several other agencies and partners that have already made commitments: the local board of education will provide a substitute teacher for me to chaperone the field trip, six parents have volunteered to assist us during our final rocket competitions as well as chaperone our field trip to the Space Camp, and the Parent-Teacher Organization has offered to provide incentives for participation.

I am excited about having the XYZ Foundation provide the additional support that is necessary for these students to have an unforgettable experience at this very impressionable age. I sincerely hope that you will give this request careful consideration. Should you require additional information regarding this request, please contact me at 111-1111. I look forward to hearing from you in the very near future.

Sincerely,

Laurel Simms, Teacher   Jeff Simon, Superintendent of Education
Central City Middle School   Central City Board of Education

Glass (1995) offered some insight from a foundation's viewpoint:

> Double-check all figures in the project budget. If you catch an addition error, you'll avoid my embarrassing phone call to ask why your summer internships costs $3,425 on page 14 and $3,388 on the budget page. Also—please—follow all submission instructions exactly. "Submit two copies" doesn't mean send four copies. "Send your IRS 501(c)(3) tax letter" doesn't mean send a letter from your lawyer saying that you're a tax-exempt institution. If instructions are unclear, call the foundation and ask for an explanation. (p. 26)

You will want to include some basics in the letter proposal: (a) brief introduction, (b) explanation of your project, (c) explanation of your need for the grant, (d) target population, (e) how you meet the eligibility criteria, (f) any partners, and (g) a contact name and number. You may want to include, or may be asked, how you are going to evaluate your project. Regarding the writing style or tone, Stowe (1995) noted, "Be brief, concise, and compelling. Do make your case with economy and logic, but don't be afraid to appeal to the reader's heart. Go ahead and use personal, dramatic examples of how your project will change the world" (p. 28). Also mention any attachments. Figure 7.9 is an example of a letter proposal.

On a final note, it stands to reason to learn as much as you possibly can about a funder as soon as you can, preferably prior to writing. Be sure to tailor your proposal to the funder's interests.

A Word About Common Applications and Common Budgets

There is a growing national trend to establish "common" application and budget procedures and forms. This is similar to the movement by federal agencies to standardize proposal submission requirements by using boilerplate forms. The Foundation Center has noted that the following groups of grantmakers are using common applications and common budgets:

- Associated Grantmakers of Massachusetts
- Association of Baltimore Area Grantmakers
- Connecticut Council for Philanthropy

Grant Tip

The obvious ramifications of such a movement as common applications and boilerplate forms are simplicity, saving time, and convenience both for the grantee and the grantor.

Figure 7.9. Example of a Letter Proposal

March 15, 2001

Ms. Anna B. Goode, Director
XYZ Foundation
123 Corporate Place
Anywhere, US 11111

Dear Ms. Goode:

Thank you for sharing information about the XYZ Foundation's areas of interests for funding supplemental educational activities in Central City. The Foundation's interest in enriching the educational opportunities for our communities' children is well documented and has helped hundreds of our youth enjoy activities that otherwise would not have been available to them.

The XYZ Foundation is a perfect match to help support the rocket science activities I want to provide for the middle school science students during the next school year. I have reviewed some of the recent projects that XYZ Foundation has generously supported in our area, and I am confident that this request will further your goal of providing enriching educational experiences for students in Central City—especially those targeted for math and science.

As we discussed, students rarely have an opportunity to participate actively in a rocket-building science unit that provides them with a holistic approach including actually building their own rocket, competitions with awards, supplemental teaching materials, and a culminating field trip to the nearby Space Camp facilities. I have objectives and purposes for requesting this funding that I feel strongly supports your mission. First and foremost, I want to spark these students' interest in science as a career and to foster their desire to become lifelong learners. Second, I want to nurture their spirit of competition, teamwork, collaborative learning, and help them to develop higher order thinking skills.

Your support will allow me to open a whole new world to these middle school students. As you are aware, it is difficult to measure the impact that this opportunity will have on a child—perhaps a future Neil Armstrong or John Glenn!

As a teacher in the Central City School District, it appears that I am eligible to receive a grant from the XYZ Foundation. This project will require the cooperation of several other agencies and partners that I have already received commitments from: the local board of education that will provide a substitute teacher for me to chaperone the field trip, six parents have volunteered to assist us during our final rocket competitions as well as chaperone our field trip to the Space Camp, and the Parent-Teacher Organization has offered to provide awards for participation.

I am excited about the possibilities that this rocket-building unit has for our middle school science students. This opportunity will provide for them enhanced learning possibilities that they can otherwise only imagine from reading a textbook.

Should you require additional information regarding this request, please contact me at 111-1111. I look forward to hearing from you after your Board of Directors meet in April.

Sincerely,

Laurel Lee Simms, Teacher   Jeff Simon, Superintendent of Education
Central City Middle School   Central City Board of Education

- Council of Michigan Foundations
- Delaware Valley Grantmakers
- Grantmakers of Western Pennsylvania
- Minnesota Common Grant Applicant Form
- National Network of Grantmakers
- New York/New Jersey Area Common Application Form
- Rochester Grantmakers Forum
- Washington Regional Association of Grantmakers
- Wisconsin Common Application Form

As the use of common applications and common budget forms grows, so does the list of foundations that currently accept them. The Associated Grantmakers of Massachusetts reported that as of January 13, 2000, there were over 70 foundations accepting the common applications, including The Gillette Company, IBM/Lotus, Digital Equipment Corporation, Bell Atlantic Foundation, and the Anna B. Stearns Charitable Foundation. With the growth and development of the Internet, this number can be expected to grow.

Obvious ramifications of such a movement as common applications and boilerplate forms are simplicity, saving time, and convenience both for the grantee and the grantor. However, hundreds of foundations do not require any formal application. Their guidelines may simply state that applicants should submit the following:

——— **Grant Tip** ———
All contacts with foundations after your proposal has been rejected should always reflect the highest professional respect.

1. Name, address, and phone number of organization
2. Contact person
3. Detailed description of project and amount of funding requested
4. Brief history of organization and description of its mission
5. Qualifications of key personnel
6. Copy of current year's organizational budget and/or project budget
7. Listing of additional sources and amount of support
8. Listing of board of directors, trustees, officers and other key people and their affiliations
9. Copy of IRS Determination Letter
10. A cover letter and a 500-word project summary

The full proposal should include items 3-9 above with no more than a 5-page description of the specific project. The key is to follow whatever guidelines are provided and to provide exactly what is requested—nothing more; nothing less.

If you are using a common application, write your proposal based on the information that has been provided by the foundation. As stated earlier, one of the major differences in writing a federal grant proposal and writing a foundation grant proposal is its length. This may be viewed in two ways: Your first reaction to writing a foundation proposal might be, "Okay, I can handle five pages." Yet many proposal writers find that writing a shorter proposal may actually be more difficult, since your writing must be absolutely clear, concise, and to the point. The challenge of writing a five-page proposal is getting your point across within a limited page restriction.

Most of the other helpful hints found in Chapter 9 apply to writing a foundation proposal. The section titles may vary, but generally you will be providing similar information as for a federal proposal. You simply will not elaborate to the extent you might in responding with a 50-page proposal. The same writing tips apply: spelling, grammar, format, ease in reading, clear, compelling, creativity, cogency, and making sure to fit your ideas into the foundation's funding priorities.

Gitlin and Lyons (1996) identified six major weaknesses reviewers of allied health grants found. For example, the grants reviewed required a Plan for Self-Sufficiency. However, half (50%) of the grants reviewed did not even include this section in their proposal. Read the guidelines carefully and include every component. Another often-cited weakness, also confirmed by Gitlin and Lyon's study, indicated that over 20% of the proposals reviewed had objectives that were not clear.

A copy of a funded proposal, will definitely give you an advantage. If you know someone who has received funding from the foundation, ask if he or she would share a copy with you. Typically, foundations do not provide copies of funded proposals. However, as you begin your research, do not overlook the Internet. Sample proposals are frequently found on sites for grantseekers, for example, http://www.seacoastweb.com/resource/grnt-app.htm (accessed on 5/6/00). Alternatively, check with a local nonprofit organization to see if employees there would be willing to share a sample proposal so that you can see what an actual proposal looks like.

Step 6. Submitting Your Proposal

John E. Marshall, III, President of the Kresge Foundation in Troy, Michigan provided this bit of information about submitting proposals:

> We put quite a bit of time into our policies and application procedures pamphlet. Why, then, do some applicants ignore it and call us to ask precisely the questions the pamphlet answers. And why do they send annual reports, case statements, and other unrelated documents instead of assembling a comprehensive narrative as requested? (The Foundation Center)

Glass (1995), a foundation representative, offered these words of wisdom about submitting proposals:

> Be punctual. This obviously means adhering to any deadlines for submitting your proposal. . . .Send your proposal well ahead of deadline day. Unlike government agencies, most foundations don't wait until the deadline to open all the sealed proposals. Put yourself in our place and imagine which proposals get more personal attention: the five that arrive in the two weeks before the deadline or the 76 that arrive after 3 p.m. on the last day. (p. 26)

Based on the experiences of these two experts, it is important to follow the specific guidelines provided for submitting your proposal.

When considering where to submit a proposal, who to approach, when to submit, and other pertinent questions, we recommend that you *think positive! Children & Youth Funding Report* (CD Publication, March 15, 2000, p. 18) reported the following when it comes to *Persistence and Understanding Donor Keys to Generating Funds.* This article, written by Donna Butts, a fundraising consultant, noted that face-to-face meetings are the most effective means of raising money. Butts (2000) cites the following reasons why many people shy away from asking for money:

- Fear of rejection. Savvy fundraisers, says Butts, believe a " no is an entrée to yes," and give up only after the third "no."

- Fear of failure. Fundraisers need to learn not to take rejection personally.

- Feeling as though they are begging. Fundraisers need to understand they are asking the donor to become a partner in a successful, important program in their community, says Butts, "not to keep the lights on."

- Lack of confidence. Butts stresses the importance of believing in the mission of the program.
- Lack of preparation. Butts says one of the best ways of learning fundraising is to go with someone who really knows what he or she is doing and is good at it (p. 18).

Regarding donations Butts offered these suggestions:

- First, identify those constituencies deemed to be most receptive to their appeals for donations.
- Remember that the fundraising world revolves around people who have already given to charities, such as members of the board and organization management.
- The next promising targets are existing general donors and people with similar interests to the nonprofits. These include beneficiaries of the organization's work, politicians, community activists, civic centers and—perhaps the best target of the whole lot—seniors.
- Knowing why people donate is key to getting them to do the same for your organization.
- People give money to worthy causes because they agree with a group's mission.
- Public relations value, especially for companies and corporations.
- The feeling of guilt from some people, which makes them try to "buy their way into heaven."
- Some givers feel good when they know they are contributing to a good cause.
- The donor has a personal relationship with the group or with the issue the group addresses.
- Donations can count as a tax write-off. (p. 18)

Butts says groups should devise a broad list of potential donors, then map out a plan of approach. "Make linkages," she says. Every person affiliated with the organization should be asked, "Who do you know?" and "Who do you know that knows . . .?" (p. 18).

"May I apply for a grant via e-mail?" needs to be asked early in the proposal development stages. Some foundations, such as the Ford Foundation, will accept a proposal via e-mail, but the guidelines state a preference for receiving proposals through the mail. The Bell Atlantic Foundation, on the other hand, recently announced that beginning in 2000 it will accept proposals *only* via e-mail. CyberGrant$, a newly formed web-based grants management system noted, "Over 300 private and corporate grantmakers have signed up for a free trial of the company's grants management system since the site's launch in December, 1999" (CyberGrant$).

The Waiting Game/The Proposal Review Process

According to the Ford Foundation, "In 1998 the Foundation received 35,700 grant requests and made 2,007 grants. Of that number, 20% were first-time grant recipients" (Ford Foundation). On the other hand, the Grant Information Center reported, "This year's success rate was around 32%, meaning that one grant was awarded for every three submitted. That's an excellent success rate" (Ford Foundation). These two sets of figures emphasize the need to find a good match between *your* ideas and a foundation's priorities.

After submitting your proposal, you must wait to hear the decision of the reviewers. The waiting period varies from foundation to foundation. The foundation's guidelines may outline the expected or normal review procedures, giving a tentative time frame. For instance, the Ford Foundation guidelines stated, "Normally applicants may expect to receive within six weeks an indication of whether their proposal is within the Foundation's program interests and budget limitations" (Ford Foundation).

Not Funded? Don't Worry!

Foundations vary in how they notify an applicant that a proposal was not funded. Again, read the application guidelines. Some foundations will state, "no notification of negative decision." Some larger foundations with adequate staff write formal rejection letters. By all means, take rejections in stride. It is part of the finding-funding game. If the foundation provides you with feedback, keep a written copy of the suggestions so that in the future, should you reapply, you can refer to this information.

Contacts with foundations after your proposal has been rejected should always reflect the highest professional respect. It only hurts your chances of future funding if you appear defensive. Begin this contact by immediately thanking the foundation for considering your request and stating that you were disappointed that you were not funded. Then you may ask if they could provide you with any constructive feedback on how to improve your proposal should you decide to resubmit it at a later date. Glass (1995) noted, "Even though a perfect proposal can't guarantee a grant, your professional attention to each proposal will help create a productive, long-term relationship with the foundation's program staff" (p. 26).

Stowe's (1995) advice for those whose proposals were rejected was, "If you don't get backing, learn from your mistakes. Follow up with the foundation and learn how to improve your proposal. Ask whether (and when) you can try again" (p. 28).

You Got Funded! Now What?

Most of the project management strategies discussed throughout this book apply to the management of your grant, albeit on a smaller scale. If appropriate, take some photographs or get some local newspaper publicity for your project. Send this to the foundation that has funded your project. Be sure to thank your funding source. You never know when you may want to apply for another project.

Sliger (1998) noted, "Small grant acquisition can be fun and beneficial. It does require a little extra effort, but . . . oh, what a feeling of satisfaction you get from knowing that your students are experiencing something from your efforts. . . . Be kind. Remember, we all had to start somewhere" (p. 11).

Finally, remember that "there is no fairy godmother for proposal writers" (Hall, 1988, p. 164). It takes hard work but the rewards are usually well worth it.

8

Writing a Proposal

Introduction

The first seven chapters have introduced you to the preliminaries of grant proposal writing and the concepts of grants. This chapter will further assist you in understanding the process of writing a grant proposal—giving you the anatomy of a successful application. Chapter 10, "Reviewing a Funded Proposal," reviews in detail a successful grant application that was funded.

Application Procedures for Federal Grants

Before beginning your proposal, review *EDGAR* so that you are particularly familiar with the following subparts:

> Subpart C • How to Apply for a Grant
> Subpart D • How Grants Are Made
> Subpart E • What Conditions Must Be Met by a Grantee?
> Subpart F • What Are the Administrative Responsibilities of a Grantee?

After reading these sections, if you still have questions, call the contact person listed in the request for proposal (RFP) and request further clarification or information.

Prior to beginning your needs assessment, you should have written to the appropriate office of the United States Department of Education to request the application packet for the proposal you want to write.

Although technically called a request for proposal (RFP) packet if you are writing a contract, and an "application" packet if you are applying for a grant, both packets are referred to as RFPs by most proposal writers. The RFP contains all forms and application information for your proposal. Review the RFP in detail. Ensure that persons connected with the proposed project are aware of their roles and what will be expected of them in the project. Seek commitments from the decision makers at your institution regarding office space and furnishings, teaching space, and adequate time for implementation, among other things. Their prior commitments will avoid problems, and possible failure, later.

After you receive the RFP and determine that you have sufficient time and resources to develop a proposal, establish a time frame. Consider federal deadlines along with adequate time for your institution's procedures and the mechanics of preparing the physical document. Do not procrastinate. List your institution's procedures for submitting an application proposal. For example, at one institution, a pre-application form must be completed that notifies certain officers and personnel of the grantwriter's intent to submit a proposal. This procedure allows the institution's leaders to decide if the proposed project is in harmony with the institution's mission statement, philosophy, and projected plans. Determine which officers or persons at your institution need to review or approve your proposal. Then ensure that the appropriate people will be available for review and approval. For example, one of the authors painstakingly developed a very difficult proposal, only to meet with failure when the approving officer was absent and no other official of the institution would accept the responsibility for approving the document. These seem like small details, but such slip-ups due to lack of communication or advance planning can result in disappointment, lost time, and energy.

Allow ample time for typing or word processing your document. *Most proposals will be subjected to three or four rewrites.* Allow sufficient time for duplication. Always assume that the copy machine will break down as your document is being printed. Allow enough time for such emergencies and unexpected obstacles. Notify your duplication service a day or two in advance that you will soon bring them a sizeable document for duplication. This will allow them to plan their work schedule to accommodate your work.

Features of a Proposal

Your proposal is the document by which your proposed project will be evaluated and a decision made as to whether or not you will receive funding. It is the only vehicle the panel of readers can use to judge your ideas; everything you say in your proposal will make an impact on the readers. You want that impact to be positive and impressive. Let's look at some features that proposal writing experts

---

———Grant Tip———

After you receive the RFP and determine that you have sufficient time and resources to develop a proposal, establish a time frame. Consider federal deadlines along with adequate time for your institution's procedures and the mechanics of preparing the physical document. Do not procrastinate.

and the United States Department of Education personnel have identified as characteristic of a good proposal, a proposal that is likely to be funded.

1. Proposals that demonstrate strong institutional, local, and private sector commitments to the project seem to be favored. This sometimes takes the form of in-kind or cash contributions that increase the likelihood for project success.

2. Good proposals always have the total commitment and support of the sponsoring institution and any other institution that serves the same target population, purposes, or both. For example, if you are writing a proposal to serve migrant and seasonal farmworkers, as does the sample proposal in Chapter 10, seek the commitment and support of the State Migrant Council, the migrant education coordinator at your state education agency, the migrant directors of appropriate local school districts, and directors or consultants at other local agencies that serve migrants, such as employment centers, training projects, health organizations, and law enforcement units?

3. A component that describes continuous monitoring of the project and participants' performance is essential. The monitoring mechanism needs to allow for ongoing modifications of troublesome areas. Often personnel do not monitor or evaluate until near the end of the cycle or project year. This precludes adjustments that could have improved performance, and hence, outcomes.

4. Good proposals are so well defined and clear that any responsible staff person can effectively operate the project according to the instructions contained in it. Readers who review the narrative should feel that they could operate the project successfully by basing their management upon the instructions and descriptions.

5. An important feature of the proposal is its physical appearance. Narrow margins, small type (elite rather than pica), charts that have been reduced or are third or fourth generation copies, or dot matrix printing may result in the reader tiring quickly and exerting little effort to understand your project. Leave white space—that is, allow ample margins, use space-and-one-half or double-spaced text, and double-space between paragraphs (unless there are page limits or special instructions to the contrary). Make sure your copier prints clear, dark-print copies. Write in plain English. Avoid professional, academic, or technical jargon when possible.

———— **Grant Tip** ————
Make your document "reader friendly" by making it physically attractive and easy to read.

6. Check to see if the RFP forbids binders; if not, use one. If you put your document in a binder, ensure that the binder does not obscure any of the text. If you punch holes for a three-ring binder, be certain the text is not so close to the margin that you punch holes in it.

7. Most grants require the *Standard Face Sheet* (Form 424) as the proposal cover. This should be completed with care.

8. Begin each major section with an overview explaining what the reader will find in that section. End each section with a summary emphasizing major points. Include a comprehensive table of contents. Detail each criterion in the table. That way, the reader may refer to the *Table of Contents* and look up specific items. An attractive cover on your proposal should bear the name of the program in large letters, the sponsoring institution and its address, the *CFDA* number of the program, and the dates of the project.

9. If the project is to help participants improve their education or obtain employment, include specific sections to describe how the project will accommodate them. The following three are examples:

   a. United States Department of Education personnel prefer that project directors conduct follow-up on their participants. Thus, you should survey those who have completed your project to ascertain its effect on them and their careers, especially if they have continued their postsecondary education.

   b. A quality proposal provides incentives for academic achievement. This does not mean gifts or additional money but, rather, support systems such as a mentoring program, peer tutoring, individualized assistance in job placement or obtaining financial aid to continue post-secondary studies. Other incentives might include individual or small-group tutoring, special skill-building classes, and frequent seminars and workshops designed specifically to meet student needs.

   c. Proposals that emphasize and strengthen the basic and higher-level skills of project participants are well received. Such emphasis and strengthening lead to the participants' becoming independent of the project. When a project fosters participant dependency, participants find it very difficult to continue their pursuit of project goals. Strive to build independence and confidence among participants.

Review your rough draft to ensure that it reflects these characteristics of a good proposal.

Understanding a Request for Proposal (RFP)

A needs assessment is required by most but not all federal programs. Outline your project and convert your outline into a narrative that details what you propose to do. The RFP tells you how to focus your needs assessment. Some programs request specific information, whereas others do not. For example, for the proposal presented in Chapter 10, the program requests specific information regarding the number of migrant and seasonal farmworkers in the target area. The application packet often contains suggestions indicating where you can obtain the information requested and in what format it should be presented.

The next few pages describe the information contained in one application for grants packet provided by the United States Department of Education. The packet used for this discussion is the *Application for Grants Under the College Assistance Migrant Program (CAMP)*, provided by the Office of Elementary and Secondary Education.

Cover Letter of Application Package

Many packets begin with a "Dear Colleague" letter. This letter officially announces that applications for funding for a grants competition are being accepted. The letter generally indicates which rules apply to the program and in which *Federal Register* they were published. A critical part of the letter is the due or closing date for proposals. Be sure you meet the deadline criterion: *There is no such thing as a late proposal.* The closing date is also printed on the cover of the application packet. The letter usually contains the name and address of a person you may contact if you need further information.

——**Grant Tip**——
The "Dear Colleague" letter is your source of important dates and information.

Focusing on Purpose

The application packet contains a variety of valuable information. It lists the purpose for which grants are awarded. Write the purpose on a card and keep it in front of you as you write your proposal. As you consider objectives, ask yourself often, "How does an objective of this project relate to the program sponsoring the grant competition?" This will help keep the grant focused, eliminate extraneous material, and ensure that you fulfill not only local need but also the needs of the sponsoring office. For example, the purpose of the College Assistance Migrant Program (CAMP) is

> *To provide grants to institutions of higher education for projects that address the educational needs of migrant and seasonal farmworker students at the postsecondary level.*

Everything in a CAMP proposal must relate to this purpose.

——**Grant Tip**——
Relate each area of your proposal to the purpose of the program.

Review by State Education Agency (SEA)

Some federal programs require state review. The review may be by the state agency (e.g., education) or by the Single Point of Contact (SPOC). The application package provides the deadline for inter-governmental review comments, if such review and comments are required. Executive Order 12372—Intergovernmental Review—requires contact with the SPOC to find out about, and to comply with, the state's process under the Executive Order. If you plan a project to serve a population in states other than your own, notify the SPOC for each state and follow the procedures established in those states under the Executive Order. Most packets include a list of the SPOC for each state. If your state does not have a SPOC, send a copy for review to the appropriate office or person in your State Education Agency. Someone at the state level must have an opportunity to review and comment on your application proposal.

What is the SPOC? Basically, Executive Order 12372 provides a vehicle by which different agencies and departments of state are advised that you plan to submit a proposal, enabling them to coordinate other similar projects with yours. They may feel that your project will contribute major services to the proposed population or that it will duplicate or conflict with existing projects. Contact someone in your SPOC and discuss your proposal prior to writing it. This may provide you with valuable information to include in the proposal and it may save you negative comments from the SPOC reviewers.

You do not need to submit your completed proposal to the SPOC office prior to submitting it to the funding agency, although some agencies appreciate seeing an abstract of your proposal. After you have completed your proposal, send a copy to the SPOC. Write a *Letter of Transmittal* and include a copy of this letter in the copies of your proposals submitted to Washington, DC, as well as in the copy you send to the SPOC. Indicate in this letter the date by which comments from the SPOC must be received in Washington, DC, and the address where the comments must be sent. *This address is different from the address to which you will send your proposal.*

Remember, if *Executive Order 12372—Intergovernmental Review*—is in effect for the program you wish to establish, *you must submit your proposal to the Single Point of Contact for review.* Failure to do so may disqualify your application proposal. Even if there is no requirement for review, it may benefit you if you send copies of your proposal to state officials interested in your project.

Facts About Funding

The "Dear Colleague" letter also indicates the amount of funding Congress has appropriated for the fiscal year (FY) of the program, the estimated range of awards, the estimated average size of awards, and the estimated number of awards. Study this information carefully. For example, the appropriation for the CAMP program was only $4,000,000 for FY 2000. The *Estimated Range of Awards* for the CAMP program represented in Chapter 10 was $263,000 to $378,000. You can be sure that, with only $2,224,000 available, if your proposal significantly exceeds the Estimated Range of Awards, your chances of being funded will be reduced. The *Estimated Average Size of Awards* for the CAMP program is $324,000. You will stand a better chance of being funded if you submit a budget near this figure.

Pay particular attention to the *Estimated Number of Awards.* For the CAMP program, the United States Department of Education estimated that only five awards would be made. The competition would be extremely keen for this program. You need to write a nearly perfect proposal in order for it to be funded. A perfect CAMP proposal receives a total of 300 points from the review panel (100 points per reader). The proposal that appears in Chapter 10 received all 300 points. In contrast, other programs such as the Student Support Services, a part of the TRIO Programs, estimated that approximately 800 awards would be made. Competition, therefore, for a Student Support Services Program may not be nearly as keen as for the CAMP program.

The "Dear Colleague" letter also indicates the *Project Period,* or number of months for which a grant may be awarded. For example, the CAMP program is funded for up to 60 months. You probably will

———**Grant Tip**———
Pay particular attention to the Estimated Number of Awards.

always request funding for the maximum number of months allowable (and you must provide objectives and an estimated budget for that duration).

The last part of the letter lists the various regulations governing the program. Review these regulations. If your proposal is funded, you will be held accountable for following them even if you do not read them. Ignorance is not an excuse. Time spent studying the regulations will pay dividends later.

Use Care in Mailing

The application packet usually contains an entire page of mailing instructions. *Read them carefully.* Do not send your proposal to the wrong address. Obtain proof of mailing, and mail early enough in the day to ensure that your package does not receive the next day's postmark.

The mailing instructions provide the correct address for mailing your proposal. Use a colored highlighter and mark this address. Be sure to type it or write it clearly on the package containing your proposal.

Carefully review the acceptable proof of mailing. A private metered postmark or a mail receipt not dated by the U.S. Postal Service is usually not acceptable. This section of the packet also contains detailed information regarding applications that are hand delivered or delivered by courier service. Study these instructions carefully if you choose to send your proposal any way except through the mail. *Make sure the postmark the post office places on your package contains the current date.* Always send your proposal by registered mail or by an official courier mail service.

Rules and Regulations

Chapter 3 discussed the *Federal Register* and the *Code of Federal Regulations.* Review carefully the *Federal Register* that contains the rules and regulations governing your application. These Rules and Regulations are usually included in the application packet. These Rules and Regulations are your "bible." They contain all criteria the Secretary of Education uses to evaluate your proposal. If you do not address the criteria, your application will not be considered. *It is as simple as that.*

The Rules and Regulations may contain a section of Supplementary Information. Study this section with care. It sometimes offers

——Grant Tip——
Include a self-addressed label for federal personnel to mail the application package back to you.

valuable insights, such as the Department of Education's (or Congress's) rationale for including certain Rules and Regulations. The Rules and Regulations list the authority under which the program is funded and additional guidelines that apply. They provide special definitions of terms that apply to the program. A key section is titled *What Types of Services May Be Provided.* List the items that appear in this section and address each service listed in this section. For example, services that may or must be provided in a CAMP project include:

- Outreach and recruitment services.

- Supportive and instructional services such as

    —personal, academic, and career counseling

    —tutoring and academic skill-building instruction and assistance

    —assistance with special admissions

    —health services

    —other services as necessary to complete program.

- Assistance in obtaining student financial aid such as

    —stipends; scholarships; student travel; career-oriented work-study; books and supplies; tuition and fees; room and board; and other assistance.

- Housing support for on-campus living.

- Exposure to cultural events; academic programs; and other activities not usually available to migrant youth.

- Other support services as necessary.

This section tells you what the Department of Education expects a CAMP project to include. The review panel looks for references to these items. As you read Chapter 10 and the *Sample Proposal,* you will find each of the above services addressed in various ways.

Some Rules and Regulations also include services that *may not be included* in the application. Avoid including any expressly excluded services.

The section *What Must Be Included in an Application?* specifies items that, if omitted, may disqualify your proposal. For example, in the CAMP program, your application will be disqualified if you do not include a budget of at least $150,000 or a management plan that contains certain specified assurances and provisions.

Evaluation of Proposal by the Secretary of Education

——— **Grant Tip** ———

The most important part of the rules and regulations describes how the Secretary evaluates your application.

The most important part of the Rules and Regulations describes how the Secretary evaluates your application. It generally specifies exactly what the Secretary (i.e., the panel of readers) looks for and how many points each criterion is worth.

Usually an application is read and evaluated by three or more panel members. The makeup and duties of this panel are discussed in greater detail in Chapter 11, "Understanding How Grants Are Awarded." Each panel member studies the application and awards points for each section of the entire application. These points are averaged and your final score is between 1 and 100. If three readers evaluate the proposal and each gives your proposal the maximum score (100 points), the total would be 300 points.

Additional points may be awarded for the successful operation of a previously funded project. These points are designated as *prior experience points* or *points for prior performance*. Usually such points are not awarded by the panel of readers but rather by personnel in the United States Department of Education. For example, Congress mandated that CAMP projects be awarded up to 15 additional points for having operated a successful project. Specific criteria are usually provided to guide the Department in awarding these additional points. Prior experience points enable a successful existing project's application to earn up to 115 points, whereas the proposal from an institution that has never operated a CAMP project can earn only a maximum of 100 points. This serves to provide continuity; it also gives an advantage to existing projects and encourages administrators to operate high quality, successful projects.

An institution in Texas had operated a federally funded project for 12 years. This project was funded through yearly competitions, which means that a complete proposal had to be submitted each year. For 12 years the institution's application was successful. However, no prior experience points were awarded; all applications were awarded between 0 and 100 points. Unfortunately, even though the Texas institution had operated its project successfully for 12 years, its last proposal was not of the highest quality. In the 13th year, an institution that had never operated this particular project submitted a well-written proposal and was funded. In spite of its history of a well-operated project, the Texas institution lost its funding because of a carelessly written application.

This example demonstrates the importance of prior experience points and the need to operate a successful project. Had prior experience points been part of the criteria, the Texas institution could have earned up to 15 points more than the other institution. These points might have been sufficient to qualify the Texas institution for funding.

If the program from which you seek funds provides prior experience points, be sure to study the criteria for those points carefully. As you write, include those criteria in your plan of operation and objectives.

Many programs do not award prior performance points. In this case, all proposals compete equally. Thus, a person with a good idea has the same chance as a person who has operated a successful project. An equal start helps assure that there can be no favoritism or friendship factors involved in the choice; each proposal is judged on its own merit. Prior experience points do make sense when continuity is a goal. They do not seem useful when innovation, efficiency, or short-term work is the goal.

Sections of an Application

The Rules and Regulations contain the actual criteria for evaluating your application. These criteria, in effect, constitute the outline you use in writing your proposal. The sections of an application vary from program to program. Below are the sections and points of the College Assistance Migrant Program (CAMP) proposal.

1. Plan of Operation (25 points)
2. Objectives and Activities (20 points)
3. Evaluation Plan (15 points)
4. Quality of Key Personnel (10 points)
5. Budget and Cost-Effectiveness (10 points)
6. Interagency Consultation and Coordination (10 points)
7. Adequacy of Resources (5 points)
8. Recruitment (5 points)

Other programs may have additional or slightly different sections such as Impact, Dissemination, or Program Factors. Each section represents a major criterion that may be divided into several more detailed criteria. The more detailed criteria of section *(a) Plan of Operation for CAMP* are reprinted in Figure 8.1. Unless otherwise instructed, address each criterion in the same order it is presented in the *Rules and Regulations.* This is important because the readers' Technical Review Form is organized in this order. The task of reading and evaluating your document is easier if readers do not have to turn from page to page, section to section, to complete their evaluations. Some programs, such as TRIO (Upward Bound, Educational Talent Search, Student Support Services, etc.), provide specific instructions in the application packet for you to arrange the criteria in a different order. If such instructions are provided, follow them carefully. The readers' Technical Review Form is probably organized according to the order requested.

Figure 8.1. Criteria for Conducting a Plan of Operation for Project CAMP

§206.31 What selection criteria does the Secretary use to evaluate an application?

(a)   Plan of operation [25 points]
    (1)   The Secretary reviews each application for information that shows the quality of the plan of operation for the project.
    (2)   The Secretary looks for information that shows the following:
        (i)   High quality in the design of the project.
        (ii)   An effective plan of management that assures proper and efficient administration of the project.
        (iii)   A clear description of how the objectives of the project relate to the purpose of the program.
        (iv)   A clear description of the way that the applicant plans to use its resources and personnel to achieve each objective of the project.
        (v)   A clear description of how the applicant will provide equal access and treatment for eligible participants who are members of groups that have been traditionally underrepresented, such as
            (A)   Members of racial or ethnic minority groups
            (B)   Women
            (C)   Handicapped persons
            (D)   The elderly

From Here to the End of Chapter 8 the Reader May Wish to Follow the Examples in the Sample Proposal in Chapter 10.

Notice that the sample proposal in the following chapter contains the face page (Standard Form 424). Most proposals must have this page. Detailed instructions for completing this and other required forms are part of the application packet. Complete Form 424 with care and ensure that it is signed in ink. A copy of this form bearing an original signature must be included with one copy of your proposal.

Include a complete Table of Contents. Often readers must refer to a previous section. A good Table of Contents will facilitate the reading process. A short Abstract will assist the readers in capturing an overview of the entire proposal. It helps them to know what to look for in the document, briefly describes the needs, and explains what the project hopes to accomplish.

Plan of Operation

The Plan of Operation provides detailed information explaining how you plan to operate the project. This section usually carries the highest number of points of any proposal section. Develop it carefully; address each individual criterion listed in the *Federal Register*. Figure 8.1 is a reprint of the criteria for the CAMP proposal (see Chapter 10) as they appear in the Rules and Regulations.

As you address each criterion, draw the reader's attention to that criterion by putting it in **bold type,** underlining it, placing it in a box, or using some other way to guide the reader. Try not to make the readers search for information they need to evaluate your proposal. Notice how the author of the proposal in Chapter 10 has carefully set apart each criterion in the order in which it appears in the *Federal Register*. The criterion, in bold type, is centered on the page with the first letter of each major word capitalized. Under each criterion, the author has cited the exact reference and the number of possible points awarded that criterion. As the readers proceed through the document, they find each criterion highlighted in this way. The readers gain confidence in your proposal and in your ability to organize as they see how carefully you follow the required criterion. Help your readers by paraphrasing each criterion and citing the numerical reference: e.g.,

———**Grant Tip**———
*As you address each criterion, draw the reader's attention to that criterion by putting it in **bold type,** underlining it, placing it in a box, or using some other way to guide the reader.*

> **Plan of Operation**
> (206.31(a) - 25 points)

You may want to preface the first section, Plan of Operation, with some background material such as why the program is needed and what special conditions exist that merit a project. Refer to the first part of the proposal in Chapter 10 for a sample of Background Information.

The background material begins with a map depicting the geographic area to be served by the proposed project. Another map appears a couple of pages later showing other areas of the country that are presently served by CAMP projects. A complete description of the need for a CAMP project is offered, including published statistics and a list of specific areas in which the target population is lacking, i.e., effective motivation, financial resource information on the part of the student and the parents, and the poor self-concepts of the farmworker students. The proposal also points out verifiable factors identified as causes for students dropping out of postsecondary programs. You are the person most familiar with your target area and institution. Tell the readers what they need to know.

A major mistake committed by many proposal writers is to assume that the reader is familiar with the conditions of the target area. Generally readers are assigned to evaluate proposals from geographical locations other than their own. Therefore, they know little about conditions that exist in your target area. In a very succinct way, provide specific and compelling reasons why a project should be established in the proposed target area.

In addressing the criteria in the *Plan of Operation*, notice how the author draws the readers' attention to the purpose of the CAMP program. The first paragraph of the Plan of Operation reviews for the reader those things that will be contained in the remainder of the document. Keep the readers' attention on the purposes for which funds are awarded. Demonstrate that the document addresses those purposes.

Notice that frequent reference is made to the *Federal Register*. This assures readers that you know the specific elements of the program as outlined. It assures them that you are trying to serve the needs of the targeted population, not trying to develop a project that centers on your needs and only peripherally on the needs of the students. Each service identified in the *Federal Register* is carefully detailed. A description and a well-planned chart are provided, indicating how the staff plans to accomplish the services.

The proposal points out that the project will be an integral part of the university structure (one major feature of a quality proposal) and that project administrators have full responsibility for its operation. This is a firm foundation for a solid plan of management. Projects whose administrators do not have full control of the implementation often do not achieve the desired results. The plan of management in this proposal places total responsibility—from submitting the application, administering the project, training and supervising its staff, overseeing the curriculum, managing the budget, to evaluating the results—upon the project administrators.

Study the remainder of the Plan of Operation, noting how each criterion is addressed. The completeness of this section helps to assure that the readers will award the full 25 points. Note the flow of the narration, the transition from one criterion to the next, and the physical appearance of the document. The author has left sufficient white space and has not crowded too much information onto one page. The author uses lists and numbers items that are of most importance, using boldface type, italics, and indenting to delineate various information. The author leaves space between each paragraph and between each numbered item. All of these details contribute to the rapid and easy reading of the proposal. The reader does not have to search for information. Because the material on each page is not crowded, the reader can create a visual image of the important aspects of each page and process that information comfortably. Readers will be more inclined to award a greater number of points for this type of writing than if they have to labor over the narration, search for obscure information, and read between the lines.

——**Grant Tip**——
Use lists, numbered items, boldface type, italics, and the like, to catch the reader's eye.

Objectives and Activities

Operationally, the Objectives and Activities section is probably the most important section. It describes to the reader, the United States Department of Education personnel, your institution, and the employees of the project (including the Director) how the project is to be operated. It is the project's road map. The proposal in Chapter 10 employs an effective format.

There is no magic number of objectives appropriate for a proposal. Do not create more objectives than necessary, but include sufficient objectives to demonstrate that all aspects of the purpose of the program are covered.

The objectives used in the sample proposal have the following components:

1. Component Title—identifies the objective topic.

2. Goal—states the broad intention for the objective.

3. Objective—tells what the author is going to do and defines it in measurable outcomes (the product).

4. Activities—instructs the staff as to the specific procedures or ways the objective is to be met.

5. Timeline—specifies when the activities of the objective will be met.

6. Evaluation—determines if, and to what degree, the objective was met.

7. Staff Responsibility—shows the staff member responsible for activities.

Component Title—This title should be descriptive and immediately indicate to the reader the content of the objective. Any reader should be able to review a list of the objectives and have a good idea of the of the scope and depth of the project.

Goal—This is a statement of the overall outcome of the objective. It is broad and does not generally specify a procedure, but rather what one might expect of the objective.

Objective—The ultimate purpose of the progam to which you are writing the proposal should be reflected in every objective. An objective describes what the program will accomplish. Some objectives may relate to intermediate aspects of the ultimate purpose. For example, the purpose of the CAMP program is *"to assist students...who are enrolled...on a full-time basis in the first academic year at an IHE."* Each objective should relate to this ultimate purpose. Some objectives will deal with financial matters, some with areas of curriculum, some with recruitment and retention, and others with social aspects of the project. Whatever the intermediate aspect of the objective is, the overall importance of the objectives is to contribute to the completion of the ultimate purpose of the program.

The objectives are among the most important elements of your proposal, particularly if the program to which you are writing awards points for prior performance. Generally, in the points for prior performance section, you will need to provide an accounting of accomplishments for each objective. Therefore, write objectives that are narrow in scope, that are not difficult to evaluate, and that are measurable. If possible, include a percentage or numerical outcome in your objective. Measurable objectives are extremely important. Unless required by the application, whether they are called program objectives, outcome objectives, performance objectives, or behavioral objectives is not

—— **Grant Tip**——
Objectives and activities are your road map to a successful proposal. Use the active voice when writing objectives and make them measurable.

important; they tell the readers what you hope to accomplish by the end of the project.

Notice the first objective of the sample proposal in Chapter 10. The objective is:

> To review and evaluate collected data on 100% of the CAMP participants and develop an Individual Educational Plan (IEP) showing special academic help and tutorial assistance needed by each student by the second week they are accepted into the program.

This objective has three major components: review, evaluate, and develop. This specific outcome objective tells what you hope to accomplish, with what number of participants, and how it will be measured. The objective is reasonable. It is attainable given the resources and level of effort described in the proposal, and it is challenging. It is not so easy that little effort will be required to attain it. Data must be collected on 100% of the participants. This may be readily demonstrated by listing all participants and identifying the data collected, i.e., Self-Report Questionnaires, High School Transcripts or GED Score Reports, ACT Score Reports, and the results of California Achievement Tests if administered. All of these items are mentioned in the activities section of the objective. A review and evaluation of this material will render a profile of the participant, from which an Individualized Education Plan (IEP) will be developed. In other words, elaboration of the IEP is proof of the review and evaluation of the data. The IEP can be included either in an evaluation or in a summary of IEPs, and the IEPs themselves can remain on file.

The purpose of this process is to develop an objective that is important, contributes significantly to the success of your participants, and produces an outcome that can be readily determined. Avoid, if possible, developing objectives that cannot be evaluated quantitatively or that describe a process only. Your objective should not depend on your opinion or on the opinion of a member of your staff in order to determine if it was successful. Of 17 objectives in the model proposal, only objective 12 does not include a specific numerical or percentage citation that can be quantitatively measured. The success or failure of the other objectives can be measured statistically.

Activities—The activities describe what the staff will do in order to accomplish the goals and have successful outcomes for the objectives. Don't outline *every* step, but do list the major steps in the order in which they will occur. Some writers list the activities numerically; others provide the activities in narrative or chart form. Several ways can be used to accomplish the purpose effectively.

Timeline—The reader wants to know when during the project the activities will occur. This also provides an excellent mechanism to pace the staff in implementing and operating the project. Be realistic with timelines; avoid too many activities at any given time. When the project is funded, make a master list of your timelines, or, using a large wall calendar, list the date of each activity. At a glance, you can survey your needs and have ample time to plan for each activity, secure the necessary supplies or materials, and have your personnel prepared.

Evaluation—The evaluation part of your objective need not be exhaustive. One criterion requires an in-depth evaluation of your complete project. The evaluation included in each objective should simply state how you will know when you have accomplished the objective and to what degree it was successful. Often the documents necessary to show this are listed in the evaluation description. For example, the evaluation could state that the IEPs, questionnaires, transcripts, and test results will be on file, or it could state that this objective will be successfully completed when an IEP is completed on 100% of the program participants.

Staff Responsibility—This clearly defines who is responsible for what. In the sample proposal, responsibility for each objective is assigned to one or more staff persons. Some writers refine it more by stating that one person has the major responsibility and is assisted by others. For example, the sample proposal states that the Associate Director, Counselor, and Recruiter/ Counselor are responsible for the successful completion of the first objective, Student Assessment. It could have been stated as follows: Responsibility: Associate Director, assisted by Counselor and Recruiter/Counselor.

———**Grant Tip**———

Make sure your objectives and activities are clear enough so a person unfamiliar with your project could successfully implement them.

Study the objectives and all of their components as they appear in Chapter 10. Use them as patterns for creating the objectives in your application. Plan to spend considerable time on the objective section. After you have completed it, ask someone unfamiliar with the program and its purposes to read your objectives. The objectives and activities should be clear to this person, who should feel that, given very little direction, they could implement and carry them out in a timely and effective manner.

Evaluation Plan

The evaluation section can present difficulties for proposal writers. The evaluation plan need not be elaborate and steeped with strategies. *EDGAR* (*CFR* 75.590) requires you to evaluate the following three areas:

1. The progress of the project in achieving its objectives.

2. The effectiveness of the project in meeting the stated purpose of the program.

3. The effect of the project on the persons being served, including any persons who are members of groups that have been traditionally underrepresented.

The evaluation section of the sample proposal in Chapter 10 provides a built-in ongoing evaluation plan. It permits the administrative staff to collect and analyze data continuously, thus allowing them to detect problems and improve strategies. An important flow chart is included to outline the evaluation plan.

The evaluation section provides a short but informative plan for assessing the effectiveness of the project in meeting the purpose of the CAMP program. The author reviews for the reader the stated purpose of the CAMP program according to the *Federal Register* and proposes to conduct a "procedural assessment" to compare the data collected with the goals and objectives as stated in the proposal. This is one of the most prevalent and useful evaluation models or designs used in social action programs. It essentially uses the program as its own comparison. It does not attempt to generalize to the degree of most quasi-experimental or experimental designs, but attempts to demonstrate success or lack of success of the project within agreed-upon and thus in one sense *validated* parameters. It gives control to project management over variables to be measured, because these are defined by project goals and objectives.

Near the end of the year, project goals and student objectives are evaluated for purposes of *summative assessment*. This overall process uses the project records, student activities, credits attempted and grades earned, and student questionnaires as the basis of the evaluation.

The sample proposal includes an elaborate chart outlining the *management by objective* plan for the project. This type of evaluation instrument provides an impressive amount of valuable information in a very small amount of space. It allows the reader to follow through the process quickly to ensure that the evaluation is meaningful and produces information that can be used for project improvement.

Quality of Key Personnel

Even though this proposal section is time consuming, develop it with care. Demonstrate that you have the personnel resources necessary to operate the project effectively. Be realistic in expectations of future project staff. Often, in an effort to impress readers, proposal developers include qualifications that are not necessary in order to carry out the project goals. Insist on well-qualified personnel and describe these qualifications in your document. However, do not require degrees and certificates that look good but do not add to the employee's expertise or ability to carry out the assigned duties.

If you require a doctorate, for example, have specific reasons in mind rather than requiring the degree for *window dressing*. Persons with doctoral degrees are often difficult to find for employment in grant-funded projects where a position carries no academic rank or tenure-track option. *Soft money* positions will last for only the project's duration with no guarantees that other positions will be available when the grant terminates. Often persons who have invested time and effort on advanced degrees prefer to seek employment that leads to academic stability. Highly trained persons demand higher salaries, which may cause a personnel budget to appear excessive. If the position can be filled just as well with a person with a bachelor's or master's degree, so be it. These persons often are interested in soft-money positions as a means of acquiring valuable experience.

Build into this section a strong affirmative action plan—one that goes well beyond your institution's affirmative action plan. Indicate how you will develop your positions to attract persons or groups of persons traditionally underrepresented in this type of employment. Describe how you will advertise such positions, even to the extent of naming the regional or statewide newspapers in which you will place advertisements. Describe how you will seek referrals from other universities or agencies, and how you will seek out and recruit such individuals. Explain how you will treat a situation in which you find that two applicants for a particular position are equally qualified in every way, except that one is a member of a group traditionally underrepresented.

Indicate how all applicants will be given equal treatment before and after they are employed. In other words, once persons are on the payroll, how will you ensure that they will not become a token person of an underrepresented population? Explain the promotion policy, how all employees share in a benefits package, and how all have equal access to the institution's various services and perks.

Describe the special qualifications and characteristics of persons already on staff who will become associated with the new project when it is funded. Explain how their preparation and experience will contribute to project success.

Develop a position description for each position in your project. Include items such as the following:

1. *Classification*—Will they be professional? Exempt, non-exempt? Termed employees? Full- or part-time employees?

2. *Employed by*—Who has the authority to review and judge the persons' qualifications for the position?

3. *Responsible to*—To whom will the people occupying the positions report? Who will supervise their activities?

4. *Purpose of the position*—A one- or two-line job description.

5. *Major responsibilities*—List the major areas of responsibility for each position. Be specific.

6. *Qualifications*—Define the training and experience you want these persons to have. Include both formal and informal training and experience that relate to the purpose, goals, and objectives of the project.

This section requires thorough planning and preparation. In developing the next section, Budget and Cost Effectiveness, you will realize that one of the largest budget line items will be personnel. Each position in the organization chart adds thousands of dollars to the budget. Plan well to ensure that all positions are necessary, well-defined, and will contribute significantly to the project's success. On the other hand, take care not to overlook an important position.

As an example, in developing the project budget for a CAMP project, one author carelessly omitted the position of Associate Director. Inasmuch as the author served only as a one-quarter time Director, the Associate Director's position was essential for the smooth and efficient operation of the project. During budget negotiations the error became apparent. By then it was too late. The Department declined a petition to add the position, and the Director was forced to operate for a year without it. This severely limited the project's effectiveness. Costly errors of this nature can spell failure for a project.

You cannot revise your project and add a position without prior approval from the sponsoring office. If you do, you put yourself in jeopardy of an audit exception and may be required to repay any salary, fringe, and other related expenses. Therefore, carefully review your document, creating both an organization chart and a chart that outlines all responsibilities involved in your proposed project. Cross-check them carefully. This will ensure that adequate personnel are listed in your budget.

Budget and Cost-Effectiveness

The line-item budget for the sample proposal in Chapter 10 is at the beginning of the application. Some proposal writers include it in the body of the proposal in the Budget and Cost Effectiveness section. If the instructions do not indicate where in the proposal you should locate the budget, you may choose to place it either at the front or in the Budget and Cost Effectiveness section. The Table of Contents should show where the budget is placed. In either location, you must carefully plan each budget expenditure.

The CAMP application packet's *"Dear Colleague" letter* gave hints as to an acceptable *cost per student*. Try to create a budget that is close to the national *cost-per-student* average. If the budget is significantly under the national average, provide ample explanation. Is it because the institution is contributing personnel, supplies, or scholarships for the project? Explain any such contributions. Although these contributions can be beneficial, they must be carefully explained.

If costs greatly exceed the national average, provide a thorough explanation. For example, one of the authors' projects requires considerable travel for recruitment. As a result, the travel budget is necessarily large, significantly increasing the overall cost per student average. Without a clear explanation, the readers may think that the budget is unrealistically inflated and may withhold points.

A good rule of thumb is to dream a little, and ask for what you need. What about the "dream a little" statement? Do not hesitate to ask for legitimate items that may not be absolutely necessary but which, if granted, would certainly enhance the project. For example, several CAMP projects have found that a summer orientation enrichment session just before the beginning of each fall term enables participants to be ready to hit the ground running. During this orientation, participants are administered a variety of tests; attend intensive workshops or seminars on study skills; become acquainted with the

———Grant Tip———
Dream a bit, but not too wildly; be creative, but realistic. Estimate costs slightly on the high side to account for inflation.

campus, its administration, policies, and rules; learn where the laundry facilities are located; and complete other such necessary but time-consuming tasks. Having done this, they are prepared to begin the term without distractions. This orientation is not absolutely necessary, but it certainly helps students and staff get off to a great start. If such a preliminary orientation would be helpful, include it in the objectives and budget. If it is accepted and funded, participants will have a head start. If it is not funded, the project will still be intact and operable.

After reviewing your line-item budget, create a narrative to explain any unclear or unusual budget requests. Don't include items that do not directly relate to the purpose of the program or to objectives outlined in the *Objectives* section. A common error is to include items in the budget, such as computers, typewriters, or additional travel that are not mentioned in the body of the proposal. When the readers review the body of your proposal, if they find no reference to such items that appear in the budget, they may believe you are attempting to use the grant not to serve the target population, but to buy equipment or allow for extra travel. If you need computers for the successful accomplishment of a specific objective, the objective itself should cite the need and provide an explanation.

For example, one of the authors designed a curriculum that used many tutorial assistants, computer-assisted instruction, and supplementary video cassette tapes. Each tutor was assigned four participants. As the tutor worked one-on-one with two participants, the other two were using computers or video cassette tapes to reinforce previously-learned material. The curriculum was well-defined, time tables were developed, and a schedule of instruction was presented. All of this was explained in the objective itself. The request for 15 computers and three video cassette recorders and monitors was well-supported within the application narrative. During budget negotiations, the negotiator questioned the need for so much equipment. After reviewing the objective that documented the need for the equipment, the negotiator granted the request. It was obvious that the project would not be as effective without the necessary equipment.

The line-item budget presented in the sample proposal in Chapter 10 is an example of a conservative budget. After you have completed your budget, divide the total cost by the number of persons you plan to serve to determine the cost per participant.

If your application is recommended for funding, an officer of the United States Department of Education, Grants and Contracts Office, will telephone you to negotiate the budget. The two of you will discuss each budget line item and modify it according to the amount of funds available for your project. Usually this means a reduction in the amount requested. Discuss each item, and if the negotiator recommends reductions, explain the reasons behind your original request and advocate for the full amount requested. However, experience will teach any person who negotiates grant budgets that there is not a significant amount of room to negotiate. Be willing to provide a quick revision of your project and amend it according to the allocation. Remember the *Time-Cost-Performance* balance that was addressed in Chapter 1. Chapter 11, "Understanding How Grants Are Awarded," discusses budget negotiations more fully.

——**Grant Tip**——

Gain the support of your target community by including its members in the planning of your proposal.

Interagency Consultation and Coordination

Earlier in this chapter, we discussed Executive Order 12372—*Intergovernmental Review*. Do not confuse that requirement with the criterion of this section. The two are not related.

This section is designed to ensure that in planning and developing the project you have consulted and coordinated with other agencies that serve similar populations, and that you will continue to consult and coordinate with them. Begin this part of your application very early in the proposal writing process. Identify the agencies or offices that serve your target population. These may include among others:

- School districts
- Welfare agencies
- Law enforcement agencies
- Other federal and state-funded programs or projects
- Centers for employment training
- Private and nonprofit training agencies
- Councils that deal with your target population
- Community centers
- Junior colleges and other postsecondary institutions in your target area
- Employment centers
- State agencies

Prior to contacting each agency, prepare a fact sheet containing an outline of the project you propose. Include a map of the target service area. Personalize each fact sheet with a few questions for the specific agency you are about to visit, or with a few suggestions of ways agency personnel can assist in serving the target population.

For example, when developing the CAMP project, one author visited high schools in the target area. He had prepared a referral form on the back of a self-addressed, postage-paid postcard. The school counselor or principal could easily complete it and drop it into the mail. Persons at each school agreed to assist in recruitment by mailing these referral cards to the Project Director.

Together with the fact sheet, the author also prepared a list of services the school or agency could provide the CAMP program. The checklist included items such as:

[ ] We will provide space for posters and advertising of the CAMP program.

[ ] We will distribute CAMP brochures and application forms to interested persons.

[ ] We will provide space for CAMP counselors to interview potential participants.

[ ] We will invite CAMP personnel to Parents Night and provide time on the program to disseminate information.

[ ] We will provide duplicating services and limited supplies for use in the CAMP program.

[ ] We will dedicate 1   2   3   4   5 (circle the correct number) school-sponsored scholarships to students who enroll in CAMP.

[ ] We will permit authorized CAMP personnel to review nonprivate school records in an effort to locate previous students who may qualify for CAMP.

[ ] The school newspaper and parent newsletters will print articles and information regarding enrollment in and the benefits of CAMP.

Ask personnel at each agency visited to submit a letter regarding your visit. The letter should include three important items: (a) a statement indicating that you discussed the project with them, (b) a statement indicating that you invited their comments and suggestions, and (c) a statement indicating their support and the contributions they will make to the project. The letter must indicate support and not just an endorsement. A letter of endorsement might simply state that agency personnel are aware of the program, consider it worthy, and extend blessings to you. A letter of support, on the other hand, includes items (a), (b), and (c) above. You may want to take a sample letter that another agency has provided or draft a sample letter to use as a model. Keep each letter on file. Create an appendix that contains these letters or representative samples. In the Interagency Consultation/Coordination section of the proposal, summarize each letter received. An example of such summaries is in the sample proposal.

Adequacy of Resources

Often, excellent proposals are developed that describe quality projects designed to meet the purpose of the program as described in the *Federal Register* and to meet the needs of the proposed target population. It is one thing to have a good project and project design. It is another to be able to implement the project if it is selected for funding. In the *Adequacy of Resources* section, describe the resources your institution has available that it is willing to commit to successful implementation and operation of the proposed project.

As you design and develop the project, list the resources the project will need in order to be successful. Then list resources currently available. Identify the persons who can supply or provide the resources you lack. For example, one of the authors proposed to establish a Student Support Services Program at his institution. A major needed resource was adequate office, counseling, and tutorial space. None being available in the building where most of the federal grants were housed, he and his dean approached the president of the university. The president determined that the Student Support Services Program would be of value to the university and set aside adequate space. He confirmed this in a letter that was included in the proposal. The proposal was successful, and the project was implemented in the newly remodeled space.

Provide a sentence or two explaining how each resource will contribute to project success. Notice that the sample proposal contains a list of 19 resources that directly contribute to project success. If you are applying for a service-oriented project, provide floor plans of housing, office, tutorial, and classroom space; menus from the food services facilities; and a list of resources and services available at the library, the student union, the media and materials center, the counseling center, the student financial aid office and career planning centers in an appendix. Include a brochure of extracurricular activities, such as theaters, cultural centers, athletic events, special events center, forums, lecture series, and social events.

Indicate also how this project will interface with other federally funded projects; explain why they do not overlap or duplicate services. Networking among projects is impressive and demonstrates that sound student services are available. For example, at one university, students are first contacted by either the Educational Talent Search or Upward Bound counselor. They receive special help to complete high school and, upon graduation, they can get help in enrolling in a postsecondary institution. These projects work closely with public school personnel to identify students who may leave high school prior to graduation. If a student qualifies for Educational Talent Search or High School Equivalency Program services, the appropriate referral is made. The university also operates a variety of service-oriented projects. It is not uncommon for a student to be contacted by an educational specialist from the Talent Search Program and, after assessment, to be referred to Upward Bound. If students complete high school through Upward Bound and meet project eligibility requirements, they may be referred to the College Assistance Migrant Program. Administrators of this project may determine that the student is interested in elementary education and needs tutorial assistance in order to be successful. Students may eventually be referred to the Bilingual Teacher Training Program to begin coursework on an elementary bilingual degree while receiving special tutoring from the Student Support Services Program.

Networking seems to contribute to positive funding decisions. A special caution is in order. Ensure that your project services do not overlap or duplicate each other, and ensure that, when prohibited, students do not receive services from two projects simultaneously. For example, a student cannot receive services from both Talent Search and Upward Bound at the same time. This is prohibited in the regulations. But a student may receive simultaneous services from Student Support Services and Bilingual Education or CAMP.

Recruitment

Inasmuch as grant programs designed to help migrant target populations often cover wide geographic areas, readers need to know how recruitment will be accomplished. When target populations are migrant, recruitment is difficult.

Build a recruitment program that will reach sufficient participants to fill all of the *slots* in your project as well as generating a *waiting list.* Often projects recruit only sufficient students to fill the vacancies. Then when a participant must leave the project unexpectedly, there is no one to fill the vacancy.

Notice in the sample proposal how the author built in a networking system of 14 agencies to receive referrals. This helps make recruiting successful. Chances of participants succeeding are greatly enhanced if they are referred by someone else. This shows they are interested in self-improvement, have initiative, and are willing to follow through. Build a network of schools, agencies, institutions, community organizations, and individuals to supply your program with potential participants. Use the list generated in the Interagency Consultation/Coordination section, for example.

Summary

This chapter has presented the meat and potatoes of proposal development and referred to a sample proposal (Chapter 10). Application procedures for federal grants were reviewed. You were encouraged to request an RFP early, study it thoroughly, and conduct your needs assessment using the RFP as a guide.

Important features of a proposal were outlined. As you develop your document, continually ask yourself, *"Does this part contribute to one of the important characteristics of a successful proposal?"*

Each aspect of one RFP was discussed. You were advised to study the RFP in detail, make notes, highlight important parts, make a list of timelines and important items to include. Make a checkoff list to ensure that you have met all requirements.

Study the system for awarding points. Determine before you begin if points for prior performance will be awarded. If so, ensure that your entire document addresses these criteria in general and that your objectives address them in particular. Never take the attitude that a particular section is difficult and that if you can earn 12 or 13 of the 15 points, you will be satisfied. Never be satisfied until you have polished your proposal to the point that you are confident you will earn all of the points. Every single point counts. Dozens of proposals fail to be recommended for funding by a point or two! One of the authors scored an average of 96 out of 100 points and still failed to make the funding cut. Never take the point system for granted. Earn every possible point available. Expend that extra hour or two to earn one additional point.

When you are ready to mail your proposal, place a note on the outside cover indicating which copy contains the original plus four

---

Grant Tip

Study the system for awarding points. Polish your proposal until you are confident that you will earn all the points. Every single point counts.

copies, as well as a courtesy copy under separate cover to the program director if the application is for a previously funded grant. This assures that in addition to the "original signature" or file copy, each of the three readers on the panel will have a dark clear copy. Feedback from United States Department of Education personnel has been positive in this regard. It makes their work easier.

Chapter 10, "Reviewing a Funded Proposal," provides one example of an application. This proposal scored 100 points, thus receiving the highest possible score. A careful study of its components will assist you in formulating a quality application proposal worthy of funding.

9

Helpful Hints From Grantwriting Professionals

Introduction

Volumes have been written about how to write grants, including journal articles, books, magazine articles, and newsletter columns. Additionally, there has been an increase in the number of grantwriting courses offered on college and university campuses, and through certification programs, workshops and seminars, as well as a proliferation of private grantwriting consultants. All these resources have been developed to make grantwriting easier.

Most experts agree that writing grants is hard work—not hard, just hard work. Successful grantwriters are able to manage multiple tasks simultaneously: research, writing, networking, and continuously expanding their grantwriting knowledge. Ward (1998) noted,

> Writing winning grant proposals does not happen overnight. It's a process that takes patience, perseverance and is not for the weak of heart! It's important to recognize that there is more to successful grant writing than just putting a proposal together, sending it in, and hoping for the best. (p. 24)

The grantsmanship challenge or the art of grantsmanship as defined by Kelley and Gay (1990) "has become more sophisticated and the process more competitive than ever before" (p. 31). They noted that the "foundation for an outstanding grant proposal rests with innovative ideas or approaches that match the prioritized purposes of a funding organization" (p. 31).

Kelly and Gay (1990) offered the following advice for those who are seriously entering the grantwriting world: "Discover the ways that work best to unleash the creative genius within you or a team, and then harness that imaginative energy into a logically organized and internally consistent fundable proposal" (p. 31).

This chapter highlights some helpful hints that we have used successfully over the years in responding to numerous requests for proposals (RFPs). These are the torn and tattered pages that we have

—— **Grant Tip** ——

Most experts agree that writing grants is hard work—not hard, just hard work.

removed from our files to share with our readers. We have organized these tips around the common sections found in a proposal. Using the information that other grantwriters have learned over the years will help you to succeed in your attempt to meet the grantsmanship challenge.

First Things First

One of your first decisions will be whether you should even try to respond to a call for proposals. Hamper and Baugh (1995) offered several considerations of when *not* to write a proposal, for example when, "the timeframe for preparing and submitting a proposal is completely unrealistic for you to do a good job" (p. 12). This may seem like an obvious consideration, but it may surprise novice grant-writers to learn how little time they will actually have to devote to putting together a proposal. It is difficult to say exactly how much time will be required because of the many variables to be considered. Unfortunately, this should be developed over a period of trial and error. One rule of thumb would be to estimate what you think it will take and then add 2 to 3 weeks.

Another example of a time when you should not write a proposal, offered by Hamper and Baugh (1995), is when "you do not have the staff or resources to prepare the best proposal your company can present" (p. 12). Experienced grantwriters take this advice seriously. Miller (1995) provided the following insight into another consideration grantwriters need to address early in the process:

> The single most important aspect of successful grant writing is knowing the mind of the grant maker. It surpasses creative writing, convincing data, and beautifully packaged presentations. It even goes beyond the compelling nature of the problem the requested grant funds are expected to solve. (n.p.)

Experienced proposal writers take the following steps to gain the competitive edge.

- Discuss in advance the grant's potential overall contribution to the agency and to the area to be served with all of the stakeholders.
- Establish a clear and direct relationship between the grant's purpose and the organization's mission and goals. Otherwise,

---

—— Grant Tip ——

Using the information that other grant writers have learned over the years will help you to succeed in your attempt to meet the grantsmanship challenge.

you may experience some administrative hesitation to embrace your proposal.

- Because you know better than anyone else, give careful consideration to your agency's size, the amount of available resources (including space to conduct the project) before you invest your time, effort, and energy into developing a proposal.

Once a decision has been made to respond to an RFP, determine who is going to write the proposal and how the proposal is going to be prepared. Kelley and Gay (1990) provided a breakdown of the types of grantwriters: the solo writer, the team-oriented writer, the mentored team, the contractor, and the professional.

The solo writer works alone. Frequently the writer will work in isolation until the major portion of the proposal is finished, at which time he or she will seek outside editorial assistance.

Many of the proposals today are being written by teams. This works well in many cases, especially when time is a factor. In the team-oriented approach, each team member has a defined responsibility, but the team must then plan for the time necessary to "get it all together."

The mentored team, less practiced and less frequently used, is a great tool for aspiring grantwriters. Experienced grantwriters are paired with those who are less experienced. A highly effective means of learning the grantwriting process, it is often difficult to find an environment in which the mentored team is nurtured. A popular means of grantwriting is to use a contractor. There are numerous considerations when using this method: costs, success rate of contractor, experience, and length of time needed to complete the proposal. Many successes have been reported; but there have also been numerous disappointing situations that have arisen, so be cautious.

Many colleges and universities as well as government laboratories have full-time professional grantwriters on their staffs. Generally these professionals write proposals submitted on behalf of their institution but the grant is awarded to the institution in which they are employed. Frequently, colleges and universities offer weekend grantwriting classes, taught by professionals, for a nominal fee. Some larger universities may also offer grant writing courses for credit.

Seasoned grantwriters know that you never wait until the last minute to begin to write or to prepare to write a proposal. A multitude of tasks can be done well in advance, before you even know a firm deadline date. Some of these are depicted in Figure 9.1.

——— Grant Tip ———
Among seasoned grantwriters it is understood that you never wait until the last minute to begin to write or prepare to write a proposal.

Applicant information can also be gathered well in advance of actually responding to a grant proposal. Why put additional pressure on yourself when you can start early?

Figure 9.1. Checklist of Information to Prepare in Advance

1. Principal Investigator's name, title, mailing address, telephone number, e-mail address, and so forth
2. Brief institutional description
3. Organization chart
4. Budgetary information including your agency's indirect cost rates, fringe benefits, travel reimbursement policy, and other related costs
5. Job descriptions and resumes
6. Sample letter of commitment along with a tentative list of individuals you plan to contact—names, addresses, telephone numbers, e-mail addresses, and a sample letter

Brewer and Hollingsworth (2001) offer a prewriting checklist outlined in Figure 9.2, which includes six simple questions to consider before you begin to write.

Consider This

It is highly recommended that you spend some time prior to actually writing the proposal studying previous proposals. Or else, spend some time researching your field for what makes a proposal successful. You will want to seek the answers to questions such as "What are the most common problems noted by reviewers?" Chavkin (1997) noted, "Although most grants are written on short notice, those that are funded often were in the planning stages many months before the application was made" (p. 166). "What sections receive most criticism?" Knowing this type of information from the get-go can help grantwriters avoid these pitfalls. Bootzin, Sechrest, Scott, and Hannah (1992) found that (a) 24.3% of the proposals' literature reviews were criticized for omitting important or relevant areas or not being thorough enough, (b) 51.5% failed to provide adequate statistical analysis strategies, and (c) over 30% demonstrated budget problems.

Bootzin et al. (1992) noted a study of NIH proposals that resulted in a list of common reasons for disapproval of proposals, for example: (a) "An apparent lack of new or original ideas, (b) a diffuse,

———Grant Tip———

It is highly recommended that you spend some time prior to actually writing the proposal to studying previous proposals.

rambling, superficial, or unfocused research plan, and (c) an attempt to conduct an unrealistically large amount of work" (p. 106). When attempting to write a highly sophisticated research proposal, make sure you take into consideration the items noted in Figure 9.3.

Figure 9.2. Prewriting Checklist

• How much time do I have to devote to writing a proposal?
• Will I be working on the grant alone or with coworkers?
• Why do I want or need to write a grant proposal?
• Does my school or school system have guidelines or procedures that I must follow?
• Am I willing to complete all required paperwork if I receive funding?
• Do I have all the information necessary for writing a grant proposal?

Berilla [source unknown] disclosed that when ranking emergency medical services systems research proposals, the top-ranked reason for failure to get funding was that the proposal was not innovative (58%). Berilla included inadequate or inappropriate description of data collection and analysis (42%), vague or missing methodology (33%), and inadequate experience, training, or knowledge of the investigator (33%).

A Good Thing—Reviewing Sample Evaluation Criteria From Actual RFPs

Anyone who is considering responding to a request for funding should spend some time reviewing sample evaluation criteria from similar requests for proposals (RFPs). This section will highlight three actual RFPs taken from the *Federal Register*. You can definitely learn from this exercise.

EXAMPLE 1
Cooperative Agreement for a Telephone Hotline for Victims of Domestic Violence. The Administration for Children and Families, Department of Health and Human Services. FR 65 FR, 14574, March 17, 2000

Figure 9.3. Research Proposal Considerations

> 1. Know what has been published in the last 5 years in the area of the interest.
>
> 2. Know the type of research that has already been done in the area of the interest.
>
> 3. Make sure that key staff are knowledgeable and experienced in the area to be researched.
>
> 4. Know and follow your agency's research proposal submission guidelines, especially for those requiring committee approval. This can often be time consuming and must be considered as you develop your timeline for submission.

Evaluation Criteria

Need for the Project (10 points)

Provide a detailed discussion of the need for a national domestic violence hotline of the scope being proposed. Provide a detailed analysis of the available data related to the problem being addressed (both domestic violence in general and the specific lack of a national domestic violence hotline), the strengths and limitations of other national and local crisis intervention and victim services hotline or referral services available, and the "state-of-the-art" relative to the problem being addressed by the proposal.

Goals and Objective (10 points)

Clearly state the project goals and objectives. Objectives should be stated in concrete, measurable terms that clearly identify the population(s) to be served, the type, quality, and level of service to be provided, the timeline for the establishment and delivery of services, and other project benchmarks. The anticipated demand for hotline services during the initial start-up period and a projection of the demand on an ongoing basis should be discussed, with supporting documentation. Describe the precise location of the project.

Approach (30 points).

Provide a sound workable plan of action (approach) that details how the proposed work will be accomplished; details how each task relates to the project's goals and activities; identifies the key staff member responsible for the specific tasks; provides a chart indicating the timetable for completing each task, the phasing in of the tasks over time, the lead staff person, and the time committed to the task; cites factors that might accelerate or decelerate the work; justifies the approach selected over other approaches; makes maximum use of existing facilities and resources and off-the-shelf technology; describes and supports any unusual features of the project, such as design or technological innovations, reductions in cost or time, or extraordinary social or community involvement; provides projections of the accomplishments to be achieved, and identifies the activities for which federal technical assistance, advice, or guidanceis anticipated and would be acceptable, as the project is implemented.

Results and Benefits Expected (20 points)

Identify, in specific terms, the results and benefits to be derived from the project and relate each result and benefit to a specific objective. Indicate the aggregate number of calls expected to be received and individuals to be assisted on an annual basis, for example, the expected volume of calls in such service areas as crisis counseling, immediate referrals to shelters, or the number of referrals made in response to non-English-speaking callers. Indicate the anticipated impact on and the subsequent benefit of the national hotline to victims of domestic violence and on the existing network of state and local shelters and services. Identify the kinds of data to be collected, maintained, and updated, and discuss the criteria to be used to assure the quality of the services provided.

Level of Effort (30 points)

Expertise, Commitment, and Support. The extent to which the applicant has nationally recognized expertise in the area of domestic violence and a record of high-quality service to victims of domestic violence, including a demonstration of support from advocacy groups, such as State Domestic Violence Coalitions or recognized national domestic violence groups; the extent of the applicant's commitment to diversity, and to the provision of service to ethnic, racial, and non-English-speaking minorities, older individuals, and individuals with disabilities.

—— Grant Tip ——

*As you develop the
proposal, look for
ways to use tables or
charts
effectively.*

Staff Background and Organizational Experience. The adequacy of the staffing pattern for the proposed project, how the individual responsibilities are linked to project tasks, and the contributions to be made by key staff. Each collaborating or cooperative organization, individual consultant, or other key individuals who will work on the project should be listed along with a description of the nature of their effort or contribution.

Competence of Staff. The background and experience of the project director and key project staff and the history and accomplishments of the organization; the qualifications of the project team including any experience with similar projects; the variety of skills, relevant educational background, and the ability to effectively manage the project and to coordinate activities with other agencies. One or two pertinent paragraphs on each key member are preferred to vitae or resumes. However, vitae or resumes may be included.

Adequacy of Resources. The adequacy of the available resources and organizational experience with regard to the tasks of the proposed project. List the financial, physical, and other resources already committed by other public and private agencies and institutions, if any. Explain how these organizations will participate in the day-to-day operations of the project. Letters from these agencies and organizations identifying and discussing the specifics of their commitment and participation must be included in the application.

Budget. Relate the proposed budget to the level of effort required to obtain the project objectives. Demonstrate that the project's costs are reasonable in view of the anticipated results.

Collaborative Efforts. The additional anticipated private sector resources that may be available to support or enhance the overall program. Discuss in detail and provide documents for any proposed collaborative or coordinated efforts with other public and private agencies or organizations. Identify these agencies or organizations and explain how their participation will enhance the project. Letters from these agencies and organizations must be included discussing, their interest and/or commitment in supporting their project, the stage of the planning and decision making, and the expected level of resource commitment.

Discussion of Example 1

Example 1 shows that there are five major sections in this proposal worth a total of 100 points. In this example, a natural starting point is with the five major criteria that are outlined. Look at each of the five sections and break the outline into more specific points to be covered. For example, your rough outline for the Need for the Project (10 points) may look something like the following:

Sample

Rough Outline for Need Section

**National Domestic
Violence Proposal**

I. Need for a National Domestic Violence Hotline

    A. Analysis of the Data
        1. Domestic Violence
        2. Lack of a National Domestic Violence Hotline
    B. Strengths and Limitations of Other National Crisis Interventions
        1. Strengths
        2. Limitations
    C. Strengths and Limitations of Other Local Crisis Interventions
        1. Strengths
        2. Limitations
    D. Victim Services Hotline and Referral Services Available

II. Goals (etc.)

For this particular section, it is easy to see that by developing an outline such as the one above, you address each element the funder has singled out as important.

    Furthermore, as you develop the proposal, look for ways that tables or charts can be used. For instance, in the Goals and Objectives section, the timeline that has been requested frequently is provided in the form of a Gantt Chart (refer to sample proposal in Chapter 10). The Level of Effort section requires that the commitment to diversity be addressed. Make certain that the information you provide is consistent with your agency's policies and procedures, and do not make promises that you cannot possibly keep.

EXAMPLE 2
Interventions for Suicidal Youth,
The National Institute of Mental Health
(NIMH) and
The National Institute on Drug Abuse
(NIDA)

Review Criteria

1. *Significance:* Does this study address an important problem? If the aims of the application are achieved, how will scientific knowledge be advanced? What will be the effect of these studies on the concepts or methods that drive this field?

2. *Approach:* Are the conceptual framework, design, methods, and analyses adequately developed, well integrated, and appropriate to the aims of the project? Does the applicant acknowledge potential problem areas and consider alternative tactics?

3. *Innovation:* Does the project employ novel concepts, approaches, or methods? Are the aims original and innovative? Does the project challenge existing paradigms or develop new methodologies or technologies?

4. *Investigator:* Is the investigator appropriately trained and well suited to carry out this work? Is the work proposed appropriate to the experience level of the principal investigator and other researchers (if any)?

5. *Environment:* Does the scientific environment in which the work will be done contribute to the probability of success? Do the proposed experiments take advantage of unique features of the scientific environment or employ useful collaborative arrangements? Is there evidence of institutional support?

In addition to the above criteria, in accordance with NIH policy, all applications will also be reviewed with respect to the following:

1. The adequacy of plans to include both genders, minorities and their subgroups, and children as appropriate for the scientific goals of the research. Plans for the recruitment and retention of subjects will also be evaluated.

2. The reasonableness of the proposed budget and duration in relation to the proposed research.

3. The adequacy of the proposed protection for humans, animals, or the environment, to the extent they may be adversely affected by the project proposed in the application.

Discussion of Example 2

There are five criteria provided for Example 2 along with three subcriteria that should also receive careful consideration. These additional criteria are not optional! If these additional criteria are overlooked because you failed to read past the first five major criteria, you have seriously jeopardized any chance that you may have had for getting funded.

Two major differences that should be noted between Example 1 and Example 2 are that Example 2 fails to provide any point value to the individual sections, and it is very short. The application guidelines provide the necessary information outlining how the proposal will be evaluated.

Our suggestion is to make a simple checklist from the criteria. Use the checklist during proposal planning and writing and after writing to be certain that all points have been addressed. For example, our checklist would look something like the one found in Figure 9.4. We use similar evaluation checklists for all of our proposals. These checklists also are used for internal evaluations to provide the grantwriter with critical feedback from coworkers. Often we find that what is clear to us as the grantwriters may not be clear to others. Once others have reviewed your proposal in light of the Evaluation Checklist, you should revise or rewrite the areas that appear weak, unclear, or add those that you have simply failed to include. This simple but effective exercise is a valuable tool and one that we highly recommend.

EXAMPLE 3
The Administration for Children and Families, Department of Health and Human Services. 65FR15336, March 22, 2000. Head Start Fellows Program

Figure 9.4. Internal Evaluation Checklist

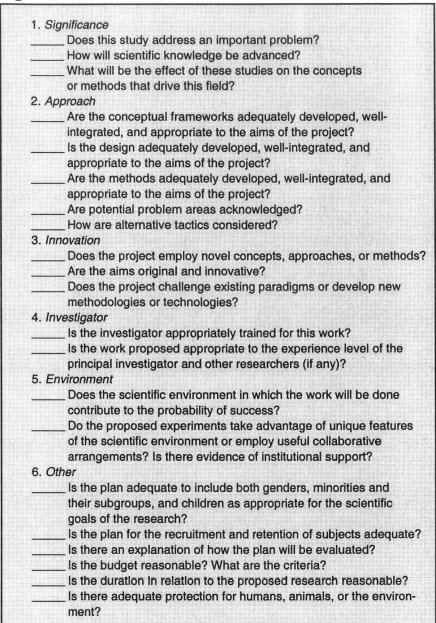

1. *Significance*
_____ Does this study address an important problem?
_____ How will scientific knowledge be advanced?
_____ What will be the effect of these studies on the concepts or methods that drive this field?

2. *Approach*
_____ Are the conceptual frameworks adequately developed, well-integrated, and appropriate to the aims of the project?
_____ Is the design adequately developed, well-integrated, and appropriate to the aims of the project?
_____ Are the methods adequately developed, well-integrated, and appropriate to the aims of the project?
_____ Are potential problem areas acknowledged?
_____ How are alternative tactics considered?

3. *Innovation*
_____ Does the project employ novel concepts, approaches, or methods?
_____ Are the aims original and innovative?
_____ Does the project challenge existing paradigms or develop new methodologies or technologies?

4. *Investigator*
_____ Is the investigator appropriately trained for this work?
_____ Is the work proposed appropriate to the experience level of the principal investigator and other researchers (if any)?

5. *Environment*
_____ Does the scientific environment in which the work will be done contribute to the probability of success?
_____ Do the proposed experiments take advantage of unique features of the scientific environment or employ useful collaborative arrangements? Is there evidence of institutional support?

6. *Other*
_____ Is the plan adequate to include both genders, minorities and their subgroups, and children as appropriate for the scientific goals of the research?
_____ Is the plan for the recruitment and retention of subjects adequate?
_____ Is there an explanation of how the plan will be evaluated?
_____ Is the budget reasonable? What are the criteria?
_____ Is the duration In relation to the proposed research reasonable?
_____ Is there adequate protection for humans, animals, or the environment?

Evaluation Criteria

Applications received by the due date will be reviewed and scored competitively, Experts in the field, generally persons from outside the federal government, will use the following evaluation criteria.

Organizational Profiles (40 points)

The extent to which the applicant provides a vitae on the project director or principal investigator and key project staff, including resumes (names, address, training, most relevant educational background, and other qualifying experiences) and a short description of their responsibilities or contribution to the applicant's work plan. The extent to which the applicant's ability to effectively and efficiently administer a project like the one proposed is described. The extent to which the mission of the organization is described as it relates to leadership development within the early childhood and family service fields and how this project fits within that mission. Applicant provides the assurance that the project director or another appropriate staff member will attend six meetings annually in Washington, D.C. to meet with federal staff to discuss issues related to the Fellows Programs implementation.

Approach (20 points)

The extent to which the applicant outlines an acceptable plan of action pertaining to the scope of the project and details how the proposed work will be accomplished. The extent to which the applicant describes the proposed approach and strategies that will be taken to design the program, to recruit potential participants, to support the implementation and maintenance of the Fellows Program, and to evaluate the program's effectiveness. The extent to which the applicant describes its understanding of the goals and purposes for the Fellows program and its relationship to developing leadership potential for the individuals in the field and for improving the quality of early childhood programs.

—— **Grant Tip** ——
Write the abstract last! It must be concise and clearly written so that the reviewer is captivated.

Objectives and Need for Assistance (15 points)

The extent to which the applicant identifies and documents any relevant economic, social, financial, institutional, or other problems requiring a solution; demonstrates the need for the assistance; and states the principal and subordinate objectives of the project. Supporting documentation or other testimonies from concerned interests other than the applicant on the need for assistance may be used.

If the proposed approach and strategies require the technical assistance of other colleges, universities, or nonprofit agencies, the proposal should include letters of commitment assuring their willingness to participate and indicating the roles they would play in the project.

Results or Benefits Expected (15 points)

The extent to which the applicant identifies the evaluation methodology that will be used to determine the specific and measurable results and benefits to be derived that are consistent with the objectives of the proposal, and indicates the anticipated contributions to policy, practice, or theory.

Budget and Budget Justification (10 points)

The extent to which the project's costs are reasonable in view of the activities to be carried out and the anticipated outcomes. Provide a budget that delineates the project administration costs versus those expenses that will directly support the Fellows individually and as a group. The budget should include stipends to Fellows. The stipend should be tiered to accommodate a range of education and experience and would parallel the Federal General Schedule 12-14 pay range. Stipends should include funds to support fringe benefits. The average stipend and total amount of the $1 million of the budget that will be used for stipends for the Fellows must be delineated. It is anticipated that the major portion of the budget will be used for stipends and direct costs of the Fellows. The other expenses to support the participation of the Fellows should also be described and budgeted within the $1 million.

Discussion of Example 3

Example 3 also has five major criteria, yet the point values are different from those found in Example 1. The names of the sections vary and the level and degree of information required also vary. For example, refer to Figure 9.5 to see a comparison of the budget sections. It is interesting to note that, even though Examples 1, 2, and 3 vary, all three require that the proposal address the budget's reasonableness.

Over the years we have found that information we have prepared for one proposal is suitable for use in another proposal. For instance, in Example 3, all we are required to do is to retrieve the previous

Figure 9.5. Comparison of Budget Evaluation Criteria

> ### *Budget Criteria From Example 1*
>
> *Budget.* Relate the proposed budget to the level of effort required to obtain the project objectives. Demonstrate that the project's costs are **reasonable** in view of the anticipated results.
>
> ### *Budget Criteria From Example 2*
>
> The **reasonableness** of the proposed budget and duration in relation to the proposed research.
>
> ### *Budget Criteria From Example 3*
>
> *Budget and Budget Justification (10 points)*
>
> The extent to which the project's costs are **reasonable** in view of the activities to be carried out and the anticipated outcomes.
>
> Provide a budget that delineates the project administration costs versus those expenses that will directly support the Fellows individually and as a group.
>
> The budget should include stipends to Fellows. The stipend should be tiered to accommodate a range of education and experience and would parallel the Federal General Schedule 12-14 pay range. Stipends should include funds to support fringe benefits. The average stipend and total amount of the $1 million of the budget that will be used for stipends for the Fellows must be delineated.
>
> It is anticipated that the major portion of the budget will be used for stipends and direct costs of the Fellows.
>
> The other expenses to support the participation of the Fellows should also be described and budgeted within the $1 million.

—— **Grant Tip** ——

The heart of the matter—the method, plan of operation, procedures, or approach section—will usually be the longest section of the proposal.

budget from an electronic file and, with some relative easy revisions, we are able to use it again for a completely different proposal. Otherwise, it might have taken us quite a bit of time to format the budget exactly like we wanted it to appear on the page. Why spend the time recreating the format when you can copy and paste it into the new proposal? It becomes a template of sorts. A word of caution though in using this method: Be sure to delete all of the previous budget information!

Now You Are Ready to Write!

Cover Letter, Title Page, and Abstract

Frequently among the last parts of the proposal to be completed, the cover letter, title page, and abstract should receive careful attention. Reeve and Ballard (1993) stated, "The cover letter is used to introduce or reintroduce you to the funding agency. It should be short (half a page) and motivating, say something different, and show dramatic need or uniqueness" (p. 31).

Although typically one of the final things completed, Reeve and Ballard (1993) noted, "The title page is one of the first pages to be read, but sometimes the last page to be written" (p. 31). How can you make yours stand out so a reviewer notices it? Reeve and Ballard suggested that "the title must be clear, descriptive of your project, express end results (not methods), describe benefits, be short, and be easy to remember" (p. 31). Most grantwriters agree that the abstract should be written last. It must be concise and clearly written so that the reviewer is captivated.

In regard to the proposal's introduction, Reeve and Ballard (1993) noted, "This is where you establish your credibility as an applicant for funding" (p. 31). This is the section that is going to set the stage for the reviewer. Normally, the information that you have prepared from the review of the current literature will be presented in the introduction. When describing a project note any strengths and be as specific as possible.

Need Section

Often cited as one of the most important sections of a proposal, the need section is one that typically carries a high point value and must receive the grantwriter's utmost attention. Heczen (1991) noted,

> Grantwriters feel very strongly about the need for their project or research, and they often assume that the funding source shares their feelings. This is usually a fantasy. The funding source has to choose among many interesting proposals, you must create a unique feelings of importance and urgency in your proposal. The funding source is in the business of buying a change or improvement. Your proposal must bridge the gap between what exists now and what should be. Document what is, but do not state your

---

> — **Grant Tip** —
>
> *The evaluation techniques do not have to be highly sophisticated, unless you are writing a research-based proposal, but they certainly need to be sound and well articulated.*

opinions. You are demonstrating your knowledge since you have reviewed the literature, Next, demonstrate what ought to be, and demonstrate how it is the mission of your proposal to deal with this problem. (p. 62)

When writing the need section keep in mind the following pointers:

- Use *current* statistics to dramatize the need for the project.

- Avoid using statistics that do not support your claims. Readers will be able to spot this instantly, and it could hurt your score.

- Keep a file of the data that you have collected including any statistics that you report in your proposal.

- If you are proposing to serve a geographic area, make certain that your data are reflective of that specific geographic area.

Writing the grant objectives can be time-consuming and confusing. But the good news is that this section can be greatly enhanced by reviewing some of the basics involved in writing sound goals and objectives. Simply stated, "Objectives are measurable steps you will take to solve the problem in the statement of need. Objectives are easy to write once the need is established, because they tell what will be accomplished" (Reeve & Ballard, 1993, p. 31). Here are some useful definitions and examples of a goal and an objective.

GOAL: A goal may be defined as a general, overarching (vague, if you will) statement involving a desired long-term outcome.

Example: The pregnant teens enrolled in Central City High School will continue to pursue their high school educations.

OBJECTIVE: An objective is generally defined in specific, measurable terms; and it is related to the goal.

Example: During year one of funding, Central City High School pregnant teens' drop-out rate will decrease by 25%. During year two of funding, Central City High School pregnant teens' drop-out rate will decrease a total of 30%; and during the third and final year of funding, Central City High School pregnant teens' drop-out rate will decrease a total of 40%.

—— **Grant Tip** ——

For more complicated budgets, you may be wise to seek the counsel of a seasoned grantwriter or someone from your accounting office.

One helpful hint that Carlson (1995) provided regarding writing objectives was, "One easy way to ensure you are writing a good objective is to state your objective so that it suggest a purpose such as: to reduce, to increase, to decrease, and to expand" (p. 16). Carlson made this important point: "Objectives do not describe methods. Opening a new spay-neuter clinic is a method. Reducing pet over-population by 10% in 2000 is an objective because it describes a result" (p. 16).

Method/Plan of Operation/Procedures/Approach

The heart of the matter—the method, plan of operation, procedures, or approach section—will usually be the longest section of the proposal. The method section describes how you will accomplish the changes that must occur to solve the problem. Describe program activities in detail. Describe sequence, flow, and relationships. Show staffing and client population. State specific time frames, and make reference to cost/benefit ratios.

Hall (1988) stated that this section "must convince the funding source that you really know how to achieve the outcomes and solve the problems that have been described earlier" (p. 115). Hall also noted that "while a proposal may sometimes get by with fuzzy or imprecise objectives, it is very hard to obfuscate inexperience or incompetence when designing and describing methodology" (p. 115). Hall noted that this section of the proposal often had problems with matching—procedures and outcomes don't match, procedures don't match objectives. Many of these problems can be avoided with careful proofreading by a colleague.

Pokrywczynski (1992) provided insight into frequently noted proposal problem areas. The most often mentioned factor leading to rejection of a proposal were

1. A lack of justification for the theoretical link to the concept(s) of interest

2. Weak arguments, often clearly showing the researcher's lack of understanding of the theory or an artificial theoretical link done simply for the sake of needing theoretical grounding

3. Methodology—often a rejected proposal fails to establish a clear contribution from the study, one that addresses relevant questions for members of the sponsoring organization (p. 72-73)

—— **Grant Tip** ——

The evaluation techniques do not have to be highly sophisticated, unless you are writing a research-based proposal, but they certainly need to be sound and well articulated.

Evaluation

President and CEO of The Pew Trusts, Rebecca W. Rimel (1999) noted,

> Outside of the foundation world, I am often asked, 'How hard can it be to give away money?' My answer is, 'It's not hard, but it's hard to do effectively.' Accordingly, we tie planning and evaluation into not only grant crafting, but also institutional planning. Evaluation has helped us to improve our grant-making programs, keep our strategy focused, and increase our accountability to the public, whom we ultimately serve. (p. 232)

Rimel also reported, "Clearly, evaluation (as we define it) is not merely a monitoring responsibility, which essentially makes sure that grantees fulfill their financial or programmatic obligations" (p. 232).

Regarding how a proposal's effectiveness may be evaluated, Rimel (1999) noted, "Did grantees carry out our strategy and the work of our shared mandate? Did those activities have a public impact? Did they educate? Change opinions? Advance the debate?" (p. 232).

An evaluation section in your proposal will state how the objectives are to be measured and will give a standard by which accomplishment is to be judged. If the objectives are written clearly, the evaluation section is much easier to write. (Pokrywczynski, 1992). Carlson (1995) stated several reasons that organizations conduct evaluation. For example, evaluation may be used to answer these questions: Did the project do what was expected? Were the objectives met? What type of impact resulted?

A clear understanding of the two major evaluation methods is imperative. The evaluation techniques do not have to be highly sophisticated, unless you are writing a research-based proposal, but they certainly need to be sound and well articulated. Frequently, grantwriters will be asked to provide both quantitative and qualitative evaluation methods.

Quantitative methods always involve data analysis techniques (such as averages, means, percentiles, and frequency distributions or descriptive statistics). Inferential statistics such as simple linear regression and chi-square analysis may also be appropriate. Popular forms of qualitative methods include interviews and observations.

An example of using a methodological mix of collecting both quantitative and qualitative data would be conducting a pretest and a posttest in a classroom to determine changes in the knowledge of

—— **Grant Tip** ——
For more complicated budgets you may be wise to seek the counsel of a seasoned grant writer or someone from your accounting office.

students (quantitative). In addition, evaluators might observe the class and the facility in which the curriculum is taught to better understand the students' experience (qualitative).

Budget

Budgets may well be the most feared element in responding to a grant proposal. However, with government proposals it has been made somewhat easier due to the use of "boilerplate" forms that are part of a standard proposal application. All figures should be carefully reviewed, because it is easy to transpose numbers and to make simple addition errors. For more complicated budgets, you may be wise to seek the counsel of a seasoned grantwriter or someone from your accounting office.

When responding to a federal proposal, budget forms are usually included in the *FR*. There are also numerous links to standard budget forms from the Internet that can be easily downloaded. According to Coley and Scheinbert (1990),

> The most common budget format . . . is a line-item budget, where each expenditure is itemized under its appropriate category. In general, costs for a project are divided into two main budget categories: personnel costs and operating expenses. Personnel costs include the salaries and benefits of the staff required to do the project as well as consultants. Operating expenses include non-personnel expenditures such as rent, printing, mailing, travel, telephone, utilities, and office supplies. (p. 84)

Hall (1988) offered the following advice to those preparing the budget: "The budget for a proposal can be developed only after the proposed program has been carefully planned and all activities have been detailed" (p. 163). Here are a few tips that we have learned along the way. They have helped us to prepare proposal budgets:

- Carefully review your proposal noting all expenses. Be sure that these are reflected in your budget.
- Unless you have an experienced staff person that you highly trust, we recommend that *you* prepare the budget.
- Keep a record of how you calculated the figures that you have projected. For instance, when calculating travel costs to and from a national conference keep the price quote that you used. This may come in handy 3 or 4 months down the road.

- Triple check all of your figures. Remember that if you make a last-minute change in the text of your proposal—you decide that only one trip to a national conference, is necessary—you must also make this change in your budget.

- Don't underestimate the importance of your budget. Funders are generally budget experts and can pinpoint questionable items with relative ease.

- Make certain that if you write in your proposal the need for a Tutor Coordinator that you have a Tutor Coordinator budgeted not a Tutor Advisor.

- Know any specific budget relationships required by the funder. For instance, you may be allowed to budget only 4% of the total for staff travel.

Appendixes

"Last but not least," noted Conrad (1980), "If you or anyone you know has ever had surgery for removal of his appendix, you know that an often forgotten and neglected organ can prove to be quite important. . . . In a grant proposal appendices contain vital information which some people tend to forget" (p. 81). Some of the common items found in appendixes include (a) letters of support, (b) resumes, (c) job descriptions, and (d) samples of project brochures or fliers.

Frequently, letters of support or letters of commitment are required by the funding agency to document the nature and level of support you enjoy (see Figure 9.6). These are basically the same thing but there may be some subtle differences. Read the guidelines carefully. If letters of commitment are required, be certain that each letter specifically documents the value of the services that will be rendered to the project. For instance, somewhere in the letter it needs to state, "The Central City Youth Center will provide space for individual counseling sessions on a weekly basis. This commercial office space is currently valued at $100 per sq. ft. or $12,000 for the three office suites (10' x 12') that will be provided to (your staff) for the duration of funding." A statement such as this provides clear evidence to the funding agency and to the reader of the nature and level of commitment that is being provided. Avoid vague and unrelated letters. Many reviewers see this as padding the proposal; usually they are not impressed. In some cases, it may be seen as a way to cover up for a lack of solid letters of commitment, and you could (or might) lose points.

Figure 9.6. Sample Letter of Support

February 15, 2001

Mr. Chris Adams, Director
Central City Youth Center
1111 First Street
Central City, USA 12345

Dear Chris,

The purpose of this letter is to offer my support and to document
my continued commitment to the work that you and your staff do
at Central City's Youth Center. I am pleased to provide you with
this letter of support so that our young people will continue to
have a safe place to go after school and in the evening. As a
Juvenile Probation Officerin Central City, I am well aware of the
need that your program fills with our young people. I have the
opportunity to interact with many of these youth who might
otherwise endup in one of the detention centers or jail.

To demonstrate my commitment, I am once again offering to
conduct monthly, year-round, after-school seminars. Each
seminar is approximately 2 hours long. As you know, the topics
vary, but include various life skills. The cost of these seminars I
have estimated to be valued at approximately: 45 seminars x 2
hours x $50 per hour = $4,500.

Again, I am pleased to have this opportunity to work with you
and wish for you much success as you seek additional funding
for Central City's Youth Center.

Sincerely,

Sarah Lanier, Juvenile Probation Office
Central City

Once a decision has been made to submit a proposal, begin to
draft a list of individuals whom you will need to contact to provide a
letter of support. "In some instances you may be asked by the
organizations to draft a letter of support for them. This is often ideal,
as you can be very specific about the items you want emphasized by
each supporting source" (Coley & Scheinbert, 1990, p. 99). Coley and

Scheinbert also noted, "As the grantwriter, be prepared to make follow-up phone calls to the agencies and to pick up the letter if you are nearing the proposal deadline" (p. 99). Generally, faxing the letters is not recommended. Request that all letters be submitted on letterhead and signed by the highest ranking official possible. We also recommend that when organizing your letters place them in the order of those you consider to be the most significant to those of least significance.

A Final Note

Volumes have been written about proposal development and grantwriting. Many of these provide excellent pointers and tips to improve proposals. We recommend that you begin your own grants library. With the Internet readily accessible in most parts of the country, most individuals have at their fingertips hours of surfing some excellent resources without ever having to leave their homes. Frost (1993) noted, "All successful writing relies upon a simple premise: no tears in the writer, no tears in the reader" (p. i). He also noted, "All of the proposals . . . communicate the passion and commitment necessary to conjure up the child whose dreams are yet to be realized or the beauty and importance of the unbuilt museum" (p. i). Frost provided the following interesting insight into proposal writing:

> What makes each proposal . . . especially effective, however, is craft. And, just as a well-crafted poem evokes clear images without cliché, these proposals elucidate the missions of institutions in a way that holds up under scrutiny. The arguments are as sound as the feelings behind them. (p. i)

As a final note, be sure to acknowledge the efforts of all the grant helpers. Recognize the efforts of those who have helped in the development of the proposal. There are many ways to recognize individuals, and certainly this will depend upon their level of involvement. For larger proposals, you may want to get together for dinner after the proposal has been mailed. Most people appreciate personal handwritten notes thanking them for their assistance. Regardless of what method you use to say thank you, just remember that it is not so much the dollar value that counts as the appreciation that the acknowledgment represents.

Advice from Reif-Lehrer (1995) is to make an outline. She noted, "An outline is like a road map or blueprint, a plan of 'what you will write' (the ideas). The text is 'how you write it' (the words and sentences that express the ideas)" (p. 317). When deciding to use charts or graphs, consider the following:

1. They must be essential to your proposal and not just a cover-up for a lack of substantive material.

2. Make sure everything is properly labeled and inserted in the right place in sequential order. Always explain a chart or table within the text. Charts and tables should follow the discussion.

3. It is not wise to assume that readers will automatically understand your chart or table. Avoid using abbreviations, acronyms, or jargon.

Conclusion

Remember that things take time, and this includes learning and developing the skills needed to be a successful grantwriter. We have found many individuals who have been willing to share their expertise. However, the majority of the learning will rest squarely on your shoulders. Be proactive. Take classes, Read books. Network. Ask questions. Listen. Learn from others who have been successful.

10

Reviewing a Funded Proposal

Introduction

This chapter contains an example of a federally funded grant proposal in its entirety except for the appendixes. It was submitted by one of the authors and funded by the United States Department of Education for a three-year period. This project was one of four funded in the United States during competition in response to an *Application for Grants under the College Assistance Migrant Program.* The main purpose of this project was to provide academic and support services and financial assistance to students who were engaged in or who were from families engaged in migrant and other seasonal farmwork. The program must have met other eligible guidelines that are outlined in the regulations.

Chapter 4, "Using the *Catalog of Federal Domestic Assistance (CFDA),*" uses this program as an example for discussing parts of the *CFDA.* "What Are the Components of a Proposal?" and "Writing a Proposal," Chapters 6 and 8, respectively, use various sections of this proposal in describing the aspects of writing grant proposals. The *Application Technical Review Form,* which is addressed in Chapter 11, "Understanding How Grants Are Awarded," shows how field readers review and evaluate a grant application such as the one presented in this chapter against selected criteria that are established by the Secretary.

Selection Criteria

The funding agency—in this example, the United States Department of Education—instructs potential applicants as to what must be included in an application and how the Secretary reviews and evaluates the proposal against the stated criteria. In this particular example, the Secretary indicated that the application would be evaluated on the following selection criteria. The maximum number of points possible for each criterion are listed.

——Grant Tip——
Selection criteria are weighted with a point value, and each one must be addressed by an applicant when developing a grant proposal.

Selection Criteria	Maximum Number of Points Awarded
Plan of Operation	25
Objectives and Activities	20
Evaluation Plan	15
Quality of Key Personnel	10
Budget and Cost-Effectiveness	10
Interagency Consultation and Coordination	10
Adequacy of Resources	5
Recruitment	5

Plan of Operation

This section provides information to show the quality of an effective plan of management that ensures proper and efficient administration of the project. The plan of operation presents a clear description of the way the applicant (university) plans to use its resources and personnel to achieve project objectives. In this section, the applicant describes how it will provide equal access and treatment for eligible participants who are members of groups that have been traditionally underrepresented, such as members of racial or ethnic minority groups, women, handicapped persons, and the elderly.

Objectives and Activities

The *Objectives and Activities* section of this sample proposal demonstrates how the applicant provided information that shows the quality in the design of objectives and activities for project participants. Because the main purpose of this proposal is to provide academic and support services and financial assistance to students engaged in migrant and other seasonal farmwork, the project's objectives and activities respond to the academic, support, and financial needs of the participating students. The applicant also addressed the size, scope, and quality of the project activities and how they contribute successfully to meeting the project objectives and program purposes.

Evaluation Plan

This section includes information that shows the quality of the evaluation plan for the proposed project. Specifically, the applicant addressed evaluation methods appropriate for the project and to the extent possible, that are objective and produce quantifiable data. Note how the applicant assesses the progress in achieving the objectives, the effectiveness of the project in meeting the purposes of the federal program, and the effect on persons being served by the project.

Quality of Key Personnel

When dealing with the *Quality of Key Personnel* section, the applicant provides information that shows adequate qualifications for the key personnel the applicant plans to use in this project. Typically in the appendixes you would provide a full résumé and job description for each person you plan to use in the project. If you have not identified a person for a specific position, include a job description. The narrative of this section includes the qualifications of the project director and each other key person in the project—this includes experience and training in fields related to the objectives of the project, the time each person will commit to the project, and the extent to which the *applicant* encourages applications for employment from persons who are members of disadvantaged backgrounds.

Budget and Cost-Effectiveness

In this section the applicant provides information showing that the project has an adequate budget and is cost-effective. Information shows how the budget will support project activities and indicates that costs are reasonable in relation to proposed objectives.

Interagency Consultation and Coordination

This section demonstrates that the applicant conducted adequate consultation and coordination with other agencies in planning and developing the proposal. In addition, the applicant describes how it consults and coordinates with appropriate agencies in implementing and evaluating the project.

Adequacy of Resources

This section shows how the applicant plans to devote adequate resources to the project. This section provides information relating to project office facilities, academic facilities, and residential facilities that will be utilized by the project. The *Adequacy of Resources* section describes resources and support activities available to the project.

Recruitment

In this section, note how the applicant provides information that shows the quality of the recruitment plan. The applicant outlined how the plan will identify, inform, and recruit eligible participants who are most in need of the academic and support services and financial assistance provided by the project.

Appendixes

The authors did not include any appendixes in the following example because of limited space. Appendixes are important in some proposals but may be prohibited in others. This particular proposal had five appendixes:

APPENDIX	CONTENT
A	Letters of Support
B	Résumés
C	Job Descriptions
D	Program Forms
E	Program Materials

If appendixes are prohibited in the proposal you wish to write, you should still seek the same kinds of support and commitments you would normally include in the appendixes. Paraphrase and condense such letters and commitments into your narrative and indicate that the documents are on file and available upon request. In this manner you can often accomplish nearly the same effect you would if you were able to include appendixes.

Sample Proposal

The sample proposal included on the following pages was initially written and submitted by Ernest W. Brewer, The University of Tennessee, Knoxville, in 1985 and rewritten for continued funding in 1987. This was one of four proposals that were funded by the U.S. Department of Education for three years in response to the grant competition of *CFDA* 84.149.

OMB Approval No. 0348-0043

APPLICATION FOR FEDERAL ASSISTANCE

2. DATE SUBMITTED *12-11-XX*	Applicant Identifier

1. TYPE OF BUSINESS

Application	*Preapplication*
☐ Construction	☐ Construction
☒ Non-Construction	☐ Non-Construction

3. DATE RECEIVED BY STATE	State Application Identifier
4. DATE RECEIVED BY FEDERAL AGENCY	Federal Identifier

5. APPLICANT INFORMATION

Legal Name: *The University of Tennessee*	Organizational Unit:
Address (give city, county, state, and zip code): *404 Andy Holt Tower Knoxville, Tennessee 37996*	Name and telephone number of the person to be contacted on matter involving this application (give area code): *Dr. Ernest W. Brewer, Principal Investigator (865/974-4466)*

6. EMPLOYER IDENTIFICATION NUMBER (EIN): ☐☐-☐☐☐☐☐☐☐

8. TYPE OF APPLICATION: ☒ New ☐ Continuation ☐ Revision

If Revision, enter appropriate letter(s) in box(es): ☐ ☐

A. Increase Award   B. Decrease Award   C. Increase Duration

D. Decrease Duration   Other (specify): —————

7. TYPE OF APPLICANT (enter appropriate letter in box) ☑

A. State	H. Independent School District
B. County	I. State Controlled Institution of Higher Learning
C. Municipal	J. Private University
D. Township	K. Indian Tribe
E. Interstate	L. Individual
F. Intermunicipal	M. Profit Organization
G. Special District	N. Other (Specify):_____

9. NAME OF FEDERAL AGENCY:

10. CATALOG OF FEDERAL DOMESTIC ASSISTANCE NUMBER: 8 4 - 1 4 9

TITLE: *College Assistance Migrant Program*

11. DESCRIPTIVE TITLE OF APPLICANT'S PROJECT:

The University of Tennessee's Southeastern College Assistance Migrant Program

12. AREAS AFFECTED BY PROJECT (cities, states, etc.):

Alabama, Florida, Georgia, Kentucky, North Carolina, South Carolina, Tennessee, and Virginia

13. PROPOSED PROJECT:

Start Date *09 01 XX*	Ending Date *08 31 XX*

14. CONGRESSIONAL DISTRICTS OF:

a. Applicant *Second*	b. Project *All of AL, FL, GA, KY, NC, SC, TN, and VA*

15. ESTIMATED FUNDING:

a. Federal	$ 476,960 .00
b. Applicant	$ 99,367 .00
c. State	$ .00
d. Local	$ .00
e. Other	$ .00
f. Program Income	$ .00
g. TOTAL	$ 576,327 .00

16. IS APPLICATION SUBJECT TO REVIEW BY STATE EXECUTIVE ORDER 12372 PROCESS?

a. YES. THIS PREAPPLICATION/APPLICATION WAS MADE AVAILABLE TO THE STATE EXECUTIVE ORDER 12372 PROCESS FOR REVIEW ON:

DATE: *12 1 XX*

b. NO. ☐ PROGRAM IS NOT COVERED BY E. O. 12372

☐ OR PROGRAM HAS NOT BEEN SELECTED BY STATE FOR REVIEW

17. IS THE APPLICANT DELINQUENT ON ANY FEDERAL DEBT?

☐ Yes   If "Yes," attach an explanation.   ☒ No

18. TO THE BEST OF MY KNOWLEDGE AND BELIEF, ALL DATA IN THIS APPLICATION/PREAPPLICATION ARE TRUE AND CORRECT. THE DOCUMENT HAS BEEN DULY AUTHORIZED BY THE GOVERNING BODY OF THE APPLICANT AND THE APPLICANT WILL COMPLY WITH THE ATTACHED ASSURANCES IF THE ASSISTANCE IS AWARDED.

a. Typed Name of Authorized Representative	b. Title *Vice-Provost for Research*	c. Telephone number *865/974-4466*
d. Signature of Authorized Representative		e. Date Signed

Previous Editions Not Usable

Authorized for Local Reproduction

Standard Form 424 (REV. 4-88)
Prescribed by OMB Circular A-102

Table of Contents
College Assistance Migrant Program
The University of Tennessee
19XX-XX Program Years

PART III--BUDGET INFORMATION

FOR THE

COLLEGE ASSISTANCE MIGRANT PROGRAM

SECTION: A BUDGET SUMMARY

OBJECT CLASS CATEGORIES	FEDERAL FUNDING AMOUNTS
a. Personnel	$ 181,500.00
b. Fringe Benefits	$ 43,500.00
c. Travel	$ 10,300.00
d. Equipment	$ 6,900.00
e. Supplies	$ 1,600.00
f. Contractual	$ 00.00
g. Other	$ 197,830.00
h. Total Direct Charges (a-h)	$ 441,630.00
i. Indirect Charges	$ 35,330.00
j. Total (lines h + i)	$ 476,960.00

iii

College Assistance Migrant Program
Base Budget 19XX-XX (one year)
{Raises and adjustments will be computed annually}

DIRECT COST

A. Personnel {Example — list and price each}
    1.   Director (25% time for 12 mos.) $18,500.00
    2.   Associate Director (100% time for 12 mos.) $51,000.00
    3.   Counselor (100% time for 12 mos.) $28,000.00
    4.   Recruiter/Counselor (100% time for 12 mos.) $28,000.00
    5.   Principal Secretary (100% time for 12 mos.) $19,500.00
    6.   *Part-time Tutors (4-5 @ 20/30 hrs/wk for 10 mos.) $36,500.00

                                 Subtotal for Personnel $181,500.00

B. Fringe Benefits $43,500.00

        (The University of Tennessee's employee benefits are calculated at
        30%. *Graduate assistants and part-time employees do not receive
        fringe benefits.) (30% x $145,000.00 = $43,500.00)

                                 Subtotal for Fringe Benefits $43,500.00

C. Staff Travel {list and describe each — e.g.}

    1.   Local Travel (pick up students at bus station, $10,300.00
        take students to service agencies, etc.)

                                 Subtotal for Staff Travel $10,300.00

D. Equipment (Two computers/monitors @ $3,450/each) $6,900.00

                                 Subtotal for Equipment $6,900.00

E. Consumable Supplies {supplies, copies, etc. — add details} $1,600.00

                                 Subtotal for Supplies $1,600.00

F. Contractual $00.00

                                 Subtotal for Contractual $00.00

G. Other

1.	Tuition and Fees (30 in-state students @ $468/ Qtr. x 1 Qtr. = $14,040 + 30 out-of-state students @ $1,186/Qtr. x 1 Qtr. = $35,580)	$49,620.00
2.	Stipends (60 students x $40/mo. x 9 mos.)	$21,600.00
3.	Student Travel (60 students x $80 = $4,800)	$4,800.00
4.	Student Dorm (60 students x $425/Qtr. x 2 Qtrs.)	$51,000.00
5.	Student Meals (60 students x $430/Qtr. x 2 Qtrs.)	$51,600.00
6.	Testing Materials	$300.00
7.	Duplication (forms, classroom handouts, etc.)	$700.00
8.	Postage	$800.00
9.	Communication (telephone service charges)	$5,200.00
10.	HEP/CAMP Dues	$350.00
11.	HEP/CAMP Scholarships (10 x $1,186)	$11,860.00

Subtotal for Other $197,830.00

H. Total Direct Cost $441,630.00

I. *Total Indirect Costs {explain details} <u>$35,330.00</u>

J. Total Cost $476,960.00

*The University is contributing indirect costs of $99,367.00 based on Modified Total Direct Costs (MTDC). MTDC are total costs less capital outlay items. 39% and 22.0% are the officially audited Indirect Costs rates by DHHS Audit Agency under OMB A-88 Negotiation Agreement, dated January 27, 19XX for UT-Knoxville on-campus and off-campus other sponsored activities.

$441,630 x 39% x .5 On/Off Campus = $86,118.00
$441,630 x 22% x .5 On/Off Campus = <u>$48,579.00</u>
Total UTK Indirect $134,697.00
Less Indirect Authorized - $ 35,330.00
Total UTK Cost-Sharing - $ 99,367.00

Background Information

Institution and Region

The University of Tennessee (UT) is a multi-campus, multi-purpose system of higher education with branches throughout Tennessee. As Tennessee's state university and federal land-grant institution, it is regarded as the "capstone of the state's educational system." *The College Money Book* calls UT the **"best buy"** for students, based on "high quality education at an economical cost." In carrying out its unique public service responsibilities, UT has a statewide mission beyond that of any other institution of higher learning in the Southeastern region of the United States. The University offers more than one hundred fields of study and sponsors a full program of student services and activities.

As the major institution in the state, UT has a RESPONSIBILITY to develop and administer programs to meet the needs of special populations. Currently, there is an overwhelming need to re-establish a College Assistance Migrant Program (CAMP) in the southeastern region of the United States. At present, UT's CAMP program was the only one that existed in this region. UT remains an IDEAL GEOGRAPHIC LOCATION to serve migrant/seasonal farmworkers and their dependents from the southeast because NINE (9) STATES BORDER TENNESSEE, and the Migrant Education Program office in Washington, D.C. furnished a report indicating that there were over 107,362 migrant students of 0-21 years of age in the eight (8) state (Alabama, Florida, Georgia, Kentucky, North Carolina, South Carolina, Tennessee, and Virginia) targeted area of the southeastern region. The reason that a large geographical area will be served is due to the fact that there are only five (5) CAMP projects in the U.S. and those are in Texas and on the West Coast. The service area, consisting of the eight states mentioned, is shown in the map below.

Map of Targeted States
Southeastern College Assistance Migrant Program

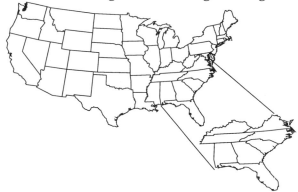

The statistical data cited in the paragraph above indicates that there are significant populations of migrant/ seasonal farmworkers in the region, many of whom benefitted from the operation of Southeastern HEP/ CAMP at UT. The University is aware of the educational and socioeconomic problems of disadvantaged students including the migrant/seasonal farmworker student. The University currently operates the High School Equivalency Program (HEP), an Upward Bound program, an Educational Talent Search program, and a Student Support Services program which have benefitted migrant/seasonal farmworker youth at the secondary and postsecondary level. The southeastern region of the United States, recognized as a major home-base area for migrant/seasonal farmworkers, is an ideal location for funding a CAMP program.

1

Program Need

Migrant/seasonal farmworkers have a unique background and possess UNIQUE educational needs that only the CAMP program can address. These students have the lowest rate of college admission, the lowest rate of college completion, and the highest rate of under- and unemployment. The University has developed and implemented programs designed to correct academic skill deficiencies, promote student self-worth, and create an environment in which students feel welcome and non-threatened by its institutional structure and academic environment. These programs, along with the specialized tutoring and counseling, enable farmworker students to have the necessary support to adjust successfully to college life and maximize their learning potentials while enrolled.

The Need for CAMP in the Targeted Area

The Southeastern CAMP Program will be the only CAMP program available in the southeastern region of the country, in spite of the fact that a very large number of youth from migrant/seasonal farmworker families have been identified in our target area. The Association of Farmworker Opportunity Programs (AFOP) has stated that its member organizations in the eight (8) target states served 40,916 farmworkers during the 1983-84 program year. The Association estimates that TOTAL farmworker population from the eight (8) state area is over 801,500 of which 267,000 were identified as migrants (according to the Department of Labor's Farmworker Farm and Rural Employment and Training Office). Furthermore, this need is supported by the USDA's ranking of the states as to the number of farms over 400 acres. Of the targeted states that we currently serve and propose to serve within this proposal, three (3) of the eight (8) states ranked as follows: Kentucky is ranked Number 4 with 101,000 farms; Tennessee is ranked Number 7 with 95,000 farms; and North Carolina is ranked Number 11 with 79,000 farms (*U.S. News and World Report*, October 22, 19XX).

In addition, very low numbers of students from migrant/seasonal backgrounds attend any kind of postsecondary program. The reasons for this can be identified by examining the barriers typically present for this type of student:

1. There is a *lack of effective motivation among farmworker youth.* It is difficult to stimulate migrant/seasonal farmworker youth to attend college. Parents discourage them from attending either because they need them to work the fields with them or because they are doubtful that they can be successful.
2. *Farmworker students often lack financial resources* to pay for a college education and are often unfamiliar with Federal aid programs designed to assist low-income students.
3. *Families of farmworker students lack financial resources* to pay for a college education and are often unfamiliar with Federal aid programs.
4. *Farmworker students have poor self-concepts and fear the unknown* situation and experiences of college life.

Our experience in administering programs for disadvantaged students has led us to identify factors which contribute to students' dropping out of postsecondary programs. These factors, which relate to problems encountered by students from migrant farmworker backgrounds, are:

1. *Lack of financial means* for school. Students have difficulty getting summer jobs and are usually unable to rely on resources from the family.

2

2. *Poor academic progress* and an *insufficient number of earned credits.* The results of inappropriately "declared majors" or change of majors cause students to lose credit for nonrelevant classes.
3. *Lack of career goals* which affect a student's sense of purpose and commitment.
4. *Feelings of alienation, fear of failure, lack of acceptance,* and *disbelief in one's ability* to succeed.

These issues and barriers are especially painful and real to students from migrant/seasonal farmworker backgrounds and will not be conquered without such programs as UT's Southeastern CAMP Program which has been designed to ENCOURAGE these students to enroll in college and receive ACADEMIC SUPPORT, FINANCIAL ASSISTANCE, and COUNSELING to help them believe in themselves and overcome those barriers which exist.

The map of the United States shown below indicates where the five (5) 19XX-XX CAMP programs are located and shows the lack of program support for the migrant/seasonal farmworker population in the southeastern region of the United States.

Map of 19XX-XX CAMP Programs

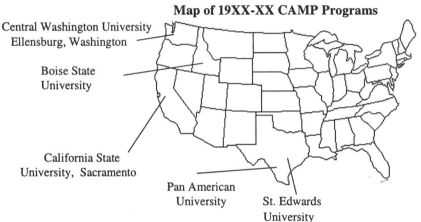

Central Washington University
Ellensburg, Washington

Boise State
University

California State
University, Sacramento

Pan American
University

St. Edwards
University

In summary, the need exists to provide CAMP services to the migrant/seasonal farmworker of the Southeastern United States and to coordinate the identification and recruitment of the migrant/seasonal farmworker population. Programs which are designed to enhance student academic performance and retention must be provided. Efforts must be made to diagnose and remediate academic difficulties so that appropriate learning programs may be prescribed. Students must be provided with tutorial services and counseling so that appropriate career objectives can be identified. And finally, efforts must be made to ensure the positive growth and development which focuses on generating pride in one's cultural and ethnic heritage. These needs provide the basis for the program design narrative which follows.

Plan of Operation
(206.31(a) - 25 Points)

Recognition of the Legislative Intent of the Project
(206.31(a)(2)(iii))

As is stated in the *Federal Register*, Volume 52, Number 126, July 1, 19XX, CAMP will provide assistance to help migratory and seasonal farmworker students in:

3

1. Making the transition from secondary school to postsecondary school;
2. Generating the motivation necessary to succeed in postsecondary school; and
3. Developing the skills necessary to succeed in postsecondary school.

Furthermore, those eligible migrant and seasonal farmworkers will be identified in accordance with the regulations described on page 24918 of the *Federal Register*, dated July 1, 19XX.

This new college experience provides a genuine opportunity for many of these individuals to leave a lifestyle of failure and poverty, an option not readily available to this population. The proposed CAMP project will combine University resources with program resources to provide assistance in all areas of student need. This project will provide students with total financial assistance for their freshman year through a combination of grants, work study, loans, and scholarships to cover tuition, fees, and other college expenses. Following their freshman year, the Financial Aid Office at UT will continue to assist students by providing financial aid awards to the full extent of the demonstrated financial need for years two, three, and four of the student's college experience.

High Quality in the Design of the Project
(206.31(a)(2)(i))

The overall project is designed in accordance with the guidelines stated in the *Federal Register*. Most importantly, in preplanning the design, assurances were made to incorporate all of the services listed in the *Register*. As is shown on page 24921, seven (7) services areas are outlined "to assist the participants in meeting the project objectives and in succeeding in an academic program of study at the IHE." Those services are as follows: (1) recruitment; (2) special counseling; (3) housing support; (4) career exploration services; (5) exposure to academic institutions, programs, cultural events; (6) inservice training for staff; and (7) tutoring and supplementary instruction including basic skills, subject areas needed by the student, related areas such as study skills, and other essential supportive services.

In addition, page 24918 of the *Register* states that the purpose of CAMP is to provide services in three major areas: (1) academic; (2) supporting; and (3) financial. These service areas as well as the services indicated in the previous paragraph have all been integrated and coordinated in the overall project design. Services to be provided are as follows (see Flowchart the following page):

1. **Student Assessment:** The CAMP staff will use information gathered from forms which the students completed during the recruitment process. ACT scores and the student's high school record or GED scores will be used to identify student's academic needs, strengths and weaknesses. In those cases where additional academic data is necessary, the California Achievement Test (CAT) and the Test for Adult Basic Education (TABE) will be utilized. From this data an Individual Educational Plan (IEP) will be established for each student. Also included in the student assessment will be an evaluation of the psychological and emotional needs of the student. Each student will have an individual interview to determine attitudinal problems which may interfere with optimal academic achievement. The CAMP staff will identify students' academic motivation and self-concept to determine the degree to which students feel secure about their educational pursuits. Students will complete a Self-Report Questionnaire to assist counselors with identification of the above mentioned concerns. Those students feeling insecure about themselves or their academic ability will participate in peer support groups to encourage the development of self-confidence and acceptance.

4

2. **Study Skill Development:** Special classes will be established for study skills development. Such skills as time-management, effective notetaking, planning, organizing and other basic academic techniques will be taught.

3. **Academic Instructional Support:** Special sections of university courses will be arranged by CAMP in the areas of English, math, and science so that regular university faculty can instruct CAMP students in a manner appropriate to their learning style and academic preparation.

4. **Tutoring:** Part of the IEP for each student will include a tentative tutoring schedule. CAMP staff will coordinate the tutoring schedule and will document all tutoring received. The Basic Skills Specialist will maintain contact with academic faculty and CAMP staff to assess student progress and determine the need for additional tutoring. CAMP students experiencing high academic success in certain subjects will be encouraged to participate as tutors in a peer tutoring program.

5. **Staff Training:** The majority of the CAMP staff members have been previously trained in working with migrant and seasonal farmworkers and additional training will continue. It is necessary for each staff member to receive information and training to help develop greater awareness and sensitivity to the needs of this particular population. In order to provide this information and training a series of preservice sessions will be planned and conducted, and each staff member will be required to attend. Those sessions will be held early in the program year and prior to the arrival of students.

> **Similar detail is provided for all additional entries (student recruitment, student orientation, counseling, career exploration, social/cultural enrichment, housing/meals, health care, transition, follow-up, financial aid, stipends, and CAMP scholarships.**

The University of Tennessee's
Southeastern College Assistance Migrant Program (CAMP)

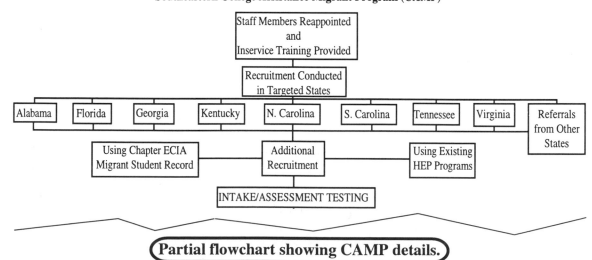

Partial flowchart showing CAMP details.

The *Flowchart of Services and Activities* shows the overall design layout and the interrelationship of each service component.   *5*

Effective Plan of Management
(206.31(a)(2)(ii))

The university is an equal opportunity, affirmative action employer and does not discriminate on the basis of race, sex, color, religion, nationality, age, handicap, or veteran status in providing employment of educational opportunities and benefits.

The program will be an integral part of the university structure within the College of Education's Technological and Adult Education Department. This university (grantee) designates the CAMP Director and Associate Director as the University Administrators responsible for program grant compliance and management. Within this context, the CAMP Director and Associate Director are responsible for:

(Three samples of nine shown.)

1. Preparing, submitting, and negotiating the College Assistance Migrant Program (CAMP) proposal and other reports required by the U.S. Department of Education (DE);
2. Administration of the program and coordination with the DE's Migrant Education Program, the University, State Farmworker agencies, and Referral/Placement Services;
3. Assuring that the coordination between the CAMP staff and students and the university administration and faculty is accomplished on a timely basis;

The CAMP staff members are employees of the univerisity, governed by university personnel and employment policies and have all rights, privileges, and benefits afforded university employees.

The Director reports to the College of Education's Technological and Adult Education Department, provides reports as necessary, and meets weekly with the CAMP staff. These meetings are augmented by progress reports and frequent communications. The organizational chart for the project and its relationship to the university administrative structure is shown below. The QUALITY OF KEY PERSONNEL Section of this proposal is located on pages 15-17 and shows the personnel which the University currently has employed in the last project and their qualifications. Resumes and Job Descriptions are located in Appendixes B and C, respectively, of this proposal.

(Partial organizational chart)

Project Organization of Personnel

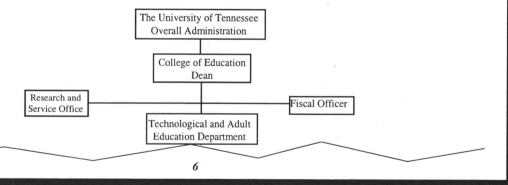

6

Relationship of Objectives to the Purposes of the Project
(206.31(a)(2)(iii))

As was stated in the design section of the plan (operation), Page 24921 of the *Federal Register* states that the purpose of CAMP is to provide academic services, supporting services, and financial assistance. All of the components of the objectives section as shown on pages 8-11 are designed to address these three (3) major service areas. The outline below demonstrates how each objective component relates to the three (3) service areas of the overall purpose of the project:

1. Academic Service Area Objectives:
    a.   Student Assessment
    b.   Study Skills Development
    c.   Academic Instructional Support
    d.   Tutoring
2. Supportive Service Area Objectives:
    a.   Staff Training
    b.   Student Recruitment
    c.   Student Orientation
    d.   Adjustment Workshops
    e.   Counseling
    f.   Career Exploration
    g.   Social/Cultural Activities
    h.   Housing/Meals
    i.   Health Care
    j.   Freshman-Sophomore Transition Assistance
    k.   Follow-Up
3. Financial Assistance Area Objectives:
    a.   Financial Aid
    b.   Student Stipend
    c.   CAMP Scholarship

In summary, four (4) objectives focus on academic service areas, eleven (11) objectives focus on supportive service areas, and three (3) focus on financial assistance service areas.

Use of Resources and Personnel
(206.31(a)(2)(iv))

We value greatly the high degree of University support and the numerous University resources that are available to the CAMP project and its participants. These resources serve to supplement and enhance the learning and social environment for CAMP students. Examples of those resources which are available include:

(Three of original 12 examples appear here.)

1. An Office of Finance which provides complete fiscal services (accounting, budgeting, purchasing, payrolls, etc.) and other financial records necessary for fiscal compliance.
2. An Office of Personnel which ensures equal employment opportunities for all staff and provides the personnel services necessary for hiring staff and processing grievance and due process hearings.
3. A Maintenance Department which provides OFFICE SPACE and equipment, other necessary space for activities, maintenance of buildings and grounds, and also performs custodial service.

7

These are representative of the resources which the university offers to enrich and enhance the academic program and to help make the students' stay at the University more fulfilling as well as enlightening. A more detailed description of the Project's resources can be found in the ADEQUACY OF RESOURCES Section of this proposal. LETTERS OF SUPPORT showing University personnel and significant others as resources are located in APPENDIX A.

Equal Access and Treatment for Eligible Participant
(206.3(a)(2)(v))

The University is in full compliance with all Federal and equal access regulations and will provide equal access and treatment for eligible participants and staff members who are members of groups that have been traditionally underrepresented such as members of racial or ethnic minority groups, women, and handicapped persons. This is outlined more explicitly in the OBJECTIVES and ACTIVITIES Sections of this proposal.

In employing CAMP staff these same Federal and equal access compliance guidelines will be adhered to. Careful consideration will be given to the experience and training of all applicants to assure that those hired have a background which is appropriately related to the objectives of the project.

Other Sections Supportive to the Plan of Operation

The following sections do NOT APPEAR in the PLAN OF OPERATION but are presented in their respective areas according to Subpart D 206.31 of the Request for Proposal (RFP) on "What selection criteria does the Secretary use to evaluate the application?" These sections are an integral part of the overall operation of the project and are presented in detail in this proposal as indicated as follows. The OBJECTIVES AND ACTIVITIES Section of this proposal, pages 8-11, has the various COMPONENTS of the project. These objectives and activities of the project are designed to respond to the academic, supportive, and financial needs of the participating CAMP students. The EVALUATION Section of this proposal is located on pages 12-15 which shows the comprehensive evaluation plan for the project. The QUALITY OF KEY PERSONNEL Section of this proposal, pages 15-18, identifies the qualifications of the project director and other key personnel, the time that each person plans to commit to the project, and the extent to which the University, as part of its nondiscriminatory employment practices, encourages applications from members of groups that have been traditionally underrepresented. The BUDGET and COST-EFFECTIVENESS Section, located on pages 18-19, documents that the budget for the project is adequate to support the project activities, and costs are reasonable in relation to the objectives of the project. On pages 21-22 the ADEQUACY OF RESOURCES Section is presented, which identifies the facilities, equipment, and supplies that the applicant plans to use. The last section of this proposal is RECRUITMENT (pages 22-23) which addresses the recruitment services of this project.

Objectives and Activities
(206.31(b) - 20 points)

⟨ **Four done in detail; others listed.** ⟩

8

Quality of the Design of Objectives and Activities for Participants
(206.31(b)(1))

Page one of the Plan of Operation, lists the three broad service areas which were cited in the *Federal Register* on page 24922. These are academic services, supporting services, and financial services. Within these broad service areas, seventeen (17) specific services were identified as necessary in order to meet the needs of project participants. For each of these services an objective with appropriate supportive activities has been written, and these are presented in the following format:

1. Component title - identifies the objective topic.
2. Goal - states the broad intention for this objective.
3. Objectives - defines the measurable outcome (the product).
4. Activities - lists the specific procedures or ways the objective is to be met (the process).
5. Timeline - specifies when the activities of the objective will be met.
6. Evaluation - determines if, and to what degree, the objective was met.
7. Staff responsibility - shows the staff member responsible for activities.

Objectives and Activities Designed to Respond to Academic, Supporting, and Financial Needs of Participants
(206.31(b)(2)(i))

This section consists of the Project's seventeen (17) objectives and activities and are presented according to the design format shown above. They respond to the academic, supportive, and financial needs of the participants.

1. Student Assessment

Goal: To create an individual profile of each participant which identifies strengths and weaknesses.

Objective: To review and evaluate collected data on 100% of the CAMP participants and develop an Individual Educational Plan (IEP) showing special academic help and tutorial assistance needed by each student by the second week they are accepted into the program.

Activities: 1. Review data on initial intake form.
    a.   Self Report questionnaires;
    b.   High School Transcript (GED Score Report); and
    c.   ACT Score Report
2.   Administer additional assessment data, such as the California Achievement Test (CAT), as necessary.
3.   Determine study skill needs of each participant.
4.   Determine special class instruction needs of each participant.
5.   Determine tutoring needs of each participant.
6.   Evaluate any special psychological, emotional, or motivational needs which exist for each student.

9

7. Develop an IEP for each participant.
8. Conduct conferences to review IEP with the each participant.

Timeline: September 12, 19XX - Collect and Review all student data.
                     September 28, 19XX - Complete IEP on each student.

Evaluation: Place all data collected in student folder. Have copy of IEP in folder with a list
                     of special academic help and tutorial assistance the project will provide each
                     participant.

Staff Responsibility: Associate Director, Counselor, Recruiter/Counselor

2. Study Skills Development

Goal: To conduct an effective study skills development program.

Objective: To provide a minimum of three hours of study skills training and instruction to
                     90% of the CAMP participants.

Activities: 1. Administer study skills pretest at beginning of first study skills class.
                     2. All students attend a study skills development class for three weeks.
                     3. Instruct students in study techniques, note taking, time management, and
                         other fundamental study skills designed to improve college class
                         performance.
                     4. Administer and score study skills posttest.
                     5. Record results of posttest gains in students' IEP.

Timeline: September 30, 19XX - Administer pretest; Students attend first session
                     October 7, 19XX   - Second session
                     October 17, 19XX   - Administer posttest

Evaluation: Maintain an attendance log recording the hours each student attended the
                     tutoring classes. Attach copies of class outlines or syllabus to demonstrate the
                     topic discussed.

Staff Responsibility: Basic Skills Specialist

3. Tutoring

Goal: To conduct a tutorial program which will focus on the individual academic
                     course needs of each student.

Objective: To provide an individualized tutorial program consisting of a minimum of ten
                     tutorial sessions per quarter to at least 95% of those CAMP participants who
                     demonstrate this service.

Activities: 1. Review student assessment data including: high school record, GED
                         scores, ACT scores, and the results of the California Achievement Test
                         (CAT) and the Test of Adult Basic Education (TABE)

10

2. Develop a list of tutorial needs from this data.
3. Include this list of tutorial needs with each student's IEP.
4. Assign tutors to each student needing this assistance.
5. Monitor student tutorial progress throughout each quarter and periodically reassess tutoring needs.

Timeline: September 30, 19XX - Assess data and develop individual needs list for each IEP.
September 30, 19XX to June 13, 19XX - Provide tutoring to students.

Evaluation: Maintain a copy of each student's individual tutorial program including an attendance sheet that demonstrates attendance at a minimum of 10 sessions.

Staff Responsibility: Associate Director, Basic Skills Specialist, Tutors

4. Staff Training

Goal: To conduct a job training program which is especially relevant to areas of recruiting, teaching, and counseling migrant/seasonal farmworker students.

Objective: To provide a minimum of five job training sessions for one hour each to 100% of the CAMP staff during the academic year.

Activities: 1. Plan and develop a training manual and a training program for CAMP staff consisting of five sessions which are designed to increase awareness of the needs of the migrant/seasonal farmworker student.
2. Conduct four (4) training sessions of one hour each.
3. Provide training on material and techniques gathered by those staff members who attended the National CAMP Technical Conference.

Timelines: July 1, 19XX — Plan and develop training program for CAMP staff
July 11, 19XX — Conduct preservice session #1
July 12, 19XX — Conduct preservice session #2 and session #3
July 13-14, 19XX — Conduct preservice session #4 and session #5

Evaluation: Maintain a log indicating attendance of staff at each session. Maintain copies of the content taught in each session. Have the Training Manual and Training Program available for inspection.

Staff Responsibility: Project Director

> **Additional objectives in the same format related to student recruitment, student orientation, college life adjustment, counseling, career exploration, social/cultural enrichment, housing/meals, health care, freshman/sophomore transition assistance, follow-up, financial aid, and student stipends.**

11

The Size, Scope, and Quality of Activities
(206.31(b)(2)(ii))

A total of eighty-four (84) activities has been presented in the section of the proposal. Each of these activities is specifically stated so it can be implemented effectively. However, the activities on the whole are broad in scope so as to include all of the aspects necessary to implement the objective properly. Quality implementation of the activities is assured through the evaluation procedure established for each component.

Evaluation Plan
(206.31(c) - 15 points)

This section of the proposal shows methods of evaluation that are appropriate for the project, and to the extent possible, are OBJECTIVE and PRODUCE QUANTIFIABLE data. The university will meet the requirements of EDGAR (CFR 75.590) and the funding agency in providing an annual evaluation covering the following three (3) areas:

1. the progress of the project in achieving its objectives;
2. the effectiveness of the project in meeting the stated purpose of the CAMP program; and
3. the effect of the project on persons being served, including any persons who are members of groups that have been traditionally underrepresented.

PROGRESS IN ACHIEVING FUNDED OBJECTIVES

The University of Tennessee's CAMP Program views the evaluation process as an essential factor contributing to its success in the quality of service. The program's multi-faceted nature requires continuous critical self-evaluation in all phases of program operation. Effective management and quality services depend on frequent feedback to document progress and detect problems. Our evaluation plan (see Flowchart below) is an integral

EVALUATION PLAN FLOWCHART

The University of Tennessee's CAMP Program

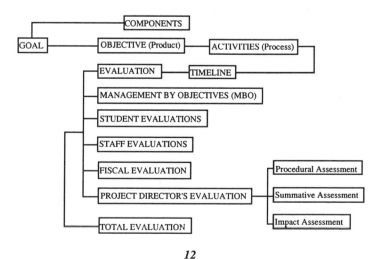

12

resource enabling the CAMP staff to plan, monitor, and refine project processes and to collect and analyze empirical information that can be used to improve strategies and control costs. The proposed CAMP Program's performance evaluation will be based on meeting the objectives (PRODUCTS) of each component as outlined in the OBJECTIVES AND ACTIVITIES Section of this proposal. Each "COMPONENT" is composed of a clearly stated NEED, GOAL, OBJECTIVE (product), ACTIVITY (process), TIMELINE, EVALUATION, and STAFF RESPONSIBILITY. Additionally, by using a Management by Objectives (MBO) approach each component is evaluated in measurable criteria. (See Management by Objectives in this section of the proposal).

PROJECT EFFECTIVENESS IN MEETING THE PURPOSE OF THE PROGRAM

The degree to which this project meets the purpose of the programs will be assessed by the CAMP staff. According to the *Federal Register*, "CAMP provides assistance to help migratory and seasonal farmworker students in - (1) Making the transition from secondary school to postsecondary school; (2) generating the motivation necessary to succeed in postsecondary school; and (3) developing the skills necessary to succeed in postsecondary school."

The design of the project, the objectives, and the activities are all constructed in a manner that will bring about the overall purposes of the CAMP program (i.e., transition from secondary schools; generating motivation, developing skills). A series of checks, balances, and evaluations have been designed to determine if, in fact, the design, objectives, and activities accomplish the stated goal.

The CAMP staff will include these criteria in its evaluation which determine whether the overall purpose has been achieved. Staff members will be required to prepare a self-evaluation showing their projected work objectives, duties, and performance indicators. This activity demands a high level of accountability and self-evaluation on the part of each staff member. Questionnaires will be submitted to the administrative office, analyzed, and the findings discussed with all staff members. Also, the Project Director will be conducting an ongoing internal evaluation for program management, modification, and improvement by including the following three elements of evaluation. Particularly important is the element of *PROCEDURAL ASSESS-MENT* whereby program activities and management procedures may be assessed and compared to the design intents expressed in the original proposal. Program goals and student objectives must also be evaluated at or near the year's end for purposes of *SUMMATIVE ASSESSMENT*. Inasmuch as many of the desired effects of a CAMP project are fairly far-reaching into the second, third, and fourth years of students' educational development, it would be appropriate to pay at least some attention to the matter of longitudinal assessments of *PROGRAM IMPACT*. These three elements are reflected in our evaluation design.

PROCEDURAL ASSESSMENT. Particularly during the new funding period, the Director should function as a special resource person to the staff. During this period, concepts and intentions for program operations, as reflected in the application proposal, are translated into specific structures and practices. Some evaluators refer to this as a *FORMATIVE EVALUATION* process.

In this assessment, the Director will determine to what degree the actual project activities and management compare with the planned activities and management. These comparative data will be analyzed, and a determination will be made by the Director as to which activities should continue, which should be changed in some way, and which should be discontinued altogether.

13

SUMMATIVE ASSESSMENT. Each of the program goals and student objectives identified in the objectives and activities section of this proposal will be evaluated according to accepted techniques of summative assessment. Project records of enrollments, student activities, credits attempted and earned, and grades awarded will constitute the basis of this assessment. A specially prepared student questionnaire will also be administered at year's end for the purpose of obtaining feedback regarding strengths and weaknesses of the program implemented, self-reported attitudinal changes that have taken place, and an assessment of the overall value of the program.

IMPACT ASSESSMENT. To the extent possible, given the uncertainty of future funding, it would be a valuable experience to conduct a longitudinal evaluation of the CAMP student population. Follow-up studies tend to be rather expensive, for as subjects leave an area the costs of pursuit frequently become prohibitive. However, to the extent that CAMP students remain on The University of Tennessee campus, academic records are easily and inexpensively obtained.

Finally, at the end of the year, the Director will analyze the demographic characteristics of the CAMP participants. The data compiled would be used to make sure that groups which have traditionally been underrepresented are represented adequately as participants. The Director will also evaluate the extent to which the program has performed and functioned as stated in the proposal.

EFFECT OF THE PROJECT ON THOSE BEING SERVED

The CAMP participants will also evaluate the program by responding to ongoing questionnaires assessing the benefits which they have derived from the program, the quality of services received, and their impressions of the program. In addition to student evaluations, the staff will evaluate the program at the end of each quarter. All data compiled on the project activities will be available to U.S. Department of Education personnel and other interested agencies. This report will be sent to U.S. Department of Education, network agencies, educational institutions, and appropriate human services organizations which are involved with migrant and seasonal farmworkers.

**SOUTHEASTERN COLLEGE ASSISTANCE MIGRANT PROGRAM
MANAGEMENT BY OBJECTIVES (MBO) FOR 19XX-19XX PROGRAM YEARS**

KEY ACTIVITY AREA	INDICATOR	STAFF	TOTAL PROPOSED GOAL	ACTUAL NO. OBTAINED	% OF PLAN ACCOMPLISHED
Student Assessment	a. No. of students receiving diagnostic achievement test	RC	225		
	b. No. of students receiving Individual Educational Plan (IEP)	RC	180		
	c. No. of Individual IEP Conferences conducted	RC	180		
Study Skills	a. No. of students attending Study Skills Instructional Program	BSS	180		
	b. No. of students completing pre-post test	BSS	180		

14

Tutoring	a.	No. of tutors available for CAMP program year	D	5
	b.	No. of students having access to tutoring services when needed	AD	180
	c.	No. of tutorial hours per student during CAMP program	T	30
	d.	No. of students receiving night tutoring services	T	20
	e.	No. of students receiving Saturday tutoring services	T	20

(Three of 17 are shown as examples.)

Quality of Key Personnel
(206.31(d) - 10 points)

This section of the application proposal provides information that shows adequate qualifications for those key personnel that the university plans to continue to use in the Southeastern CAMP Project. Qualifications of key personnel, the duration which staff will be appointed to the project, and the university's nondiscriminatory employment practices are also presented here.

Nondiscriminatory Employment Practices
(206.31(d)(2)(iv))

The University will adhere to the Affirmative Action Plan as an equal opportunity employer. The procedures used in implementing an affirmative action plan are as follows:

1. Advertising copy prepared to announce available positions at UTK shall comply in all regards with Federal, state, and local regulations for faculty and staff-exempt positions; copies of advertisements placed will be maintained on file by the unit advertising the vacancy. The UT Personnel Office will place all advertisements for staff-nonexempt position vacancies and will maintain on file copies of all such advertisements.
2. Sources of referral utilized by UT units are to be informed in writing of this policy and of UT's intention to SEEK OUT and to employ qualified applicants without regard to race, color, religion, sex, age, national origin, handicap, or veteran status. A copy of such notification shall be maintained on file by the head of the unit contacting the source of referral, in the case of faculty and staff-exempt positions. The UT Personnel Office will notify sources of referral for staff-nonexempt positions and will maintain on file copies of the notification.
3. Employment decisions shall be based solely upon individuals' qualifications for the position for which they are being considered.
4. Promotions shall be made in accordance with the principles of equal employment opportunity. Only valid, job-related requirements for advancement will be established.
5. No employee shall be excluded from participation in any university-sponsored activity or denied the benefits of any University program on the grounds of race, color, religion, sex, age, national origin, or veteran status. The university is prepared to make reasonable accommodations to allow participation by the handicapped in its programs, activities, and benefits.

15

Members of traditionally underrepresented groups will have equal opportunity for employment (i.e., members of racial or ethnic minority groups, women, handicapped persons, and/or the elderly). Full-time vacant positions will be advertised through the University Personnel Office. Due to the nature of the project, its intended participants, and the requirements in the Federal regulations, special efforts will be made to attract and employ members of groups traditionally underrepresented. For example, if two persons, both equally qualified, apply for a given position, and one is a member of a group traditionally underrepresented, that person will be given preference for the position. The Director will interview applicants and make the final decision in the selection process after consulting with the Dean of the College of Education. Upon notification of the grant award, current staff members would be retained from the current CAMP Program. An organizational chart is presented in this section of the proposal which depicts the structure of project personnel. Although the proposed CAMP Program will utilize the services of numerous University offices and programs within the academic and student affairs divisions of the campus, it will staff only those positions that provide exclusive service to CAMP students (refer to EMPLOYMENT DURATION CHART).

These positions include the following: project director, associate project director, counselor, recruiter/counselor, basic/skills specialist (graduate student, 50% time), residential counselor (graduate assistant, 25% time), secretary, and five (5) tutors (graduate students and upperclass students, hired hourly on an as-needed basis). Volunteers from the College of Education who are majoring in education, counseling, community service, and/or certain related areas will also be recruited for the project.

Employment Duration Chart
Southeastern College Assistance Migrant Program
(206.31(d)(2)(iii))

POSITION	% TIME	DURATION	S	O	N	D	J	F	M	A	M	J	J	A
Director	25%	12/mos	X	X	X	X	X	X	X	X	X	X	X	X
Associate Director	100%	12/mos	X	X	X	X	X	X	X	X	X	X	X	X
Counselor	100%	12/mos	X	X	X	X	X	X	X	X	X	X	X	X
Recruiter/Counselor	100%	12/mos	X	X	X	X	X	X	X	X	X	X	X	X
Secretary	100%	12/mos	X	X	X	X	X	X	X	X	X	X	X	X
*Basic Skills Specialist	50%	9/mos		X	X	X	X	X	X	X	X			
*Residential Counselor	25%	9/mos		X	X	X	X	X	X	X	X			
*Tutors (5)	hrly	9/mos		X	X	X	X	X	X	X	X			

*The Basic Skills Specialist and Residential Counselor will be master's or doctorate degree candidates (graduate assistants).

Qualifications of the Project Director
(206.31 (d) (2) (i))

The Project Director will be responsible for the CAMP as proposed and will report directly to the College of Education's TAE Department Head. The specific responsibilities of the Director, employed 25% time with the CAMP program for twelve (12) months, would include staffing, public relations, program planning, writing and negotiating the proposal, conducting inservice, conferring with key project personnel, evaluating the project, expending the budget, and overseeing the general operation of the CAMP participants (see Job Description, Appendix C).

(Name), who is currently Executive Director of the University of Tennessee's High School Equivalency Program (HEP), Upward Bound, Veterans Program, Educational Opportunity Center, Talented Minority

Research Fellowship Program, Math and Science Regional Center, and Educational Talent Search, has a doctorate degree in education with an emphasis in administration and a master's degree in rehabilitation counseling education. He has directed CAMP and HEP projects at the University and has many years' working experience with migrant/seasonal farmworkers, economically deprived youth, drop-outs, and potential drop-outs. Prior to (Name) current position, he was the Project Director and Associate Director of other University Federally funded programs. He is a professional educator with over twelve years of experience in education with several national counseling certifications. Before coming to the University, he served as Executive Director of a comprehensive rehabilitation facility and has served on numerous human service advisory committees.

(Name) appointment as Director for the College Assistance Migrant Program project is convenient to his current employment with the University (see Resume, Appendix B).

Qualifications of Other Key Personnel
(206.31(d)(2)(i))

Associate Director

The Associate Director's primary responsibility will be to be in charge of the daily running of CAMP. The Associate Director will report directly to the Director. Specific responsibilities of the Associate Director, employed 100% time, 12 months, would include supervising the day-to-day operations of the project, assisting in in-service, recommending budget expenditures, supervising CAMP staff, and assisting in evaluation (see Job Description, Appendix C).

(Name), who is currently Project Director for the HEP program, has a master's degree in Adult Education. Prior to (Name) appointment to the HEP project, she served as a personnel administrator/trainer for the National Farmworkers Association, where she had responsibility for all staffing and training. She also worked as a Job Placement Coordinator and was responsible for operating a Federally funded program (see Resume, Appendix B).

> **Follow similar format for each position that you include in your application.**

Additional Staff (Tutors)

Additional information on all the staff personnel is shown on the RESUMES in Appendix B of this proposal. JOB DESCRIPTIONS for each of the staff positions are located in Appendix C.

As indicated on the RESUMES in Appendix B, most of the CAMP staff members have worked previously with the CAMP/HEP project. This past working experience with migrant and seasonal farmworker participants, years of academic and Federal program experience among the staff members, master's and doctoral degree graduates/candidates who have been available for two to three years, along with the staff's participation in a comprehensive in-service training program, serve as key factors of a knowledgeable, motivated, and involved staff.

17

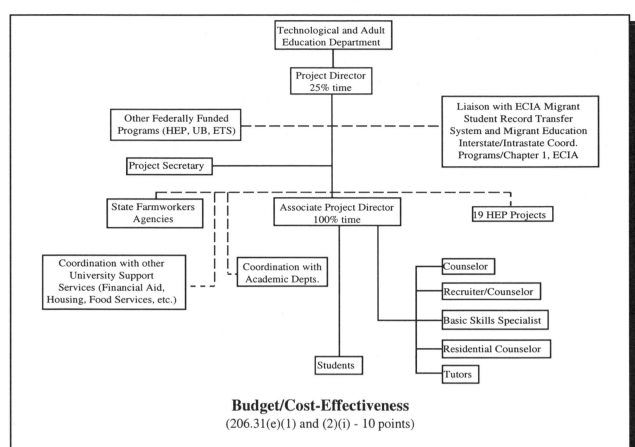

Budget/Cost-Effectiveness
(206.31(e)(1) and (2)(i) - 10 points)

COST-EFFECTIVENESS

This section of the proposal elucidates the project budget's adequacy and cost-effectiveness. In addition, it describes how the budget is adequate to support the project activities and how the costs are reasonable in relation to the objectives of the project.

The project proposes to serve 180 students on a low-cost basis due to the fact that numerous university resources are available and will be utilized by the current proposed CAMP program at NO COST to the program itself. According to the Department of Education's Migrant Education Program Office, the current average cost per student in all existing CAMP programs runs up to $6,784.00 per student. Our budgeted cost per student is $6,710.

The proposed budget is highly cost-effective in relationship to services provided because, of the total CAMP staff, only the Director, Associate Director, Secretary, Counselor, Basic/Skills Specialist, and Recruiter/ Counselor are twelve (12) month appointments (see Employment Duration Chart in the Personnel Section of this proposal). In addition, upperclassmen and graduate students will be serving as tutors, counselors, and dorm staff in the project. By utilizing these students as tutors, lower cost wages can be paid and will be expended only on an hourly, as-needed basis. Although part-time employment is cost effective, it does NOT compromise service delivery or neglect the quality herein proposed. In addition, the university does not pay part-time staff fringe benefits, thereby eliminating these extra costs. Efficient utilization of part-time employment seems to be an appropriate vehicle for maintaining high quality services in a cost-effective manner.

It should be noted that, in addition to the services directly provided to CAMP participants, students will continue to receive benefits of University and other specially funded programs. Moreover, the cost per participant ($6,710) reflected in the budget does not include university contributions of OFFICE SPACE, UTILITIES, EQUIPMENT, and other "direct cost" items that are considered "in kind." Free speech and hearing exams, eye exams, community donations, etc., keep the cost very reasonable. Self-instruction materials and standardized test materials previously purchased by other projects are currently available and would not have to be purchased for this project.

Costs Are Reasonable in Relation to the Objectives of the Project
(206.31(e)(2)(ii))

This program will provide the following types of services to assist CAMP participants in completing their first academic year of college successfully: recruitment services for enrolling project participants; instructional services in academic subject areas; special academic, career, and personal guidance, counseling, and testing services; residential program services; stipends and transportation; and services designed to expose participants to academic institutions and programs, cultural events, and other activities not usually available to the participants yet important to their intellectual, cultural, social, and personal development.

Interagency Consultation/Coordination
(206.31(f) - 10 points)

This section describes how the project will continue to coordinate with other agencies within the eight (8) state targeted area. In addition, this section addresses the coordination and consultation with agencies which serve migrant/seasonally employed farmworkers and their dependents.

Information That Shows Adequate Consultation
and Coordination With Other Agencies
(206.31(f)(1))

While responding to CAMP/HEP proposals and receiving funds since 19XX, the Director of this program has continually involved institutional and migrant/seasonal state farmworker officials in requesting input from respective states with respect to the overall purpose of this Federally funded program. He has consulted and coordinated with appropriate agencies in planning, developing, implementing, and evaluating the initial project in 19XX-XX, as well as subsequent years. At present, about fifty (50) agencies are actively participating through referral, consultation, services, transportation, etc. Many officials have already sent letters of COMMITMENT AND ENDORSEMENT showing their support for the program (see Appendix A). Upon receiving notice of the award, the university will continue to consult other community agencies to elicit their cooperation and support to be used to implement this project.

The CAMP program will continue the development and expansion of interagency consultation and coordination for the purpose of augmenting and improving the quality of services to our CAMP participants. Innovative suggestions and recommendations will be implemented whenever possible. The project will actively contact existing linkages and establish new ones with appropriate agencies which provide consultation, coordination,

19

and other free services. Also, the project plans to release public service announcements to targeted state newspapers and radio stations, distribute program brochures and posters, and speak to other agency staff about the proposed services. Local institution and community resources will be used to motivate and provide skills to participants which are necessary for success in college. The university's commitment of $83,757 (see budget breakdown) as an "in-kind" contribution will provide the necessary office space, classrooms, recreational and cultural facilities necessary for the project's operation. Speech and hearing services will provide the necessary evaluations at NO COST to the project. Local businesses have donated supplies to the project and certain individuals have donated money and clothing (see Letters of Commitment and Support in Appendix A).

Information That Shows the Project Will Consult and Coordinate Adequately With Other Agencies in Implementing the Project
(206.31(f)(2))

The project plans to continue to inform the targeted state farmworker organizations and the educational communities of the goals and objectives of the Southeastern CAMP Project at the university and the selection criteria for acceptance into the CAMP program.

As program needs dictate, there has been a focus on developing and maintaining linkages with agencies that provide services to migrant and other seasonally employed farmworkers and their dependents (see Flowchart below). This interagency consultation and coordination has permitted the staff to plan, develop, and implement programs which can interface with PEEM to meet the educational needs of farmworker youth. Additional contact has been established in linkages with 303 Programs, Dept. of Agriculture Farmworker Organizations, and DOL. These linkages demonstrate the benefits that can accrue from extensive program interfacing and coordination.

Institutional and Community Support

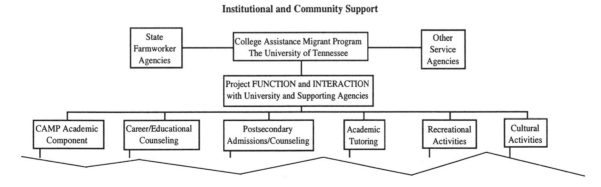

The staff will apprise all significant agencies and institutions in the targeted areas of the goals and objectives of the CAMP program. Regular contacts will be made with state farmworker professionals, school administrators, counselors, teachers, community agencies, parents, and students to provide updated information concerning the program goals and activities and to explain information concerning the program goals and activities and to explain changes in the program. The orientation of the targeted states will be more readily accomplished because the university is service oriented, well-known, and well-respected in the targeted states.

20

Moreover, upon the initiation of recruiting activities in the fall, the CAMP Recruiter/Counselor will work with project participants to establish a liaison relationship and publicize project goals, purposes, and activities. Other liaison relationships will be developed with postsecondary institutions in the vicinity for the provision of information to CAMP participants regarding various educational options.

In summary, the project has strong institutional and community support (see Flowchart below) which will enhance the opportunities available to the CAMP students at the University. In addition, the LETTERS OF COMMITMENT and ENDORSEMENT indicate that the project will have a close and cooperative working relationship with targeted states. And finally, the extensive interagency linkage developed during the operation of our HEP Program will greatly assist our staff in the initial stages of program publicity, participant identification, and student recruitment.

The following are samples of interagency consultation and cooperation currently in place:

(Seven in orginal—two shown.)

1. The Telamon corporation, which assists migrant and seasonal farmworkers in four (4) states within our targeted area, has been very supportive of our migrant program. Telamon involves itself with every facet of the program allowable to an outside agency including offering financial support/ incentives when possible. The agency has a solid network established within itself as well as with the community (and its agencies) it serves. Telamon provides for personal, as well as educational needs and tries to eliminate as many obstacles as possible for those clients choosing to continue their education. For example, Marguerite Brown, Regional Manager of the Aiken, South Carolina office, has referred several students and has provided continuous support for the program. Mrs. Brown enthusiastically proclaims her patronage of our program and is a strong source of encouragement to those clients qualifying along with providing placement assistance.

2. Genesco Migrant Center's Project Trainer, Mr. Bob Lynch, states that the program provides opportunities and alternatives to migrants who have few advantages available to them. Not only has Mr. Lynch referred candidates to the program, he has also provided additional sources of agency contacts throughout the service area and letters of encouragement and support to those students who were enrolled. The Genesco organization also offers the Mattera Educational Scholarship for migrants as an incentive for secondary and post-secondary education. In addition, the job development component has provided another avenue of service which assists HEP with placement. Mr. Lynch has also expressed his readiness to continue his working relationship with our migrant program.

Adequacy of Resources
(206.31(g) - 5 points)

The university has a wide variety of resources and support to the College Assistance Migrant Program. As a land-grant institution and major graduate and research center in Tennessee, the University has excellent staff and facilities to support the CAMP Program. As the major university in the state, UT has tremendous resources (laboratories, libraries, cultural enrichment, and recreational activities and facilities) available at no cost to the project. The CAMP Program will be able to use campus resources including media equipment and materials, learning centers, laboratories, recreational facilities, educational films and libraries, in addition to the University Center with its programs. These facilities are modern and exceptionally well-equipped. The

College of Education has a large and fully-equipped media center and support units such as the Bureau of Educational Research and Service (BERS) through which the CAMP Program would be administered as a restricted account.

The University also conducts other compensatory educational programs from which the project could seek professional inservice training, consultation, and to a certain degree, services, at NO COST to the project. The special services for disadvantaged students include the Upward Bound, the Educational Talent Search, the Educational Advancement, and the High School Equivalency (HEP) Programs.

Some of the resources and support activities that will be available to this program include:

(Four samples of 19 listed items appear as an example.)

1. An OFFICE OF FINANCE which provides complete fiscal services such as accounting, budgeting, purchasing, payrolls, etc. and other financial records necessary for fiscal compliance.
2. An OFFICE OF PERSONNEL which ensures equal employment opportunities for all staff and provides the personnel services necessary for hiring staff and processing grievance and due process hearings.
3. A MAINTENANCE DEPARTMENT which provides the office space and equipment and other necessary program space for activities, maintenance of buildings, grounds, and custodial service.
4. A fully-equipped MEDIA CENTER offering a wide variety of audio-visual equipment, student learning carrels and television studio facilities.

Additionally, the University's College of Education has been awarded a number of other human service programs because of its strategic location and large target population. Through continuous application for these human service awards, the University's commitment to assist the poor and educationally disadvantaged with their academic, social, cultural and personal development is well-demonstrated.

SUMMARY

In summary, extensive resources of the University more than adequately meet the needs of the participants in the proposed College Assistance Migrant Program. In addition to providing adequate classroom and office space, the proposed project has access to the University Center for students' social activities, ACT testing facilities, Career Planning and Placement Center, Media Center, Teacher Materials Center, Learning Resource Center and school libraries, and many university recreational and educational support facilities. The project also has access to dorm rooms and vans and buses for field trips at low-cost rates.

Recruitment
(206.31(h) - 5 points)

At the beginning of the program year, recruitment services will be performed by a Recruiter/Recruiter Counselor, along with other staff members, who will identify, inform, and recruit eligible participants who are in need of the academic and supporting services and financial assistance provided by the project. The linkages already developed between the University's migrant programs and the farmworker organizations in the Southeast will provide a high degree of accessibility to farmworker populations in the eight (8) state targeted

22

areas (see Recruitment Flowchart). The recruiters will contact these farmworker organizations and other community agencies in each target state to inform them of the program and seek referral of potentially eligible candidates. Besides telephone and face-to-face contacts made by the recruiter, public service announcements and previously developed brochures and posters will be placed in establishments visited by farmworkers to alert potentially eligible candidates of the program's existence. Special emphasis will be placed on the recruitment of women, social and ethnic minorities, and the handicapped.

Recruitment Flowchart

The University of Tennessee
College Assistance Migrant Program

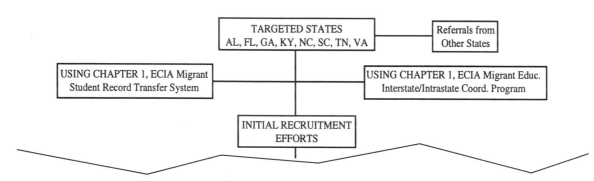

The recruiter will visit each target state and individually interview potential candidates to determine eligibility, discuss the program, and enroll participants. A pre-assessment, using the Test of Adult Basic Education (TABE) and the Wide Range Achievement Test (WRAT), will be performed on all applicants. The recruiter and other project staff who are participating in recruitment will explain the three basic components of the admission process to CAMP applicants. These components are: (1) the UT Application; (2) the ACT Test; and (3) the Financial Aid Form (FAF).

The Recruiter/Counselor will be employed for a twelve (12) month period. Initially, the recruiter's full-time responsibility will be recruitment. When all CAMP students have been recruited, the recruiter's responsibility will then shift to counseling and other on-campus student support duties.

The need for a Recruiter/Counselor was identified due to the large geographical area to be covered, namely eight (8) Southeastern states. The Recruiter/Counselor, along with the Counselor and the Associate Director, will be assigned specific geographical areas in which to recruit. It is anticipated that the recruiting staff will be on the road three (3) nights per week initially in order to perform these duties. The recruitment staff will be working toward assigned goals, and recruitment productivity will be monitored by the Associate Director. At the end of the program, a questionnaire will be sent to farmworker agencies and other community organizations to determine the effectiveness of the recruitment campaign. Throughout the operation of the CAMP Program, a system of linkages and coordination will continue to be established with government agencies, private institutions, schools, private citizens and businesses for the purpose of identifying the target population to be served by this project and to initiate the application and verification process of each potential candidate. At this time, the University's CAMP program plans to work with the following:

23

1.	State Farmworker Organizations	8.	Office of Voc. Rehab.
2.	HEP Programs	9.	Agric. Extensions
3.	State Dept. of Labor	10.	Schools/Churches
4.	Employment Security	11.	PEEM
5.	Dept. of Human Services	12.	Farmwork Unions
6.	State Migrant Educ. Offices	13.	Farm Owners
7.	State Dept. of Education	14.	Food Stamp Offices

Other possible contact locations such as rural gathering places, country stores, tobacco barns, produce markets, and feed distributors will also be explored and utilized as appropriate.

V. CERTIFICATIONS AND ASSURANCES

Required certifications are appended. The total Law was included. For this *handbook*, only the names are provided.
•Certification Regarding Drug-Free Workplace Requirements
Grantees Other Than Individuals
•Certification Regarding Debarment, Suspension, Ineligibility and Voluntary Exclusion
Lower Tier Covered Transactions
•Civil Rights Certificate

VI. APPENDIXES

APPENDIX A - Letters of Support
APPENDIX B - Résumés
APPENDIX C - Job Descriptions
APPENDIX D - Program Forms
APPENDIX E - Program Materials

24

11

Understanding How Grants Are Awarded

Introduction

An important aspect of proposal writing is understanding what happens to your document once it gets to the funding source. This chapter discusses common procedures used to evaluate your proposal by personnel of the agency to which it is sent. Each agency has its own procedure, so this chapter deals in general terms.

Funding agency staff assign a control number to the proposal and subject it to a preliminary review to ensure that it addresses the purpose of the program. Usually panels of readers thoroughly read, evaluate, and score the proposal. From the reading process, the proposals are often rank ordered, and the budget is reviewed. Funding agency personnel estimate the number of awards that the appropriated dollars will support and establish a *cutoff* point. Proposals scoring above the *cutoff* point are then *negotiated*. Usually unsuccessful applicants are not notified until all successful proposals have been negotiated. An award document is issued, at which time the grant award becomes official. Additional details for each step are outlined in the following sections.

Agency Review and Approval

Given the large number of applications that may be submitted in a competition, funding agency personnel endeavor to ensure that only those addressing the purposes of the program or statute are evaluated by the readers. Some competitions are very small. As few as 25 or 30 applications may be submitted, whereas other competitions may receive 1,500 or more applications.

Staff persons usually review the proposal abstract, table of contents, and perhaps the objectives. They look for indications that the proposal includes all necessary information such as original signatures, standard face page, and required assurances. They also ensure that the proposal addresses the criteria outlined in the application, that it is within the scope of the authorizing legislation, and that the expected outcomes are in accord with overall program goals. Proposals missing vital information are judged inappropriate and may be returned to the institution without further review.

Each agency or program may have its own specific criteria for evaluating proposal applications. For example, the Fund for the Improvement of Postsecondary Education (FIPSE) utilizes three outside readers, but there is no group discussion of the proposals among the three. The Office of Special Education and Rehabilitation Services (OSERS) uses three readers in addition to an evaluation by an ad hoc panel. The Office of Postsecondary Education (OPSE) submits proposals to three readers who then meet and discuss their evaluation to arrive at a group score. Other agencies may have still different review procedures.

In the abstract, you should clearly state the purpose of the proposal, such as *"The purpose of this proposal is to establish an international studies project for 30 students to study one academic year in the People's Republic of China."* Use bold face type, underline, or in some other way highlight this important statement. As you begin various sections of the document, restate the purpose. For example, as you elaborate the objectives, preface the section with a statement such as, *"The following section contains the objectives of our international studies project that will support an academic year of study for 30 students in the People's Republic of China."*

Both the preliminary reviewers and review panel will be reading or will have read many similar proposals. After reading 12 to 14 proposals discussing the same general topic, a reader could confuse the contents of one proposal with others previously read. By re-stating your purpose several times throughout the document, you will reduce the possibility of error and confusion and keep the reviewers' attention focused on *your* application.

Panel Reading, Review, and Scoring

The most important phase of the proposal review process is the work of the reader panel. If the readers understand and like your proposal, they will score it high and it will go on to be considered by the department or agency. If your proposal doesn't make it past the readers, the department or agency will never see it. The review process may take from a few days to two or more weeks to complete. In an effort to make the selection process as fair as possible and to eliminate bias, the funding agency implements its specific review process previously described.

——Grant Tip——

Restate the purpose of your proposal in a variety of different ways. Each panel of readers may review 15 to 20 proposals. Make yours stand out.

Try to learn how your proposal will be evaluated. This may help you in terms of how you present your material. If your reviewers will be persons highly specialized in your grant area, they may be more critical of your plan of operation, facilities, and how you will evaluate your efforts. You may want to seek the advice of experts to help you write these sections. If your reviewers come from broader, less specialized backgrounds, you may want to be less technical and emphasize the importance and need of the services you propose to provide and how those services will benefit the target population.

One researcher in the area of proposal development and writing suggests that there tends to be a *cumulative effect* among readers. This suggests that if the readers find excellence in the proposal in the first few areas, their perception of the remainder of the document will be positively influenced (Cavin, 1984). On the other hand, if the first areas of the proposal are weak or inadequate, the readers will tend to perceive the remainder of the document as being weak and inadequate.

Persons interested in serving as reviewers may submit a letter of application and their resume to the agency. After a review of these documents, readers are selected and invited to Washington, DC or another designated site to receive orientation for reviewing and scoring the applications. Readers are selected from all walks of life. They may not be educators and thus may be unfamiliar with educational programs funded by the United States Department of Education. They may not fully understand the application and funding process employed by the Department. They may represent the group(s) to be served by the proposed projects.

Sometimes employees of various other divisions within the Department serve as reviewers. For example, a Department employee who works in programs for the physically impaired may review proposals for vocational education programs. In such cases, the panels are generally composed of one federal reviewer and two nonfederal reviewers.

In selecting reviewers, care is taken to avoid persons who may have a conflict of interest. A conflict of interest exists if the reviewer reviews an application that involves (a) him/herself, (b) a spouse, (c) an organization for which the reviewer serves as an officer, director, trustee, partner, or employee, (d) a person or organization that employs the reviewer or from which the reviewer derives financial interest, or (e) an agency with which the reviewer has any personal ties such as the university the reviewer attended. If reviewers think they

——**Grant Tip**——
The readers are your first audience. Write in terms they understand.

have a conflict of interest, they must report it to the program staff immediately.

Those selected to review applications must agree to maintain confidentiality. Confidentiality means that the reviewer may not discuss the application with others who are not members of the review team, and the reviewer may not remove the application from the review location.

Because of the varied backgrounds of the reviewers, their orientation is of enormous importance. The Department of Education issued a document titled *Reviewing Applications for Discretionary Grants and Cooperative Agreements: Orientation Trainer's Manual* (Horace Mann Learning Center, 1988). It describes in detail the orientation received by members of the review panels prior to reading and scoring the application. The process is designed to ensure that projects are worthwhile and that awards are fair and impartial.

Figure 11.1 outlines the funding and decision framework for discretionary funds and the review process that involves 15 distinct steps *(Reviewing Applications . . .)*. Understanding these steps will give you a better sense of how the review panels fit into the process. Steps one through seven are preparatory to the review process. Step eight is the actual review and scoring of the application. Steps 9 through 15 describe what happens after the review is completed.

Figure 11.1. Steps in the Funding and Decision Framework for Discretionary Funds

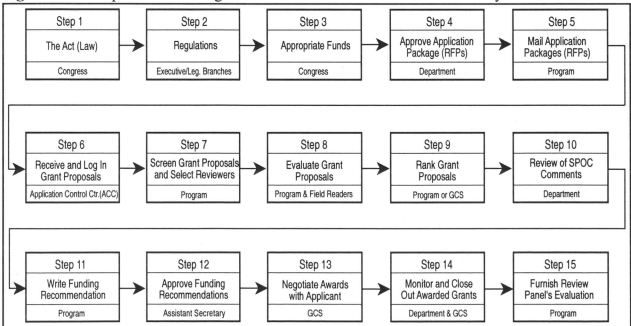

Step 1 • Congress passes an education *act (law)*. This becomes the enabling legislation to fund a specific program. It lists the authorized funding.

Step 2 • Department *establishes regulations* governing how the act's objectives are to be carried out.

Step 3 • After Congress *appropriates funds,* the Department conducts a process designed to award those funds.

Step 4 • Department establishes a schedule of awards and approves an *application package* (RFP) for each funding program.

Step 5 • Department *mails out application packages* (RFPs) as requested.

Step 6 • Department's Application Control Center (ACC) receives and *logs in applications*. These are date-stamped on receipt and assigned an application control number.

Step 7 • Program office personnel *screen applications* for eligibility and conformity to general administrative regulations, select reviewers, and assign applications to panel. Applications that do not conform to some basic administrative requirements do not enter the review process.

Step 8 • The review panel *reviews the application*. This review is the foundation for funding recommendations made at later stages in the cycle. Program officers verify accuracy and sufficiency of written evaluations.

Step 9 • *Applications are ranked* according to scores assigned by the review panel. Staff members at the control centers review, check, record, and enter raw scores or normalized scores in computer.

Step 10 • *Review SPOC comments*. Those applications requiring the Executive Order 12372 process will go through the SPOC and are reviewed as part of the funding and award process.

Step 11 • Department prepares a summary of *funding recommendations* using the evaluations of the review panel, SPOC comments, and other factors such as equitable geographical distribution of awards and unnecessary duplication of effect or services.

Step 12 • Department reviews and approves or disapproves the funding recommendations, and *a recommended slate is forwarded for approval.* Congress is notified of results and receives a list of awards.

Step 13 • Funding levels are negotiated for approved applications. The Grants and Contracts Services (GCS) *negotiates the final funding of each project.*

Step 14 • *Monitoring and closing out* of awarded grants. Typically, those applicants who were not selected are notified by letter.

Step 15 • Distribution of the *review panel's evaluation* to applicants, as requested.

Technical Review Form

During orientation, panel members receive instructions for reviewing and scoring the application according to the Technical Review Form the Department provides. The summary page of the *Technical Review Form* of the CAMP of the Office of Elementary and Secondary Education is presented in Figure 11.2. It contains most of the information that the application package guidelines include. There is a detailed page for each criterion and readers summarize the details on this summary page.

This emphasizes the importance of organizing an application in the same order and sequence suggested in the application packet. The panel of readers will find your document easier to read and score if the order and sequence are carefully followed. Chapter 8, "Writing a Proposal," deals with this in more detail.

After receiving the orientation, the reviewers are assigned to panels usually consisting of three members each. A team leader is responsible for coordinating team efforts. Generally the team will receive three to six or more proposals to read each day. Sometimes the teams read as a group, and sometimes members read separately and then convene to review and discuss each proposal.

As an example, assume that the individual readers receive the proposal from the team leader and retire to their hotel rooms or other designated areas to evaluate it. Using the *Technical Review Form* which contains the criteria for each section, the reviewers carefully study each section of the proposal according to the instructions provided in the orientation. The reviewers provide written comments on the strengths as well as on the weaknesses found in each section.

——**Grant Tip**——
The Technical Review Form *contains the criteria for each section. Readers will find your document easier to read and score if the order and sequence are carefully followed.*

Figure 11.2. Example of a Technical Review Form Cover Page

Application Technical Review Form

**Special Educational Programs for Students Whose Families are Engaged in Migrant
and Other Seasonal Farmwork-High School Equivalency Program (HEP)
and College Assistance Migrant Program (CAMP)**

FY 19XX PR No. _____

Type of Application: [   ] High School Equivalency Program (HEP) (CFDA 84.141)
(Check one)   [   ] College Assistance Migrant Program (CAMP) (CFDA 84.149)
Name of Applicant: _____
Address of Applicant: _____
Name of Project Director: _____
Title of Application: _____

Instructions: This Application Technical Review Form contains eight criteria published in the *Federal Register* (December 30, 19XX and July 6, 19XX) which must be used in reviewing the attached application. After reading the application and completing the identification information on this page of the Review Form, begin recording your assessment of the application. On the following pages, please write specific review comments in the space provided with regard to the strengths and weaknesses of the application as judged against the specified criterion. Circle the descriptor on the scale for each criterion which describes the adequacy of the application. Finally, for each criterion, assign a score consistent with the descriptor which denotes your rating. Complete pages 2 through 9 in that order and rate each criterion independently. The maximum score per application cannot exceed 100 points. After completing pages 2-9, return to this page and complete the bottom. Sign your full legal name and date your review.

		Individual Rating	Post-Panel Rating
1. Plan of Operation	(25)		
2. Objectives and Activities	(20)		
3. Evaluation Plan	(15)		
4. Quality of Key Personnel	(10)		
5. Budget and Cost-Effectiveness	(10)		
6. Interagency Consultation and Coordination	(10)		
7. Adequacy of Resources	(5)		
8. Recruitment	(5)		
Total	(100)		

Complete This Section After Pages 2 Through 9

Total points given application: _____
(Maximum is 100)

Summarized Strengths:

Summarized Weaknesses:

_____   _____
            Reviewer's Signature   Date

The comments may eventually be made available to the author of the application for use in future proposal writing. *If you desire a panel's comments on your proposal, submit a written a request to the agency or department that administers the program.*

The maximum number of points possible appears at the top of each section of the technical review form. The reviewer assigns a score within the range of possible scores for that section. After each reviewer has studied and scored each section of the proposal, the three reviewers reconvene as a panel to discuss the proposal and their scores. Through discussion with other panel members, concepts are often clarified. During this discussion, a reviewer may choose to adjust a score. The reviewer may find an important item that was overlooked or misunderstood. Generally during the discussion process, the reviewers arrive at an agreement of the quality of the application, and their scores do not differ greatly. (If there is great disparity in scores, another panel may read the proposal.)

The panel leader usually collects the completed review forms containing the written comments and scores then submits the forms to the Department supervisor. This completes the review process as performed by the panel of reviewers. The responsibilities of the reviewer can be summarized as follows:

1. Report any conflict of interest which will remove a reader from the panel reviewing the proposal for which there is a conflict.
2. Provide a specific and well-documented critique of each application including constructive written comments.
3. Evaluate applications independently of personal feelings.
4. Participate in panel discussions.
5. Maintain confidentiality.

Rank Ordering of Reviewed Proposals

The review panel's forms are checked to ensure that each section was carefully reviewed, written comments describing the strengths and weaknesses were included, and that a score was assigned. The Department representative then proceeds to rank order the applications according to the total score assigned. Figure 11.3 provides an example of how the rankings may appear for a specific program. Sometimes the scores of the reviewers are averaged; sometimes they are adjusted by a formula that assigns a numerical value to the raw scores. At any rate, the Department organizes a slate of proposals recommended to be funded arranged in rank order.

Figure 11.3. Example of a Technical Review Summary

PR NUMBER/FILE KEY APPLICATION NAME	PANEL NUMBER SCORES			MEAN SCORE	FUNDS REQUESTED	FUNDS RECOMMENDED
842AH2663 173365 X University	98	21 99	93	96.67	368,983.	323,358.
842AH2113 163432 Y Universtiy	93	18 100	97	96.67	398,368.	356,322.
842AH0021 153342 University Z	97	25 94	96	95.67	402,930.	365,334.
842AH3225 165332 X State University	93	19 99	89	93.67	297,006.	292,338.
842AH3326 163325 Y Central Washington	96	22 93	89	92.67	433,226.	00.
842AH2263 163323 X Institute of HumanResources	89	21 91	93	91.00	532,335.	00.
842AH1221 153223 W University	88	18 89	92	89.68	493,335.	00.
842AH9531 151091 XY University	85	25 79	83	82.33	491,219.	00.
842AH8335 162322 XYZ, Inc.	79	15 83	86	80.28	168,000.	00.

Note: Partial listing of proposals considered under this competition (names changed for practical reasons).

Cutoff Point

After the proposals have been rank ordered by score, the Department uses the slated cutoff score that is usually established in the regulations. The Department personnel again review each proposal with particular attention to the proposed budget. Usually during the Departmental review of the budget, reductions and modifications are suggested. The Department then recalculates the anticipated total budget of each proposal and subtracts that amount from the total appropriated by Congress or assigned by the Department for the program. An operational cutoff is established at the point where the totals of the budgets of the highest ranked proposals equal the funds appropriated or assigned by the Department.

In competitions with many applications, several proposals may receive the same score. It is not uncommon for the cutoff to fall at a point where two or more proposals are tied with the same score. In such cases the Department often reviews the *Needs* or other comparable section of the tied proposals. The scores on that section are rank ordered, and the two scoring the most points on that particular section will be recommended for funding. Sometimes, the competitions have requirements for regional distribution of monies or projects. That may be another factor taken into consideration.

In recent years competition for federal grants has become extremely keen. The operational cutoff point may include scores only in the middle to high nineties. Frequently only a half point or less may separate a funded proposal from an unfunded proposal. This emphasizes the necessity for careful elaboration of each part of every section of the proposal.

The readers on the review panel are your first and most important audience. Often proposal writers direct their writing to agency or Department personnel, assuming that they are familiar with the program requirements, target population, and acceptable activities. Writers have a tendency to omit detail, clarification, and *obvious* information. Remember, the review panel scores your proposal, not the agency personnel. If the review panel does not score your proposal high enough, the agency or Department personnel will never see it. Therefore, write to the review panel, which is your first and most important audience.

Negotiations

After the slate of proposals to be funded has been completed and the budgets reviewed and revisions recommended by the Department program staff, a negotiator from the grants/contracts office will telephone the contact person designated in the application. The purpose of the first telephone call is generally to set a time and day to *negotiate* the budget. At times during this initial call, the negotiator will indicate the recommended *bottom line* figure for the budget. This gives you an idea of the amount of money available or set aside for your project.

Negotiation simply means that you or another designated person will, through a telephone conversation with a grants officer, negotiate the line items of the budget of your application. The total amount of your budget is seldom open to negotiation. After you have

———Grant Tip———

Write to the review panel, your first and most important audience.

received the call to set a date and time to negotiate, prepare yourself. Reread your document several times. Make sure you are completely familiar with each part of the proposal and how each particular part is supported through the budget. Review your budget carefully. Assuredly, the Department will negotiate your budget downward.

The program officer assigned to your project will carefully review your proposed program and the supporting budget and make suggested revisions and reductions. That officer will write down suggestions for budget revisions and forward them to the grants officer (negotiator) who will call you. The negotiator who works with you will rely on notes prepared by the program officer, who may not be familiar with all of the details of your project. Be prepared to defend your budget in order to be able to operate a successful and efficient project. To prepare, you should ask yourself, and then answer, these critical questions.

──**Grant Tip**──

A program officer will discuss the program; a grants and contracts officer will discuss monies.

1. Can I reduce my proposed budget without changing other parts of the proposal? (Probably not, if the proposal was well done in the first place!) If not, there will be choices.

2. Can I reduce personnel and still carry out each objective? If I eliminate a position, will I have to eliminate one or more objectives? Can I still operate the project within the guidelines by eliminating the position and corresponding objectives? Can I reduce a position from full time to part time and still maintain the objectives?

3. If I reduce personnel, should I reduce the number of participants to be served or the services provided for the participants?

4. Can I get by with fewer supplies and materials? Could my department provide some of the supplies and materials or rent-free space to help reduce the budget?

5. Can I reduce or consolidate travel? Are all of the training conferences and other proposed travel absolutely necessary?

6. Is all equipment absolutely necessary? Can I get by with one less typewriter or computer and still perform at an acceptable level? Can I lease or rent rather than buy?

7. Can I modify my evaluation plan and reduce costs, perhaps by using a local evaluator rather than a person from out of state? Could the staff perform some of the evaluation functions, such as collecting and compiling data needed by the evaluator?

8. Will my institution allow me to use all or part of the indirect cost money derived from the grant in the form of supplies, travel, or equipment?

By answering these types of questions in advance, you will be better prepared to conduct negotiations. The process of negotiating a new budget may take an hour or more by telephone. Bear in mind as you negotiate that the negotiator from the Department probably is not familiar with your application. The negotiator will be relying on notes provided by your newly assigned program officer. *Do not be afraid to defend your budget.* On one hand, answer the negotiator's questions courteously; explain and clarify points carefully as needed. On the other hand, be prepared to reduce your budget in certain areas. Travel, equipment (especially computers), personnel, and evaluation are often questioned by negotiators. Therefore, either be prepared to reduce your budget in these areas or be prepared to provide a cogent defense.

A well-developed proposal is a tight relationship among *time, cost,* and *performance.* If the negotiator requires a budget (cost) reduction, you will need to adjust either or both of the other variables: *time* and *performance.* After you and the negotiator have arrived at a final figure, you will have time to develop a revised *scope of work* and budget estimate. When you send this to the Department, send copies to each person who received the original proposal.

In developing a budget there are several ways to hedge against severe reductions at the time of negotiations. One is to include a *throwaway item* that would enhance your project but is not critical to operating a good, effective project. As an example, one institution submitted an application to fund a project aimed at assisting high school dropouts obtain a GED. The application guidelines said nothing about including an English as a Second Language (ESL) component as part of the project. An unusually large number of Hispanics who were very much in need of ESL assistance resided in the institution's target area. The proposal included a modest but adequate ESL component as one project objective. During negotiations, the ESL component was eliminated. It reduced the budget by a significant amount but did not impair overall project effectiveness. Had the negotiator decided to leave the ESL component intact, it would have enhanced the project's outcomes and provided a needed service to the target population. The writer was able to reduce the budget significantly by *throwing away* the ESL component without seriously jeopardizing the integrity of the project. During the next

——**Grant Tip**——

The negotiator probably is not familiar with your application. Do not be afraid to defend your budget.

——**Grant Tip**——

If the negotiator requires a budget (cost) *reduction, you will need to adjust either or both* time *and* performance *to make your proposal work.*

competition, the writer again included the *throwaway* ESL component, but it was not eliminated by the negotiator, resulting in a major project improvement.

Use caution if you choose to include a *throwaway* item. Do not include items that, if funded, will be impossible to implement or will be so time-consuming and cumbersome as to detract from the effectiveness of your project. *Throwaway* items must be sound, reasonable items or components that clearly are acceptable for inclusion. They should be *self-contained* and have an impact on the budget.

You might include a target area a little larger than what you really expect to serve, both in physical area and also in the number of students or clients to be served. As an example, in proposing to assist high school students in better preparing for college, a logical service area would include schools within 25 miles of the institution. However, by extending the proposed service area to approximately 35 miles, many more schools could receive needed services. The enlarged service area would require more funds for personnel, travel, and numbers of participant books and supplies. Although with the increased funds the project could serve the larger area, the project still could provide efficient service in the reduced area for reduced costs.

Sometimes during negotiations, the negotiator insists upon eliminating a line item that you believe is absolutely essential to your project. In such cases be prepared to defend your need for the line item, even if you cannot save the total amount requested. For example, you may submit a budget that includes $1,000 for duplicating services, handouts, classroom materials, and exams. Because of severe budget cuts, the negotiator wants to cut the item and have you convince your institution to supply duplicating services. Rather than lose the line completely, negotiate a reduced amount. The purpose is not so much to preserve the amount as it is to preserve the line.

If you preserve the line, at a later date you might submit a budget revision and transfer additional funds into the line. However, if you lose the line completely, it is difficult to receive approval to create a line item through a budget revision. For example, a project director requested funds to continue a newsletter that had been approved in the previous year's budget. Because of a smaller appropriations for the Department, the project officer recommended eliminating the newsletter. Having recognized the importance and the value of the newsletter, the project director was successful in retaining the line item but accepted a reduced amount for it. During the first months of operation, he had

————— **Grant Tip** —————
Estimate on the high but actual cost side. Use tourist air fares to build a budget but hope that you might be able to use super-savers.

savings in other areas and through a budget revision transferred sufficient money into the newsletter line to continue its publication.

After negotiating the budget determine what effects these reductions will have on the objectives and the way you planned to operate the project. Often project directors accept a budget without realizing that severe reductions may render certain objectives impossible to achieve. Such a determination is critical if your project receives points for prior performance. Leaving an objective in your document for which the budget has been severely reduced or eliminated may have a negative effect on the number of points you receive in a "prior performance" review later. Before you finalize your negotiations, decide where you will have to modify your objectives. You may need to eliminate an objective or two, or you may need to reduce the number of participants you originally planned to serve. You may decide to keep all of your objectives but to reduce the services each participant will receive. For example, you may have originally proposed to visit each participant a minimum of once each month and to provide each participant with one-on-one weekly tutoring sessions. After negotiation, you might reduce that objective to visit each participant once each quarter and to provide weekly tutoring sessions for groups of six participants rather than following the originally proposed one-on-one format.

You do not have to complete the negotiation process during the first telephone call. If you are in doubt about certain items, tell the negotiator that you must have more time to make the decision or that you must consult with your director, chairman, dean, or other superior. When you have had sufficient time, call the negotiator and complete your negotiations. Chances are good that you will be able to modify your proposal to the point that you can accept the recommended budget. Or perhaps the negotiator will be in a different frame of mind during the second conversation. You are not required to accept passively every budget reduction recommended to you. You must deal with that revised or reduced budget for a complete year. In all likelihood you will not be able to increase the recommended amount. Ensure that reductions are in areas that you can deal with and still have a project that can produce acceptable results. Remember, the decisions you make during that brief time of negotiations are the decisions you will have to live with for at least a year!

After budget negotiations, you will receive instructions to submit a revised budget reflecting the negotiated changes. Rework your budget while your telephone negotiation conversations are still fresh in your mind. As you rework the budget, also go back through your application and revise and adjust objectives and other items that were affected as a result of negotiations. You will be held responsible for the completion of objectives in their original form unless you provide revisions. You may need to submit a new face page (Form 424) or other required form that bears the signature of an administrative financial officer for your institution. You may want to do a *revised scope of work* after negotiations. This two- to five-page document brings negotiated budget and revised objectives and activities into line.

The Grant Award Notification

A short time after you have submitted your revised budget, you will receive an official *Grant Award Notification.* A sample Grant Award Notification is reproduced in Figure 11.4. This is your official notification that your application has been accepted and funded. Each item on this document is important.

Block 1 indicates the official name of the award recipient as recorded in the records and files of the Department.

Block 2 indicates the official name of the project. Each time you correspond with Department personnel, be sure to indicate the official name as indicated on this document.

Block 3 contains the names and telephone numbers of persons important to your grant award. These are the people most directly involved in your grant and who will make important decisions as to directions you will take.

Block 4 contains the *PR/Award Number.* This is the control number assigned to your grant. Include it on all correspondence with the Department.

Block 5 indicates the dates for which your project is funded and also approved. This example is the second year of a three-year project. The *budget period* indicates the one-year dates of funding for this particular grant. The *project period* indicates that the proposal was approved for a four-year period. The funding agency may approve a second, third, and fourth year of funding on a noncompetitive basis under the conditions specified in *Block 9.*

Block 6 tells the funding level for this funding period. The line entitled Project Period indicates the total amount received for this award up to and including the current year.

Block 7 provides the administrative information. This information will assist the recipient in completing the approved activities and

——Grant Tip——
Decisions you make during negotiations are decisions you will have to live with for a year!

Figure 11.4. Example of a Grant Award Notification

	U.S. DEPARTMENT OF EDUCATION WASHINGTON, D.C. 20202 **GRANT AWARD NOTIFICATION**	GRANTS AND CONTRACTS SERVICE

1	RECIPIENT NAME UNIV OF TENNESSEE/KNOXVILLE COLLEGE OF HUMAN ECOLOGY/HRD DEPT 404 ANDY HOLT TOWER KNOXVILLE, TN 37996

4	AWARD NOTIFICATION
	PR/AWARD NUMBER P066A40135 ACTION NUMBER 01 ACTION TYPE NEW AWARD TYPE DISCRETIONARY

2	PROJECT TITLE EDUCATIONAL OPPORTUNITY CENTER

5	AWARD PERIODS
	BUDGET PERIOD 10/01/99 - 09/30/00 PROJECT PERIOD 10/01/99 - 09/30/03

3	PROJECT STAFF RECIPIENT PROJECT DIRECTOR ERNEST W. BREWER 865-974-4466 EDUCATION PROGRAM STAFF BOB SMITH 202-708-4804 EDUCATION GRANTS STAFF SUSIE BROWN 202-708-6818

6	AUTHORIZED FUNDING
	THIS ACTION 365,403 BUDGET PERIOD 365,403 PROJECT PERIOD 365,403 RECIPIENT COST SHARE 0%

7	ADMINISTRATIVE INFORMATION
	PAYMENT METHOD ED PMS ENTITY NUMBER 1-626001636-A1 REGULATIONS EDGAR, AS APPLICABLE 34 CFR 644 ATTACHMENTS ABCS

8	LEGISLATIVE & FISCAL DATA AUTHORITY: HIGHER EDUCATION ACT OF 1965 P. L. 102-325, AS AMENDED PROGRAM TITLE: EDUCATIONAL OPPORTUNITY CENTER CFDA 84.066A

APPROPRIATION	FY	CAN	OBJECT CLASS	AMOUNT
96 40201	99	E003033	4115	365,403

9	TERMS AND CONDITIONS OF AWARD THE FOLLOWING ITEMS ARE INCORPORATED IN THE GRANT AGREEMENT: 1) THE RECIPIENT'S APPLICATION (BLOCK 2), 2) THE APPLICABLE EDUCATION DEPARTMENT REGULATIONS (BLOCK 7) THIS AWARD SUPPORTS ONLY THE BUDGET PERIOD SHOWN IN BLOCK 5. THE DEPARTMENT OF EDUCATION WILL CONSIDER CONTINUED FUNDING OF THE APPLICATION IF 1) FUNDS ARE AVAILABLE, 2) THE DEPARTMENT DETERMINES THAT CONTINUING THE PROJECT WOULD BE IN THE BEST INTEREST OF THE GOVERNMENT, AND 3) THE RECIPIENT SHOWS SUBSTANTIAL PROGRESS TOWARD THE GOALS OF THE PROEJCT AND SUBMITS A CONTINUATION APPLICATION. OTHER INFORMATION AFFECTING THIS ACTION IS PROVIDED IN THE ATTACHMENTS SHOWN IN BLOCK 7. (SIGNATURE) _____ JULY 11, 1999 John Doe DATE GRANTS OFFICER

Ver.   1

ED - GCS 007 (11/88)

managing the project in accordance with United States Department of Education procedures and regulations.

Block 8 gives the name of the authorizing legislation for this grant and the *CFDA* title of the program through which funding is provided.

Block 9 provides the terms and conditions of this grant award. Note some of the terms and conditions in Figure 11.4.

Study the Grant Award Notification document carefully. The reverse side usually contains an item-by-item explanation. If you have questions or you think a mistake has been made, contact your Education Program Staff Officer or Education Grants Staff Officer immediately. Their names and phones numbers are provided in *Block 3* of the Grant Award Notification document.

Unsuccessful Applications

Many more proposals are submitted than funded. As a result, many good proposals are not successful in receiving funds. Usually, after all successful applications have been negotiated, the Department notifies the unsuccessful applicants. This may be accomplished by returning the unsuccessful proposals to the submitting institution and notifying the institution by letter that its proposal was not recommended for funding.

If your application was unsuccessful, there are several things presented in Figure 11.5 that you should do. Immediately request in writing that the reviewers' rating sheets and comments be sent to you. In the same letter request that the Department indicate the *cutoff* score and your score as it was calculated by the Department. When you receive the rating sheets and comments, review them to ensure that an error was not made in calculating your score. Review the comments to determine if they relate to your proposal. Very seldom will a funding agency entertain an *appeal* or a *review* of the scores and comments of the panel that rated your application proposal. If you should find a grave error, such as obvious bias or comments totally unrelated to your document, you may wish to contact the Department and request a review. Experience, however, indicates that such requests seldom result in reversals of Department decisions.

Keep the reviewers' rating sheets and comments in a file. As you prepare your document to submit during the next funding cycle, review the comments and incorporate the pertinent items into your new application. Remember, however, that the next time you submit

——**Grant Tip**——
If your application was unsuccessful, request in writing that the reviewers' rating sheets and comments be sent to you. Review and incorporate the pertinent items into your new application.

Figure 11.5. Steps to Take With Unsuccessful Applications

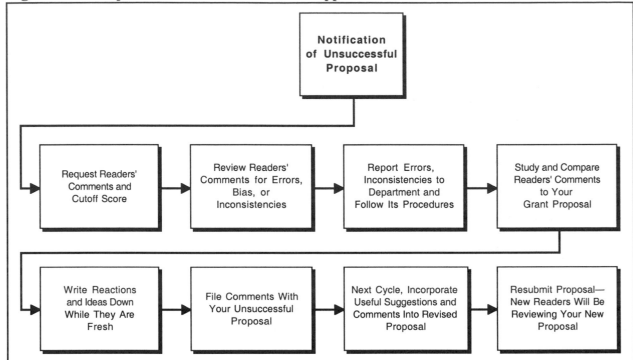

your application, a different review panel will score it. Therefore, even though you respond to every comment and detail outlined by the first review panel, there is no guarantee that your document will now meet the expectations of the next panel that reviews it.

To help you improve your application the next time, write to the Department and request a copy of the two top-ranked proposals from the previous competition. Once funded, under the Freedom of Information Act, the proposals become part of the public domain, and you have every right to request and review them. These may serve as good models. You may need to pay for duplication of the documents. Remember, top-ranked proposals are only models: Your set of circumstances, needs, and target area will be different. Even though you may glean some good ideas, be sure you address your specific needs, circumstances, and target population.

—— **Grant Tip** ——

To help you improve your application the next time, request a copy of the two top-ranked proposals from the previous competition.

12

The Players and Their Roles in the Process

The Process Starts Long Before You Begin to Write

Before you get your hard-earned grant money, quite a few different groups and people will have been involved. This chapter defines some of those who are involved and sketches out the roles that each is likely to play in your life as a proposal writer. As described in Chapter 1, a proposal is typically an instrument that you use to develop a project that will carry forth the purposes and objectives of a particular program, often a federal program.

A program generally comes into existence in response to a need recognized and championed by some group, often an advocate or special interest group that brings the need to public attention. At some point, the group generates enough interest in the need that the need is perceived as a *problem*.[1] Someone in a position of influence may now recognize the political benefits to be gained in responding to the problem. Thus the first players in the federal or state grants process are the persons or groups who focus a need into a problem and then promote the problem to prominent, public attention. This social definition of the problem may be quite general and not well focused.

Political Definition of Need or Problem

The next step is formal political definition of the problem, generally as expressed by a legislative body. The legislature may hold hearings to sample opinion and collect information before developing a bill (legislation) to support attempts to remedy the expressed need. In this way the legislative branch is the first *formal* actor. The

---

[1]Paul Warren (1980) expressed the first levels of "players" in the grants process as those who bring about a social definition, a political and legislative definition, and an agency or administrative definition. We have borrowed his terms here as they seem eminently expressive and sensible. See especially Chapters 1 and 3. Warren's other "definitions" of the problem were the institutional definition (the proposal document) and the operational definition (the way the project actually operates).

legislative branch defines the need or problem in a political sense and provides legislation for the program to come into existence. A bill, successfully passed by a legislature and signed by the executive branch, becomes an act, or a Public Law (PL). In federal parlance, public laws are numbered by designating the Congress that passed them and the chronology of the passage. Thus, PL 94-10 (the original Elementary and Secondary Education Act, or ESEA) was the tenth act passed by the 94th Congress.

The Key Committees

—— Grant Tip ——
The House Postsecondary Education Subcommittee deals with reauthorizing the Higher Education Act (HEA).

The federal legislative process works through a committee structure. In both the Senate and the House of Representatives, a major committee works with education and education-related problems, needs, issues, and concerns. In the Senate the major standing committee is the Senate Committee on Labor and Human Relations; the primary subcommittee to work with education is the Subcommittee on Education, Arts and Humanities. In the House of Representatives, the major committee is the House Committee on Education and Labor. Several important subcommittees work on education issues. Figure 12.1 shows the standing committees for education in the Senate and House of Representatives and one example of a subcommittee for each committee. Appropriations committees in both the House and the Senate make important decisions about how much federal support the various programs will receive each year.

The Regulation Process: Agency Definition

After the bill becomes law, representatives of the executive branch take over. Personnel of the agency that will eventually administer the law now develop *regulations*. These regulations go through several steps before they become final. Although it is not our intent to explain in detail the rule-making process in this *book*, a brief summary is necessary because during the rule-making process, a prospective proposal writer does have some opportunity to influence the outcome of the rule making. Agency personnel first publish in the *Federal Register* a notice of an Intent to Develop Regulations (see Chapter 3 for details of the *Federal Register*). This notice typically says that the agency is proceeding to develop regulations to govern the implementing of a particular piece of legislation. The notice invites interested people to submit ideas that seem appropriate for

Figure 12.1. Key Congressional Committees That Deal With Education Issues

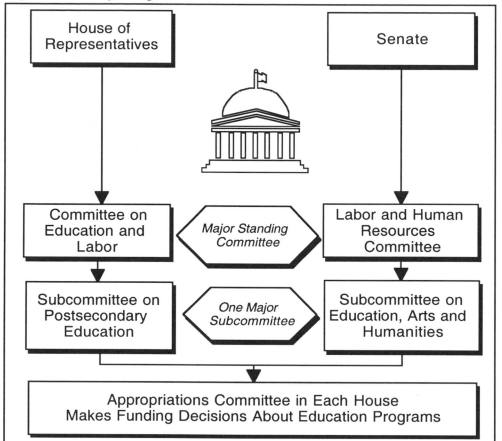

implementing the intent of the legislation. The notice will include the name, address, and phone contact of the government agency employee in charge of the rule-making process.

At some later date, usually several months in the future, federal agency personnel will publish in the *Federal Register* a notice of *proposed rules and regulations*. This constitutes the agency personnel's initial attempt to translate the intent of the legislation into an operational framework. Accompanying the proposed regulations is information about how an individual or a group can respond to those proposed rules and regulations. At this time individuals, or individuals representing groups or agencies, have an opportunity to comment on the rules and suggest changes. If the regulations are important to many groups, the agency may hold hearings on the proposed regulations at various central points throughout the nation. There is a cutoff date for the comments and suggestions. After that date agency personnel will review the comments and, based upon the intent of the legislation, may make some changes in the rules and regulations or may specify why no changes were made. The agency will publish in the *Federal Register* what are now designated as *Final Regulations*. If the Congress does not take some action to stop the regulations from becoming final, the regulations as published in the *Federal Register* as Final Regulations will become final after 45 days. In reality, the process usually takes much longer. The legislative and administrative branches also have additional prominent roles as major actors in the process at later stages.

Using the Regulation Process

Why is understanding this process important? If you or your organization wish to influence the way a program will be run, you have several opportunities to make your wishes known during the rule-making process. You may write comments to the agency or even appear in person at hearings. If you appear in person, remember also to provide a written statement for the record. You may review the comments of others during this comment period. You may encourage your elected officials to comment, or you may work through a professional association to make your points known about the regulations in process.

The proposed rules constitute an agency's best estimate of how agency personnel believe the law should be implemented. The compromise between the proposed rules and final rules can be instructive and may help you develop a stronger grant application. For example, if the proposed rules suggest that stipends for personnel should not be allowed, and if the final rules suggest that stipends can be allowed, you might develop a proposal that has some matching funds for stipends. This would show an intent to meet the agency's best estimate of the way the law should be implemented while still taking advantage of the provision to allow stipends for participants.

Once published in the *Federal Register*, the final regulations have essentially the force of law. They describe the way the agency will implement and administer programs authorized under the legislation. The final regulations become the agency's definition of the need brought to the attention of the legislative branch. Except for legislative oversight and periodic reports from the agency to the legislature, once the rules and regulations have become final, the agency, which is part of the executive branch, will have responsibility

——Grant Tip——
Registered lobbyists on Capitol Hill: 36,599; per member of Congress: 68. Average years served in House in 1991: 12.4 years; in Senate in 1991: 11.1 years.

for implementing the programs under the legislation. This is "the bureaucracy." Figure 12.2 shows the general picture of how a social need or problem eventually becomes the program to which you submit a proposal.

Figure 12.2. Process of a Social Need/Problem to a Competitive Grant

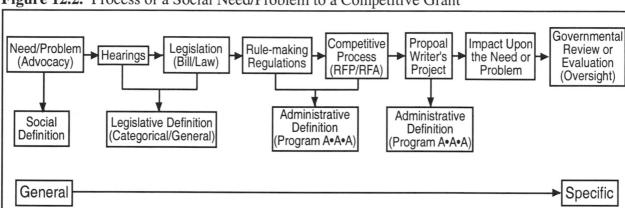

The Federal Budget Process

The federal budget process consists of the following three main phases that you should be aware of as you plan, write, and administer grants: (a) executive formulation and transmittal, (b) congressional action, and (c) budget execution and control. These phases are interrelated with each other.

Executive Formulation—The United States federal budget sets forth the President's financial plan and indicates his priorities for the federal government. The primary focus of the budget is on the budget year—the next fiscal year for which Congress needs to make appropriations. The President transmits his budget to Congress early in each calendar year, typically nine months before the next fiscal year begins. The process of formulating the budget is at least 18 months before the fiscal year begins.

Congressional Action—Congressional review of the budget begins shortly after it receives the President's budget proposals. Congress approves, modifies, or disapproves them. It can change funding levels, eliminate programs, or add programs not requested by the President. Congress does not enact a budget as such. It enacts appropriations bills and other legislation. Prior to making appropriations, Congress usually enacts legislation that authorizes an agency to carry out a particular program and, in some cases, includes limits on the amount that can be appropriated for the program. Some programs require annual authorizing legislation.

Budget Execution and Control—As approved or modified through the appropriation process, the President's budget becomes the basis for the financial plan for the operations of each agency during the fiscal year. Under the law, most budget authority and other budgetary resources are made available to the agencies of the executive branch through an apportionment system. The Director of OMB distributes appropriations and other budgetary resources to each agency by time periods and by activities (*The Budget Process,*1990).

United States Department of Education Key Personnel

The United States Department of Education's organizational structure consists of some key positions and offices with which you, as an individual interested in responding to a grant, should be familiar. Figure 12.3 is an organizational chart of the United States Department of Education, and it is followed by a brief statement of the key positions within that structure (*United States Government Manual,* 1999).

United States Secretary of Education—The United States Secretary of Education advises the President on education plans, policies, and programs of the federal government. Another major function of the Secretary is directing the Department staff in carrying out the approved programs and activities of the Department and promoting the public understanding of the Department's goals, programs, and objectives.

Under Secretary—The Under Secretary serves as Acting United States Department of Education Secretary in the absence of the Secretary and performs on behalf of the Secretary such functions and duties as the Secretary may designate and coordinates federal-state relations.

Deputy Under Secretary for Intergovernmental and Interagency Affairs—This office is responsible for providing overall leadership in coordinating regional and field activities as well as establishing and directing intergovernmental and interagency

Figure 12.3. Organizational Chart of the United States Department of Education

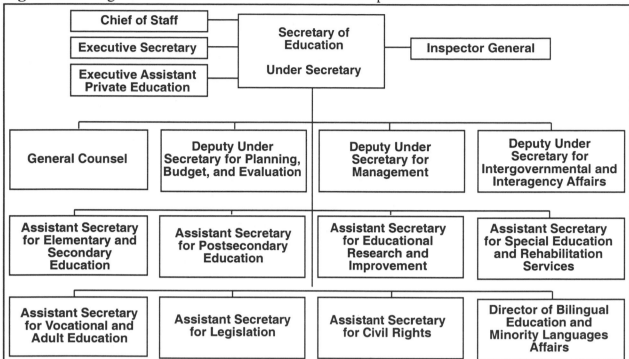

services for the Department. The office is also responsible for hearings and appeals related to Departmental programs.

Deputy Under Secretary for Managment—The Management Office provides advice and guidance to the United States Secretary of Education on administrative and financial management and provides for the direction and coordination of these activities throughout the Department on a day-to-day basis. These activities include financial management, personnel, training, grants and procurement management, and other supportive services.

Deputy Under Secretary for Planning, Budget, and Evaluation— This office coordinates the Department's activities in the preparation of the Departmental budget, program analysis, and planning activities, and ensures that Department policy and program planning appropriately reflect the results of these activities.

Inspector General—The Inspector General is responsible for conducting and supervising audits and investigations relating to programs and operations of the Department. The office provides leadership, coordination, and policy recommendations to promote economy, efficiency, and effectiveness and to prevent and detect fraud and abuse in the administration of the Department's programs and operations. The Inspector General is also responsible for keeping the Secretary and Congress fully and currently informed about problems and deficiencies relating to the administration of such programs and operations in the Department.

General Counsel—The General Counsel provides legal advice to the United States Department of Education Secretary and to the various operations within the Department.

Assistant Secretary for Legislation—The Assistant Secretary serves as the principal adviser to the United States Secretary of Education on matters concerning the Department's legislative program and congressional relations.

Assistant Secretary for Civil Rights—The Assistant Secretary is responsible for the administration and enforcement of civil rights laws related to education and the handicapped. In addition, this office monitors compliance in programs and activities receiving federal financial assistance.

Assistant Secretary for Elementary and Secondary Education—This office formulates policy for, directs, and coordinates the activities related to preschool, elementary, and secondary education in the Department. Included are programs of grants to SEAs and LEAs, programs of financial and technical assistance to school districts to meet special needs incident to the elimination of discrimination, and grants for the education of neglected and delinquent students.

Assistant Secretary for Educational Research and Improvement—The OERI administers functions of the Department concerning research, statistics, development, demonstration, dissemination, and assessments. In addition, this office oversees a wide variety of discretionary grant programs to maximize individual program impact on school improvement.

Assistant Secretary for Vocational and Adult Education—The Assistant Secretary of this office is responsible for grants, contracts, and technical assistance for vocational and technical education, community schools, and comprehensive employment and training.

Assistant Secretary for Special Education and Rehabilitative Services—This office administers special education programs and services expressly designed to meet the needs and develop the full potential of handicapped children. In addition, this office is responsible for comprehensive rehabilitation service programs specifically designed to reduce human dependency and to fully utilize the productive capabilities of all handicapped persons. Programs under this office include support for training of teachers and other professional personnel, grants for research, and financial aid to help states initiate, expand, and improve their resources.

Assistant Secretary for Postsecondary Education—The Assistant Secretary of this office formulates policy, directs, and coordinates programs for assistance to postsecondary educational institutions and students pursuing a postsecondary education. Programs include assistance for the improvement and expansion of educational resources, grants to improve instruction, and construction assistance for academic facilities. This office oversees the various financial aid programs such as Pell Grants and GSLs.

Director of the Office of Bilingual Education and Minority Languages Affairs—The Director of this office assures access to equal educational opportunity and improves the quality of programs for limited English proficiency and minority languages populations by providing support for programs, activities, and management initiatives meeting the special educational needs of those populations.

Regional Offices—Ten Regional Offices serve as points for the dissemination of information and provide technical assistance to SEAs, LEAs, and other institutions and individuals interested in federal education activities. These Regional Offices are located in Atlanta, Boston, Chicago, Dallas, Denver, Kansas City, New York, Philadelphia, San Francisco, and Seattle.

Program Officers

The agency employs persons to work with the program to ensure that its goals and purposes are met and that the program operates according to the regulations. These are *program officers.* They work within the agency, disseminate information about the program, answer questions about the program, and administer the program for the agency. In their role as program administrators, they may well be responsible later for working with the project which the successful proposal writer has developed.

——**Grant Tip**——
Program officers hold the grant competition and may also serve on review panels. After the grant competition, they oversee and administer successful projects for the agency.

Before proposals are funded, program officers have numerous responsibilities. One responsibility is to hold the grant competition. In this role the program officers prepare application packets, announce the competition, mail out application packets, and check proposals when they come to the federal government. Program officers may also serve on review panels. In this role, the program officer will generally assure that the grant competition is held according to appropriate rules and regulations, that the proposal review process is fair, and that all persons receive the appropriate communications. Program officers may also hold seminars or briefing sessions for persons planning to develop proposals for the program.

After the grant competition successful projects are assigned to program officers who will oversee and administer that project for the agency. The program officer becomes the contact person for the principal investigator or director of the successful project. The program officer generally works with the project for its entire duration and usually gets to know the project and project personnel quite well. The program officer answers questions and is a liaison between your project and the program at the agency. The program officer makes decisions regarding program quality and about the way a program is conducted. The program officer does not make final decisions regarding funding or expenditure of project funds. Funding decisions are the responsibility of the grant and contract officer.

Grant and Contract Officer

──Grant Tip──
After notification that your proposal has been selected for funding, the grant officer assigned to your project negotiates final budget figures with you.

The grant and contract officer is the person who knows thoroughly the federal rules and regulations regarding expenditure of funds for grants and contracts. This person will assist you with any questions about your budget or about appropriate expenditures. After notification that your proposal has been selected for funding, the grant officer assigned to your project will negotiate final budget figures with you for the federal government. This negotiation is based upon discussions with and recommendations from the program officer, but final decisions regarding money matters will rest with the grant and contract officer.

If you plan to make a major deviation from your budget, or if you plan to request a budget change, you will contact the grant and contract officer. You should, of course, have discussed these changes with your program officer in advance. Indeed, you should send a copy of any correspondence with the grant and contract officer to your program officer, and vice versa.

Implementation and operation decisions are made by a program officer; the project's fiscal issues are addressed by the grant and contract officer. Each has a particular role in the process. The program officer's responsibility begins long before the grant competition starts. The grant and contract officer's responsibility begins after successful proposals have been funded and the proposal writer has become a project director or a principal investigator.

Some Part-Time Players on the Roster

There is another team of players in the grant process. Members of this team are only part-time players, but they are very important. These are the readers for your proposal. Most grants are awarded after a peer review and scoring or ranking of proposals. In this process a team of readers will review proposals and grade or rate and often rank the proposals. A typical proposal reading team might consist of two persons from outside the federal government and one person from inside the federal government. Agency personnel may mail proposals to reviewers for them to read, or they may invite the readers to Washington and establish a review panel in that manner. (Detail of the review process is provided in Chapter 11, "Understanding How Grants Are Awarded.")

Although the readers will have only a short tenure in working with your proposal, their decisions will have a significant impact on whether or not your proposal receives funds. The peer review process (readers) helps keep politics out of the grant process to some degree and allows the federal government to get outside, expert opinions on the value of various projects proposed to implement the purposes of a program.

Some Early Players Have Dual Roles

The legislative and executive branches have at least one other role in the grant process. When the legislative branch passes a law, one portion of that law will specify how much money is authorized to be expended for each section of the law. This *authorization* is generally a figure considerably higher than that which will eventually be available. In passing a law, the legislature usually intends that the law will be in effect for several years. By authorizing more funds than are appropriated, the legislative branch maintains continuity and flexibility and can make changes without passing a new law.

—— **Grant Tip** ——
The U.S. Department of Education's Application Control Center serves as the point of receiving all grant proposals.

If it decides to support activities under a law, the legislature will include the funds in an *appropriations* bill. An appropriations bill designates the amount of funds available to carry forth the purposes of the law. Appropriations are generally for one year, but if the agency is successful in meeting the purposes of a particular program, the legislature is likely to include funds for the agency's program in an appropriations bill in succeeding years, thus ensuring that the program will have some life of its own.

Once monies have been appropriated, the executive branch through the administering agency will *allocate* funds to particular program categories. These three steps, authorization, appropriation, and allocation (AAA) are important because they help the proposal writer understand the value of the program to the funding source. This importance can be inferred from the amount of funding authorized and appropriated and the way the appropriated funds are allocated.

The amount authorized is almost always considerably more than the amount appropriated. Cynics suggest that legislators discuss the amount authorized when they speak to groups in favor of particular legislation, but speak only about appropriations or allocations when questioned seriously about their care in watching over public funds.

There are many actors in the grant process. Some important ones are the legislative branch, the executive branch, the program officer, the grants officer, and the proposal readers. Using Warren's (1980) conceptualization, the social definition of a problem is when it becomes evident and is made apparent to the legislature. The legislative definition of a problem is the law passed because of the need. The administrative definition of a problem is the rules and regulations and final allocation of funds for the program.

The Project Director/Principal Investigator (PI)

There is one more extremely important actor. That is the project director or the principal investigator. A project director is the person designated to administer a project. This person is in contact with the program officer and the grant and contract officer in Washington and has the day-to-day responsibility for managing the funded project. The director is responsible to the federal government for meeting timelines and for expending funds in accordance with rules and regulations. The federal government provides rules and regulations to govern the administration of a project, and the director must know those rules and regulations.

Often the project director is the person who wrote the proposal. A cooperative working relationship between the project director and the administrative personnel in Washington will help ensure that a particular project is well run, well administered, and successful in meeting its objectives and purposes.

State-Level Reviews

In the federal grants process, there are also state-level roles. Federal Executive Order 12372 requires that you *may* need to review your proposal with a State Single Point of Contact (SPOC). Note that *not all* federal programs are covered under the review requirements of Executive Order 12372. Instructions about this requirement are in the regulations and may also be in the grant application packet.

The SPOC process is designed to see that there is appropriate *coordination* between and among federally supported programs.

Executive Order 12372 notes that persons at SPOC can send comments on the project (proposal) to the federal agency that administers the program. The comments usually have to be at the federal agency at a specific cutoff date, generally 30 days after the proposal's due date. The address for sending SPOC comments to the federal agency is not the same address as that to which you send the proposal. Read these instructions carefully!

The SPOC agency requirements vary from state to state. Some want only copies of a project abstract; some want entire proposals. Learn about your SPOC; *know* the SPOC address, phone number, and preferred process for review.

A grant application may require that you submit your proposals for another state review—for education this may be the State Education Agency (SEA). The application packet or regulations will provide the exact directions you should follow.

Be courteous and communicative. Regardless of the requirements for sending your proposal to agencies or places for review, you should send a copy to appropriate agencies. If you are developing a project to improve pupil reading, be sure to share your proposal with the reading personnel and possibly the dropout, compensatory education, or other personnel in the SEA. If your project deals with health, send a copy to the state agency that works with health issues in the state.

In sending courtesy copies of your proposal, you need only send the basics—the idea and the plan. You will want to remove excess

——— Grant Tip ———
The address for sending SPOC comments to the federal agency is not the same address as that to which you send the proposal. Read these instructions carefully! State Players: Executive Order 12372, Single Point of Contact in States, and State Agency Review or Information.

——— Grant Tip ———
Learn about your State Single Point of Contact; know the SPOC address, phone number, and preferred process for review. Appendix B contains a list of SPOC addresses (2000).

pages, appendixes, and the budget. Not only is this information usually private, but slimming down the packet will save on duplication and postage. Your purpose is to be informative—to communicate your interest in the problem and in developing a project to work with the problem.

Conclusion

This section provides a summary of the key actors or players in the federal grant process. While omitting some academic and bureaucratic details, we have tried to include ideas and steps to help the grantwriter understand the entrance to the labyrinth and to have a successful start down the twisting path toward competency in the federal grant game. If you move to the major leagues, you'll need a more detailed scorecard!

PART III

Implementing, Operating, and Terminating a Project

In Part III, Chapters 13-16, we examine the implementing, operating, and closing out of a funded project. The Federal guidelines that must be followed *(EDGAR)* while operating a project and the nature of site visits and audits are also discussed. In each chapter, we offer a variety of tips and examples that are helpful to a grant administrator.

13

Implementing a Funded Project

Introduction

Now that you have negotiated your grant and have received your Grant Award Notification, you are ready to implement your project. This phase of your grant can be exciting and fun if you are well prepared and organized. This chapter is designed to help you develop a plan and get you started on the implementation procedures.

Grant Award Notification

Often, the time you have to actually implement your project is very short. It is common to have less than two months between the time you receive your Grant Award Notification and the start up date of your project. You need to be well organized and ready to "hit the road running" the moment you receive the Grant Award Notification. When you negotiated your grant, you were told by the negotiator that the negotiations did not constitute a grant and that you were not to announce your grant or spend any money from it until you received the Grant Award Notification document. Many times it takes between two and five weeks to receive this document.

—— Grant Tip ——
Be well organized and ready to "hit the road running" the moment you receive the Grant Award Notification.

Pre-Implementation

In the meantime, you can begin to organize your plans for implementation. Some of the areas you need to organize include:

1. Prepare in-depth, comprehensive positions descriptions.
2. Prepare position announcements.
3. Plan the distribution of the announcements.
4. Prepare advertisements for positions for newspapers.
5. Develop interview rating sheets.
6. Select an interviewing committee.

7. Hire personnel.

8. Locate and modify physical space for the project (office, classroom, tutoring, and storage).

9. Set up bookkeeping and accounting procedures.

10. Prepare procedures for participant recruitment and application forms.

11. Outline selection procedures for participant selection.

12. Prepare class schedules, curriculum materials, and participant handbook or manual.

13. Outline procedures for gathering evaluation and annual performance report data.

14. Set up files and filing procedures.

——— Grant Tip ———
Have all the financial procedures in order prior to the expenditure of money from your grant.

Your institution may not provide bookkeeping and accounting services for your project. Therefore, you will have to have someone on your staff perform this function. It is of extreme importance that you employ a person with experience in working with federal grants. Your business office may provide you with assistance in hiring such a person or you may need to seek the assistance of a private accountant. At any rate, determine this early and make the appropriate arrangements. You will probably expend money from your budget long before you begin to offer services to the target population. Do not delay in having all of the financial procedures in order prior to the expenditure of money from your grant.

Participant Selection

In the case of grants that serve individuals, another vital part of your project that you can organize while you are waiting for applications to come in and be processed is the recruitment of participants. Take care to make your application form reflect the applicant qualifications as specified in your proposal. Ask questions that will provide the information needed to make wise selection decisions. No matter how great your personnel may be or how well-organized your project is, if you do not have a good quality of participants according to the guidelines, you will have difficulty in achieving success.

In selecting participants, remember that your project cannot be all things to all participants. You must be selective in choosing those to receive services. You need to devise a rating scale to help you be objective. For example, one project director designed an application form that gathered information in three separate areas. He gave each question in the three areas a numerical value. The scale was from 0 to 27. He and his staff determined that, even though the applicant met the criteria required in the application, if he/she scored above 23 points, he/she really did not need the services of the project in order to succeed. On the other hand, if an applicant scored seven or less, the project did not provide the services necessary to help him/her. These applicants were referred to other agencies whose programs were designed for such persons.

This rating scale ensured that the project did not "cream" the applicant pool by choosing only those who would succeed regardless of what the project did, and the other extreme, it protected the project from inadvertently selecting those who could not succeed in spite of the efforts of the project.

Do not underestimate the importance of participant selection. The success or failure of your project in a large measure depends upon wise selection criteria and implementation.

Preparing for the Participants

For those grants that serve program participants, especially those that may have a campus residential component—impress your participants by being completely ready for them. As you meet them individually or in an orientation meeting, have their schedules ready, complete with course or project titles, credit hours, classroom numbers, instructors' names, textbooks required, and campus map. To do this, you must involve your instructional staff and plan well.

Have a packet of materials ready for each participant. Include special items, such as instructions where different services are available, the library, administrative office, health services, bookstore, snack shop, student union or lounge area, tutorial services, directions to the dorms and cafeteria. If your project is to furnish certain materials such as a notebook, pencils, paper, or backpacks, have them ready for your initial contact. Often it is helpful to put together a participant handbook. Most of the items listed above could be included in an attractive handbook. There are always things that a participant should not do. Often the "do nots" out number the "dos." By putting the other items in the handbook, it does not give it such a negative tone.

A handbook will give all participants an even opportunity to be successful. At the first meeting or contact, they will probably be nervous, surveying the situation to see who their potential friends might be and sizing up the instructors and administrative staff. They may even be fighting back a little homesickness. Having everything written down in a handbook allows them to read it and study it when they are more at ease. It also provides you and your staff with a point of reference in dealing with situations that might arise in the future.

Participants will be impressed by your well-organized and designed initial contact with them. An investment of time in this area will pay dividends.

Record Keeping System

It is very important while setting up your record keeping system that you read and understand the following *Education Department General Administrative Regulation (EDGAR)* that governs federal grants for the United States Department of Education. *EDGAR* is described in more detail in Chapter 14. In record keeping, you need to be familiar with 75.730 thru 75.734 regulations that are outlined in Figure 13.1.

Establish a comprehensive record keeping system that includes at least (a) expenditures records (invoices and transfer vouchers.); (b) personnel records; (c) participant records, if serving participants; and (d) incoming and outgoing correspondence. Often in an audit or a site visit, your visitor will want to review such records. Keep all the information your employees sent you as they were applying for the position. Put their job description in their file. Make sure you have a copy of their signed contract, vacation schedule, and sick leave policy. Place copies of any correspondence you have with them, in addition to commendations and reprimands in their files.

If you maintain a complete file on each participant, include his/her application form and related correspondence, a clear reason why he/she was accepted into your project, and what specific needs qualified him/her for participation. Also include your plan for intervention that will assist that participant in successfully completing the project. Place copies of progress sheets, test scores, and interest inventory results in the file. Summarize any counseling or advising sessions you may hold with the participant, along with a report of special action taken as a result of superior performance or disciplinary problems.

When the participant exits your project, take a few minutes and "close" the file by indicating the participant's reasons for exiting

——Grant Tip——

It is very important while setting up your record keeping system that you read and understand EDGAR.

Figure 13.1. *EDGAR* Guidelines for Recordkeeping

§ 75.730 **Records related to grant funds.**
A grantee shall keep records that fully show:
(a)   The amount of funds under the grant.
(b)   How the grantee uses the funds.
(c)   The total cost of the project.
(d)   The share of that cost provided from other sources.
(e)   Other records to facilitate an effective audit.
(Authority: 20 U.S.C. 1232f)

§ 75.731 **Records related to compliance.**
A grantee shall keep records to show its compliance with program requirements.
(Authority: 20 U.S.C. 1221e-3(a)(1))

§ 75.732 **Records related to performance.**
(a)   A grantee shall keep records of significant project experiences and results.
(b)   The grantee shall use the records under paragraph (a) to:
   (1) Determine progress in accomplishing project objectives.
   (2) Revise those objectives, if necessary.
(Authority: 20 U.S.C. 1221e-3(a)(1))
CROSS-REFERENCE. See 34 CFR 74.103 (b) and (c)--Procedures for revising
   objectives.

§ 75.733   **[Reserved]**

§ 75.734 **Record retention period.**
Unless a longer period is required under 34 CFR Part 74, a grantee shall retain records
for five years after the completion of the activity for which it uses grant funds.

Source: *EDGAR* (1999).

(successfully completed the program, became ill, was expelled, or had financial problems), the progress he/she made while in the program, and, if possible, an exit evaluation the participant completed. All of this information will be extremely helpful in maintaining the constant focus of your staff on each participant and being "on top" of any problems or areas of weakness or concern. In addition, in the event of a site visit or in the preparation of your annual performance evaluation, you will have valuable information systematically collected. Financial records are of utmost importance. All program expenditures must be well-documented with receipts or purchase orders. Although the fiscal officer of your institution or agency may keep the original copy of the financial invoices you should maintain a backup copy for your files.

Maintain a complete file of all correspondence, which should include any responses you may receive. Your correspondence becomes important documentation of your performance and organization.

It serves as a reference and you will find that, if you systematically keep and file this correspondence, it will be an important source of information.

Annual Performance Report Data Gathering

Almost all federally funded projects must submit an annual performance report of some type. Some departments and offices in the United States Department of Education have very detailed outlines and requirements for information that must be submitted annually. Other departments and offices provide almost no guidelines or suggestions. If your particular office or agency provides information, study it carefully. Even before your project begins, determine the types of information you need to gather. Make a list of all the items you need to preserve in order to respond to the annual performance report criteria. Decide now who will be responsible for gathering what information and make sure that these employees are aware of their responsibilities and that they know when the information should be submitted to you.

Select a drawer in a file cabinet that is close to your desk and prepare a file entitled Annual Performance Report Data. A good rule of thumb is to document everything and save copies of everything you do. Put all of this material in your Annual Performance Report Data file.

For example, keep an "official" copy of all the position descriptions you may develop. Buy the newspaper(s) that carry your advertisements of position vacancies and cut the advertisements out. Be sure to cut out the name of the newspaper and the date. Tape them on a piece of paper and put them in your Annual Performance Report Data file. If you send out position vacancy announcements to sister institutions or agencies, put a copy in your Annual Performance Report Data file.

Save a copy of your employee application rating sheet and the participant selection rating sheet. Compile a complete list of all of your participants, their qualifications and needs, and why you selected them to be in the program. Keep a copy of your participant handbook, forms, information sheets, and accounting and bookkeeping information and put all of it in your Annual Performance Report Data file. Be sure to keep accurate information on those participants who successfully complete your project. Keep newspaper clippings, articles, or other published accounts of your project.

—— Grant Tip ——

Even before your project begins, determine the types of information you need to gather for an annual performance report.

—— Grant Tip ——

A good rule of thumb is to document and save copies of everything you do.

When the time comes for you to compile your Annual Performance Report, you will probably find that you have collected much more information than you need. It is much better to be able to "pick and choose" information from your Annual Performance Report Data file than it is to have to sit down and have a "creative writing session."

Summary

This chapter has attempted to provide you with suggestions that will help you to implement your project. You will find there are many other things you will need to do, depending on the type of project you have, your institution or agency's policies, and your previous experience. Plan to spend additional time and effort at the start up of your project. It may be difficult, but you will be pleased you did. The smooth operation of a project is impacted heavily by the way you have it organized prior to the actual delivery of services. Give yourself, your staff, your participants, and your institution or agency every advantage of having a successful project by being well prepared.

14

Understanding *EDGAR* and GPRA

Introduction

This chapter deals with two important federal government documents: the *Education Department General Administrative Regulations* (*EDGAR*) and the Government Performance and Results Act (GPRA). We recommend these as standard documents in your grant library because of their importance in proposal development, proposal writing, and program administration.

Another relatively new provision, enacted in 1994 by the Congress, is Section 427 of the General Education Provisions Act (GEPA). It requires new applicants to create a plan for ensuring equitable access to, and participation in, their federally funded program. In other words, how are all students, teachers, and those with special needs going to be guaranteed equal access to the program you are proposing? The federal government identified six barriers that you must address in your proposal: gender, race, national origin, color, disability, and age. Frequently the Government Performance and Results Act (GPRA) and General Education Provisions Act (GEPA) are confused, but they are substantially different. For more information about GEPA refer to Grants Policy OMB Bulletin #10, issue date 12/7/98.

Introduction to *EDGAR*

EDGAR is an acronym for *Education Department General Administrative Regulations*. This handbook of regulations is published by the U.S. Department of Education and is revised often. The latest revision is dated September 16, 1999. This edition took effect April 7, 1997, except the removal of 34 *CFR*, Part 630, which took effect on October 1, 1997. The September 16, 1999 edition of *EDGAR* (orange in color) applies to all currently funded projects. You can obtain a copy of *EDGAR* by contacting the research office of your institution, by requesting one from your federal program officer, or via Internet access at http://ocfo.ed.gov/grntinfo/edgar.htm. You need your own copy of *EDGAR* so you can mark the important parts that pertain to your project.

Read *EDGAR* before beginning to write your grant application. Usually the grant application or, in the case of a contract, the Request for Proposal (RFP) will refer you to several parts or subparts that relate directly to the proposal you intend to write. Familiarity with EDGAR may save you many hours of revision and possibly legal problems or audits.

The September 16, 1999 revision of *EDGAR* contains 13 parts. The cost principles are replaced by the appropriate Office of Management and Budget (OMB) Circular. In the case of educational institutions, this is OMB Circular A-21 "Cost Principles for Educational Institutions." If your agency is a non-profit organization, the cost principles in OMB-Circular A-122 apply to you. Figure 14.1 outlines the major parts of *EDGAR*.

This chapter reviews a few highlights of *EDGAR* to give you a head start on your project. Space does not permit an in-depth discussion of each topic covered in *EDGAR*. You are encouraged, however, to read and study *EDGAR* prior to writing a proposal. Become

Figure 14.1. Major Parts of *EDGAR*

Part 74	Administration of Grants
Part 75	Direct Grant Programs
Part 76	State-Administered Programs
Part 77	Definitions that Apply to Department Regulations
Part 79	Intergovernmental Review of Department of Education Programs and Activities
Part 80	Uniform Administrative Requirements for Grants and Cooperative Agreements to State and Local Governments
Part 81	General Education Provisions Act (Enforcement)
Part 82	New Restrictions on Lobbying
Part 85	Government-wide Debarment and Suspension (Nonprocurement) and Government-wide Requirements for Drug-Free Workplace (Grants)
Part 86	Drug and Alcohol Abuse Prevention
Part 97	Protection of Human Subjects
Part 98	Student Rights in Research, Experimental Programs, and Testing
Part 99	Family Educational Rights and Privacy

thoroughly familiar with each part, especially the part or parts that apply to programs of interest to you. After receiving funding for a project, thoroughly review *EDGAR* again prior to implementing your project. This will help you set up and initiate your project correctly. Part 74 of *EDGAR* relates to the administration of grants.

Part 74: Administration of Grants

Part 74, *Administration of Grants and Agreements with Institutions of Higher Education, Hospitals, and Nonprofit Organizations.* Each Part, except for Part 77, begins with a comprehensive index that divides the contents into subparts, each bearing an identifying number. For example: Part 74, Subpart A-General, begins with 74.1, The purpose and scope of the part; 74.2, Definitions as used in this subpart; 74.3, Effect on other issuances; 74.4, Deviations; and 74.5, Subawards. Subpart B-Pre-Award Requirements deals with pre-award policies, forms for applying for federal assistance, debarment and suspension, special award conditions, and certifications and representations. Subpart C-Post-Award Requirements focuses on financial and program management, property standards, procurement standards, reports and records, and termination and enforcement. The last Subpart section of Part 74 is Subpart D-After-the-Award Requirements. Closeout procedures, subsequent adjustments and continuing responsibilities, and collection of amounts due are outlined in this section. The remainder of this chapter points out important parts and subparts and touches on them briefly in relation to grant administration.

Retention and Access
Requirements for Records

Record keeping is an important aspect of managing any funded project. Specific instructions tell you how long you must keep records and who shall have the right to review your records. Keep all programmatic and financial records, supporting documents, statistical and other records required by the specific program in order to operate the project efficiently and effectively.

Retention

Records must be kept for a minimum of three years from the starting date of your project. If the project is a *direct grant program,*

——— **Grant Tip** ———
Retain your records at least three years from the starting date of your project.

—— Grant Tip ——
You must submit an annual report 90 days after your grant year ends.

—— Grant Tip ——
You cannot change the scope or objectives without prior approval.

—— Grant Tip ——
74.25
Prior Approval Procedures
• *When requesting prior approval, make requests to your Grants Specialist and/ or your Program Officer.*
• *Make sure you include your Grant Number on all requests.*
• *Approvals are not valid unless they are in writing and are signed by the authorized ED Grants Officer.*

you must retain your records for a minimum of five years. If litigation, claim, negotiation, audit, or any other action has been initiated regarding the project prior to the end of the three- or five-year period, you must retain all records until such action or litigation has been completed, even though it may extend far beyond the ordinary required limit.

If the project is renewed annually or at certain intervals, the three- or five-year retention period begins on the date you submit your expenditure report for that period. In other words, assume your grant was awarded for three years, is not a direct grant, and that your first funding period expires on March 31. You submit your expenditure report to the appropriate office on May 15. The three-year retention requirement for that funding period begins on May 15. If you must submit an expenditure report quarterly, your retention period begins on the day you submit your report for the last quarter of the fiscal year. If an expenditure report has been waived, retention begins on the day the report would have been due.

EDGAR discusses other aspects of retention as it pertains to equipment, income transactions, and indirect cost rate proposals. For details, read the subpart carefully.

Access

The Secretary or the Comptroller General or any of their authorized representatives have the right to inspect project books and records. This is true even if you subcontract part of the project to another agency.

EDGAR also prohibits you from imposing grant terms that would limit public access to your records and documents. Nevertheless, you are not required to invite public access and inspection of your records. You may refuse public access to certain confidential records and documents if such records would be excepted from disclosure under the *Freedom of Information Act* (FOIA). Such a determination must be made by the Department of Education and not by the recipient of the grant award.

Monitoring and Reporting of Program Performance

Monitoring and reporting of program performance provide general timelines and guidelines that apply to the annual performance report. Unless otherwise specified in the particular project, the annual report is due 90 days after the grant year ends. Your grant award document may contain instructions as to the content of the annual report. However, some programs do not have a required outline or form requesting specific information. In such cases, use this section of *EDGAR* as a guide. It requires a comparison of the actual accomplishments of the goals established in your proposal. If goals were not met, it requests reasons for the slippage. It also requests information regarding unexpectedly high costs and, when appropriate, a cost-per-student or cost-per-unit analysis.

Programmatic Changes and Budget Revisions

Programmatic changes and budget revisions are very important. During the course of a project, especially one funded for three years or more, it often becomes necessary to make program or budget revisions. Check the guidelines in *EDGAR* if you need to make changes in the project or in the budget.

What constitutes a change? A change has occurred if the project's scope or objectives have changed from those contained in the approved application. A good rule to follow: *If your performance does not match the scope and/or objectives of the approved application proposal, submit a request for prior approval for a programmatic revision.* You cannot change the scope or objectives without prior approval. Assume, for instance, that one objective states that the project will serve 90 students. For various reasons this becomes impossible, and you can serve only 60. Submit a request for prior approval to reduce the number of students served from 90 to 60. Do not make the reduction until you receive written approval from an authorized Department of Education Grants Officer.

In preparing a request for prior approval for a programmatic revision, indicate the modification desired. Include a statement such as:

> Objective A states that the project will assist 90 students to earn graduate degrees in secondary science education. We hereby request approval to amend Objective A as follows:
>
> *Objective A:* The project will assist 60 students to earn a graduate degree in secondary science education.

—— **Grant Tip** ——
74.25 Programmatic Changes Requiring Approval

• *Changes to the scope or to the objectives.*

• *Changes in key people.*

• *The absence for more than three months, or a 25% reduction in time devoted to the project, by the approved project director or principal investigator.*

• *The need for additional Federal funding.*

• *Transferring to a third party, by contracting or any other means, the actual performance of the substantive programmatic work.*

• *The transfer of funds allotted for training allowances (direct payments to trainees) to other categories of expense.*

Provide justification for requesting the modification. Support the request with current facts and figures, letters of support or concurrence, and a good rationale for change. Other modifications that require prior approval include:

1. Continuing the project during a period of more than three months without a project director.

2. Replacing the project director or principal investigator or other key project people.

3. Reducing the amount of time spent on the project by a key person.

4. Transferring to a third party the actual performance of the substantive programmatic work.

5. Providing medical care to individuals under research grants.

A request for prior approval will stand a better chance of approval if it does not require additional money. If a modification requires more funds in a particular budget line or causes excess funds in a line, adjust other budget areas to accommodate the difference.

A budget revision also requires prior approval. According to 74.25, Budget Revisions—Nonconstruction Projects, prior approval to revise the budget is required to:

—— **Grant Tip** ——
*Carefully review
OMB Circular A-21
for allowable cost
principles.*

1. Transfer amounts budgeted for indirect costs to absorb increases in direct costs.

2. Transfer amounts previously budgeted for student support (tuition waivers, stipends, and other payments to or for trainees).

3. Increase the total amount of the grant.

4. Transfer funds from one budget line to another if large amounts of funds are involved.

Some budget changes may not require prior approval. Try to avoid requesting transfers from student services to other line items such as equipment, travel, and personnel. Such requests often are not approved. Requests that receive a more favorable response seek request transfers from one "non-student support" item to another "non-student support" item, such as from equipment to travel or from travel to supplies.

Subpart L is one of the most important subparts of *EDGAR*. Protect yourself, your institution, and your project by adhering closely to its guidelines. In addition, become familiar with the Office of Management and Budget (OMB), Circular A-21—Cost Principals for Institutions of Higher Education, and OMB A-122—Cost Principals for Non-Profit Organizations.

Property

Property provides information regarding property, equipment, and supplies. This subsection of *EDGAR* describes these items and when they are considered part of the grant. It defines several important terms, among them equipment and supplies. *Equipment* is generally defined as tangible personal property having a useful life of more than one year and an acquisition cost of $5,000 or more per unit unless your agency uses the Cost Accounting Standards Board standard of $5,000 or more per unit and useful life of two years. This differs from *supplies,* defined as "all tangible personal property other than equipment." This section also discusses the use and disposition of equipment acquired for a project.

Allowable cost principle. For each kind of organization, there is a set of federal principles for determining allowable costs. For educational institutions, you should refer to OMB Circular A-21. Within it you will find valuable information regarding allowable and unallowable costs.

Part 75: Direct Grant Programs

Part 75, *Direct Grant Programs,* describes the procedures used by the U. S. Department of Education to award direct grants. The Department of Education may have developed implementation rules and regulations that apply to a specific grant program that falls within the category of Direct Grant Programs. In such cases, the implementation rules and regulations supersede the regulations contained in Part 75. However, if no specific implementation rules and regulations have been established, applicants must use the criteria established in the authorizing statute and the regulations contained in Part 75.

Section 75.60 is important to you if your project plans on providing financial assistance to students. A description of criteria which makes a participant ineligible to receive assistance is provided. For example, an individual who is not current in repaying a debt or is

———— **Grant Tip** ————

Make sure that your participants who receive financial assistance are not in default in repaying other Federal loans or fellowships.

—— **Grant Tip** ——
*You must make
substantial progress
in meeting your
objectives in order to
receive your funds
for the next year of a
multi-year project.*

in default on a debt under a scholarship, fellowship, discretionary grant, or loan program or who has not made satisfactory arrangements to repay the debt, is ineligible to receive assistance. You should read this section very carefully to determine if your proposed recipients of assistance meet the new criteria.

This part also requires certification of eligibility of a participant seeking assistance. The participant must certify that he or she is not in default and is current in repaying a previous debt as described in section 75.60 and that he or she has not been debarred or suspended under section 5301 of the Anti-Drug Abuse Act of 1988. Grant funds should not be awarded to participants until such certification has been obtained and is on file. This section of *EDGAR* requires your careful attention.

Much information in Part 75 is similar to or the same as information contained in a RFP or a grant application packet. It describes eligible applicants, how to apply for the grant, mailing instructions, deadlines, and the criteria the department uses for scoring the application and making awards. Part 75 allows the Secretary to distribute an additional 15 points among the criteria as a way of placing more weight in selected areas of the criteria. This procedure often favors applicant institutions or agencies with prior experience in organizing and operating grants of a similar nature. This part describes the process used in dealing with your proposal. (This was discussed in detail in Chapter 8, "Writing a Proposal.")

Part 75 clarifies the difference between a *project period* and a *budget period.* The project period is the total number of months for which your project is funded. The department cannot fund a project for more than 60 months. The budget period is usually one year. The budget for a multiyear project is negotiated each year of the project period.

Instructions for continuing a multiyear project after the first budget period are in this part. Follow the procedure outlined here to receive funding for the subsequent budget periods of the project. Note a small but significant change here: Previously you were required to show "satisfactory" progress in meeting your objectives. This has now been changed, and you must demonstrate "substantial progress toward meeting the objectives" or receive approval to change your program so long as it does not increase the cost of the grant and it will enable you to meet your objectives in succeeding budget periods.

Special circumstances may make it necessary for you to seek an extension of the project period. Instructions for filing for an extension are found in this part. You must submit your request at least 45 days before the end of the project period and follow the remainder of the instructions carefully.

Part 75 also contains the three criteria that you must address in the Evaluation Section of your proposal:

1. The grantee's progress in achieving the objectives in its approved application.

2. The effectiveness in meeting the purposes of the program.

3. The effect of the project on persons being served by the project, including ethnic minorities, women, handicapped persons, and the elderly.

Part 75 contains instructions for grants containing construction and also instructions for dealing with publications, copyrights, inventions, and patents.

Another important part, Subpart F, of Part 75 describes the general administrative responsibilities you have in relation to your project. This includes fiscal control and fund accounting procedures, obligation of funds, instructions relating to subgrants, a section on reports and records, retention period for direct grants, and how to handle the privacy of records.

Part 75 also provides procedures the department uses to get compliance, including suspension and termination of projects. This section notes that no official, agent, or employee of the Department of Education may waive any regulation that applies to a department program, unless the regulation specifically provides that it may not be waived. Even if a department official acts on a certain item, or fails to act, this cannot affect the authority of the department to enforce regulations.

Part 76: State-Administered Programs

Part 76, *State-Administered Programs,* establishes general requirements that a state must meet to apply for a federal grant. A state must have on file with the U.S. Secretary of Education a general application or state plan that meets certain requirements of Section 435 of the General Education Provisions Act (GEPA). State plans fall into 20 different areas, such as compensatory education, migrant children, basic skills, community schools, career education, adult education, and math-science programs.

Part 77: Definitions That Apply to Department Regulations

Part 77 contains a glossary of terms used in *EDGAR*. Often the definition of a term in the glossary is narrowed or modified to fit a specific rule or regulation within *EDGAR*. When used in a RFP or other official document, the term must be defined and interpreted as it appears in this part or in another part. You will enhance your application and increase the confidence readers will have in you if you use these terms as they are defined. Many terms appear on the technical review form that the readers use when they evaluate your proposal. By using the terms correctly in your proposal, you demonstrate that you have studied them, you are familiar with *EDGAR,* and that your interpretation and the department's interpretation are the same.

───── **Grant Tip** ─────

Use terms as defined in Part 77 in the body of your grant.

Part 79: Intergovernmental Review

Part 79, *Intergovernmental Review of Department of Education Programs and Activities,* is an attempt to foster intergovernmental partnerships and to strengthen federalism by relying on state processes and on state, area-wide, regional, and local coordination for review of proposed federal financial assistance. Not all programs are subject to this part of *EDGAR.* Periodically, a list of Department of Education programs under this part is published in the *Federal Register.* Write to the Department of Education for an updated list.

Part 80: Uniform Administration Requirements for Grants and Cooperative Agreements to State and Local Government

Part 80, *Uniform Administrative Requirements for Grants and Cooperative Agreements to State and Local Government,* establishes uniform administrative rules for federal grants and agreements with state, local, and Indian tribal governments. It begins with a lengthy section of definitions of terms followed by an explanation as to which recipients are affected by this part. Among those included in this part are states, institutions of higher education, hospitals, and block grant recipients.

Part 80 explains pre-award and post-award requirements. If you are writing a proposal for an agency or entity other than a government hospital or institution of higher education, read this section carefully.

Part 81: General Education Provisions Act—Enforcement

Part 81 established the Office of Administrative Law Judges (OALJ) to govern the enforcement of legal requirements under applicable programs administered by the Department of Education and to implement Part E of the General Education Provisions Act. OALJ has jurisdiction to conduct proceedings concerning an application program such as (a) hearings for recovery of funds, (b) withholding hearings, (c) cease and desist hearings, and (d) other proceedings designated by the Secretary.

Part 82: New Restrictions on Lobbying

Part 82 provides restrictions on lobbying activities. Its opening statement is worth restating here: "No appropriated funds may be expended by the recipient of a Federal contract, grant, loan, or cooperative agreement to pay any person for influencing or attempting to influence an officer or employee of any agency, a Member of Congress, an officer or employee of Congress, or an employee or a Member of Congress in connection with any of the following covered Federal actions: the awarding of any Federal contract, the making of any Federal grant, the making of any Federal loan, the entering into any cooperative agreement, and the extension, continuation, renewal, amendment, or modification of any Federal contract, grant, loan, or cooperative agreement" (p. 134).

Part 85: Government-wide Debarment and Suspension

Part 85, *Government-wide Debarment and Suspension (Non-procurement)*, sets out the rules pertaining to persons who have been debarred by the government. Such persons may not participate in financial and nonfinancial assistance or benefits under federal programs and activities. *Debarment,* as defined in this part, is "an action taken by a debarring official in accordance with these regulations to exclude a person from participating in covered transactions. A person so excluded is 'debarred'" (p. 146).

Debarment

Debarment may be imposed for any of these major factors: (a) conviction of fraud or criminal offense in connection with attempting to obtain, or performing a public or private agreement or transaction; (b) violation of federal or state antitrust statutes; (c) commission of embezzlement, theft, forgery, bribery, falsification or destruction of records, making false claims, receiving stolen property, making false claims, or obstruction of justice; and (d) commission of any other offense indicating a lack of business integrity or honesty that seriously and directly affects the present responsibility of a person.

Suspension

Suspension is defined as "action taken. . . that immediately excludes a person from participating in covered transactions for a temporary period, pending completing an investigation" (p. 148) and other legal action. Suspension may be imposed upon adequate evidence of offenses such as those indicated under debarment. Both of these actions have serious legal consequences. Upon submitting most proposals, the submitting institution or agency must sign and include an assurance regarding debarment and suspension. Failure to adhere to this provision "may result in disallowance of costs, annulment or termination of your award, issuance of a stop work order, debarment, or suspension, or other remedies, as appropriate" (p. 148).

Another section of Part 85 is designed to carry out the Drug-Free Workplace Act of 1988. It requires that a grantee, whether an agency or an individual, certify that, as a condition of the grant, a drug-free workplace will be maintained, that no one connected with the grant will "engage in the unlawful manufacture, distribution, dispensing, possession, or use of a controlled substance in conducting any activity with the grant" (p. 148).

Part 86: Drug and Alcohol Abuse Prevention

Part 86 is titled *Drug and Alcohol Abuse Prevention*. Its purpose is to "implement section 22 of the Drug-Free Schools and Communities Act Amendments of 1989, which adds section 1213 to the Higher Education Act and section 5145 to the Drug-Free Schools and Communities Acts. These amendments require that, as a condition of receiving funds or any other form of financial assistance under any federal program, an institution of higher education (IHE), state educational agency (SEA), or local education agency (LEA) must certify that it has adopted and implemented a drug prevention program as described in this part" (p. 167).

Part 97: Protection of Human Subjects

Part 97 is one of three new parts added with the September 16, 1999 printing. It deals with all of the research that involves human subjects, including the Institutional Review Board (IRB). This section is critical to any grantwriter who will be involved with research-oriented proposal development. The six categories detailed in Part 97 are

1. Research conducted in established or commonly accepted educational settings, involving normal educational practices, such as (i) research on regular or special education instructional strategies, or (ii) research on the effectiveness of or the comparison among instructional techniques, curricular, or classroom management methods

2. Research involving the use of educational tests (cognitive, diagnostic, aptitude, achievement), survey procedures, interview procedures, and observation of public behavior

3. Research involving the use of educational tests (cognitive, diagnostic, aptitude, achievement), survey procedures, interview procedures, or observation of public behavior that is not exempt under paragraph (b)(2)

4. Research, involving the collection or study of existing data, documents, records, pathological specimens, or diagnostic specimens, if these sources are publicly available or if the information is recorded by the investigator in such a manner that subjects cannot be identified, directly or through identifiers linked to the subjects

5. Research and demonstration projects that are conducted by or subject to the approval of department or agency heads and that are designed to study, evaluate, or otherwise examine

   (i) Public benefit or service programs
   (ii) Procedures for obtaining benefits or services under those programs
   (iii) Possible changes in or alternatives to those programs or procedures
   (iv) Possible changes in methods or levels of payment for benefits or services under those programs

6. Taste and food quality evaluation and consumer acceptance studies

Part 98: Student Rights in Research, Experimental Programs, and Testing

Part 98 is one of three new parts added with the September 16, 1999 printing. As noted in this section, Part 98 was transferred to the department by the Department of Education Organization Act (DEOA). This section includes information about definitions; access to instructional material used in a research or experimentation program; protection of students' privacy in examination, testing, or treatment; information and investigation office; reports; filing a complaint; notice of the complaining investigation and findings and enforcement of the findings.

Part 99: Family Educational Rights and Privacy

Part 99 is another of three new parts added with the September 16, 1999 printing. This section's purpose is to set out the requirements for the protection of privacy of parents and students under section 444 of the General Education Provisions Act, as amended. It should be noted that most of this section applies to an educational agency or institution to which funds have been made available. This section has five subparts, including: Subpart A—General, Subpart B—What Are the Right of Inspection and Review of Education Records? Subpart C—What Are the Procedures for Amending Education Records? Subpart D—May an Educational Agency or Institution Disclose Personally Indentifiable Information From Education Records? and Subpart E—What Are the Enforcement Procedures?

Some Basic Questions and DOs

The following are some basic questions that you should consider concerning grantee accountability. The answers to these questions indicate how effective you are managing your grant and if you are staying within the *EDGAR* requirements.

- Are the travel expenditures in conformance with the grant agreement?
- Did you hire the number of employees as stated in the approved budget?
- Do the time commitments of each employee agree with the grant agreement?

- Has equipment been received and is it being used as outlined in the approved application?

- Are proper records maintained by the Project Director?

Review carefully the Terms and Conditions section of your grant that typically comes with the Grant Award Notification (refer to Block 9), all applicable program regulations (refer to Block 7), and *EDGAR*. The grant administrator is responsible for managing the grant in accordance with these regulations. The program officer, the grants officer (refer to Block 3), or the Regional Grants Representative will be able to assist in answering specific questions. Some of the following *dos* that were provided by a program official at a workshop may assist on what to do in relation to *EDGAR:*

- Do fulfill all grant Terms and Conditions (e.g., send in a performance report within 90 days after the grant ends) as outlined in program regulations and *EDGAR*.

- Do a continuation application each year in accordance with the grant Terms and Conditions.

- Do manage equipment bought with grant funds.

- Do use the equipment, during and after the project, in accordance with the guidelines.

- Do develop adequate record-keeping systems for financial and programmatic records, and keep all records for at least three years after the grant expires.

- Do document cost-sharing contribution if it is required for your grant award.

- Do follow the financial management standards in accordance with the regulations.

- Do monitor your project in accordance with the regulations.

- Do inform the program officer of any significant developments (positive or negative) in the project.

- Do seek prior approval in writing from the grants officer for budget revisions.

- Do seek prior approval in writing from the grants officer for program changes, changes in project scope, or changes in key personnel.

- Do administer and supervise the project, and keep records in accordance with the regulations.

- Do notify the grants officer if the project will be without a project director for more than 90 days.

- Do procure supplies, equipment, and other services in accordance with your own procurement policies provided they are in accordance with federal regulations.

- Do pay project staff members in accordance with regulations.

- Do coordinate your project with others. However, do not duplicate your project with other activities that serve similar purposes or target groups.

- Do evaluate your project according to the standards established in the regulations.

- Do certify that your participants are not in default on previous federal assistance.

- Do complete certifications concerning lobbying.

- Do complete certifications regarding Drug-Free Schools and Campuses.

- Do consult the regulations if you intend to publish or copyright material.

- Do anticipate a site visit or a program audit.

EDGAR Summary

This section reviews important areas of *EDGAR,* the official document that contains the rules and regulations that govern your grant. Become familiar with the entire document. Take time before you begin to write your application to study *EDGAR.* After you receive notification of your grant award, again review especially those parts that pertain to your grant and project. It will be time well spent and most profitable for your institution and for your project.

Introduction to GPRA

GPRA is an acronym for Government Performance and Results Act and is also known as the Results Act. In a recent publication, *Demonstrating Results*[1], the Director of the Office of Management and Budget noted,

[1]*Demonstrating Results* is a document found on the U.S. Department of Education's web site at http://www.ed.gov/pubs/DemoResults/title.html that was accessed on 5/7/00. There are extensive references to this document in this section.

This is an era of fiscal limits. Resources are scarce. Not every priority can be met, nor all needs satisfied. Every program must count. So we must ask: Which programs are effective, and which are not? Which programs are efficient, and which are not? . . . Budgeting under the regimen of a long-term balanced budget agreement can be seen as a zero-sum game. Within the discretionary spending cap, choices about which programs receive funding increases, remain level funded, or shrink, should increasingly be governed by performance.

In an era of reduced discretionary funds, Congress has a mandate to require federal agencies to improve performance and document that they are administering effective programs. GPRA should substantially increase the management and accountability of all federal agencies and the programs that fall under their jurisdiction. GPRA will require federal agencies to

- Establish agency-wide strategic plans
- Develop performance goals for every program
- Link strategic plans and performance goals to budgets
- Measure performance against goals
- Provide a mechanism for reporting to the public their success

—— **Grant Tip** ——
Even if a program is desirable, appropriations will be forthcoming only to the extent that positive outcomes can be demonstrated.

These requirements are currently having a direct impact on federal agencies. For instance, they are seeing a transformation in their management approaches, increasing the public accountability for expenditures, and making all federal programs more effective in achieving their purposes.

Background

According to a recent report, discretionary spending accounted for 17.2% of the federal dollar in FY 1998, down from 23.9% in FY 1980, and it is projected to decrease to 15.7% in FY 2003.

It should come as no surprise that federal agencies are becoming increasingly concerned with the "bottom line." Programs need to anticipate receiving less annual funding than that appropriated during the previous year. Agencies that expect to receive increases must demonstrate their effectiveness to ensure continued funding. Stevens, Chairman of the Senate Appropriations Committee, noted the following:

With the Results Act, we can ask other important questions about federal programs, such as what will the program accomplish, what will it cost to accomplish it, how will the results be achieved, and how will the agency monitor the program's effectiveness. If properly implemented, the Results Act can assist Congress in identifying and eliminating duplicate or ineffective programs. *(Demonstrating Results)*

——— Grant Tip ———

Remember GPRA is the law.

Even if a program is desirable, appropriations will be forthcoming only to the extent that positive outcomes can be demonstrated. GPRA was designed to enable the Congress to obtain quantifiable data about a program's performance to determine what programs will be funded in the future.

Requirements of GPRA

GPRA will require all federal agencies to take a serious look at their management practices. Agencies will be required to (a) clearly state intended accomplishments, (b) identify the required resources, and (c) report progress to the Congress. These three steps will (a) increase accountability for expenditures of public funds, (b) improve congressional decision making, and (c) focus on outcomes, service delivery, and customer satisfaction.

Previously, effort was often mistaken for results but not any more. Rather than being determined by the number and cost of academic interventions, accountability (for example, in a program designed to help youth enter college) will require that the interventions actually result in more youth entering college and an increase in student achievement.

Each agency must provide the Congress with a business plan. This is a similar plan to those that corporations complete for banks. The new GPRA requirements state that each agency must submit three items:

1. A strategic 5-year plan. The first plans were submitted to Congress on September 30, 1997 and are to be updated every 3 years.

2. An annual performance plan. The first one was submitted to the OMB with the FY 1999 budget request and transmitted to the Congress in February 1998. These agency plans formed the basis for a government-wide performance plan, which also was submitted to the Congress in February 1998.

3. An annual report on program performance. This is to be provided within 6 months of the end of a fiscal year; the first report was due by March 31, 2000 (*Demonstrating Results*).

Strategic Plans

Remember that GPRA is law. As such, it requires each agency to develop a 5-year strategic plan. An additional requirement to ensure a plan's relevance is that it must be revised at least every 3 years. GPRA specifies six distinct elements for each agency's strategic plan:

1. A comprehensive mission statement that sets forth the fundamental purpose of the agency. The Department of Education's mission is "to ensure equal access to education and to promote educational excellence throughout the nation" *(Demonstrating Results)*.

2. General strategic goals and objectives that are results oriented and that reflect tangible accomplishments that justify the existence of the agency's programs.

3. A description of how the goals and objectives are to be achieved, that is, the strategies to be employed and the resources needed to attain the goals and objectives.

4. A description of how the annual performance goals are related to the general goals and objectives of the strategic plan.

5. An identification of those key factors external to the agency and beyond its control that could significantly affect the achievement of the agency's goals and objectives.

6. A description of the program evaluation methods used in establishing or revising agency goals and objectives with a schedule for future program evaluation (*Demonstrating Results*).

Other elements that may be included in an agency's strategic plan are a vision statement and an assessment of the economic, social, cultural, demographic, political, legal, and technological trends.

Annual Performance Plans

Another GPRA requirement is an annual performance plan. The annual performance plan, including annual performance goals, fo-

—— **Grant Tip** ——

The annual performance plan, including annual performance goals, focuses on only one year, while the strategic plan is a much more long-term plan.

cuses on only 1 year, while the strategic plan is a much more long-term plan.

A critical aspect of the annual performance plan is the agency's performance objectives and performance indicators: Both indicate the success of the agency and both must be quantifiable and measurable.

Annual Performance Reports

The requirement for annual performance reports submitted to the President and to the Congress within 6 months after the end of the fiscal year are now also a part of the GPRA law. Performance reports compare actual results with the goals identified in the annual performance plan. Beginning in March 2000, agencies are required to account for their performance during FY 1999.

What happens when goals have not been met? GPRA provides agencies an opportunity to explain the reasons. Agencies may be allowed to redirect their efforts in light of changing circumstances beyond an agency's control. The strategic plan then becomes a living document that remains current and relevant.

Performance Budgeting

By requiring annual performance plans as a part of the agency's budget request, GPRA makes the budget an explicit aspect of the "managing for results" concept. The importance of strategic planning and of performance measures is dramatically increased because they are linked to the agency's budget process and thus allow the expenditure of resources to be compared to performance as the means to improve decision-making.

—— **Grant Tip** ——
Program assessment will require agencies to develop performance measures that impact the higher levels, namely output, outcome, and impact.

Performance Measures

The Results Act (GPRA) has defined five categories of measures for programs and projects: (a) impacts, (b) outcomes, (c) outputs, (d) activities, and (e) inputs. These categories may be viewed as a hierarchy. Under GPRA, agencies must account for both the activities that arise from programs and the results attributed to those activities. Program assessment will require agencies to develop performance measures that impact the higher levels, namely output, outcome, and impact. According to GPRA, agencies must be prepared to the demonstrate the level of expected results, provide objective information, and compare actual program results with the proposed goals.

Programs or agencies that previously have dutifully submitted the number of hours of tutoring provided or the number of students who attended study skills classes will now be required to change their processes for collecting, analyzing, and reporting their data.

Assessment of Performance

GPRA has two purposes. "One is to report to the Congress on the results being obtained by the various programs. But, equally important, is the continual improvement of the programs, and the projects they support, to assure that the purposes for which the programs were established and funded are achieved in the best way possible. Program measurement and assessment are the means that lead to the accomplishment of both of these purposes" (*Demonstrating Results*).

Project Monitoring

How will individual projects be monitored? How will individual project's effectiveness be measured? These issues will be addressed through the projects:

- Original application
- Project objectives
- Performance agreements between the grantee and HEP[1]
- Performance reports that the grantee submits annually to the program staff
- Site visits

In the past, site visits typically have been conducted to assure compliance. However, future site visits under GPRA will focus on a project's performance as directly related to the project and program objectives. *Demonstrating Results* provides further explanation of the often-feared site visit:

---

[1] Higher Education Programs (HEP) is a branch of the Office of Postsecondary Education housed within the U. S. Department of Education. For discussion purposes, HEP guidelines have been referenced in this section. However, because GPRA impacts each federal agency, you should consult specific agency literature as you develop and write your proposal.

—— Grant Tip ——

*Program
evaluations are
not the same thing as
performance
monitoring.*

Site visits are an excellent opportunity to provide technical assistance to the grantee visited. This assistance can take the form of suggestions on how to improve the operation of the project, provide information on similar projects that are successful and can be used as models, or explain aspects of the program regulations or operations with which the grantee may not be familiar. Some site visits will be conducted by HEP program officers. Others will be conducted by or under the auspices of Area Representatives. The grantee should not take as mandatory any suggestions made during a site visit unless they are said to be required by the grantee's program officer who has direct responsibility for the project being visited.

Program Assessments

Program assessments as described in GPRA are not designed to address individual projects but to focus on:

• Strengths of the program

• Perceived weaknesses

• Changes that have occurred since the last report

• Summary of how the program is meeting its performance goals

• Suggestions for program improvement

Assessment results will be used by federal administrative and management personnel to increase program effectiveness, generate annual performance reports, develop budget justifications, determine how projects contribute to the program goals, and compare individual projects to the program as a whole.

Program Evaluations

Program evaluation as defined by GPRA is "an assessment, through objective measurement and systematic analysis, of the manner and extent to which federal programs achieve intended objectives" (*Demonstrating Results*). Program evaluations are not the same thing as performance monitoring. *Demonstrating Results* explained the important difference between the two:

The latter involves the ongoing review of performance data to manage program performance. Program evaluations, on the other hand, are intended to illuminate broader, longer-term aspects of program performance. While monitoring is done by or under the direct control of the HEP staff, program evaluations, especially those dealing with long-term impacts, are often done by third parties, who are experts in the analytical methodologies of evaluation, working in conjunction with the HEP staff. These broader, in-depth evaluations are often coordinated by or done under the auspices of the Department's Planning and Evaluation Service.

Role of the Grantee

The role of the grantee in the success of GPRA should not be underestimated. GPRA's success will be directly related to those who are closest to the actual outcomes—the grantee. What are some of the ways that grantees can be expected to help? As noted in *Demonstrating Results*, grantees will be called upon to:

- Identify the most important factors that are truly critical to a program's success

- Identify the appropriate level of annual performance for each output

- Suggest ways to reformulate the performance indicators when needed

- Provide qualitative and quantitative evidence of their individual project's achievements

Obviously, project administrators who demonstrate successful performance while keeping budgets intact will receive more favorable reviews by the Department of Education and by the Congress.

GPRA Summary

The Government Performance and Results Act has changed the way federal agencies and grantees conduct programs. "Given the dramatic challenges facing public governance as we enter the 21st Century, GPRA offers those committed to the ideal of public accountability for the expenditure of public funds an unprecedented opportunity to link high-minded program goals with a clearer idea of the resources needed and a means of assigning responsibility for the

——— **Grant Tip** ———

Knowing the fundamental aspects of EDGAR *and* GPRA *are instrumental in proposal development, proposal writing, and project administration.*

delivery of those goals. By any measure, this will be a significant step forward" (*Demonstrating Results*).

Conclusion

Knowing the fundamental aspects of *EDGAR* and GPRA are instrumental in proposal development, proposal writing, and project administration. You need not memorize them, but you should be very familiar with their contents and how they relate to your project. Familiarity, we have found, comes with repeated use.

Want More Information?

The Strategic Plan for the Department of Education can be found at http://www.ed.gov/pubs/StratPln/. To subscribe to the GPRA Report E-mail list, a free service, via e-mail, send the following information to ombwatch@ombwatch.org:

- List you are subscribing to (specify "gpra")
- Name
- Organization and title (if any)
- Address
- Phone
- Fax
- E-mail address

15

Understanding Site Visits and Audits

Introduction

During the life of a federal grant, project officers or other officials from the sponsoring government agency may conduct site visits or audits. Your project may be selected for attention.

Site visits are generally for the purpose of reviewing the progress of your project and to ensure that you are operating the project according to the terms of your approved application, the authorizing legislation, and the federal regulations. The federal visitor reviews project files and documents, the eligibility guidelines for participants, and the procedures for fiscal accountability. He/she will generally interview staff members, an institutional administrator or two, and a representative sample of the project participants and then prepare a narrative describing the findings. Usually this narrative highlights the successes of your project and emphasizes those outstanding elements that may be shared with other similar projects; if deficiencies are found, he or she makes recommendations for improvement. If major deficiencies are discovered, the visitor may request that a formal audit be conducted to provide guidelines to rectify deficiencies and put your project back on track.

Audits are much more formal than site visits and may be conducted by persons more specialized than a project officer. Audits may be conducted as a result of suspected operational deficiencies or questionable expenditure of federal funds. An audit may result in formal requirements being imposed upon the project. These requirements may deal with program compliance, financial requirements, or both. Generally the grant recipient must provide evidence that the requirements are being met.

The remainder of this chapter will help you plan and operate your project in such a way that you will be ready for a site visit or an audit at any given time without having to spend many long hours of preparation.

—— **Grant Tip** ——
Proper attention to internal controls, compliance, and record keeping is essential.

Site Visits

A site visit to a funded project can be the single most important factor in the funding agency's deliberations regarding the project's worthiness and prospects for future funding. Creating positive images of the project during a site visit depends on several factors, including: (a) progress made in carrying out the specific activities for which funding was granted, (c) effectiveness of planning for the site visit, (c) how the visit is organized and how material is presented, (d) how the visitors are treated, and (e) the general climate established during the visit.

A site visit is a funding agency's review of a funded project, conducted at the location of the project. It may be held for one or more of the following purposes; (a) to review, monitor, and assess project accomplishments, (b) to review and assess project management, including financial systems and controls, (c) to examine and discuss a particular problem that has occurred, (d) to negotiate change(s) in the project's program or budget, (e) to assess the project in terms of decisions to continue and/or refund the project, (f) to provide technical assistance to the project, and (g) to receive and discuss project final reports.

Often a project is selected for a site visit if it is experiencing serious problems. Such problems may be brought to the Department or agency's attention by another department, a project employee, or a participant. Some departments or agencies also give priority for site visits to grantees who have several grants totaling a specific amount, such as $200,000 or more. Other projects are selected because they fall into a "geographic package" that may include other institutions close by with similar grant projects. Length of time since a project was last visited is another factor that may determine when a site visit occurs.

Site visits are designed to assist you, to point out potential problem areas, and to highlight areas of success. When the project looks good, the sponsoring agency looks good. The sponsoring agency does not want to preside over projects that are failures. The site visit is the agency's way of trying to identify problems before they become major. Cooperation with the site visitor and the preparation you put into the site visit will pay dividends in the long run.

Site Visit Activities

You may ask yourself, "What happens on a site visit?" Typically, the first thing that happens is that the agency or department notifies the program by phone and letter to set a convenient date for the visit. Figure 15.1 is an example of a site visit letter that may be sent to your institution or agency. To prepare, the visitor may obtain a copy of your approved proposal, previous site visit reports, and other pertinent information regarding your project. The visit generally begins with an "entrance interview" with appropriate institutional personnel, the president, vice-president, or dean, to explain the purpose of the visit.

Figure 15.1. Example of Site Visit Letter

UNITED STATES DEPARTMENT OF EDUCATION
WASHINGTON, D.C. 20202

July 13, 2000

Dr. John Doe, Dean
College of Human Ecology
State University of Jonesville
20 Claxton Education Building
Jonesville, Tennessee 37996

Dear Dr. Doe:

This is to confirm the arrangements made by Mrs. Madeline Adams of my staff with Dr. Robert Seaton to review the College Assistance Migrant Program (CAMP) at State University of Jonesville on July 29, 2000. The site monitoring team will consist of Mrs. Michelle Lanter and Ms. Jean McAdams.

The on-site review will cover the following: (1) the management of the CAMP project; (2) eligibility policies; (3) recruitment policies and procedures; (4) program effectiveness; (5) progress in meeting program objectives; (6) fiscal accountability; and, (7) compliance with existing regulations governing the CAMP projects. It is requested that you have the project records for the past three years available for the review team.

A written report will be forwarded to you within 30 days following the on-site review.

We look forward to continuing to work with your staff in carrying out our mutual responsibilities under these programs.

Sincerely,

Kenton Sweckard, Director
Office of Migrant Education

xc: Dr. Dennis Overton, Project Director

Site visit activities typically follow this progression:

- Phone Call
- Formal Letter
- Entrance Interview
- Site Visit Activities
- Exit Interview
- Formal Written Letter or Report of Findings

The Site Visitors

Site visits may be made by a single person representing the funding agency, or by a team of two or more. It is important for the project staff, including principal investigator, project director, and other key staff, to understand who the site visitors are in terms of their relationship to the funding agency. Visitors may be direct employees of the funding agency, privately contracted consultants, technical experts in the field related to project activities, members of an independent government review panel, corporate or foundation directors or officers, or government auditors. Project managers have the right to inquire as to the identity and qualifications of those chosen for the site visitation team in order to determine how to structure the content of the site visit in appropriate ways. The funding agency program officer who arranges for the site visit can provide specific information on the site visitors.

Roles of Project Staff and Site Visitors

The site visit involves the project staff and the site visitors in a complex set of roles and communication patterns. Site visitors and project staff alike are nervous over the conduct of the site visit. Site visitors are under the pressure of needing to make quick but valid assessments of complicated programs and situations in a very short period of time. Project staff members are under the pressure of making favorable impressions on the site visitors and on their project superiors as well. Primary responsibility for the conduct of a well-planned and well-managed site visit rests with the principal investigator or project director, with the assistance of the chief project aides.

Entrance Interview

Interviews with the project director and other key personnel may center around the areas of administration, budget, objectives and allowable activities, or record keeping. For projects that provide direct services to program participants, the person conducting the site visit will typically interview a representative sample of program participants regarding the program and review the services that they are receiving. On the other hand, if a project was funded to develop curriculum materials, the development process will be discussed and the materials will be reviewed. The visitor will want to spot-check your files, records, and other documents. The reviewer will be particularly interested in determining if your project is carrying out its funded objectives. He/she will also try to become aware of areas in which you may appear to be out of compliance with the rules and regulations.

The visitor may visit with personnel from your business office as well as with several program participants. If you provide services to participants at remote sites from your institution or agency, the reviewer may want to visit these sites and talk to some of the program participants.

Your visitor generally will be willing and pleased to provide technical assistance and suggestions if you ask. Take advantage of this person's expertise, experience, and knowledge while he/she is visiting you.

Primary Areas of Concern

The site visit personnel will generally review and monitor the project in the areas of project administration, fiscal operations, project activities, and procedures used in evaluating the project. Figure 15.3, *Items Typically Reviewed by Site Visitors,* addresses these four major areas.

Exit Interview

At the conclusion of the visit, exit interviews are generally held to provide the project director, key employees, and institutional administrators with a preliminary oral report of the visitor's findings and observations, recommendations, and probable required action. The exit interview also provides the project and institutional administrative personnel the opportunity to respond verbally, clarify, and provide important input.

The site visitor will provide a written report of his/her findings, recommendations, and required actions. Because of internal

─────**Grant Tip**─────

The site visit personnel will generally review and monitor the project in the areas of project administration, fiscal operations, project activities, and procedures used in evaluating the project.

Figure 15.2. Items Typically Reviewed by Site Visitors

Administration of the Program Project personnel (staff hired; hiring procedures; etc.) Organizational structure (as proposed and approved) Director (full-time if waiver not approved) Adequate record keeping (personnel, etc.) Adequate space/location Compliance with laws and regulations Institutional commitment Affirmative action procedures Training and staff development Compliance with *EDGAR* guidelines	**Scope of Work—Program Activities** Documentation of services/activities Achievements to date Time frames—as scheduled, revisions, slippages Are you deviating from approved activities? Are you complying with the laws and regulations that govern your program? Is there duplication of services? Are you serving eligible participants? Are you producing and/or serving those items/individuals whom you proposed to serve?
Fiscal Procedures and Operation Documentation of expenditures Cost effectiveness of project Monthly budget reports and current ledger records Time and effort certification Equipment accountability/inventory Sound purchasing procedures Travel limitations Equipment limitations Contracts (formalized; amounts; etc.) Stipends—if any (cannot move monies from participant support without written approval)	**Evaluation Procedures** Do you have an internal evaluation procedure implemented? Will you have an external evaluation of your project? Do you have internal reporting and management procedures? Can you conduct performance outcomes? Do you evaluate your project staff members on an annual basis? Do you have a monitoring system in place to evaluate progress being made on a monthly basis?

——— **Grant Tip** ———

The key to successful site visits and audits begins the day you start to write your application. Defining and documenting are important elements.

procedures, the written report or letter from some departments and agencies may not be available to you for several months, whereas others may have the report to you in a few weeks. Figure 15.3 is an example of a site visit form.

When you receive the report, you must respond in writing as to how you intend to correct any problems found and to implement suggested recommendations for improvement. Most problems identified in a site visit can be rectified by program management. In some instances, however, problems may be serious enough to merit the involvement and assistance of the office of the Inspector General. Such involvement usually constitutes an audit. Audits are discussed later in this chapter.

Defining and Documenting

The key to successful site visits and audits begins the day you start to write your application. Defining and documenting are important elements for successful site visits. The previous chapters

Figure 15.3. Example of Site Visit Forms

U.S. Department of Education
Higher Education Programs
Region IV

On-Site Visit Report

Dates of Site Visit:_____
Name of Institution/Agency: _____
Address:_____City:_____State:_____Zip:_____

Classification: ___Agency ___Institution: __ 2 year __4 year __public __ private

Name of President or Chief Administrator: _____Title:_____

Name of Principal Investigator/Project Director: _____

Project Telephone Number: (   )_____Fax Number ( ) _____

Title of Project: _____CFDA #:_____

Type of Project: _____Grant #: _____

Grant Award Cycle : From ___/___/___ To ___/___/___
Total Number of Years of Participation in Program (years and months): _____

Funding History: Amount of Current Grant: $_____
Total Amount of Funds Received Under This Program: $_____

Persons Interviewed:

_____ *Name* _____ _____ *Title* _____ *Phone* _____ _____ *Address.* ____ _____

Site Visit Report Format

Institution/Agency:_____

Program:_____Grant Amount: $_____Dates of Visit:_____

I.   Administration

   Findings (strengths, weaknesses)

   Recommendations

   Required Actions

II.   Fiscal Operations

   Findings (strengths, weaknesses)

   Recommendations

   Required Actions

III. Program Activities

   Findings (strengths, weaknesses)

   Recommendations

   Required Actions

IV.   Evaluation Procedures

   Findings (strengths, weaknesses)

   Recommendations

   Required Actions

V.   Other

VI.   Summary

NOTE: *Each item will be typically addressed in terms of compliance with the laws and regulations that the program is funded under; the degree of success in meeting the funded goals and objectives; the cost-effectiveness of the project; and the identification of any exemplary practices.*

---

explained the preparation and documentation necessary to design and implement a project. Your needs assessment documented reasons for which you requested funds. The needs assessment provides a significant portion of the groundwork necessary for a successful site visit. In your assessment you demonstrated that your target population needed the services you proposed to provide. Each need should have been carefully documented and defined. Keep a well-organized file of all the sources you consulted, the individuals who provided you with important information, the surveys you may have conducted or relied upon, and the steps you went through to establish the basis for your project. During a site visit these all constitute important evidence to show that the proper foundation exists for your project.

As you begin to organize your project, take special care to define in writing the procedures you will use. You may wish to compile a notebook with important "site visit" information in it. A section on evidence to show that a proper foundation exists as well as a section detailing the procedures you use would be an excellent way to begin the notebook. Even though these procedures may have been listed in the Plan of Operation section of your application, you need to fill in the details of exactly how you implemented them. For example, as you prepare to hire your staff, ensure that you have well-defined position descriptions that clearly identify the necessary qualifications. Set up reasonable timelines for receiving applications, making sure that you allow sufficient time to reach a large population of potential applicants and that they have enough time to gather the information you request and return it within your time frame. Sometimes seemingly insignificant problems are not properly addressed, and they quickly grow into major problems that may precipitate site visits or even an audit. Items that should be included in a notebook may consist of the following items:

- Copy of award letter
- Copy of approved budget
- Copy of approved plan
- Organizational chart of project in relationship to the structure of the institution or agency
- Inventory of equipment purchased with grant funds
- A copy of the project objectives, progress, and performance measures
- If serving participants, a list of the participants
- Performance reports
- External evaluation reports, if any
- Copies of recent audits, if any
- Documentation of nonfederal matching funds, if required

As you form a pool of potential project participants, carefully define the eligibility recruitment and application requirements and then ensure that your staff and potential participants are fully aware of these requirements. One project director was careless in defining the requirement for demonstrated academic need of potential participants. He was careful to ensure that each met the citizenship or residency requirements, and the age, income, and occupational requirements. He did not document well the academic need requirements.

After a year or so of operation, several students who met the requirements, including demonstrated academic need, were rejected for enrollment into the project because there was no room left for them. These students investigated the requirements and discovered that the academic need of several students was not documented. They filed a protest with the sponsoring agency and, as a result, the sponsoring agency conducted a site visit. Even though the major purpose of the site visit was to investigate the protest regarding academic need, the visitors reviewed the entire project and all of the supporting documentation.

In organizing each project component, carefully define the criteria and determine the documentation needed to support them. For example, assume that you are preparing to hire personnel for the position of Educational Specialist and the qualifications you establish require (a) a letter of application, (b) a current résumé, (c) a master's degree in education, (d) three years of experience in similar programs, (e) three letters of recommendation, and (f) because the position requires travel between service delivery sites, a valid driver's license and a reliable vehicle.

In the position announcement explain these specific requirements. Then prepare for the folder of each applicant a check-off list that indicates the documentation you will accept to support each qualification. The check-off sheet may look like the example in Figure 15.4.

Figure 15.4. Example of a Position Announcement Check-Off List

Check-Off List—Educational Specialist	
Requirements	Documentation Received
(1) Letter of Application	_____
(2) Current Résumé	_____
(3) MA Degree Transcripts	_____
(4) Experience—Letters	_____
(5) Letters of Recommendation	_____
(6) Copy of Driver's License	_____
(7) Copy of Vehicle Registration	_____

Attach a check-off sheet to each applicant's folder. As the required information is received, date the check-off sheet and file the document inside. This will ensure that each applicant submitted the required documents, each was evaluated on the same criteria, and each had an equal opportunity for the position.

Use a similar check-off sheet for the selection of project participants. List each selection criterion and the documentation needed to support it. Attach this list to each participant's folder. Document all eligibility criteria mandated in the Request for Proposals (RFP) and also for the requirements that your specific project or institution may impose. For example, to satisfy the RFP eligibility criteria, you may need to require documentation of age (birth certificate), citizenship or legal residency status (birth certificate or immigration documents), income status (IRS tax information), and occupational history (check stubs showing current or former employment). Your institution and project may require additional criteria, such as residency in your state, to determine tuition charges (rent or utility receipts), enrollment or acceptance in your institution (certificate of acceptance for admission), academic need (high school and previous college transcripts), student housing (dormitory deposit or acceptance certificate), financial need (statement of anticipated income and expenses), and other financial support (copies of Financial Aid Form, scholarship applications, and letters of recommendation).

Other areas in which you should carefully organize your procedures and staffing patterns are (a) *organizational structure,* including organizational chart and lines of authority for reporting purposes; (b) *staff,* with information such as position descriptions, tenure, academic rank, years with the project, background, affirmative action nondiscriminatory policy, and committee assignments; (c) *institutional involvement,* such as space, equipment, location on campus, in-kind contributions, availability of administrators, monitoring and supervision of grant activities and personnel; (d) *staff training,* who receives and who provides the training, how often, kinds of training, i.e., formal classes, workshops, conferences, in-services, and observations; (e) *records and reporting,* including personnel, participant, budget, and project records, who receives them, what they contain, and what they are used for. Some of these areas are discussed in further detail in the following paragraphs.

Fiscal Accounting Systems

Establish a procedure for expending project funds. This procedure should conform to the institution's approved procedures and federal regulations that may apply. Include documentation required for requisitions, purchase orders, and interdepartmental transfers, such as receipts, letters of services rendered, anticipated expenditures, estimates, airline ticket receipts, and so forth. Indicate who is authorized to create requisitions and purchase orders, and who must approve and sign these documents. Set up your ledger sheets that would be in line with your final approved budget breakdown. For example

- Personnel
- Fringe Benefits
- Travel (Professional, Local, and Participant)
- Equipment
- Supplies
- Services
- Postage
- Telephone
- Participant Room and Board, If Needed
- Stipends, If Needed
- Other

Outline a clear description of who receives stipend money, the criteria for receiving a stipend, amounts, when and how paid, and how you document that the participant received the stipend. Establish the route these documents must follow to ensure payment, how they will be filed, and who may have access to the files. Describe the types of financial records that will be kept, official and unofficial, specific responsibility for creating the reports (business office, grants accountant, program director, and secretary), the frequency with which they are created, and who has access to them. Establish the length of time financial documents must be retained for review, conforming to guidelines established in *EDGAR* and by your institution. Write these procedures down and ensure that all project employees have a copy of the procedures, understand them, and follow them. Periodically review them with your staff during staff meetings. Document each time that you review them through minutes of staff meetings or in a log.

Staff Evaluation

Establish staff evaluation guidelines that include the evaluation criteria (general criteria, specific areas such as management techniques, student interaction, peer interaction, and instructional effectiveness), the frequency of evaluation (semi-annually or quarterly), the results of the evaluation (commendation, recommendations for improvement, or dismissal), appeal and rebuttal procedures, and timelines. Document that each employee is aware of the evaluation procedures, by providing each with a copy and by placing a copy in each employee's personnel folder with a signed statement indicating that he/she has received, read, and understands the procedures.

Review each objective and the activities proposed to achieve the objective. Determine the documentation needed to demonstrate successful achievement of each objective. This information is included in the Objective section of the proposal. You may need to expand and refine it. A check-off list of activities for each objective that must be accomplished may include timelines, equipment and supplies needed, person responsible, date completed, and results. Maintain copies of agendas, printed programs, announcements, registration receipts, and sign-in lists that demonstrate the activity was accomplished.

Any time you need to change or modify the procedures for project operation, inform all staff and other related persons (dean or provost) by circulating a copy to all concerned personnel with a signature sheet that will eventually be returned to you. Figure 15.5 is a sample that you may want to follow.

A Recent Site Visit

Such documentation and paperwork are time-consuming. You may think that it can wait until things slow down a little. Things seldom slow down, and the time and energy spent on it now are nothing compared to what you will spend if your have to recreate this information from memory several months or years in the future. For your own sake, document all that you do.

In a recent site visit a project officer arrived with a large pad of columnar accounting paper. He proceeded to review the proposal to determine the federal and local criteria for virtually every aspect of the project. Under student eligibility criteria, he listed one of the following categories at the top of each column on the accounting pad: age, citizenship/residency, low income, parental college status, academic need, personal need, social need, grade-point average, counseling appointments, and follow-up. He then randomly selected ten student folders and reviewed each one for the items listed. As he found the documents, he noted if they were complete, current, and contained acceptable documentation.

He then listed the criteria for hiring personnel on another sheet. He randomly selected five employees and reviewed their files for

Figure 15.5. Example of a Circulation Copy to all Concerned Personnel

---

STUDENT ACADEMIC EXCELLENCE PROJECT
State University of Jonesville

MEMORANDUM

TO: All Personnel
FROM: Dr. Bob Epley, Project Director
SUBJECT: Change in Employee Evaluation Policy
DATE: January 15, 2001

The current employee evaluation policy requires that all employees be evaluated on an annual basis. Effective February 1, 2001 all project employees will be evaluated once each semester. The same evaluation form that each of you has in your file will be used. If you have questions regarding this change in policy, please contact me immediately.

Sign this memorandum and forward it to the next person.

Bill Spencer   _____ Date_____
Brenda Belt   _____ Date_____
Eric Johnson   _____ Date_____
Lupe Gonzalez   _____ Date_____
Ed Smith   _____ Date_____
Ben Campbell   _____ Date_____
Ron Brown   _____ Date_____
Greg Petty   _____ Date_____
Michelle Lanter   _____ Date_____

Dr. Dennis Overton, Chair_____
Dr. James Moran, Dean _____
Dr. Tom Reesor, Affirmative Action_____

RETURN TO: DR. ROGER GILBERT, PROJECT DIRECTOR

---

completeness and uniformity. He was complimentary when he found things in order but did not hesitate to note irregularities. On a third sheet, he listed the activities and required documentation of two of the project objectives. The last area he reviewed in detail concerned expenditures from the budget. He selected approximately 15 requisitions and interdepartmental transfers and checked each for appropriate approvals, signatures, receipts, and invoices.

He repeated this procedure for three federal projects that had been awarded to that particular institution. Two project directors had taken the time on an ongoing basis to ensure that all files and documentation were in order. The visitor's review and subsequent report of these projects were positive and complimentary. The director of the third project had not been so careful in his organization and documentation. Even though the program was running equally as smoothly as the first two, he was unable to demonstrate it. As a result the site visit report imposed many requirements for improvement and remediation and required a follow-up site visit within six months to verify compliance.

The best way to prepare yourself for a site visit is to *define* and *document:* define your criteria, define what is acceptable documentation, and then gather and organize the documentation.

Review Procedures for Conducting Formal Evaluation

Review and outline your procedures for conducting formal evaluations designed for each individual objective, annual performance reports, external evaluation, in-house evaluations, and project participant evaluations. Place in your notebook copies of the final report of all evaluations that have been completed. If you use any standard evaluation forms, you should also include copies in your notebook.

Another important area requiring attention is samples of exemplary practices or components of your project. Site visitors are always interested in parts of your project that are functioning exceptionally well and that may be shared with other similar projects. Analyze the components of your project that have worked extremely well or that have brought exceptional results. Describe why you feel the component has been so successful, including tips and suggestions that others can incorporate into their projects. Include such exemplary components in your notebook.

Audits

Each sponsoring agency, at its discretion, can request that a given project be audited. Such requests usually are the result of serious alleged problems, unusual reports or information that has reached the department or agency, or a series of smaller events that point to possible major problems or concerns of noncompliance. Audits are not as frequent or as common as site visits. Site visits are usually performed by project officers or others who deal with the project from the implementation perspective. Audits are more formal and often involve persons from the sponsoring agency's audit division.

——Grant Tip——

Auditors examine the "financial statements of an organization, reviewing that organization's (i) compliance with applicable laws and regulations, (ii) economy and efficiency of operations, and (iii) effectiveness in achieving program results."

Source: U.S. Department of Education

The scope of audits may include areas such as the following:

- Review the reliability and integrity of the project's financial system.

- Review procedures established for complying with policies, plans, laws, and regulations.

- Review how assets are safeguarded and verify the existence of assets acquired through the project.

- Review the effective and efficient use of project resources.

- Review project operation to ascertain if it is meeting the established objectives and goals as described in the approved application.

- Review compliance with laws and regulations governing the project.

As with site visits, the best way to prepare for an audit is to document. Become familiar with the laws and regulations that govern your particular project. Most of these are found in *EDGAR* and in the RFP you followed in preparing your application. Ignorance of the laws and regulations regarding your project is not an acceptable excuse for non-compliance. Study thoroughly all laws and regulations that pertain to your project. As you review each law and regulation, compile a detailed list of the specific things you should and should not be doing. Collect documentation to demonstrate that you are doing those items required and that certain practices you are doing do not border on or resemble unacceptable activities. If doubts persist, consult your project officer.

When financial records are audited, you are expected to justify all expenditures through proper supporting paperwork. Auditors look for evidence that you have followed generally accepted accounting practices, such as supplying reliable invoices and receipts for expenditures, and complying with required bidding procedures. If documentation is not available, attach an explanation. For example, your institution may require receipts for reimbursement of small expenditures such as meals, supplies, or taxi fare. Some taxicab services do not use standardized receipts. In such cases note the pertinent information on a slip of paper containing, if possible, the driver's signature. Submit this in lieu of a standard receipt. Generally small items of this nature do not arouse suspicion. Nevertheless, you should document even small expenditures including taxi fare, meals, tips, and over-the-counter supplies.

———**Grant Tip**———
Become familiar with the laws and regulations that govern your particular project.

If supporting documentation has been misplaced, lost, or destroyed, duplicate copies are generally available from the vendor or supplier. Every effort should be made to obtain such duplicates to support expenditures. Make it a habit of requiring your employees to obtain such documentation. Avoid purchasing supplies, books, or registration fees with your personal funds and then "turning in receipts for reimbursement." The standard procedure is to plan ahead, submit requisitions, and obtain the proper approval prior to expending the funds. This ensures compliance with acceptable procedures and allows for shared responsibility through prior approval of expenditures by a department chair, dean, or the accounting office.

An auditor may look for evidence that each project employee is working the appropriate amount of time. This is particularly important when one employee is employed by two projects. For example, an institution may have two related grants, such as a High School Equivalency Program (HEP) and a College Assistance Migrant Program (CAMP). The recruiter, secretary, and director may share responsibilities in both projects. Assume that the recruiter is contracted for 30% of his time to recruit for the CAMP and 70% for the HEP. Document that he/she not only spent the required amount of time in each project, but that his/her pay is appropriately divided between projects. If you share employees with other projects, ensure that you can account for their time and that each project is being charged accordingly. This is often done through the accounting office on a payroll verification form or other standard document.

This same principle is true when two or more projects share rented equipment, space, and services. If equipment, such as a photocopy machine or a computer, is used by nongrant entities, such as the host organization, have a way to assign appropriate charges to that entity. Equipment purchased by a federal project should be restricted for the use of that project unless provisions are made for other users to share in the cost. Be prepared to demonstrate how those costs are shared.

An audit may also include a review for compliance with the purpose of the project. For example, if your project was to serve low-income, ethically diverse participants, the auditor may review your records to ensure that only program participants with those characteristics are being served; if your project was funded to serve a specific number of participants at any given time, the auditor may want to verify that you are serving that number. Therefore, create a student profile that highlights the required characteristics of each participant.

Include important information such as the number in the applicant pool and number actually being served, data concerning the geographic distribution of participants, their income levels and academic achievements, and any other important data that will contribute to a successful audit. Prepare for these aspects of an audit as you did for a site visit.

If your auditor finds you out of compliance in any aspect, he/she has various options. For example, he/she may recommend that a percentage of your assistance be withheld until compliance is achieved or that payment for disallowed services or equipment be withheld. He/she may also recommend that you or the institution be required to repay funds if assistance has been misused. A final and drastic recommendation would be that all funds for your project be withdrawn and the project terminated.

Typical Problem Areas Detected by Auditors

According to the United States Department of Education's Office of Inspector General, the following are examples of common problem areas.

- Inadequate record keeping for payroll distribution and improper charging.

- Supplanting or replacement of existing support of an activity, position, or program with federal support. For example, an employee continues to perform the same functions as he/she did prior to the receipt of federal funds but is now paid partially or completely with federal funds. Another example would be if funds that are regularly budgeted at your institution or agency for travel, supplies, or equipment are replaced with federal funds.

- If required, matching requirements have not been met.

- Funds have not been allocated based on counts of eligible program participants or funds have not always been used to benefit the intended recipients.

- Poor documentation on eligibility determinations of program participants.

- Not receiving formal approval for changing scope of work.

As with site visits, the best way to prepare for an audit is to document. Preparation does *not* begin with the notification that the auditors are coming. Preparation begins when you (a) start to write your proposal, (b) do the needs assessment, (c) receive the Grant Award Document, and (d) begin to organize the project. Preparation begins as you set up files, define criteria, and collect documentation. Do this work up front and save many hours of work and headache later.

Summary

This chapter has described how to prepare for a site visit or an audit. Define your criteria and document your actions. Preparation for site visits and audits is an activity carried out throughout all phases of the project. Major problems arise when you procrastinate. It is difficult, if not impossible, to construct a "paper trail" months or years later. The only assurance of a successful site visit or audit review is to prepare for it from the beginning.

Remember, your sponsoring agency, project officer, and others at the federal level want you to be successful. Your success is their success. Rely on them and consult with them for advice and counsel. Read and thoroughly study *EDGAR* and the laws and regulations that pertain to the project. Plan ahead and be consistent in your information gathering and you will be successful in your site visit or audit.

16

Closing Out a Project

Introduction

For a variety of reasons and circumstances, an institution or agency may need to close out or terminate a grant. When this occurs, it is important to ensure that steps are taken expeditiously to complete the proper paperwork, to file the appropriate forms and reports, and to dispose of the assets accumulated by the grant. This chapter addresses some important considerations for properly terminating a grant.[1]

Why Are Grants Terminated?

Grant termination may be initiated by one of three general processes: (a) from the review process, (b) by the host organization, or (c) by the funding source. One of the most common reasons grants are terminated is because the application to continue the project fails to receive sufficient points in the review process. Rarely in such cases does an appeal to the Department result in restoration of the grant.

A host institution may decide to end a project. Some grants are awarded for a determined period of time after which the host institution must fund all or part of the project activity or phase out project efforts. An institution may determine that the need for which the grant was obtained no longer exists and choose to terminate the grant. In some instances a school board or other governing body may decide the grant is too restrictive and either not renew it at the end of a cycle or not submit a continuation proposal for subsequent years; hence, the grant ends.

At times grants are ended by Department action. The Department may determine that all applicable administrative actions and

---

[1]Complete details for the administration of a Department of Health and Human Services and most Department of Education Grants—including grant closeout—are in the *CFR* 45, Part 74. A project administrator should have, know, and follow this "bible."

required grant work have been completed by the grantee and the Department, therefore, initiates the process of *grant closeout.*

The Department may determine that grant conditions are not being met and may choose one of several options to deal with the situation. It may implement a *suspension* of the grant, which means a "temporary withdrawal of the grantee's authority to obligate grant funds pending corrective actions by the grantee or a decision to terminate the grant" (*EDGAR* 74.110).

The Department may decide to effect a *termination*, which means "permanent withdrawal of the grantee's authority to obligate previously awarded grant funds before that authority would otherwise expire. It also means the voluntary relinquishment of that authority by the grantee" (*EDGAR* 74.110).

Whatever the reason for ending the project, the host institution or agency is responsible for closing out the grant as promptly as is feasible after expiration or termination and to ensure that the proper closing procedures are implemented and the assets are divested. Upon request, the Department will pay the grantee for any allowable reimbursable cost not covered by previous payments. On the other hand, the grantee must immediately refund or otherwise dispose of, in accordance with instructions from the Department, any unobligated balance of cash that may have been advanced.

Reports

Most federal grants require that annual performance reports be submitted to the granting department or office within 90 days after the end of a project fiscal or performance year. The contents for such reports are generally prescribed in the regulations or in the documents that accompany the grant award. If the grant is terminated or allowed to expire at the end of the program year, the project personnel would complete and submit regularly required reports. These reports include information relating to the accomplishments realized during the reporting period, completion of objectives, evaluation of the project (often in formative and summative terms) in relation to the effect the grant had on the participants, and a complete financial statement.

Year-end reports include a financial report usually due 90 days after the grant is terminated or expires. The financial report discloses the total amount of funds received, the total amount expended by object or category, and the rate of indirect costs and any remaining, unobligated funds. The business or financial office frequently prepares and submits the financial reports, but the project director is responsible for reviewing those reports and verifying their accuracy.

Upon receiving a justifiable request, the Department may extend the due date for any report or may waive any report that is not needed. It will do neither, however, unless you request it.

The closeout of a grant does not affect the retention period for, or the federal rights of access to, grant records. Records are to be retained for a minimum of five years after the completion of the activity for which the grantee uses grant funds. If your grant ends and is not renewed in subsequent years, be sure that people remaining at the site understand that the records must be retained for the specified amount of time.

Equipment

If your project has acquired equipment with a high value, the Department will generally indicate the proper disposal, such as transferring it to another federally funded project at your institution or to another institution. Often the "ball park" figure for such transfers is around $5,000. In any case, work closely with the Department to ensure proper disposal of property purchased or lease-purchased with project funds.

Equipment not transferred elsewhere may be used by the recipient or host institution in the project for which it was acquired as long as it is needed even though the project will no longer receive federal support. When it is no longer needed for that project, it may be used in other projects or programs currently or previously sponsored with federal funds at the recipient institution.

In all cases of grant termination, work closely with the appropriate officers in the Department to ensure that the disposition of or continued use of equipment is handled properly and in accordance with the latest Department regulations.

Notification of Grant Termination

Should the Department initiate termination proceedings against your grant, it will only be after both you and representatives of the Department have discussed the reasons and the Department has determined that the situation cannot be remedied satisfactorily. These types of terminations are relatively few and seldom come as a surprise to the grantee.

Often, however, a project that has been successfully operated for one or more funding cycles does not score sufficient points in the reading process to fall within the funding range and, therefore, the Department must close out the grant. The Department generally begins negotiating and funding those programs that are at the top of the funding slate. After all available funds have been awarded, the Department notifies unsuccessful applicants. Generally this is within a few weeks or months of the would-be start up date of your project for the next year's cycle.

If your project is already operating and you have applied for funds to continue for another cycle, timely notification is essential. You may have employees who will need to seek other employment and students who will need to find other means of funding their schooling.

Check and update all employee and student files as soon as you know the project will be ending. Employees will be searching for work elsewhere. You will receive calls and requests from future employers seeking information about your former staff members. You may want to prepare in advance a letter of recommendation with important information to help you respond to such requests and to assist staff members in their search for employment. Most will have little time to find other employment, especially if the grant cycle follows a regular academic year. By the time you know you will not be funded, many jobs in education will have already been filled.

The same is true for any students who may be supported on the project. They will need all the help possible to locate funds (if the project previously supplied tuition and/or stipends) or a new program into which they can transfer. As soon as you receive notification, begin contacting other similar programs in your area. Prepare a fact sheet for your students listing options for them including the names of the programs, start dates, cost, services provided, eligibility requirements, and application procedures. This will save time that you use to close out the grant instead of repeating time after time the same information to each student. At the time you receive notification of termination, notify other similar programs in the area. They may send representatives or recruiters to visit with your students to provide choices for them to relocate.

Immediately notify other agencies or institutions with which you work. If you recruit students from or provide services to local school districts, make sure they realize you will no longer be able to receive students into your program nor will you be able to provide services. For example, Educational Talent Search programs, a part of the Federal TRIO Programs, provide extensive academic and financial counseling to large numbers of students in local school districts. Services include assisting students to determine career goals and completing college application and financial aid forms. The loss of the services of an Educational Talent Search program may cause severe hardships on school districts previously served. Counselors, administrators, and others need lead time to prepare alternative services for persons who had been served by the grant.

Future Plans

When you know you are not going to be funded for the next cycle, set up an appointment with your chair, supervisor, dean, and other administrators. Plan for the future. Determine at that time whether you will submit an application at the next cycle to see if you can win a new grant to renew the program, or if the institution has the funds to continue your program even though it may be at a greatly reduced level. What will happen to your employees and physical facilities (office, telephone, and office furniture)? Discuss the academic impact the loss of the grant will cause. Be sure to discuss personnel plans and the need for keeping records for at least five years.

—— Grant Tip ——
Keep all financial and other important records for 5 years— safe and accessible.

For example, if you determine to submit an application the next year, try to negotiate to keep your office space, equipment, furniture, and other things necessary to operate an office even though during the interim others may use the facility or share it with you. It is easier and much less cumbersome to make such arrangements than to start over if you receive a new grant.

If your grant supported an academic program of study, such as an associate, undergraduate, or graduate degree, visit with those involved in academics to assess the impact of project termination on the students' degree plans. Has the academic program been institutionalized, i.e., has it been approved and accepted by the institution and, if appropriate, the State Education Agency? Does it appear in the institution's catalog? Have classes been scheduled for the subsequent semester? What impact will loss of the grant have on the continuation of the degree program? Can individual education plans be created so the student can transfer the majority of classes already taken to a related program? For example, assume that a grant was terminated that supported an undergraduate degree in elementary bilingual education. The project director may be able to negotiate with the chair or the dean to allow students enrolled in the bilingual program to transfer credits to the regular education program or to a related special program.

Summary

Although losing a grant is never a pleasant experience, it is a reality to institutions that seek federal grants. Often the loss of a grant is considered by the institution as a temporary condition inasmuch as a person may submit a new application the very next year. Even so, the necessary steps must be taken to close out the existing grant properly. By working closely with the Department and following the procedures outlined, the chances of obtaining a new grant may even be enhanced.

Become familiar with the close-out procedures from a federal standpoint, and create close-out procedures to meet local needs. Help others understand that what has happened is part of the *competitive* nature of federal grants and that through following the proper procedures and maintaining a good attitude, services may be restored at a future time with another grant. Start planning immediately to seek new funding if such funding is important to you and to the institution.

Preserve as much goodwill within your institution and your service community as you can. In all likelihood, if you stay in the grant business, you will need to call upon them again. Learn from the experience. Going through the processes of closing out a grant will provide valuable insight. Learn from all parts of the grant process. Your actual operation of a grant may be improved to the point that the likelihood of losing another one becomes remote, unless you or your institution choose not to continue.

Just as certainly as there is no such thing as a late proposal, that you can't win a competition without entering it, and that you won't win all competitions, you will also find out that grant-supported projects eventually end. Approach termination with the same zeal you used to seek funding. Do the close-out activities professionally. Learn from the process. Try again!

Bibliography

General

In developing the material we have relied on many federal sources. These are identified throughout the text as appropriate. They include

Catalog of Federal Domestic Assistance (CFDA)

Code of Federal Regulations (CFR)

Education Department General Administrative Regulations (EDGAR)

Federal Management Circulars

Federal Register (FR)

Government Performance and Results Act (GPRA)

Grant Application Packets

Office of Management and Budget Documents

We have relied upon materials (and quoted as appropriate) from such sources as:

Education Funding Resource Council

The Foundation Directory

The Grantsmanship Center

Specific

A Directory of U.S. Government Depository Libraries. (1990). Washington, DC: United States Congress—Joint Committee on Printing. *All About ERIC* (1990). Washington, DC: U.S. Department of Education.

Achilles, C. M. (1986). *A grantwriter's manual.* Knoxville, TN: Bureau of Educational Research and Services.

Applied Research and Development Institute. Associated Grantmakers of Massachusetts. Retrieved March 4, 2000, from the World Wide Web http://www.agmconnect.org

Bootzin, R. R., Sechrest, L., Scott, A., & Hannah, M. (1992). Common methodological problems in health services research proposals. *EGAD Quarterly, 1*(3), 101-102, 106.

Brewer, E. W. (1999). Grantseeker's toolkit for writing grant proposals [Monograph]. *Journal of Educational Opportunity, 18*(1), 9-97.

Brewer, E. W. (1993). New directions for adult and continuing education. In P. Mulcrone (Ed.), *Managing multiple funding sources and writing grant documents* (pp. 21-37). San Francisco: Jossey-Bass.

Brewer, E. W. & Hollingsworth, C. (2001). Applying for education grants. In Holt Science & Technology (Eds.). Professional reference for teachers (pp. 124-129). Austin, TX: Holt, Rinehart and Winston.

The Budget Process. (1990). Washington, DC: Government Printing Office.

Butts, D. (2000). *Persistence and understanding donor keys to generating funds.* Silver Spring, MD: CD Publications.

Carlson, M. (1995). *Winning grants step by step.* Support Centers of America. San Francisco: Jossey-Bass.

Cavin, J. I. (1984). *Understanding the federal proposal review process.* Washington, DC: American Association of State Colleges and Universities.

Chavkin, N. F. (July, 1997). Funding school-linked services through grants: A beginner's guide to grant writing. *Social Work in Education, 19*(3).

Coley, S. M., & Scheinbert, C. A. (1990). *Proposal writing.* Sage Human Services Guides (63). Newbury Park, CA: Sage.

Conrad, D. L. (1980) *The quick proposal workbook.* San Francisco: Public Management Institute.

Council on Foundations. Great grant archives. Retrieved May 7, 2000, from the World Wide Web: http://www.cof.org/applications/search/index.cfm

CyberGrant$. (2000, January 24). Three hundred grantmaker users sign up for CyberGrants' new online grants management system. Retrieved May 7, 2000, from the World Wide Web: http://www.cybergrants.com/news2.htm

Demonstrating Results. U. S. Department of Education. Washington, DC: Government Printing Office. Retrieved May 7, 2000, from the World Wide Web: http://www.ed.gov/pubs/DemoResults/title/html

Education Department's Guidelines for Administrative Regulations (EDGAR). (1999). U. S. Department of Education. Washington, DC: Government Printing Office.

Ferguson, J. (1996, July). *School Business Affairs*, p.12.

Ford Foundation. Retrieved on February 13, 2000, from the World Wide Web: http://www.ford found.org/about/faq_mail.cfm

The Foundation Center. Retrieved May 7, 2000, from the World Wide Web: http://www.fdncenter.org

The Foundation Center. (1996-1997). *In-depth profiles of the 1000 largest U.S. foundations.* New York: The Foundation Center.

Foundation Giving on the Rise. (2000). *Philanthropy News Digest, 6*(6). Retreived on May 7, 2000 from the World Wide Web: http://fdncenter.org/pnd/20000208/003158.html

Fox, R. D., Nanovic, J., & Sowada, E. (1994). *Document drafting handbook.* Washington, DC: National Archives and Records Administration.

Frost, G. J. (Ed). (1993). *Winning grant proposals.* Rockville, Maryland: Fund Raising Institute.

Gitlin, L. N., & Lyons, K. J. (1996). *Successful grant writing: Strategies for health and human service professionals.* New York: Springer.

Glass, S. A. (1995). *The Perfect Proposal I.* Currents, XXI, *26.*

Hall, M. S. (1988). *Getting funded: A complete guide to proposal writing* (3rd ed.). Portland, OR: Continuing Education Publications.

Hamper, R. J., & Baugh, L. S. (1995). *Handbook for writing proposals.* Chicago: NTC Publishing Group.

Heezen, R. R. (1991). Take money for granted: Grant proposals that work. *Library Journal, 115*(18), 62.

Horace Mann Learning Center. (1988). *Reviewing applications for discretionary grants and cooperative agreements: Orientation trainer's manual.* Washington, DC: Government Printing Office.

Kelley, J. A., & Gay, J. T. (1990). Elements of grantsmanship: The process. *Nursing and Health Care, 11*(7).

Koch, D. (2000). *Funders like to see their money go a long way, expert says.* Silver Spring, MD: CD Publications.

Kraft, M. (1999). *Toward equity in funding of secondary art programs,* Art Educator, 52(57).

Krauth, D. (1979). *How to use the Catalog of Federal Domestic Assistance.* Los Angeles: The Grantsmanship Center.

Locke, L. F., Spirduso, W. W., & Silverman, S. J. (1987). *Proposals that work.* Newbury Park, CA: Sage.

Miller, R. (1995). *Grants—Your Key to Prosperity.* Fund Raising Management, 27*(4).*

Office of Research. (1994). *Abstracts of the educational research and development centers.* Washington, DC: Office of Research and Improvement.

The Packet Guide to ERIC. (1994, Spring). Washington, DC: Government Printing Office.

Pokrywczynski, J. (1992). Peer reviewers describe success in grant writing. *Journalism Educator, 47*(3).

Reeve, E. M., & Ballard. D. V. (1993). A faculty guide to writing grant proposals. *Community College Journal, 63*(4).

Regional Educational Laboratories. (1994). *Institutional projects funded by OERI.* Washington, DC: Office of Educational Research and Improvement.

Reif-Lehrer, L. (1995). *Grant application writer's handbook.* Boston: Jones & Bartlett.

Rimel, R. W. (1999, May/June). Strategic philanthropy. Pew's approach to matching needs with resources. *Health Affairs, 18*(4).

Sliger, B. (1998). The ABCs of small grant acquisition for social studies teachers. *Social Education, 62*(1).

Steiner, R. (1987). *Total proposal building.* Albany, NY: Trestletree.

Stowe, B. (1995). The perfect proposal II. *Currents, XXI,* 28.

United States Government Manual. (1999). Washington, DC: Government Printing Office.

Ward, D. (1998). Grantwriting dos and don'ts. *Technology and Learning, 18*(10).

Warren, P. (1980). *The dynamics of funding.* Boston: Allyn & Bacon.

What should I know about ED grants? (1995). Washington, DC: U.S. Department of Education.

Appendix A

Abbreviations

AAAH	American Association for the Advancement of Humanities
AAAS	American Association for the Advancement of Science
AAC	Association for American Colleges
AACD	American Association of Counseling and Development
AACUO	Association for Affiliated College and University Offices
ACC	Application Control Center
ACE	American Council on Education
ACLS	American Council for Learned Societies
ACYF	Administration for Children, Youth and Families
ADAMHA	Administration on Drug Abuse, Mental Health and Alcoholism
AFDC	Aid to Families with Dependent Children
AFOSR	Air Force Office of Scientific Research
AID	Agency for International Development
AOA	Administration on Aging
ARI	Army Research Institute
ARO	Army Reserve Office
ASAP	As soon as possible
AVA	American Vocational Association
BIA	Bureau of Indian Affairs
BLS	Bureau of Labor Statistics
CASE	Council for the Advancement and Support of Education
CBD	*Commerce Business Daily*
CFDA	*Catalog of Federal Domestic Assistance*
CFR	*Code of Federal Regulations*
CIES	Council for the International Exchange of Scholars
CPB	Corporation for Public Broadcasting
CURI	College and University Resource Institute
CWS	College Work Study
DEA	Drug Enforcement Administration
(D)HHS	Department of Health and Human Services
DOD	Department of Defense
DOE	Department of Energy
DOT	Department of Transportation
EDGAR	*Educational Department General Administrative Regulations*
EEO	Equal Employment Opportunity
EO	Executive Order
ERIC	Education Resources Information Clearinghouse
ERS	Economic Research Service
ESEA	Elementary and Secondary Education Act
ETA	Employment and Training Administration

	Fund for the Improvement of Post Secondary Education
	Federal Management Circular
	Freedom of Information Act
	Federal Register
FY	Fiscal Year
FYI	For your information
GAO	Government Accounting Office
GEPA	General Education Provisions Act
GPRA	Government Performance and Results Act
GPO	Government Printing Office
GSA	General Services Administration
GSL	Guaranteed Student Loan
HEA	Higher Education Amendment
HEARS	Higher Education Administrative Resource Service
HED	Higher Education Daily
HENA	Higher Education and National Affairs
HHS	Department of Health and Human Services
IHE	Institution of Higher Education
IREB	International Research and Exchanges Board
LEA	Local Education Agency
NA	Not applicable
NCES	National Center for Educational Statistics
NCURA	National Council of University Research Administrators
NEA	National Education Association
NEA	National Endowment for the Arts
NEH	National Endowment for the Humanities
NIA	National Institute on Aging
NIAAA	National Institute on Alcohol Abuse and Alcoholism
NIDA	National Institute on Drug Abuse
NIE	National Institute on Education
NIH	National Institutes of Health
NIHR	National Institute for Handicapped Research
NRA	National Rehabilitation Association
NSF	National Science Foundation
OERI	Office of Educational Research and Improvement
OFCC	Office of Federal Contract Compliance
OFR	Office of the Federal Register
OGPS	Office of Grants and Program Systems
OMB	Office of Management and Budget
ORM	Office of Regional Management
OSHA	Occupational Safety and Health Administration
OTA	Office of Technology Assessment
PHS	Public Health Service
PIC	Private Industry Council
RFP	Request for Proposal
RSPA	Research and Special Programs Administration
SBA	Small Business Administration
SEA	State Education Agency
SRA	Society of Research Administrators

Appendix B

State Points of Contact (SPOC)

ARIZONA

Joni Saad
Arizona State Clearinghouse
3800 N. Central Avenue
Fourteenth Floor
Phoenix, Arizona 85012
Telephone: (602) 280-1315
FAX: (602) 280-8144

DISTRICT OF COLUMBIA

Charles Nichols
Office of Grants Mgmt. & Dev.
717 14th Street, N.W. Suite 1200
Washington, D.C. 20005
Telephone: (202) 727-1700 (direct)
(202) 727-6537 (secretary)
FAX: (202) 727-1617

INDIANA

Renee Miller
State Budget Agency
212 State House
Indianapolis, Indiana 46204-2796
Telephone: (317) 232-2971
FAX: (317) 233-3323

ARKANSAS

Tracy L. Copeland
Manager, State Clearinghouse
Office of Intergovernmental Services
Dept. of Finance and Administration
515 W. 7th St., Room 412
Little Rock, Arkansas 72203
Telephone: (501) 682-1074
FAX: (501) 682-5206

FLORIDA

Cherie Trainor
Florida State Clearinghouse
Department of Community Affairs
2555 Shumard Oak Blvd.
Tallahassee, Florida 32399-2100
Telephone: (850) 414-5495
FAX: (850) 414-0479

IOWA

Steven R. McCann
Division for Community Assistance
Iowa Department of Economic
    Development
200 East Grand Avenue
Des Moines, Iowa 50309
Telephone: (515) 242-4719
FAX: (515) 242-4809

CALIFORNIA

Grants Coordination
State Clearinghouse
Office of Planning & Research
1400 Tenth Street, Room 121
Sacramento, California 95814
Telephone: (916) 445-0613
FAX: (916) 323-3018

GEORGIA

Deborah Stephens, Coordinator
Georgia State Clearinghouse
270 Washington Street, S.W.
8th Floor
Atlanta, Georgia 30334
Telephone: (404) 656-3855
FAX: (404) 656-7901

KENTUCKY

Kevin J. Goldsmith, Director
Intergovernmental Affairs
Office of the Governor
700 Capitol Avenue
Frankfort, Kentucky 40601
Telephone: (502) 564-2611
FAX: (502) 564-0437

DELAWARE

Francine Booth
Executive Department
Office of the Budget
540 S. Dupont Highway, Suite 5
Dover, Delaware 19901
Telephone: (302) 739-3326
FAX: (302) 739-5661

ILLINOIS

Virginia Bova
Illinois Department of Commerce
    and Community Affairs
100 West Randolph, Suite 3-400
Chicago, Illinois 60601
Telephone: (312) 814-6028
FAX (312) 814-1800

MAINE

Joyce Benson
State Planning Office
184 State Street
38 State House Station
Augusta, Maine 04333
Telephone: (207) 287-3261
FAX: (207) 287-6489

MARYLAND	NEW HAMPSHIRE	RHODE ISLAND
Linda Janey Manager, Plan & Project Review Maryland Office of Planning 301 W. Preston Street - Room 1104 Baltimore, Maryland 21201-2365 Telephone: (410) 767-4490 FAX: (410) 767-4480	Jeffrey H. Taylor, Director Office of State Planning Intergovernmental Review Process 2 1/2 Beacon Street Concord, New Hampshire 03301 Telephone: (603) 271-2155 FAX: (603) 271-1728	Kevin Nelson, Review Coordinator Department of Administration Division of Planning One Capitol Hill, 4th Floor Providence, Rhode Island 02908 Telephone: (401) 277-2656 FAX: (401) 277-2083
MICHIGAN Richard Pfaff Southeast Michigan Council of Governments 660 Plaza Drive - Suite 1900 Detroit, Michigan 48226 Telephone: (313) 961-4266 FAX: (313) 961-4869	**NEW MEXICO** Nick Mandell Local Government Division Room 201 Bataan Memorial Bldg Santa Fe, New Mexico 87503 Telephone: (505) 827-3640 Fax: (505) 827-4984	**SOUTH CAROLINA** Omeagia Burgess Budget and Control Board Office of State Budget 1122 Ladies Street - 12th Floor Columbia, South Carolina 29201 Telephone: (803) 734-0494 FAX: (803) 734-0645
MISSISSIPPI Cathy Mallette, Clearinghouse Officer Dept. of Administration 550 High Street 303 Walters Sillers Building Jackson, Mississippi 39201-3087 Telephone: (601) 359-6762 FAX: (601) 359-6758	**NEW YORK** New York State Clearinghouse Division of the Budget State Capitol Albany, New York 12224 Telephone: (518) 474-1605 FAX: (518) 486-5617	**TEXAS** Tom Adams, Director Intergovernmental Coordination P.O. Box 12428 Austin, Texas 78711 Telephone: (512) 463-1771 FAX: (512) 936-2681
MISSOURI Lois Pohl Federal Assistance Clearinghouse P.O. Box 809 Jefferson Building, 9th Floor Jefferson City, Missouri 65102 Telephone: (314) 751-4834 FAX: (314) 751-7819	**NORTH CAROLINA** Jeanette Furney Dept. of Administration 116 West Jones Street - Suite 5106 Raleigh, North Carolina 27603-8003 Telephone: (919) 733-7232 FAX: (919) 733-9571	**UTAH** Carolyn Wright Office of Planning and Budget Room 116 State Capitol Salt Lake City, Utah 84114 Telephone: (801) 538-1027 FAX: (801) 538-1547
NEVADA Heather Elliot Dept. of Administration State Clearinghouse 209 E. Musser Street, Room 220 Carson City, Nevada 89710 Telephone: (702) 687-6367 FAX: (702) 687-3983	**NORTH DAKOTA** Office of Intergovernmental Assistance 600 East Boulevard Avenue Bismarck, North Dakota 58505 Telephone: (701) 224-2094 FAX: (701) 224-2308	**WEST VIRGINIA** Fred Cutlip, Director Community Development Division Building #6, Room 553 Charleston, West Virginia 25305 Telephone: (304) 558-4010 FAX: (304) 558-3248

TERRITORIES

WISCONSIN

Jeff Smith, Section Chief
Federal/State Relations
101 East Wilson Street - 6th Floor
P.O. Box 7868
Madison, Wisconsin 53707
Telephone: (608) 266-0267
FAX: (608) 267-6931

WYOMING

Sandy Ross
Dept. of Admin. and Information
2001 Capitol Avenue, Room 214
Cheyenne, WY 82002
Telephone: (307) 777-5492
FAX: (307) 777-3696

GUAM

Joseph Rivera, Acting Director
Bureau of Budget and Mgt Research
Office of the Governor
P.O. Box 2950
Agana, Guam 96932
Telephone: (671) 475-9411
FAX: (671) 472-2825

NORTHERN MARIANA ISLANDS

Alvaro A. Santos, Executive Officer
Office of Management and Budget
Office of the Governor
Saipan, MP 96950
Telephone: (670) 664-2256
FAX: (670) 664-2272
Contact person: Ms. Jacoba T. Seman
Federal Programs Coordinator
Telephone: (670) 664-2289
FAX: (670) 664-2272

PUERTO RICO

Jose Caballero-Mercado, Chairman
Puerto Rico Planning Board
Federal Proposals Review Office
Minillas Government Center
P.O. Box 41119
San Juan, Puerto Rico 00940-1119
Telephone: (787) 727-4444
FAX: (787) 724-3270

VIRGIN ISLANDS

Nellon Bowry, Director
Office of Management and Budget
#41 Norregade Emancipation
   Garden
Station, Second Floor
Saint Thomas, Virgin Islands
   00802

In accordance with Executive Order #12372, "Intergovernmental Review of Federal Programs," Section 4, "the Office of Management and Budget (OMB) shall maintain a list of official State entities designated by the States to review and coordinate proposed Federal financial assistance and direct Federal development."

Appendix B represents the designated State Single Points of Contact. The jurisdictions not listed no longer participate in the process but grant applicants are still eligible to apply for the grant even if your state, territory, or commonwealth does not have a "State Single Point of Count." States without a "State Single Point of Contact" includes Alabama, Alaska; American Samoa; Colorado; Connecticut; Hawaii; Idaho; Kansas; Louisiana; Massachusetts, Minnesota; Montana; Nebraska; New Jersey; Ohio; Oklahoma; Oregon; Palau; Pennsylvania; South Dakota; Tennessee; Vermont, Virginia; and Washington. This list is based on the most current information provided by the States. Information on any changes or apparent errors should be provided to the Office of Management and Budget and the State in question. Changes to the list will only be made upon formal notification by the State. Also, this listing is published biannually in the *Catalogue of Federal Domestic Assistance* (see Chapter 4).

If you have any questions, direct all questions and correspondence about intergovernmental review to: Linda Clarke. Her telephone is (809) 774-0750 or fax number (809) 776-0069. To request that copies of this list be faxed to your office, please call the publications office at (202) 395-9068.

Appendix C

Glossary of Terms

Administrative Regulations. Regulations that implement (1) guidance from the Office of Management and Budget (OMB) contained in circulars that apply to the administration of all federal grants and cooperative agreements, (2) Presidential Executive Orders (where regulation is necessary), and (3) legislation that affects all applicants for or recipients of federal grants and cooperative agreements; see also *EDGAR* (defined below).

Application Control Center. The area of the Department of Educational [in the *Grants and Contracts Service* (defined below)] that is officially authorized to receive applications for discretionary grants and cooperative agreements.

Application Notice. A notice published in the *Federal Register* that invites applications for one or more discretionary grant or cooperative agreement competitions, gives basic program and fiscal information on each competition, informs potential applicants when and where they can obtain applications, and cites the deadline date (defined below), for a particular competition.

Application Package. A package that contains the application notice for one or more programs and all the information and forms needed to apply for a discretionary grant or cooperative agreement.

Appropriations Legislation. A law passed by the Congress to provide a certain level of funding for a grant program in a given year.

Assurances. A listing of a variety of requirements, found in different federal laws, regulations, and executive orders that applicants agree in writing to observe as a condition of receiving federal assistance.

Audit Finding. A conclusion about a monetary or nonmonetary matter related to an auditor's examination of an organization, program, activity, or function, which frequently identifies problems and provides recommendations for corrective action in order to prevent their future recurrence.

Audit Resolution Process. The process by which the Department determines whether costs under a grant that have been identified in an audit report as questioned or unsupported are actually allowable or unallowable and initiates action to have recipients return unallowable expenditures.

Audit Resolution Specialist. The Department staff member who reviews audit reports on recipients' projects and develops the proposed recommendations to management for settling cases of expenditures not allowed under discretionary grants or cooperative agreements; these recommendations become the basis for decisions issued in the *program determination letter* (defined below).

Authorizing Legislation. A law passed by the Congress that establishes or continues a grant program.

Budget Period. An interval of time into which a project period is divided for budgetary purposes, usually 12 months.

Catalog of Federal Domestic Assistance. Publication and database produced by the General Services Administration that lists the domestic assistance programs for all federal agencies and gives information about a program's authorization, fiscal details, accomplishments, regulations, guidelines, eligibility requirements, information contacts, and application and award process; also called the *CFDA.*

Certification. A statement, signed by an applicant or recipient as a prerequisite for receiving federal funds, that it (1) meets or will adhere to certain conditions and/or (2) will undertake or not undertake certain actions.

CFDA Number. Identifying number for a federal assistance program, composed of a unique two-letter prefix to identify the federal agency ("84" for the Department of Education), followed by a period and a unique three-digit code for each authorized program.

Closeout. The process during which the Department determines that the recipient has performed all required work of a discretionary grant or cooperative agreement and undertakes all necessary administrative actions to make any final fiscal adjustments to a recipient's account.

Code of Federal Regulations (CFR). Compilation of all final regulations issued by federal agencies and published annually by the National Archives and Records Administration; divided into numbered "Titles"; Title 34 contains the regulations of the Department of Education.

Competitive Review Process. The process used by the Department of Education to select applications for discretionary grants and cooperative agreements for funding, in which applications are scored by subject-area experts and the most highly scored applications are recommended for funding.

Continuation Grant. Additional funding awarded for budget periods following the initial budget period of a multiyear discretionary grant or cooperative agreement.

Cooperative Agreement. A type of federal assistance; essentially, a variation on a *discretionary grant* (defined below), awarded by the Department when it anticipates having substantial involvement with the recipient during the performance of a funded project.

Deadline Date. The date by which the Department must receive a discretionary grant or cooperative agreement application for it to be considered for funding.

Discretionary Grant. An award of financial assistance in the form of money, or property in lieu of money, by the federal government to an eligible recipient, usually made on the basis of a competitive review process.

ED. The acronym for the U.S. Department of Education (i.e., Education Department).

ED Board. An electronic bulletin board service (BBS) of the Department of Education that gives information on discretionary grant, cooperative agreement, and contract opportunities at the Department.

EDGAR (Education Department General Administrative Regulations). Administrative regulations governing ED discretionary grant and cooperative agreement programs found in Parts 74, 75, 76, 77, 79, 80, 81, 82, 85, and 86 of Title 34 of the *Code of Federal Regulations* (defined above); a book issued by the Department that contains a reprint of these regulations.

Employer Identification Number (EIN). The number the Internal Revenue Service assigns to every employer; used by the Department as the basis for the *entity number* (defined below).

Entity Number. The number the Department creates, using the *employer identification number* (defined above), to identify a recipient (as distinct from the award itself) in its dealings with the Department; enables the Department to be able to establish an account and to identify the correct recipient to receive the funds awarded under a discretionary grant or cooperative agreement.

Federal Register. Daily compilation of federal regulations and legal notices, presidential proclamations and executive orders, federal agency documents having general applicability and legal effect, documents required to be published by act of Congress, and other federal agency documents of public interest; prepared by the National Archives and Records Administration for public distribution by the Government Printing Office; publication of record for ED regulations.

Financial Operations Division (Accounting and Financial Management Service). The administrative unit of the Department of Education that makes payments of federal funds to recipients of discretionary grants and cooperative agreements and receives recipients' completed SF-272 reports. (See *financial report,* below).

Financial Report. A document the recipient sends to the Department showing the amounts and/or types of expenditures made under an ED discretionary grant or cooperative agreement; usually made on a federal form, SF-272; for some grants, the financial report is also made on another federal form, SF-269.

Formula Grant. A grant that the Department is directed by Congress to make to recipients, for which the amount is established by a formula based on certain criteria (e.g., population) that are written into the legislation and program regulations; directly awarded and administered in the Department's *program offices* (defined on the next page).

Funding Priorities. Activities, identified by the Department in advance of a discretionary grant or cooperative agreement competition, that applicants are asked to include in an application so as to receive preference in the review process; they include *absolute priorities* (the applicant must address them in order to be considered for funding), *competitive priorities* (the applicant can choose whether or not to address them and the application might receive additional points for doing so, depending how well the applicant addresses the priority), and *invitational priorities* (the applicant is encouraged to address the stated priorities, but the application does not receive extra points for doing so).

Grant Application Reviewer ('Reviewer'). An individual who serves the Department by reviewing new discretionary grant and cooperative agreement applications; also referred to as "field reader" or "peer reviewer."

Grant Award Notification. Official document signed by the grants officer stating the amount and the terms and conditions of an award for a discretionary grant or cooperative agreement.

Grant Program. For the purposes of this booklet, a program of discretionary grants and/or cooperative agreements administered by the Department of Education.

Grants and Contracts Service (GCS). The organizational unit of the Department of Education that has authority for overseeing the Department's assistance (grants) and procurement (contracts) processes; holds responsibility for the related functions of establishing indirect cost rates and developing automated systems for processing grants and contracts.

Grants Division. The administrative unit of the *Grants and Contracts Service* (defined above) responsible for negotiating, awarding, administering, and closing out all of the Department of Education's discretionary grants and cooperative agreements.

Grants Officer. The only person in the Department of Education who has the authority to award its discretionary grants and cooperative agreements and to establish or revise their terms and conditions.

Grants Specialist. The staff person in the *Grants Division* (defined above) who reports to the grants officer and who negotiates discretionary grants and cooperative agreements and handles the details of administering them on a daily basis.

Indirect Costs. Costs of an organization incurred for common or joint objectives, which cannot readily and specifically be identified with a particular grant project or other institutional activity.

Monitoring. Activities undertaken by ED staff members to review and evaluate specific aspects of a recipient's activities under a discretionary grant or cooperative agreement; they include (1) measuring a recipient's performance; (2) assessing a recipient's adherence to applicable laws, regulations, and the terms and conditions of the award; (3) providing technical assistance to recipients; and (4) assessing whether a recipient has made substantial progress.

Negotiation. Preaward discussions conducted by the *Grants Division* (defined above) to establish the conditions and amount of a discretionary grant or cooperative agreement; based on recommendations from the cognizant Principal Office, a cost analysis of the applicant's budget, and a review of proposed activities.

Notice of Proposed Rulemaking. An announcement published in the *Federal Register* (defined on the preceding page) of proposed new regulations or modifications to existing regulations; the first stage in the process of creating or modifying regulations.

Obligation. An entry made by a grants officer in the Department's automated accounting system that authorizes the *Financial Operations Division* (defined on the preceding page) to make payments of federal grant funds to a recipient.

Office of Management and Budget (OMB) Circulars. Administrative policy documents that give instruction to federal agencies on a variety of topics, including the administration of federal grants and cooperative agreements.

Payment Identification Number (PIN). A number associated with a recipient's entity number (defined above), which enables the recipient to draw down cash payments authorized by a discretionary grant or cooperative agreement award.

Performance Report. A report of the specific activities the recipient of a discretionary grant or cooperative agreement has performed during the budget period or the project period.

Principal Officer. The Department official who is head of one of the six principal offices listed above; holds the rank of assistant secretary or its equivalent.

Program Office. A subunit of a principal office that conducts the daily work of administering ED discretionary grant and cooperative agreement programs, including the review and ranking of applications.

Program Officer. Program office staff person responsible for (1) developing *program regulations* (defined below), *application notices,* and *application packages* (defined above); (2) overseeing the review and ranking of applications submitted under their programs; (3) providing detailed funding recommendations to the Grants Division for applications; (4) participating in negotiations, as necessary; (5) providing technical assistance to applicants and recipients; (6) monitoring funded projects; and (7) making recommendations to the Grants Division about recipients' requests for revisions to project activities and budgets.

Program Determination Letter (PDL). An official written notice from an authorized Department of Education management official to an audited recipient that sets forth the Department's decision on findings in an audit report, including all necessary actions and repayment of funds for which the recipient is responsible.

Program Regulations. Regulations that implement legislation passed by Congress to authorize a specific grant program; they include applicant and participant eligibility criteria, nature of activities funded, allowability of certain costs, selection criteria under which applications will be selected for funding, and other relevant information.

Project Period. The total amount of time (sometimes several years) during which the Department authorizes a recipient to complete the approved work of the project described in the application; project periods of more than one year are divided into *budget periods* (defined on page 369).

PR/Award Number. The identifying number for a discretionary grant or cooperative agreement award, composed of seven parts (e.g., H029A31234-01C):

1. Principal office designator   (H)
2. *CFDA* numeric suffix of the program   (029)
3. Alphabetic subprogram identifier   (A)
4. Last digit of the fiscal year of the competition   (3)
5. Unique application identifier   (1234)
6. Fiscal year of the funding   (01)
7. Sequential order of the most recent funding
   action in a Fiscal Year   (C)

The first five parts remain the same throughout the life of the project period while the last two parts change by budget period.

Regulations. For purposes of this booklet, federal rules of general applicability that are authorized by federal laws or other federal authority and contained in the *Code of Federal Regulations* (defined on page 370).

Slate. The official list of recommended applicants and award amounts in a discretionary grant or cooperative agreement competition.

Standard Form 424 or SF-424. A standard grant application form, sometimes referred to as the application "cover page," used by the Department of Education and other federal agencies.

Source: *What Should I Know About ED Grants?* (1995). U.S. Department of Education, Washington, DC.

Index

-F-

CORWIN
PRESS

The Corwin Press logo—a raven striding across an open book—represents the happy union of courage and learning. We are a professional-level publisher of books and journals for K–12 educators, and we are committed to creating and providing resources that embody these qualities. Corwin's motto is "Success for All Learners."